Reagan, God, and the Bomb

Reagan, God, and the Bomb

From Myth to Policy in the Nuclear Arms Race

F. H. Knelman

Prometheus Books
Buffalo, New York

Library of Congress Catalog Card No. 84-043328
ISBN 0-87975-310-2

Acknowledgments

This book is dedicated in general to all those people, young and old, who wage the just cause of peace throughout the world. In particular, I would like to express my gratitude to Suzy Gordon, without whose tireless and devoted assistance this book would never have been completed; to Jack McClelland, who provided a critical word of encouragement at a discouraging time; to Robert Aldridge, who selflessly read the manuscript and made a significant contribution; and to my editor Barbara Konie Bergstrom, who provided the discipline that I lack and significantly improved the book.

Contents

1

Two Minutes to Midnight

An outrageous novelty has been introduced into our lives . . . and now it seems . . . nothing we learnt before . . . is of the slightest use.
W. H. Auden

As soon as men decide that all means are permitted to fight an evil, then their good becomes indistinguishable from the evil they set out to destroy.
Christopher Dawson, *The Judgement of Nations*

The *Bulletin of the Atomic Scientists,* undoubtedly the most significant forum on nuclear issues in the world, was founded in 1945 at the very dawn of the nuclear age. The journal's cover features the famous Bulletin Clock, a "symbol of the threat of nuclear doomsday hovering over mankind." When the clock originally appeared in 1945, its hands were set at fifteen minutes before midnight. For a twelve-month period beginning in January 1980, the clock's hands remained at seven minutes before midnight. This indicated the destabilization and deterioration of the superpowers' so-called "military balance" represented by the concept of deterrence, and symbolized by the acronym MAD—mutually assured destruction. The essential instability of deterrence is directly affected by the interaction between politics and technology. By January 1981, the enhanced chill of the cold war brought with it the official rejection of deterrence and advanced the counterforce first-strike as operational policy. The clock's hands on the cover of the *Bulletin* moved forward to four minutes to midnight, bringing us closer to the brink of a "nuclear holocaust." The "unthinkable" had not merely become "thinkable"; instead, the deliberate delusion of winning a limited or protracted nuclear war became firmly installed as official policy. The distinction between conventional and nuclear war has blurred into a continuum. To the possibility of nuclear war being initiated by madness, miscalculation, malice, or accident, one can now add the possibility of nuclear war being precipitated by a belief in victory that is sanctioned by religion. Policy has become the conversion of mythology into nuclear means; thus, the politics of containment has become a suicide pact for the planet.

1

Once again, on its January 1984 cover, the *Bulletin* moved its clock forward one minute closer to midnight, i.e., to three minutes to midnight. But this author feels that events would indicate an even more serious symbol and would propose that 1984 justified a depicted time of two minutes to midnight. In accord with the editors of the *Bulletin,* this suggestion does not signify despair but indicates a state of extreme alert. Only once before has the *Bulletin* clock moved to two minutes to midnight: in 1953, on the advent of the hydrogen bomb. In retrospect this was not as great a danger as exists today, when a leader of a superpower believes he is leading a holy crusade against an "evil empire" and the "focus of evil" in the world, and also apparently believes that nuclear wars can be invoked and won in pursuit of his cause. The reelection of Ronald Reagan in November 1984 justified moving the clock to one minute to midnight. In pursuit of reelection, he may have spoken more softly, but he plans to build a huge nuclear stick in the next four years. In the end, weapons are made for use, not dismantling.

It is important at the outset to attack some major myths about nuclear warfare, and at the same time to affirm the reality of "nuclear holocaust." The myths are the concepts of "limited damage," "survivability," and "winnability" in a limited and/or protracted nuclear war between the superpowers. Even as early as 1967, official figures cite about 100 million fatalities on both sides in an all-out nuclear war (McNamara, 1967). But myths of "limited damage" still persist. These myths, based on counterforce first-strike accompanied by civil defense, count only the number of immediate deaths from blast, fire, and radiation, as derived from various scenarios of nuclear war. These scenarios discount damage to the biosphere and the global ecosystems that support all life on the planet. They also credit civil defense with the ability of limiting damage amid the global impact of a gigatonnage war, i.e., the explosion of thousands of megatons of nuclear weapons. The complexity of these global impacts permits us only to deal with risk probabilities based on limited experience, but if any risk can be judged unacceptable, then a war that could destroy the future and the basic environmental life-support systems on this planet must be unacceptable to almost all. *The Fate of the Earth* (Schell, 1983) and the *Final Epidemic* (Adams and Cullen, 1981) provide a great deal of evidence and analysis for our assertion that survivability after a protracted nuclear war is not only mythic for the peoples of the two superpowers, but also that the mere risk of nuclear war is totally unacceptable, since it threatens the continuity of life on our planet. We feel strongly that evidence of a "holocaust effect" is being denied. An assessment of analyses by relevant experts indicates that the risk is real (National Academy of Science [NAS], 1975; Arms Control and Disarmament Agency [ACDA], 1979; Office of Technology Assessment [OTA], 1979; Peterson, 1983; Leaning and Keys, 1983).

As mentioned above, in January 1984, the Bulletin Clock moved to three minutes to midnight, despite some editorial soul searching about whether it should be moved forward again. The clock, sensitive through analyses of both negative and positive events, represents a judgment of the relative dynamics of war and peace. At the outset of this book we acknowledge that the most positive new factor, the most hopeful development in the cause of peace and disarmament, is the role of people all over the world, most dramatically in North America and Europe. The public has now become a legitimate actor in the policy debate on the nuclear arms race. Together with public interest scientists and other experts, they are becoming a formidable force. The potential impacts are far-reaching and may, in fact, become pivotal in turning back the momentum toward war. In Western Europe and the United States, relatively open societies compared to those in the communist bloc, the failure to hoard and distort information has led to major opposition to the arms race. Nevertheless, in this book our major analysis will be aimed at what we consider unique developments attendant to the Reagan administration. The problem is that mirror-image rhetoric of the cold war is no longer mere rhetoric or political posturing in Washington; it has become incorporated into ideology and even theology.

It is our hypothesis that the Reagan administration has introduced and/or revived policies that introduce a quantitative and qualitative change in the dynamics of the arms race. We consider this the most dangerous new element in its potential to lead us to nuclear war. This in no way relieves the USSR from its share of the responsibility. In many ways, both superpowers incorporate a mirror image of paranoia and aggression, but we contend that in the bipolar nuclear arms race, with few exceptions, the U.S. acts (and leads) and the USSR reacts and overreacts. This credibility issue also involves methodological flaws that we intend to analyze. What is clear is that each sees the other as the ultimate villain (or even demon), and itself as the embodiment of good for all. Each seeks its own ways of subverting the other. The Soviet intervention in Afghanistan in 1980 was a serious blunder that played into the hands of those opposed to SALT II and was generally reprehensible. But when it comes to the dynamics and anatomy of the nuclear arms race, there are built-in strategic, technological, geopolitical, and economic inequalities that have favored and continue to favor the U.S. The USSR, with some exceptions, is constrained to act in the nuclear arms arena within the bounds of Eastern Europe and, at that, not homogeneously (Romania is a reluctant ally). The U.S. has the capacity to act almost everywhere, in terms of its nuclear military capability. Thus, Euromissiles can rightfully be viewed as strategic, an extension of the strategic force of NATO and the U.S., while confined largely to the role of "theater" weapons in the case of the USSR.

In 1955, Bertrand Russell and Albert Einstein issued a declaration as both a warning and a plea. In the clearest statement on nuclear war ever made, the Einstein-Russell declaration both sounded the alarm—"man whose continued existence is in doubt"—and called for the waging of peace beyond the bounds of sovereignty and ideology: "Remember your humanity and forget all other things." If only all of us, Russians, Americans, and others, could do just that, but the obstacles are profound. There are real issues of conflict between powers by virtue that their game is power. In the post-World War II era, the world was made small by technology, and geopolitics heightened confrontation. The superpowers vied for an extension of power and developed surrogate wars. The Soviet Union used naked aggression—in Hungary, in Czechoslovakia, and in Afghanistan, with other adventures in Angola and Ethiopia. The U.S. went through Vietnam and finally Grenada, the last a Soviet-type intervention. The U.S. overthrew Allende in Chile, it invaded Cuba, and now it is in Nicaragua, all "unofficial" clandestine operations, but everybody knows. The Soviets claimed they were invited into Afghanistan by the legitimate government. That is what happened with the U.S. in Vietnam and, in a small way, in Lebanon. The excuse for Grenada was more tenuous.

In all previous wars up to and including World War II, even the profoundest of horrors had finite results. The fate of the earth was not in question. In each successive war the weapons of destruction grew exponentially and so did the cost of destruction. Each war was prefaced by the development and stockpiling of military technology and by conflict between contending states over sovereignty and its extension. One almost suspects that British historian Michael Howard was correct when he said war is "a continuing activity within human society." Moreover, before each great war those who prepared for war were confident that peace was best sought through strength. Unfortunately, each of the contestants believed this, and so there was an inevitable peacetime arms race. The Russian proverb that an unloaded gun will fire sooner or later seems true. Nevertheless there were apparent winners and losers in previous wars. Wars were for winning. We killed each other in the millions. We destroyed entire cities, particulary in the mass bombings of World War II. The innocent increasingly became the prime victims. But the weapons of destruction and their modes of delivery could only destroy stone and flesh. Buildings and people were the major victims. All this changed on the sixth of August 1945, with the nuclear bombing of Hiroshima. War would never be the same again (NAS, 1975; ACDA, 1979; OTA, 1979). The world would never be the same again. The next war would be without winners. And the stakes have also been qualitatively altered. The next world war can murder our planet. To paraphrase Einstein, everything in the world has changed except the way some people think. Unfortunately, the generals and the political leaders are living in the nuclear, age with minds that belong in the prenuclear past. They have the power to unleash World War III but continue to use the arguments of World War II. They have learned nothing from the history of war. They are not alarmed. For them and their advisers, nuclear weapons are an extension of conventional ones by other means. Tactical nuclear weapons were the first to be sanitized. Now they have developed a complex doctrine of surgical strategic strikes. They have removed biology from the physics of nuclear war. They are concerned with counter-vailing (prevailing) strategies, flexible response, and, above all, escalation dominance. Their phrase for the "fog of war" is "collateral damage." Their preference is winning a "limited" nuclear war. Their delusions threaten the future. In fact their target is time itself. Their target is the future.

But where does this leave us? The only possible consensus is that we must avoid nuclear war. And the only answer is that we cannot leave this necessary avoidance to our leaders on any side. They are locked into a mutual perception of the other as the force and "focus of evil." They are locked into an arms race based on the mutual assumption of peace through strength. They are lighting matches in the dark space of a tinderbox. Both sides have legitimate reasons to fear the other. But again we must separate the citizens from their leaders. There is a profound difference between the U.S. and the USSR. The difference is basically that the former is relatively open and the latter is relatively closed. But on the other hand, it would be difficult to find a Soviet citizen who is not fearful of another war, and who does not believe it is possible. This is not true of Americans. There are some who believe their leaders' assertions that nuclear wars can be won and are not something to be feared. They believe survival would be possible. That is what their administration has told them. Fortunately there are increasing numbers of Americans, perhaps even a majority, who are speaking out against this monstrous illusion. It is a great benefit to the world that they have the right to speak out. Despite the residual questions of who is right and who is wrong, now or in the past, or when or who started it, we, the people of the world, must find the paths to peace. We must not allow our leaders to make the agenda or pose the questions. It is not peace at the expense of slavery or slavery at the expense of peace that is the real question. Peace and justice are legitimate twins and legitimate goals. We cannot fragment the unity of human rights. Peace is the core but justice and equity make a unity out of a trinity of essential goals. "Peace is indivisible."

Nevertheless there remains an inescapable paradox in the current issue of peace and war. Nobody can explain how the continued competition for power can be justified by the mutual annihilation of war. It does not seem possible that the U.S. and the USSR have signed a suicide pact rather than a survival pact. Nor can anybody explain goals of a struggle that cannot be realized. Yet both sides are seemingly locked into a nuclear collision. We are all traveling on a nuclear Titanic and the command is "full speed ahead." Only people waging peace can alter that command. Ordinary people everywhere, not obsessed by power or paralyzed by fear, still love life and the earth more than mutual and meaningless extinction.

We cannot overemphasize our contention that the Reagan administration heralds a significant historical discontinuity in the dynamics of the nuclear age. This is neither to deny the continuity of the Soviet threat nor the precursor elements in U.S. nuclear military policy that preceded the advent of the presidency of Ronald Reagan. In fact, the seemingly more benign Jimmy Carter accepted the doctrine of "flexible response" and incorporated it in Presidential Directive #59 (PD-59). Flexible response is a euphemism for a warfighting doctrine that includes first use of nuclear weapons. President Carter also made the "dual-track" decision regarding the new missiles in Europe, but he seemed to mean "dual-track" seriously, i.e., as both a position of strength and an invitation for serious arms control. After all, Carter supported the second strategic arms limitation treaty (SALT II). While this treaty incorporated some elements of a freeze while allowing a warhead build-up, it was an important step in reducing tensions and halting the arms race. Reagan, who helped defeat SALT II, was bent on superiority from the beginning. After stalling talks for a year, every proposal put forth was designed to be refused by the Soviet Union. This may appear to be a strong statement of negative intent, but we intend to document our argument.

It is a major aspect of this book to supply evidence that the Reagan administration is the first since the end of World War II to make nuclear warfighting plans and to translate into operational programs the central and implicit goal of the decapitation of the Soviet state. The Soviet Union will not be given options such as détente or peaceful coexistence or competition. Nothing short of voluntary dissolution or defeat will be acceptable.

In effect, the Reagan administration has transformed mythology into policy, plans, and operational programs based on the assumption that the USSR is a "permanent adversary" that can and must be destroyed by any means, including a nuclear war. The following myths constitute the basis of these plans and programs:

1. That a nuclear war, limited or protracted, is winnable;
2. That such a war is survivable through a strategy of civil defense known as the crisis relocation program (CRP); that the U.S. would recover from such a war to its present state of "civilization";
3. That arms control is to be eschewed in favor of an arms race designed for superiority, and that such superiority would assure Soviet capitulation or defeat, either in war or through economic suffocation;

4. That the U.S. actively confront the USSR or its surrogates by any means, including interventionism, provocation, and clandestine operations, a new form of aggressive isolationism;
5. That the doctrine of deterrence is invalid and has been replaced by first use, flexible response, and escalation domination, all warfighting strategies, and that there is no real difference in destructive ca⁻abilities between conventional and nuclear weapons or between theater and strategic weapons.

A holy nuclear crusade supported by a "holocaust lobby" and based on a mythology of nuclear warfighting now occupies Washington (Mann, 1982). This book will document the existence of these myths as official policy and will provide evidence to refute them. This evidence will all be drawn from the public record and from official, supersecret documents of the Reagan administration, i.e., the "Five-Year Defense Plan," the Single Integrated Operational Plan #6, and the National Security Decision Document (NSDD-13) (Halloran, 1982; Pringle and Arkin, 1983). Our thesis is that nuclear war is now more imminent, both in intentional and unintentional modes. There is now ample documentation of what we have called "the day before," "the day after," and "one year later": in order, the probability and causes leading to nuclear war; the immediate short-term effects; and the long-term environmental, ecological, and biological consequences. Some significant new studies regarding the long-term consequences commonly refer to them as "twilight at noon" (Peterson, 1983) or the "nuclear winter" (Turco et al., 1983). With this information, why isn't nuclear war outlawed? Why isn't the use of nuclear weapons prohibited?

Former President Harry Truman made the first declaration of "no first-use" on 4 February 1950, during the intense debate on the development of thermonuclear weapons or H-bombs in the late 1940s and early 1950s (Jungk, 1958). Truman said categorically, "We believe no nation has the right to use such a bomb, no matter how righteous its cause. . . . its use would be a betrayal of all standards of morality and of Christian civilization. . . . we urge that the United States, through its elected government, make a solemn declaration that we shall *never use this bomb first* [Italics mine]." Then Mr. Truman's "never" begins to waver. "The circumstance which might force us to use it would be if we or our allies were attacked by this bomb. There can be only one justification for our development of the hydrogen bomb and that is to prevent its use." This is the beginning of the history and the tragedy of the nuclear arms race but also of the "no first-use" doctrine, now officially subscribed to by the USSR but consistently disclaimed by the U.S. ever since Truman. It appears that Harry Truman and Ronald Reagan have very different views of what is "righteous" or of "morality" and "Christian civilization."

Why would the U.S. not declare a "no first-use" policy? Why would the

U.S. insist on the so-called "flexible response"? The usual answer is that the Warsaw Pact conventional forces are superior to NATO's and NATO's nuclear theater forces present the only barrier to the Russians attacking and overrunning Western Europe. This contains two erroneous assumptions: first, Warsaw Pact forces are not superior to NATO's conventional forces; second, no historical or political precedent exists for the idea of a Soviet attack on Western Europe. Since Napoleon's fatal incursion, Russia has been invaded three times. Of all peoples in Europe, the Russians recognize the enormous cost of war with powerful adversaries. Invading Afghanistan or Hungary or Czechoslovakia bears no relationship to an all-out attack on Western Europe, any more than Grenada is a precursor for a U.S. invasion of the USSR. We can agree that "no first-use" has more symbolic or propagandistic value than operational meaning, but it would still be significant for both superpowers to at least minimally agree with the original Truman declaration. But now that the Reagan administration has consolidated power, there is no hope for such an initiative.

In effect, foreign and military policy under Reagan has been captured by a strange amalgam: the Old and New Right, Strangelovian defense intellectuals, and religious fundamentalists formed into lobbies, such as the Committee on the Present Danger (CPD), that act as "peddlers of crisis" (Sanders, 1983), and constitute a "conspiracy of the like-minded" (Knelman, 1976). This author recognizes the risk of being labeled as "scapegoat" or, worse, as "agent," giving "comfort to the enemy." It must be accepted that these kinds of attacks are the last refuge of anti-intellectualism, and that they cannot be nullified by protesting one's opposition to the Soviet regime. These accusations contain the "genetic logical fallacy," i.e., that an idea can be dismissed because of where it came from (the USSR supports the nuclear freeze), or guilt by association of ideas.

The argument that one often encounters regarding peace activities is that such actions are either absent or manipulated in the USSR. Thus, the argument runs, peace activities in the West directly or indirectly, naively or deliberately, support the policies of the Soviet Union. This argument is invalid and, in the case of the major issue of the Nuclear Freeze Initiative, it is irrelevant. A majority of American, Canadian, British, West German, and, presumably, Soviet citizens support a mutual and verifiable freeze on the development and deployment of new weapons and weapon systems, followed by serious, phased reductions. That the Soviet government supports this while the U.S. government remains opposed is revealing. From our analysis, given the relative superiority of the U.S. and its momentum toward significant superiority in the next five to ten years, together with its warfighting doctrine, then it is easy to understand the countries' relative positions on a freeze. The main point, however, is that the support of the freeze by the

USSR does not render the policy invalid in this case. On the other hand, the issue of peace dissidents in the USSR and the manipulation of their peace movements is a legitimate question of the violation of human rights that in no way alters the legitimacy of the freeze proposal, or the fact that a majority of the peoples of the two superpowers seem to support it.

An important but minor aspect of this book deals with the U.S.-Canada relations relevant to the nuclear arms race. Canada and the U.S. are the largest bilateral trading pair in the world, and Canada has a long history of accommodation, if not complicity, in support of U.S. militarism. The history of continentalism as U.S. intervention and nationalism as Canadian resistance has not seemed to affect integration of military policy. Although Canada is a member of NATO and NORAD and also has a Defense Sharing Production Agreement with the U.S., the Reagan administration has tended to "harden" negotiations between the two countries. In part, Ronald Reagan and Pierre Trudeau were the most incompatible coleaders the two countries have ever had. Lack of respect and trust was mutual. Lawrence Eagleberger said of Trudeau's peace initiative that it was "akin to pot-induced behavior by an erratic leftist" (*Washington Spectator*, 15 April 1984, p. 4). Unfortunately, the cruise missile debate in Canada was largely conducted in a contextual vacuum. NSDD-13 programs a "decapitation" strike against the Soviet body whereby the "head" of the state is decapitated. The critical weapons for this, quite explicitly described and explicitly designated as "strategic," are Pershing II's and cruise missiles. Canada's complicity in accommodating Reagan's nuclear warfighting program cannot be denied. With a renewed interest in "Canadian Studies" in U.S. universities, the part of the book dealing with military relations between the countries should be of interest on both sides of the "longest undefended border" in the world. In the nuclear age, Canada's geostrategic position could make it the nuclear Belgium of World War III.

Aside from the major theses of this book, this author remains convinced of the essential vitality and sanity of the American democratic tradition in a society that unseated and unmasked a national leader in full public view. Watergate was remarkable: it represents a living tradition of openness, due process, and accountability. These cornerstones of a democratic society may be violated in America, but such violations carry with them the potential of investigation, public scrutiny, and correction. Thus it is no accident that two senators, Kennedy and Hatfield, the first a Democrat and the other a Republican, should be among the major proponents of nuclear sanity, the Nuclear Freeze Initiative. The hundreds of thousands of Americans who march for peace, environmental sanity, and human rights carry the banner of all that is best in the country. It can only be hoped that the liberal democratic tradition of America can overcome the primitive cowboy conservatism of the present regime.

In November 1984 Ronald Reagan was reelected president in an over-whelming victory at the polls. The surveys had told us this for months, but Mondale's clear victory in the first debate engendered some false hopes. The question that remains is, does this vote constitute a transformation of con-stituents into some more permanent re-alignment or de-alignment? While the vote also clearly reflected black and white divisions, the *macho* image of "hanging tough" found its resonating chord in the minds of millions of Americans. Reagan had luck riding on his side, particularly in the guise of an apparent U.S. economic recovery (potentially a house of straw that appeared like reinforced concrete), and won the vote of the youth of the 1980s. The election said as much about those who voted as those who did not vote. For those who voted for Reagan, it was rallying around the flag, hanging tough, and enjoying the "good" times. For those who didn't vote at all, it was the persistent alienation from the political process. These chords run deep. Mondale could not match the former or overcome the latter. Those of us who felt that the low turn-out turned the race into a default have little left on the political banquet table but sour grapes. Reagan became president of the United States with just over 30 percent of the total vote, but the race ended with the second presidential debate. Mondale lost largely because he was forced to echo the president's tough policy vis-à-vis the Soviet Union.

We believe there is now a real danger of right-wing subversion of policy. The alliance of New Right groups that brought victory in 1980 could now complete their planned take-over. The stage is set for the puppeteers to write a new script for the puppet. There seems little question that the danger of nuclear war has increased as a result of Reagan's new mandate for four more years. The burden on those who must try and save the peace will be very great. We do not subscribe to the view that if things get bad enough they are bound to get better, so we view the future with apprehension. But those who must continue to struggle for peace must not allow themselves to be disarmed by the dangerous possibilities of anxiety or apathy. In 1975 Ronald Reagan said, "The United States has much to offer the Third World War" (Trivial Pursuit)—a slip of the tongue or the truth in the mind? There are also positive aspects to the results of the 1984 election. Reagan did not win an ideological majority in the House and, possibly, the Senate—there is a sane fringe in the Republican party. The nature of U.S. politics is that Reagan has perhaps a year of opportunity to force his policy on America; after that, he becomes the terminal incumbent, a lame duck president, and the struggle to maintain his policies begins to be directed toward the 1986 midterm elections and the 1988 race for president. However, that Reagan will ultimately be replaced does not lessen the significance of his 1984 victory.

We must accept that the old frontier spirit, the opening up of the West at the expense of the near genocide of native peoples, runs deep in the psyche of

Americans. A few days before the 1984 presidential election, Reagan, who once hosted "Death Valley Days," visited the grave of the throwback hero John Wayne—who always rode tall in the saddle, who always hung tough, and always gave them hell as he defeated evil in the final shoot-out. The past has not died.

The new frontier of Kennedy and Johnson contained elements of traditional folk heroism also, but Kennedy at least had vigor, intelligence, and, seemingly, the ability to learn from history, not return to it. One cannot imagine the relatively articulate Kennedy saying "you ain't seen nothin' yet" or "over my dead body" or even "America is back," lines from a grade-B movie or even a comic strip. After the second debate a British speech analyst stated that Reagan showed indications of early stages of senility (*Gazette,* Tuesday, 30 October 1984, Montreal). Reagan may be impeached (replaced) for incapacity before the end of his term, but he may also complete the assured damage his regime has begun.

Reagan, a man of 1884, had the gall to use the word "revolution" in respect to his 1984 presidential victory. In one sense he is right. The amalgam of forces that returned him to power contains elements of revolutionary doctrine in its discontinuity with the twentieth-century trend. Thus it is a counterrevolution by a new counterculture: it is a revolution to the past, for the past, and by the past.

The CBS-*New York Times* 25 October poll during "campaign 84" was extremely revealing. Mondale won overwhelmingly on issues but lost on choice of leader, i.e., on voting alignment. Mondale was generally favored by the old, the ethnics, and women. White males provided Reagan with his major source of support. Given the president's position on school prayer, the Republican platform's criteria for new Supreme Court justices, and the New Right alliance's fervor for Armageddon, it is not difficult to see that Reagan will represent the worst traditions in America—racism, chauvinism, and political bullying. The macho man is once again in the White House, riding high in the political saddle of America. It is a return to the old frontier, equipped with all the most deadly and sophisticated technology of the newest of frontiers.

How frightening it is that increasingly, prime-time soap operas—"Dallas" and "Dynasty"—now create role models for many young people. They have dropped out of the issue-oriented universe and are now prepared to trust a man of seventy-four to get a piece of the action, to join the system, and to become the problem. Then there are the eight million members of "moral" majorities and their fundamentalist leaders with their vision of Armageddon, who were registered to vote for "Right, Might, and God." They and the "strategy scholars," with their actuarial accounts for winning and surviving nuclear war, seem dedicated to do final battle with evil or force its total capitulation.

Individuals and even government leaders make the serious assertion that some things are more valuable than peace. The American tradition of "Give me liberty or give me death" is not without historical validity, particularly on a personal level. "Better dead than Red," on the other hand, is the refuge of the ultraright. It is not a declaration of the love of liberty but a statement of fear of the threat of the loss of property. It is not concerned with universal human rights and the restoration of global equity. Those who equate the policy of containment interventionism with some generalized concept of protecting the "American Way of Life" are not being dishonest; they are concerned with protecting a way of life that has no reference to the issue of human rights for the world's populations or even for the majority of U.S. citizens. For the Right, the "American Way" means protecting the rights of ruling groups, entrenching the traditional power structure, subsidizing CARE programs for large corporations, and callously disregarding the plight of the poor, the old, the women, and the minorities. The plight of dissidents in Eastern Europe evokes an extension of cold-war politics, rather than an evaluation of the broad issue of the right to dissent. Recent and past Eastern European emigrés, consumed with implacable hate for the Russian system, view dissent in their newfound homelands as equivalent to treason, while dissent against the USSR answers the true call of liberty.

All the factions of the right-wing coalition, together with certain neo-psychotic strategic scholars, believe containment is the ultimate good: if containment is not enough, it must be augmented with interventionism; if both are not enough, then war is necessary. Unfortunately some who think there are worse things than nuclear war have found high position in the U.S. government. For them, the strength of the U.S. is a virtue in a vacuum; they are abstracted from the dynamics of the arms race. The comfort of denial dispenses with the consequences of nuclear wars: wars, even nuclear wars, are for winning and surviving. The containment cold war achieved what are viewed as victories in the two mirror-image Olympic boycotts of 1980 and 1984 and the abandonment of serious arms control. Isolationism now means the process of isolating the Soviet Union, as well as "going it alone" in defense of the American empire. U.S. hegemony is being expressed by new equations, the world domination of the dollar, the export of supply-side economics to the United Kingdom, West Germany, Canada, and others. The huge, persistent U.S. deficit has a profound negative impact on Western economies. The net effect is the export of unemployment and the attack on trade unions in the West. This is a natural consequence of the economic downturn in Western Europe. This leads to the erosion of social services for the most needy and the most vulnerable. The U.S. is waging economic warfare, not merely against the USSR, but against its allies. It also means the rapid evolution into a militarized industry and culture.

Politics is now making stranger bedfellows than ever before. Segments of the far left, imbued with the psychotic hatred of the USSR, find themselves choosing Reagan in the conflict. This hatred is the emotional dysfunction characteristic of betrayed love, truly "an infantile disorder." The amalgam of all of the above forces brought and bought victory for Reagan. His election with a blank check on policy portends "You ain't seen nothin' yet."

In the next four years we may still see nothing, but extreme vigilance is the order of every concerned person. The *Bulletin*'s clock could well be moved to one minute to midnight.

2

The Secret Agenda

The United States should plan to defeat the Soviet Union and, to do so at a cost that would not prohibit US recovery.
Colin Gray and Keith Payne, "Victory Is Possible,"
in Foreign Policy

Once a nation bases its security on an absolute weapon, such as the atom bomb, it becomes psychologically necessary to believe in an absolute enemy.
P. M. S. Blackett

If those we trust adopt strange policies; if they turn out, in office, to be double agents—one hand to pat our babies, the other raised in salute to the Bomb— then we have the right and the duty to dismiss them as unfit.
Nicholas Humphrey, *Four Minutes to Midnight*

THE SECRET AGENDA

Ronald Reagan was elected president of the United States in 1980 and re-elected in 1984 with the support of a unique amalgam of political forces, generally a mix of traditional conservatives and members of the New Right. In addition, the luck of an economic upturn attracted the vote of many persons who benefited, or who saw the potential for benefit, including large numbers of Yuppies and young voters. At the same time the psyche of a large number of Americans was finely tuned to the Reagan appeal through certain national traumatic experiences, not least of which was the humiliation of the Iran hostage incident. We intend to present a historical analysis of Reagan's road to power and return to power, with our major concern the analysis of policies and programs relating to the nuclear arms race, strategic doctrine, and the countermovements of peace and disarmament. While the politics of the Reagan administration comprises a unity of approach to both social and military policies, we are constrained to deal mainly with the latter.

We propose that the composition and policy of the Reagan administration constitute a radical discontinuity in American political history, although precursors exist. In addition, we believe that a secret agenda effectively guides the military policies and programs of this administration. Since we reject conspiracy theory in general, we are not proposing its existence as such; instead, we suggest that U.S. foreign and military policy has been captured by an amalgam of groups that share a common world view that in effect expresses the social myopia of the Old and New Right: their visions of American supremacy, their virulent anticommunism and consequent containment militarism—an entire spectrum of ultraconservative beliefs and values. Thus what we are experiencing is what this author in another context termed a "conspiracy of the like-minded" (Knelman, 1976). The groups that comprise the like-minded are not homogeneous in the total conglomerate of their views, but they share a powerful convergent consensus in their persistent perception of the Soviet threat. They are not interested in arms parity and thus reject arms control or the mutual verifiable freeze at present levels. In fact they rejects arms control per se as a form of unilateralism predisposed to the Soviet Union. They favor, promote, and seek nuclear superiority to match their self-assessment of moral superiority engaged in a fundamental contest between good and evil—a mirror image of the Soviet view except the Soviets seek parity. Thus, in one way or another, oversimplified or sophisticated, the various support groups behind Reagan and the key members of his administration implacably view the Soviet Union as an "evil empire" and communism as an ultimate threat. This has now become a paradox: an administration equipped with twentieth-century—even twenty-first-century—tools of destruction is operated by men with nineteenth-century minds. They steer the U.S. through the rearview mirror of their historical redundancy.

The amalgam of groups has found an almost ideal spokesperson, an almost perfect representative, in Ronald Reagan: a made-for-TV president, part puppet and part fellow-conspirator of the like-minded. In turn, Reagan has surrounded himself with cabinet members, of the formal and the kitchen variety, who share his own world view of cowboy capitalism, rugged individualism, fundamentalist faith, and, above all, an implacable hatred of the USSR and communism. Undifferentiated in its oversimplification and, tragically, dedicated to the notion of winning an unwinnable game, this perspective has dire consequences for all.

Basic to the major analytic mode of our book is the anatomy of the "hidden agenda," a group of key top-secret guidance, memoranda, decision, and directive documents relating to national security and to U.S. nuclear military policy. We believe that continual reference to this secret agenda makes sense and creates coherence out of the myriad of seemingly diverse voices and sometimes conflicting signals, official and unofficial, that emanate from the White House. The largely unstructured media response compounds the misdirection of these conflicting signals, as if the networks intend to cover the end of the world.

Fortunately, the secret agenda operates within the context of an open society. The members of the House and Senate, the various courageous critics in public life, in the universities, and among the people, and the various movements of nongovernment organizations dedicated to peace and justice all help to rewrite the script that is the text of the secret agenda. The secret agenda itself may be eroded by time, altered perceptions, and new influences within and outside of government.

In summary, the mutually reinforcing mind-sets of the various groups comprising the amalgam of Reagan supporters, combined with an almost autonomous set of technological means and a context of a political economy of war, provide a powerful systemic dynamic directed to the induction of nuclear war. In addition, the bipolar aspect of the struggle between the superpowers, both infected by a mirror-image paranoia and a mirror-image picture of the other as evil and themselves as good, presents the open-ended justification of means that so often accompanies such extreme polarization.

In this chapter we will examine the hidden agenda that we believe guides the military policies and programs of the Reagan administration. Many of the key actors who helped formulate the secret agenda have maintained a remarkably consistent approach in their continued roles over time. Of great significance is the revealed fact that the military balance, an assessment of the relative strategic strengths of the two superpowers, has been manipulated in order to disguise U.S. strength, distort Soviet strength, and justify U.S. superiority. Those who participated in these deceptions in the past remain active today; many of them are in positions of considerable power, multiplied by the leverage of influence as "advisers to the prince." Their analysis and documentation legitimates the decisions of the administration. They play a critical role in the search for nuclear superiority.

To this day each attempt to control nuclear arms has been opposed on the grounds that advantages would accrue to the Soviets. Even parity is such an advantage. The Strategic Arms Limitation Treaty II (SALT II), signed by the U.S. and USSR in 1979 but never ratified by the U.S. Senate, became the target of focused, organized opposition. The election of Ronald Reagan in 1980 became an equally significant goal. The mask of the argument, then and now, was that all previous treaties were merely a facade for permitted build-ups. But the real face of those who opposed SALT II was the active search for superiority, to defeat what they saw as appeasement (détente, above all, was appeasement). The debate over nuclear arms and arms control intensified from 1975 to 1980, a period that included the last year of the Ford presidency and the four years of Carter's presidential term. A critical element in this debate emerged in a special-interest organization, the Committee on the Present Danger (CPD), that alleged itself to be nonpolitical and dedicated to the defeat of SALT II and all its supporters. Integrated with the CPD's various activities was an attempt to subvert the national intelligence estimate of the military balance between the superpowers—the "Team B" report.

THE COMMITTEE ON THE PRESENT DANGER

The Committee on the Present Danger was founded in 1975 by Eugene V. Rostow, recently ousted head of the Arms Control and Disarmament Agency (ACDA). The Committee on the Present Danger has sixty-one directors, twenty-nine of whom hold, or held, key positions in the Reagan cabinet, the defense establishment, the intelligence services, and foreign affairs (Scheer, 1982, pp. 144-146). Among the most powerful are Ronald Reagan, president of the United States; Max Kampelman, chief counsel and founding director of CPD and new chief arms negotiator; Eugene Rostow and his recommended replacement, Kenneth L. Adelman, now head of ACDA; James L. Buckley, undersecretary of state for security assistance; William J. Casey, director, Central Intelligence Agency (CIA); John S. Foster, Jr., member, President's Foreign Intelligence Advisory Board (PFIAB); Francis P. Hoeber, Donald M. Rumsfeld, William B. Graham, Colin S. Gray, members, General Advisory Committee on ACDA (Graham is chairman); Charles Burton Marshall, John P. Roche, Paul Seabury, Laurence H. Silberman, and E. R. Zumwalt, Jr. (all members of the General Advisory Committee); W. Glenn Campbell, John B. Connally, Clare Boothe Luce, Peter O'Donnell, Jr., Edward Bennett Williams (all members of PFIAB); Amoretta M. Hoeber, deputy assistant secretary of the army for research and development; Fred Charles Iklé, undersecretary for defense of policy; Geoffrey Kemp and Richard Pipes, on the staff of the National Security Council (NSC); Jeane J. Kirkpatrick, former U.S. representative to the United Nations; John F. Lehman, secretary of the navy; Paul H. Nitze, former chief negotiator for theater nuclear forces; Richard N. Perle, assistant secretary of defense for international security policy; George P. Shultz, secretary of state; R. G. Stilwell, deputy undersecretary of defense for policy; Charles Tyroler II, president of CPD and member of the President's Foreign Intelligence Oversight Board; and a few others. This list does not include former and present members (not directors) of CPD, such as General Edward Rowny, former chief U.S. arms negotiator and now a Reagan adviser.

One thing is certain. At the time, CPD claimed to have captured state power and Reagan acknowledged their influence (Scheer, 1982, pp. 37-50, 41). The Committee on the Present Danger's Public Relations Director Paul Green said, "So the Committee's philosophy is dominant in the three major areas in which there is going to be US-Soviet activity" (Scheer, 1982, p. 39). This appears to still hold true.

The dominant philosophy of the U.S. defense establishment is more than ever the organized destruction of arms limitation and/or reductions, the total disavowal of détente, the total defeat of the Soviet communist state, the restoration of the "national will to defend the Free World against the spread of communism," and the restoration of American supremacy—a position that presupposes that nuclear war can be kept limited, survivable, and winnable, even if protracted, i.e., "We are living in a pre-war and not a post-war world" (Eugene Rostow, quoted in Scheer, 1982, p. 5). The CPD plan "for deterring or prosecuting a global war with the Soviet Union" (Scheer, 1982, pp. 5–6) is the moving force behind Reagan's "Five-Year Defense Plan" (Scheer, 1982, pp. 7, 8). The Committee on the Present Danger chose SALT II as its first target and effectively scuttled it.

THE "TEAM B" PLAYERS

The continuity of lineage from the fringe to the center to the seats of power is clearly identified by the key actors in the creation of CPD and the so-called "Team B." They now control the triad of key government functions—foreign policy, defense policy, and intelligence services. Basically the background is as follows. Until George Bush became director of the CIA in 1976, "it did not assume Soviet supremacy nor the notion that the USSR expected to win and survive a nuclear war." One of Bush's first tasks during the last year of Ford's presidency was to appoint a special team of "outsiders" and super-hawks that would break the CIA's code of secrecy and be given carte-blanche access to its most sensitive information. This group was called Team B, Team A being the professionals within the intelligence establishment. A *New York Times* report stated that Team B members had to "hold more pessimistic views of Soviet plans than those entertained by the advocates of the rough parity thesis" (Scheer, 1982, pp. 53–55). According to Ray S. Cline, former deputy director of the CIA, the process of making national security estimates "has been subverted" by employing "a kangaroo court of outside critics, all picked from one point of view" (Scheer, 1982, p. 153). The Team B chairman was Richard Pipes, Eastern European Harvard history professor, Polish emigree, and violently anti-Soviet former director of CPD. Nitze and Van Cleave were also members of Team B and CPD and shared Pipes's views. Pipes's views incorporate the galaxy of positions of CPD itself but, if anything, are more virulent. He dismisses the distinction between conventional and nuclear war, believes in "meaningful superiority," and is convinced that the Soviet's civil defense program is proof of its expectation of survival. Team B's report remained classified, but the official CIA estimates for 1976, although admitting increased Soviet spending, contradicted Team B's conclusions. Unsubstantiated rumor, referred to as "new evidence," in effect became the basis of policy through the personal judgment of Bush. It has been suggested that Richard Perle, now an assistant secretary of defense, but formerly adviser to Senator Jackson (D-Wash.), was provided with Team B's report and leaked it (Clarke, 1981). The Foreign Intelligence Advisory Board, resurrected by Reagan, is also captive of CPD. Pipes's famous 1977 article in *Commentary* (whose editor was a founding member of CPD), reaches new heights of Strangelovian but "scholarly" hysteria, only slightly less than mad (Pipes, 1980). Entrenched in the seats of power, the circle has become completed—Reagan, CPD, and Team B, one and the same (Clarke, 1981). Topping this inbreeding is the appointment of Max Kampelman as the new chief arms negotiator.

THE HOLOCAUST PROPHECY: THE FIVE-YEAR DEFENSE PLAN (FISCAL YEAR 1984–88, DEFENSE GUIDANCE)

The ironically titled "Five-Year Defense Plan" (derived NSC title, "National Security Decision Document #32" [NSDD-32]), presented and signed by Caspar Weinberger for Reagan's approval in 1981, was "leaked" and first reported in detail by the *New York Times* (Halloran, 1981, 1982; Bethe and Gottfried, 1982; *Washington Post*, 1982; Scheer, 1982, pp. 7–8). The essence of the plan is "decapitation" of the Soviet state through defeat in a limited or protracted or initiated nuclear war, using both military and economic diversions, psychological warfare, sabotage and guerrilla warfare, and the use of fear and alarm to justify their strategy of nuclear blackmail and coercion. Above all, the plan requires the will and means to fight a nuclear war and win it through nuclear superiority. Using a basketball term equivalent to "all-out attack," Reagan called for a "full-court press" against the Soviet Union. Richard Perle called for the will "to move up the escalation ladder" (Scheer, 1982, pp. 7, 13). The plan represents the literal take-over of military strategy and policy by the superhawks of CPD and, more seriously, "comes close to a declaration of war on the Soviet Union" (Bethe and Gottfried, 1982). Even the generals were alarmed. General David C. Jones, upon leaving office as chairman of the Joint Chiefs of Staff, derided the plan and the strategy as unreal and incredibly extravagant (*Washington Post*, 1982). Former Secretary of State Cyrus Vance used the word "madness" to describe the five-year plan (Scheer, 1982, p. 33). The plan embodies the views of the "scholars" of apocalypse like Colin Gray, now a key adviser to the defense establishment. Gray and coauthor Keith Payne wrote the script in "Victory Is Possible," a *Foreign Policy* article of 1980:

> Victory or defeat in nuclear war is possible . . . . The United States should plan to defeat the Soviet Union, and to do so at a cost that would not prohibit U.S. recovery. . . [to] contemplate the destruction of Soviet political authority and the emergence of a post-war world compatible with Western values [using]

. . . a combination of counterforce offensive targeting, civil defense, and ballistic missile and air defense [should] . . . hold U.S. casualties down to a level compatible with national survival and recovery [about 20 million dead] . . . . American strategic forces do not exist solely for the purpose of deterring a Soviet nuclear threat . . . [but] are intended to support U.S. foreign policy.

Vice President George Bush echoes the NSDD-32 goals. When asked if 5 percent of people would survive in a nuclear war, he said, "You have a survivability of command and control, a survivability of industrial potential, protection of a percentage of your citizens, and you have a capability that inflicts more damage on the opposition than it can inflict on you. That's the way you can have a winner . . . . and if everybody fired everything he had, you'd have 'better' than that survive" (Scheer, 1982, p. 29). Survival capability depends on civil defense or the relatively more acceptable, but also more euphemistic "crisis relocation" (plus missile defenses, of course, and abrogation of the Anti-Ballistic Missile [ABM] Treaty). To quote Thomas K. Jones, deputy undersecretary of defense and formerly of Boeing, "If there are enough shovels to go around, everybody's going to make it . . . . it's the dirt that does it" (Scheer, 1982, p. 18). Bechtel, Boeing, and other major "defense contractors" are well represented in the Reagan administration. One should respond to T.K. Jones by paraphrasing Hemingway's injunction to young authors, i.e., that they learn to distinguish between the shovels and the b.s. Yet the myth of civil defense has persisted for almost three decades, despite thorough refutation by independent assessors and official studies (ACDA, 1978; OTA, 1980; Physicians for Social Responsibility [PSR], 1981) and the resistance of many U.S. cities.

The myths of the nuclear arms race and other sociopolitical myths have now become entrenched policy. The dominant actors in this nuclear theater of the absurd are a strange amalgam reinforcing each other through a single common denominator, i.e., that victory is necessary and possible. Hopes for arms limitation, reduction, and control have radically diminished. Fear, ignorance, and religious mission have captured policy. Looking backward, the Carter administration, despite PD-59, appears benign and sane. The Moral Majority and the New Right, with their punitiveness and ignorance, have captured policy, i.e., "The Russians could walk right in and take over without firing a shot . . . . they could do that any time between now and the mid-1980s . . . and long after that if we continue the Carter administration's non-defense policy" (Jerry Falwell, evangelist of the Moral Majority). When asked how the Russians could walk in, Falwell replied, "Across the Mexican border" (Fitzgerald, 1981). It would be ludicrous if it were not deadly serious. That is Ronald Reagan's position and that is the unique new danger the world faces. Only the hopeful involvement of people, attested to by the anti-nuclear Easter parades of Europe, together with sane Americans in and out of office can change this course of destruction. Mutually Assured Destruction, or MAD, has been displaced by NUTS (Nuclear Utilization: Tactics and Strategies) or, as it was originally used, Nuclear Utilization Target Selection, a form of "surgical attack" (Keeny, Jr., and Panofsky, 1981/82).

THE COMPLETION OF A VICIOUS CYCLE

Cold war containment policies peaked twice in post-World War II U.S. history. In each case special-interest groups composed of a strange amalgam of direct representatives of the industrial-military complex, psycho-Sovietologists, hawkish strategy experts imbued with the "win syndrome," "crackpot realists," neoconservatives, and more extreme members of the New and Old Right emerged as a potent force, aptly named the "peddlers of crises" (Sanders, 1983). Disgruntled liberals, the American-Jewish Committee, racists, Daniel Patrick Moynihan, all became bedfellows of containment hardness. During the Truman administration Paul Nitze, who once again stands center stage in nuclear diplomacy, masterminded the secret policy study of "containment militarism," National Security Memorandum #68 (NSC-68). An earlier version of the Committee on the Present Danger (CPD-1) came together in the environment of NSC-68 to counter a perceived Soviet threat (Sanders, 1983). They disbanded in 1953 but their members infiltrated the foreign-policy establishment. After President Carter's election in 1976, the Committee on the Present Danger formed to promote U.S. supremacy and the "containment" of the Soviet Union. The CPD took SALT II and the "doves" of ACDA as their targets; yet Carter himself is the author of Presidential Directive #59 (PD-59), which tended to entrench counterforce doctrine into U.S. nuclear strategy (*National Journal,* Tuesday, 20 October 1979, p. 1751).

The new CPD sought a huge build-up in U.S. military might to achieve "containment," if not destruction, of the USSR as a political system. Disguised as politically nonpartisan, the Committee on the Present Danger nevertheless functioned as candidates of Reagan's shadow cabinet. After a January 1979 dinner meeting in Washington with key members of CPD, Ronald Reagan became a member of its executive committee *(National Journal,* Tuesday, 20 October 1979); after Reagan's 1980 election, CPD members became his cabinet.

The creation of mythical gaps between the relative military strengths of the U.S. and USSR became the cornerstone of CPD interventions in U.S. military expenditures and strategies. While the members of CPD-1 (1950) were ultraconservative isolationists who resisted U.S. involvements abroad, the strength (and weakness) of CPD today is that its ultraconservatives have become interventionists. The present CPD also has had the advantage of Soviet cooperation. First Afghanistan, the suppression of Solidarity, the trials of the dissidents, then KAL-007—all these actions fed the paranoia of the new apocalyptics with their sum-zero approach and their denial of even the possibility of détente, dialogue, negotiated conflict, and arms reduction. In the evolution of U.S. policy from NSC-68 through PD-59 to NSDD-32 and SIOP-6, we have come full circle, but at a much higher level of cold-war intensity, with enhanced nuclear arsenals to incinerate humanity. However NSDD-13, the first official document to state that U.S. strategic forces must be able to win a protracted nuclear war, is a doctrine identified as "suicidal" (Rodberg, 1982). Charles Kupperman, former defense analyst for CPD, stated categorically, "I think it is possible to win in a classical sense" (Scheer, 1982, p. 131). NSDD-32 also calls for "internal reform in the Soviet Union and shrinkage of the Soviet empire" (Scheer, 1982, p. 7).

The Committee on the Present Danger not only killed SALT II, but it also destroyed the eminently sensible director of the Arms Control and Disarmament Agency (ACDA), Paul Warnke. President Carter yielded to the CPD assault by deciding to replace Paul Warnke with General George M. Seignious II, and to develop the Rapid Deployment Force, a 100,000-man intervention army group, for availability "wherever . . . there might be a contingency outside the jurisdiction of NATO" (Sanders, 1983).

SALT II's defeat in the Senate represented the most intense coalition of the containment interventionists. Allied in the battle were the Committee for the Present Danger, the intellectual hawk establishment, the Coalition for Peace Through Strength (191 members of Congress), the American Security Council, the Conservative Caucus, the American Conservative Union, the Moral Majority Evangelicals, etc. They outspent the proponents of SALT II by a fifteen-to-one margin (Sanders, 1983, p. 265). But, if this victory was sweet, the capture of U.S. foreign and defense policy under Reagan was pure saccharin. And remember a protocol in SALT II would have banned the deployment of cruise missiles and this was critical in the attack on ratification.

The CPD continues in the heart of military policy and containment politics. Even as Max Kampelman was named new chief arms degotiator, an article in the *New York Times Magazine* of 27 January 1985 coauthored by him laid the real basis for negotiation expectations. The article says that Soviet arms control compliance is "sufficiently troubling to warrant skepticism regarding the likelihood of implementing any such complex and farreaching agreement" and would "require a much more felicitous political climate than currently exists." Kampelman attempted to have his name withdrawn from the article but it was too late. These same authors would enthusiastically support the "Star Wars" development, a much more complex and difficult technological feat than arms verification, and yet reject arms control because of the imperfectibility of verification. This is the politics of deception or at least self-deception. In effect, the new chief arms control negotiator is dedicated to the goals of nuclear superiority and not to arms control. This is typical of every overture and initiative on nuclear weapons made by the Reagan administration.

Jeane Kirkpatrick, UN ambassador during Reagan's first term, made the clearest statement on arms control, "I am willing to be just as generous as we possibly can be as long as that's consistent with maintaining clear supremacy" (Sanders, 1983, p. 149). Kirkpatrick has now become a Republican and is slated for a new, senior position in Reagan's second-term administration. The completion of vicious circles goes on.

REAGAN: THE PRESIDENT WHO WENT OUT INTO THE COLD

The essential elements of the Reagan administration's military/political policies, plans, and programs, as represented by the supersecret Defense Guidance FY 1984–1988, Single Integrated Operational Plan #6 (SIOP-6), and National Security Decision Documents/Directives #13, 32, and 85 (NSDD's), are:

1. A dedication to the destruction of the present Soviet political system, i.e., "to render ineffective the total Soviet (and Soviet-allied) military and political power structure"; the American nuclear forces "must prevail and be able to force the Soviet Union to seek earliest termination of hostilities on terms favorable to the United States"; to require the assured destruction of "nuclear and conventional military forces and industry critical to military power"; to be able to maintain "through a protracted conflict period and afterward, the capability to inflict very high levels of damage" on Soviet industry. The plan is to confront the Soviet Union anywhere in the world by every means required to reduce its influence and effectiveness. In effect the documents are a declaration of technical and economic war against the USSR.
2. Explicit in these documents is the doctrine of nuclear warfighting, i.e. to fight, win, and survive a limited or protracted nuclear war; in fact, the documents are dedicated to the defeat of the Soviet Union at any level of conflict, from insurgencies to nuclear war. The preferred attack technique would be a "decapitation" strike to destroy Soviet command, control, communications, and intelligence (C^3I) systems, as well as the political and intelligence headquarters, i.e., the Kremlin and KGB, to remove the head from the body politic by destroying "the political power structure."
3. The above warfighting plan is to be supported by a program of economic suffocation of the USSR through a variety of means, i.e., trade restrictions, technology transfer boycotts, and a costly arms race, including

deliberately deceptive elements designed to drain Soviet resources and to lead them into false and costly activities, i.e., a technical strategy to erode the Soviet economy by focusing "investment on weapons systems that render the accumulated Soviet equipment stocks obsolescent" and impose "costs on the Soviets by raising uncertainty regarding their ability to accomplish some of their higher-priority missions"; to develop weapons that "are difficult to counter, impose disproportionate costs, open new areas of major military competition and obsolesce previous Soviet investment."

4. Also explicit in these documents is the doctrine of active interventionism, including the wide use of "special operations," meaning guerrilla warfare, sabotage, and psychological warfare. "We must revitalize and enhance special operations forces to project United States power where the use of conventional forces would be premature, inappropriate or infeasible," including such target areas as Eastern Europe. A Special Defense Acquisition Fund would be established for providing aid, including aircraft, to troubled allies or friendly nations. For Europe, in order "to exploit political, economic and military weaknesses within the Warsaw Pact and to disrupt enemy rear operations, special-operations forces will conduct operations in Eastern Europe and in the northern and southern NATO regions" and will force their way into Southwest Asia or the Persian Gulf if necessary, i.e., to stop Soviet infiltration or invasion, without waiting for an invitation from a friendly government.

5. The plan also explicitly mandates the Defense Department to develop a weapons procurement program and technological research and development to fulfill these plans. Of particular interest here is the development of communications systems that "must provide the capability to execute ad hoc plans, even subsequent to repeated attacks . . . that these systems should support the reconstitution and execution of strategic reserve forces, specifically full communications with our strategic submarines" and "the services should program resources to insure that intelligence support is adequate." The key is a survivable C^3I system to persist "throughout crisis situations up to and including protracted nuclear." SIOP-6 and DG FY 1984–1988 emphasize this.

6. The Pentagon is also directed to begin a "prototype development of space-based weapons systems," including those weapons to destroy Soviet satellites, known as the Strategic Defense Initiative (SDI) or "Star Wars." The development of all ballistic missile defense systems (ABM) including those that are space based (SBABM) would be accelerated. In fact DG FY 1984–1988 is explicit in its warning that the U.S. might seek a revision in the ABM Treaty. The latter may be linked to defend MX silos. SBABM is now represented by the Strategic Defense Initiative (SDI) (or "Star Wars"). Thus, contrary to media speculation, Reagan's speech of 23

March 1983 did not launch us into space. An operationally separate, but deceptively connected program is the development of antisatellite weapons (ASAT's).

The Strategic Defense Initiative has a more subtle aspect to it. The top-secret agenda also proposes "investment on weapons systems that are difficult to counter, impose disproportionate costs, open new areas of military competition and obsolesce Soviet investment." Thus SDI may also be deliberate hoax, an absurd example of technological faith, or both. There may be Machiavellians as well as true believers behind the plan and, most likely, in the Soviet military and political bureaucracy as well. This would account in part for Soviet insistence on preventing the militarization of space, whether it stems from economic or military apprehensions or both. Regardless of motive, SDI has moved to the top of the negotiating agenda.

7. Both implicitly and explicitly, these documents present a general denial of deterrence strategy, in favor of a nuclear warfighting doctrine that includes a first-strike option. Countervailing has become prevailing.
8. Explicit and implicit statements support the notion of survivability after a limited or protracted nuclear war; thus, such wars should end on "terms favorable to the United States."
9. Explicit statements also deny the distinction between conventional and nuclear weapons and between threats and strategic weapons, i.e., regional and intercontinental weapons. In fact, the defense guidance document deliberately calls for the joint employment of medium- and long-range weapons to eliminate "any arbitrary division between categories of nuclear weapons systems," and in SIOP-6, Pershing II's (the so-called "Euromissiles") are also described as "executing non-strategic nuclear options may be tasked for [strategic] missions" (Arkin, 1983, p. 12). This is a direct contradiction of the NATO "dual-track" decision, giving the clear lie to the arguments provided to rationalize this.
10. The defense guidance document details the identification of new weapons systems and even the projected defense budget. Surprisingly, the media or other analysts make scant reference to a document so revealing in its description of future programs and policies that extend through fiscal years 1984–1988, the second Reagan term. It is also surprising that the degree of compliance with the secret agenda is so complete.

Many of these plans have already been translated into programs and actions: the mining of harbors in Nicaragua, the CIA terrorist manual for use by the contras, the invasion and occupation of Grenada, the Middle East incursion, the implementation of the "Star Wars" system, and the general program of weapons development. Some tactics were designed to strain and drain the Soviet economy; others contributed to the "heating up" of tensions with the Soviet Union, mainly by rhetoric but also by exploitation of strained situations (KAL-007 and Reagan's statement disavowing Soviet authority over Eastern Europe).

Readers should be aware of the tentative nature of our hypothesis that the military/foreign policies of the Reagan administration are guided by what we have termed the "secret agenda." Tentativeness is endemic to this hypothesis because we are dealing with "top-secret" documents defined under a secrecy classification: documents dealing with "the national defense and foreign relations of the United States" (U.S. President Executive Order 12065: Sections 1-2, 28 June 1978). Nevertheless, key elements of some of these supersecret documents have been leaked. They form a compelling context in which to assess the military and foreign policy milieu of the Reagan administration. They thus provide a model whereby the major decisions are knitted into a more consistent thread, set within the more complex and often contradictory patterns of public statement, action, and reaction. This hypothesis is reinforced by publicly documented materials, written and spoken in the present and the past by key actors in the policy script. The degree of agreement between the "secret agenda" and the public agenda, as well as between policy, mind-set, and world view, is quite striking.

However, readers are to be further cautioned that the real world is situated in a matrix of opportunities and obstacles, of constraints and contexts, that tend to modify simple correlations. Even Ronald Reagan was eventually forced to capitulate radically on the defense budget, nevertheless managing to call it a victory. What he called "irresponsible" on the part of the Senate suddenly became responsible on his part. The budget he had said was indispensable was reduced by 8 percent.

For some basic reasons, that part of our hypothesis dealing with the policy of "economic suffocation" is less certain than military and foreign policy. The level of secrecy maintained on which particular actions or military systems are deliberately designed to drain Soviet resources, as described in item #3 of the secret agenda on page 23, is such as to make analysis speculative by nature. It is also quite possible that some deliberately "false trail" military developments may not be consistently perceived as such within the policy and planning group. "Star Wars" may be such a mixed development, designed at the same time to drain Soviet resources, scuttle arms negotiations, obsolesce Soviet offenses, and yet remain believably viable for some. "Economic suffocation" takes a variety of forms involving aid and trade, commodity market manipulation, price fixing, embargoes, and even political provocation.

One further aspect of the "secret agenda" relates indirectly to military policy, but directly to the crisis mentality of the Reaganites: the highly classified NSDD authorizing the program code-named "Rex 84." This program provides the design for a mass round-up and arrest of hundreds of thousands of persons, mainly illegal aliens but also the politically "undesirable." The authors are two of the California gang, Edwin Meese, former special attorney general of California in charge of civil disorder and now U.S. attorney general, and Louis O. Guiffrida, former commandant of the Crime Training Institute of California and now head of the Federal Emergency Measures Agency (FEMA). Rex-84 is connected with military preparedness exercises for nuclear war, code-named "Night Train 84" and "Global Shield." It also prepares for the intervention in Central America that Guiffrida believes would trigger an invasion by illegal aliens, rushing across the borders in a six-hour period (Ridgeway, *Village Voice,* Friday, 3 March 1985). According to Jack Anderson, this plot against basic civil liberties is even more sinister in that General Guiffrida is requesting "standby" legislation to suspend the Constitution and the Bill of Rights in the event of a "national emergency." Meese has found power in Washington, while Guiffrida has room to move into the office of director of the FBI.

We can also authenticate the content of these documents by examining the published views and political history of those few men and women who hold real power in the defense and foreign policy establishments of government. When we do this, we find a curious correspondence of style and content between the open, published views of these "scholars of apocalypse," or "wizards of Armageddon" as they have been so aptly described, and the top-secret documents. This correspondence reinforces, if not establishes, our contention that the Reagan administration has declared "war" on the Soviet Union. If we go one step further and examine the writings, statements, and politics of Reagan's support groups, i.e., the New and Old Right, then the correspondence runs beyond the realm of rationalized, intellectual analysis, down deep into a peculiar mind-set, into a deeply entrenched belief system consistent with the view that the battle between the superpowers is a battle between good and evil that must be fought to the end.

"The cold war . . . has broken loose from its historical moorings and acquired an independent inertial thrust of its own. What is the cold war now about? It is about itself . . . . We face here in the grimmest sense, 'the consequences of consequences' . . . . the entrepreneurs have lost control of it, as it has thrown up its own managers, administrators, producers and a large supporting cast, all of whom have a direct interest in its continuance, in its enlargement. Whatever happens, the show must go on" (E.P. Thompson, *Nation,* 10/17 July 1982). This is not unlike the nuclear power industry whose managers plan for perpetuity with their "Faustian bargains." What Amory Lovins said is increasingly true, "What is not specifically forbidden becomes compulsory." The compulsion has two components: the technical component, the "ensemble of means" (Ellul, 1965), tends to become autonomous and usurp human ends; the organizational component, the technocratic/managerial group whose self-interest reinforces technological autonomy, converts the technological to the logical!

David Halloway's concept that the victory of the Reagan administration constituted the beginning of a second cold war adds the political component to the above Ellulian concept. The conventional left will remain to argue about continuity or discontinuity. It is their historical burden to attack liberal Democrats in preference to conservative Republicans. Whichever the interpretation, it would appear that by policy and action the Reagan administration represents not a mere continuity of past trends but a unique departure from them, a stance possibly dedicated not to mere brinkmanship but to taking us over the brink. The military budget itself sets the stage for self-fulfillment. As former senator J. William Fulbright stated, "This budget, together with the propaganda to sell it to the public and Congress, has the effect of shifting the focus of our policy from deterring nuclear war to the waging and winning of nuclear [even a protracted war]" (*National Catholic Reporter,* 26 March 1982, Ad Hoc Congressional Committee, Chairman Congressman Ronald Dellums, April 1982).

Given the good will and common sense of most of the public, hardly anyone, informed or otherwise, seems to believe that there is a weapons' managerial group totally dedicated to the proposition that nuclear war is winnable, survivable, and even necessary. The Reagan administration has not merely reintroduced the game of nuclear chicken or reenacted the doctrine of nuclear warfighting; it has altered the belief system. The analogies made to Carter's policy with PD-59, Brown's "countervailing" doctrine, Schlesinger's "counterforce," or Kennedy's collision game in the Cuban missile crisis are not valid. It is not the "willingness to use atomic weapons" (Eisenhower) that is now at issue; it is the dedication to use them should the Soviets not capitulate or self-destruct. National Security Decisions Directive #13 is the logical yet mad extension of PD-59, the former being based on "flexible options" and "victory denial," while the latter is victory assuring: it transforms the "countervailing" policy into a "prevailing" policy. It is amazing that Walter Mondale did not use the leaked material from the Defense Guidance FY 1984–1988 document or the later national security decision documents signed by Reagan to set the record straight. These documents explain the refusal to negotiate seriously the warfighting program, the clandestine operations in Nicaragua, the position in the Middle East, and the invasion of Grenada.

During the 1984 presidential campaign Reagan made the politically astute decision to support the former regime of John Kennedy. Reagan's speeches were filled with praise for Kennedy and denigration of the Carter-

Mondale years, comparing the former's strength with the latter's weakness. Yet, in a letter to his crony Richard Nixon in 1960, Reagan viciously stated that Kennedy's ideas came from Karl Marx and Adolph Hitler: "Shouldn't someone tag Mr. Kennedy's bold new imaginative program with its proper age? Under the tousled boyish haircut is still old Karl Marx—first launched a century ago . . . . There is nothing new in the idea of a government being Big Brother to us all. Hitler called his 'State Socialism' and way before him it was 'benevolent monarchy'" (*New York Times,* Monday, 24 October 1984, p. A-24).

Let us examine a more fundamental difference between John Kennedy and Ronald Reagan. On 10 June 1963 at the American University, Kennedy delivered a prophetic speech of undying wisdom. In part, he said:

> I speak of peace because of the new face of war. Total war makes no sense in an age where great powers can maintain large and relatively invulnerable nuclear forces and refuse to surrender without resort to those forces. It makes no sense in an age when a single nuclear weapon contains almost ten times the explosive force delivered by all the Allied air forces in the Second World War. It makes no sense in an age when the deadly poisons produced by a nuclear exchange would be carried by wind and water and soil and seed to the far corners of the globe and to generations yet unborn . . . .
>
> I speak of peace, therefore, as the necessary rational end of rational men . . . . Some say that it is useless to speak of peace or world law or world disarmament—and that it will be useless until the leaders of the Soviet Union adopt a more enlightened attitude. I hope they do. I believe we can help them do it. But I also believe that we must re-examine our own attitude—as individuals and as a Nation—for our attitude is as essential as theirs. And . . . every thoughtful citizen who despairs of war and wishes to bring peace, should begin by looking inward—by examining his own attitude toward the possibilities of peace, toward the Soviet Union, toward the course of the cold war and toward freedom and peace here at home.
>
> No government or social system is so evil that its people must be considered as lacking in virtue. As Americans, we find communism profoundly repugnant as a negation of personal freedom and dignity. But we can still hail the Russian people for their many achievements—in science and space, in economic and industrial growth, in culture and in acts of courage.
>
> Among the many traits the peoples of our two countries have in common, none is stronger than our mutual abhorrence of war. Almost unique among the major world powers, we have never been at war with each other. And no nation in the history of battle ever suffered more than the Soviet Union suffered in the course of the Second World War. At least twenty million lost their lives. Countless millions of homes and farms were burned or sacked. A third of the nation's territory, including two thirds of its industrial base, was turned into a wasteland—a loss equivalent to the devastation of this country east of Chicago.
>
> . . . both the United States and its allies, and the Soviet Union and its

allies, have a mutually deep interest in a just and genuine peace and in halting the arms race. Agreements to this end are in the interests of the Soviet Union as well as ours—and even the most hostile nations can be relied upon to accept and keep those treaty obligations, and only those treaty delegations, which are in their own interest.

So let us not be blind to our differences—but let us also direct attention to our common interests and the means by which those differences can be resolved. And if we cannot end now our differences, at least we can help make the world safe for diversity. For, in the final analysis, our most basic common link is that we all inhabit this small planet. We all breathe the same air. We all cherish our children's future. And we are all mortal. [*Public Papers of the Presidents of the United States, J. F. Kennedy, Washington, D.C., 1963, pp. 459–64*]

Now, forgetting the frightful gulf in style between the eloquent Kennedy and the loquacious Reagan, or the emotive difference between a caring Kennedy and a card-reading Reagan, let us read what Reagan said on the same subject.

In his first press conference after his 1980 victory, Reagan stated that one can never trust the Soviet leaders who "reserve unto themselves the right to commit any crime, to lie, to cheat, in order to obtain their objective . . . . Communists are not bound by our morality. They say any crime, including lying, is moral if it advances the cause of socialism." Earlier, he had said, "I wouldn't trust the Russians around the block. They must be laughing at us because we continue to think of them as people." Thus Reagan's attack on the leaders is extended to the people. While some may even agree philosophically with Reagan's views of the Soviet leadership, it is incredible that they would also believe Reagan's self-created image as peacemaker at the very end of the 1984 campaign. You cannot have it both ways. You cannot have arms reduction treaties with someone who will cheat because it is not possible to have absolute verification. You cannot negotiate from "strength" and "superiority," the expressed goals of the Republican platforms of 1980 and 1984, in a dynamic arms race whose enhancement decreases global security. You cannot deal with nuclear arms reduction from a position of fundamentalist Christian morality in the sense of a struggle to the death between good and evil. If you are Reagan, you must destroy, in one way or another, this "evil empire" and "focus of evil in our time." You cannot "compromise our belief in God with [their] dialectical materialism" (G. Ball, *New York Review,* 8 November 1984, pp. 5–11). How could anyone believe that Reagan's arms reduction proposals are genuine and acceptable when he rejects parity and insists on superiority! The Reagan administration has stalled talks until public and world opinion dragged him into them after long delays. (The first meeting occurred one-and-a-half years after Reagan took office.) This same Reagan administration considered it a victory when the Soviets walked out of INF talks on 23 November 1983; the triumph was complete when the Soviets walked out of START on 8 December 1983. Only on the eve of the 1984 election did Reagan alter his rhetoric.

THE LEGITIMATION OF NUCLEAR WAR

The key administrators in the Reagan administration truly believe in a nuclear warfighting, warwinning, and warsurviving doctrine. They truly believe in this nuclear mythology and base plans and programs on their belief. They spend billions to create the technical basis for victory in nuclear war. For example, Louis O. Guiffrida, head of FEMA, has said that nuclear war "would be a terrible mess but it wouldn't be unmanageable" (Scheer, 1983, p. 3). His assistant William Chipman also believes in survivability: "As I say, the ants eventually build another anthill" (Scheer, 1983, p. 3). Eugene V. Debs Rostow, the man Reagan chose to head the Arms Control and Disarmament Agency, has clear views. "We are living in a pre-war and not a post-war world." Charles Kupperman, another Reagan appointee to ACDA, said, "Nuclear war is a destructive thing but still in large part a physics problem" (Scheer, 1983, p. 6), and Colin Gray notes, "The U.S. must possess the ability to wage war rationally" (*Washington Post,* Friday, 16 April 1982).

By 1981, Defense Secretary Caspar Weinberger told the House Budget Committee that the U.S. capability "for deterring or prosecuting a global war with the Soviet Union" would be expanded (Scheer, 1983, p. 6). Of the most fanatical and outspoken of the "strategy scholars" brought in by the Reagan administration—Richard Pipes, Colin Gray, and Richard Perle—it is Perle who, as assistant secretary of defense, wields the power behind the throne of Caspar Weinberger, "born-again" cold warrior–crusader (Talbott, 1984).

Richard Pipes, another pathological Soviet hater, is at once more fanatic and more candid than many more subtle voices on surviving doomsday. He insists that the administration's goal is not "punishing the aggressor [but] rather . . . defeating him" (Scheer, 1983, p. 6). Pipes has clearly enumerated official Reagan policy: "Soviet leaders would have to choose between peacefully changing their Communist system . . . or going to war" (Scheer, 1983, p. 8). Colin Gray, a member of key defense committees and senior adviser to the National Security Council, has written an article with Keith Payne that states, "To advocate . . . targeting flexibility and selectivity is not the same as to advocate a war-fighting, war-survival strategy . . . . victory or defeat in nuclear war is possible . . . . the clearer the vision of successful termination, the more likely war can be waged intelligently at earlier stages" (Gray and Payne, 1980). Later in this same article, Gray wrote, "The United States should plan to defeat the Soviet Union and to do so at a cost that would not prohibit U.S. recovery. Washington should identify war aims that in the last resort would contemplate the destruction of Soviet political authority and the emergence of a post-war world order compatible with Western values." Gray argued further that in such a war, U.S. casualties could be held "down to a level compatible with national survival and recovery." Compatibility for Gray is itself as monstrous as it is an underestimation, a mere twenty million dead. What is clear, on the other hand, is the striking resemblance between this article and the actual policy documents to which we have referred. In 1979 Gray wrote a series of articles that introduced many aspects of the "secret agenda." One in particular, "Nuclear Strategy: The Case for a Theory of Victory" (Gray, 1979), provides a clear, theoretical analysis of the real policy expressed in the "secret agenda."

Richard Perle is much more clever than his associates, a true modern Machiavelli. He also advocates winning a war without actually waging it. Perle has probably written most of Reagan's arms reduction proposals that are deliberately designed to be rejected by the Soviets. In addition, Perle also probably originated the idea of using deliberate exaggerations of the Soviet threat to achieve superiority. Perle's role in subverting arms agreements has been admirably documented (Talbott, 1984); like Rostow, Perle has a history of playing such games, with strategies that go back to Herman Kahn's game of nuclear chicken. Today Perle is more concerned about the national will to "move up the escalation ladder." Having once been national security adviser to the late, hawkish Senator Henry Jackson (D-Wash.), Perle later joined a law firm with Rostow and John Lehman, the current secretary of the navy and advocate of "superiority." Robert Scheer's interview with Richard Perle illustrates Perle's ignorance of both history and the arms race (Scheer, 1983, pp. 96-97). When asked about peace and protest movements in the U.S., Perle commented that "we've pretty much recovered from that." Six months later, the largest peace demonstration in U.S. history took place in New York City.

One should not misunderstand Perle's position. He has declared economic and technical war on the USSR and is dedicated to winning that war by every means. He is also dedicated to a vast nuclear superiority and if deterrence, intimidation, subversion, and economic suffocation fail, he is dedicated to winning a nuclear war. Perle shows particular dedication to escalation dominance, which means, literally, to act beyond conventional and well into nuclear warfighting stages. Like his colleagues Kenneth Adelman, new head of the Arms Control and Disarmament Agency and a less knowledgeable clone of his predecessor, superhawk Eugene Rostow; Fred Iklé, undersecretary of defense for policy; Richard Allen, former national security adviser to President Reagan; Colin Gray of the Arms Control Agency Advisory Committee, ACDA, and Verification Review Committee; and to a fair degree Richard Burt, director of the State Department's Bureau of Politics–Military Affairs, all reject arms control as a hoax, the net effect of which is unilateral U.S. disarmament. In 1981, Burt wrote in *Daedalus,* "There are strong reasons for believing that arms control is unlikely to possess much utility in the coming decade" and "regardless of whether the SALT II is ratified, the United States, in any follow-up negotiations should not seek severe quantitative reductions or tighter qualitative constraints" (Burt, 1981). It is true that Burt of State and Perle of Pentagon are in an interdepartmental power struggle (Talbott, 1984), but in the end they share a strategy that Senator Edmund Muskie said "may be a secret agenda for sidetracking disarmament while the United States goes on with rearmament" (Scheer, 1983, p. 84).

With the possible exception of Burt, the writings, speeches, interviews, and general behavioral and attitudinal history of these men and others in positions of advisory as well as administrative power validates our notion that they constitute a "holocaust lobby" and deeply subscribe to all the proposals and plans in the relevant secret documents for fighting, winning, and surviving a limited or protracted nuclear war. If one adds to these the other former members of the Committee on the Present Danger who are in the seats of real political power—Ronald Reagan, president of the United States, George P. Shultz, secretary of state, and John F. Lehman, secretary of the navy—then the entrenchment of the rigid right, with a mind-set dedicated to the destruction of the Soviet state by nuclear war if necessary, is almost complete. We are left with the Dr. Strangelove of U.S. politics, Secretary of Defense Caspar Weinberger, claimed and acknowledged friend of CPD, "born-again" fundamentalist, and true believer in Armageddon (because it's in the Bible). Perhaps the hardest of hard-liners, Weinberger's religious belief, ideological belief, and political power contrive to produce the ultimate conversion of myth to policy in the military area. We would reiterate our argument that this present U.S. administration represents a unique discontinuity in American politics. We do not subscribe to conspiracy theories, yet we acknowledge that a cohesive and organized collective of the New and Old Right has captured policy power in the U.S. government. We are dealing with something far more dangerous than an ordinary conspiracy: we now deal with the "conspiracy of the like-minded" (Knelman, 1976). We are now witnessing the legitimation of nuclear war as an extension of peace. In their prescient article, Colin Gray and Keith Payne spelled out the policy of "preemptive retaliation" or "counterforce offensive targeting" (Gray and Payne, 1980). They wrote, "American strategic forces do not exist solely for the purpose of deterring. . . . they are intended to support U.S. foreign policy. . . . such a function [defending Europe] would enable a president to *initiate* [Italics mine] strategic *nuclear use for coercive, though politically defensive purposes*" (Gray and Payne, 1980). With the concept of defensive offense, Orwell's prediction on the politics of language is self-fulfilling.

RANT, CANT, AND RAND

Of all the institutions in America, the Rand Corporation (RAND stands for Research and Development) of Santa Monica, California, spawned the greatest number of influential strategic doctrines and strategy intellectuals. As early as 1 March 1946, this corporation began its studies of "air warfare" with Army Air Force contract #MX-791, known as Project Rand (F. Kaplan., 1983, p. 59). The early group at Rand included such luminaries as John Williams, Bernard Brodie, Ed Paxson, Albert Wohlstetter, Andrew Marshall, Tom Schelling, Herman Kahn, Henry Rowen, Daniel Ellsberg, and William Kaufman. This community of strategy scholars, aptly called the "wizards of Armageddon" by Fred Kaplan, developed the entire notion of the rational use of nuclear weapons. The basic assumptions behind their thinking that nuclear wars could be fought, won, and survived stemmed from their omniscient, yet mad "rationality." Nuclear Options or NU-OPTS, more properly termed NUTS (Nuclear Utilization: Tactics and Strategy), became the fashionable field of study.

By the 1960s, a new generation of "defense intellectuals" had arrived at Rand. Among them were Fred Iklé and James R. Schlesinger, who contributed the rationale for NU-OPTS, a rationale for the irrational. The counterforce die was cast: the top-secret National Security Decision Memorandum (NSDM-242) resulted from this rationale. Schlesinger's warfighting doctrine became entrenched U.S. policy when Schlesinger became Nixon's secretary of defense in July 1973. Schlesinger appointed Andrew Marshall, one of Rand's founding fathers, to the Pentagon. National Security Decision Memorandum #242 became the basis for unlimited weapons procurement. Jimmy Carter's Presidential Directive (PD-59) of 25 July 1980 reinforced a nuclear warfighting policy. The seminal influence of the Rand defense intellectuals' contribution continued.

Not surprisingly, Andrew Marshall, Fred Iklé, and Richard Perle wrote Weinberger's notorious "Defense Guidance" document (Kaplan, 1983, p. 387). Paul H. Nitze, Richard De Lauer, and T. K. Jones also joined the circle of holocaust planners. T. K. Jones, the former Boeing engineer famous for his succinct commentary on the aftermath of a nuclear exchange—"If there are enough shovels to go around, everyone's going to make it"—had served as Nitze's chief technical assistant on the U.S. SALT team. Nitze, now the new arms control ambassador of the U.S., masterminded the National Security Council Memorandum #68 of 7 April 1950: the first purely ideological statement of the permanent struggle between the superpowers, and the U.S. mandate "to foster a world environment in which the American system can survive and flourish" (F. Kaplan, 1983, p. 140). Nitze candidly admitted that NSC-68's purpose was "to bludgeon the mass mind" of top government officials (F. Kaplan, 1983, p. 140). A later, second report, "Deterrence and Survival in the Nuclear Age," drafted for President Eisenhower, solidified the cold-war image of the Soviet threat.

In an article in the January 1976 issue of *Foreign Affairs*, Nitze used comparisons of survival estimates in describing how the Soviets could begin and win a nuclear war. Nitze's scenario—actually a replay of Kahn's—posits that the Soviets launch a counterforce first-strike after evacuating their cities; the Soviets then threaten to attack U.S. cities if the U.S. retaliates. Nitze based his argument on quantifying the numbers of people left on both sides. He declared the winner the one with the greater portion of survivors, missiles, and megatons remaining—an obscene, totally unreal level of abstraction. Nitze helped create the Committee on the Present Danger in 1976 to help defeat SALT II. In the 1960s, Nitze, Wohlstetter, and Dean Acheson had created an earlier committee to support antiballistic missiles. This Committee to Maintain a Prudent Defense Policy hired Richard Perle as its chief research assistant. The influential advisory group of Marshall, Iklé, Perle, Wohlstetter, and Kahn has left a deep imprint on U.S. military policy. They are the real "wizards of Armageddon." Reagan's receptive, relatively simplistic team of William P. Clark, Michael K. Deaver, Edwin Meese III, Caspar Weinberger, Craig Fuller, Lyn Nofziger, and David C. Fuller proved ideal customers for the influence-peddling "strategy scholars." When the neoconservatives Jeane Kirkpatrick, Michael Novak, Max Kampleman, and the Committee for the Present Danger join these two groups of "strange bedfellows," we witness a formidable force gathering behind the "secret agenda."

Our New Right amalgam incorporates diverse elements: the New Right, the Old Right, the Religious Right, the "strategy scholars," and the neoconservatives. Indeed, some neoconservatives, for example, the disaffected liberal left and former Democrats, support the Reagan administration because of their hatred for the Soviet Union, and not because of their affection for Ronald Reagan. Nevertheless, the entire New Right amalgam looks to Reagan as the vehicle for its brand of interventionist/containment politics.

Reviewing what we have now covered, Reagan approved Weinberger's supersecret defense guidance document, euphemistically called the "five-year defense plan," and then embodied it in another supersecret decision document, National Security Decision #32. The defense guidance document had called for "deployment plans that assure United States strategic nuclear forces can render ineffective *the total Soviet military and political power structure through attacks on political/military forces and industry critical to military power . . . also provide for limiting damage to the United States* [Italics mine]." While the attack focuses on surgical "decapitation," the word actually used, the force of the attack aims at the destruction of the USSR as an industrial state. This is reaffirmed in the "guidance document," i.e., "forces that will maintain, *throughout a protracted conflict period and afterward, the* capability to inflict very high levels of damage against the industrial/economic base of the Soviet Union . . . so that they have a strong incentive *to seek conflict termination short of an all-out attack on our cities and economic assets* [Italics mine]."

While this author is not qualified to make a judgment of insanity, it would appear that this use of the words "protracted" and "conflict termination" is effectively insane. To assume the destruction of the Soviet political, military, and economic base while limiting damage to the U.S. or eliminating countervalue strikes, i.e., attacks on cities, or for that matter to propose deterrence by attack, is surely insane. However, the official document goes further and talks of "United States strategic nuclear forces and supporting C^3I . . . capable of supporting controlled nuclear counterattacks over a protracted period while maintaining a reserve of nuclear forces sufficient for trans- and post-attack on our cities and economic assets." Thus, we have the ultimate contradiction: a protracted nuclear war with limited damage to the U.S. despite "counter-attacks over a protracted period," followed by an even-longer period of "trans- and post-attack"; in other words, a protracted nuclear war "won" by the U.S. (Some sections of this material were taken from Halloran [1982], and others from L. H. Gelb, *New York Times Magazine,* Thursday, 4 March 1984, p. 29.)

We cannot overemphasize the Reagan administration's commitment to destroying their ultimate enemy, the "focus of evil." Without an acknowledgment of the Soviet Union's right to exist, war becomes inevitable. Anti-Soviet sentiment and fear of nuclear war now contend in the American psyche, but the "professionals" see no contradiction. Richard Perle, assistant secretary of defense for international security policy, states this explicitly. "Every time we create the impression that we and the Soviet Union are cooperating and moderating the competition, we diminish that sense of apprehension" necessary to protect U.S. security (*Defense Monitor* 13, 1984, p. 7).

Finally, the question arises: Could anyone who had real power and was not insane seriously advocate fighting, winning, and surviving a nuclear war? Unfortunately, the issue here is neither sanity or strategy. Rather, the issue has become almost systemic, given the convergence of industrial, military, technological, and political components that override recognition that nuclear weapons cannot be rationally used. Myth has been consolidated into policies, plans, and programs, as the leaking of the three supersecret nuclear warfighting documents shows.

The first of these, National Security Decision Document #13 (NSDD-13), was leaked to Robert Scheer and reported in the *Los Angeles Times* of Sunday, 15 August 1982. It apparently had been adopted by the National Security Council in the fall of 1981. The next document was the 124-page "Fiscal Year 1984–1988 Defense Guidance," parts of which were leaked to Richard Halloran and reported in the *New York Times* on 30 May 1982 and again on 24 August 1982. The National Security Council incorporated DG FY 1984–1988 into a new decision document signed by Ronald Reagan himself (NSDD-32) and adopted as a "strategic master plan" in August 1982 (*New York Times*, Sunday, 20 January 1984). The third document, the latest Single Integrated Operational Plan #6 (SIOP-6), has been revealed in considerable detail by Arkin (Pringle and Arkin, 1983). In sum, all of these top-secret documents prove the administration adheres to a policy of fighting, winning, and surviving a limited nuclear war, or a protracted one lasting as long as six months (Draper, 1984, p. 38).

These documents and the quoted material from them have never been denied; yet the response and the damage they provoked were not as great as expected. Moreover, by 1983 they seem to have been forgotten and certainly neglected, even by many serious critics of the Reagan administration. The Mondale-Ferraro campaign ignored them. Nevertheless, U.S. Secretary of Defense Caspar Weinberger responded in a most unusual manner. On 23 August 1982 he wrote to thirty U.S. and foreign publications, charging that "news accounts" contained "completely inaccurate" stories about the administration's nuclear war policy. This letter never denied or in any way referred directly to the factual material contained in the leaked documents (Draper, 1984, pp. 34–36); nor did Weinberger offer any denial in an interview with Richard Halloran (*New York Times*, Monday, 9 August 1982, with further material quoted directly from the "five-year war plan").

In a devastating article in the *New York Review of Books*, 4 November 1982, Theodore Draper wrote a point-by-point rebuttal and revelation of contradictions and violations of elementary logic in Weinberger's letter of August 23. Weinberger does nothing to disclaim or contradict the content of these documents, but discusses them in a way transparently designed to both deny and affirm them. The policy of nuclear warfighting has been enshrined officially and denied publicly. Deterrence and nuclear warfighting have been twinned in the new strategic doctrine. Draper dismantles Weinberger's nuclear double-talk to reveal its true intent, that "a nuclear war can be fought and a meaningful victory achieved."

If we add to these top-secret documents the published views and political history of certain key actors in the defense and foreign policy establishment, we can conclude that the hidden policy of the Reagan administration is dedicated to the destruction and/or capitulation of the present Soviet regime by every means, including nuclear war.

Although the umbrella phrase "should deterrence fail" may have prefaced the top-secret war plans (Weinberger complained of contexts), the content indicates that defense is again a euphemism for offense. These plans are not merely to fight and win a nuclear war, but to fight and win an all-embracing war—economic, clandestine, political, technological, and, if that fails, physical and actual.

Lord Zuckerman has aptly described the present arms race with the phrase "war is indivisible," paraphrasing Litvinov's famous dictum "peace is indivisible." Zuckerman's statement gains further credibility from our knowledge of the phenomenon of "nuclear winter," which alters all strategic theory. A pledge of no-use, if it were more than a simple declaration, would make more sense. Such a pledge can only be made operational if nuclear weapons are eliminated. Even a state of "minimum deterrence" would not make the world safe since escalation could cross the boundary between conventional and nuclear war, or an accident, miscalculation, or act of malice could initiate nuclear war.

To set the record straight on Weinberger's real views is difficult, since it means unraveling the contradictions of double-speak. At one point he says, "Nowhere do we imply that nuclear war is winnable . . . . That is exactly why we must have the capability for a 'protracted' response—to demonstrate that our strategic forces could survive Soviet strikes over an extended, that is to say protracted, period. Thus we believe we could deter an attack" (*New York Times,* Friday, 4 June 1982, p. 10). This translates to nuclear war is not winnable but we must prepare to win it in order to avoid it. At the Army War College on 25 June 1982, Cap the Knife said, "We do not believe nuclear war is winnable. However, successful deterrence does require responsible and effective contingency plans should deterrence fail and we are attacked. In those plans we are not planning to lose." He then continued, "The only war we want is the war-which-never-was. But the war-which-never-was is a war which was never fought because we were prepared to fight and win it" (Gertler, 1982). Now Mr. Weinberger is again saying that while war is not wanted or winnable, if the U.S. is attacked, it is planning to win it. How do you win an unwinnable war, Mr. Weinberger? But we can document our argument further.

At the 1982 hearings of the Defense Appropriations Committee, Senator de Concini (D-Ariz.) asked General Bernard Davis, "What is our policy called, in place of mutually assured destruction?" "Counter-force or warfighting, the two are synonymous," the general replied (Arkin, 1983, p. 9). As Weinberger himself said before the Senate Foreign Relations Committee in November 1981, "The new twist is to prevail" (Arkin, 1983, p. 9).

For sheer chilling candor, the statements of James Wade, principal undersecretary of defense for research and engineering, are difficult to top. He speaks of "the victor in nuclear war" and "we must not fear war" (Pringle and Arkin, 1983, pp. 241, 244). Now we have unmasked the face of nuclear warfighting policy: there is a victor and nuclear war is not to be feared but to be won—a somewhat more candid statement than Weinberger's predictable hedging. But Paul Nitze exhibits the ultimate actuarial approach to nuclear war in his contention that there could be a decisive winner if the word "win" is "used to suggest a comparison of the post-war position of one of the adversaries with the position of the other" (Arkin and Pringle, 1983, p. 248). Perhaps this comparison might be made by counting the dead—or more simply, the living—or weighing the rubble or measuring the postattack GNP, since all these are essential indicators of "winning." A more meaningless or dangerous view of nuclear war would be difficult to imagine, yet this exercise in meaninglessness continues to have significance for all of us.

The sum of the "five-year war plan" or NSDD-32 and SIOP-6 is zero for the entire world. To use ICBM's, SLBM's, and Pershing II's for the "decapitation" of the USSR, i.e., for the political assassination of an entire government and its bureaucracies, epitomizes the madness of the strategists of apocalypse. The "collateral damage" from the so-called decapitation attack will involve the deaths of tens of millions, but hundreds of millions will die when the total "hit list" of SIOP-6 is executed.

The deliberate policy of Reagan's notorious "five-year war plan" is to use the weapon of economic suffocation against the USSR. But with $1.6 trillion already allocated over fiscal years 1984–1988, and with the knowledge that this could be greatly exceeded now that Reagan has a second term, this orgy of obscene spending on death-dealing technologies could lead to mutual economic suffocation.

The late Senator Richard Russell gave the "actuarial attitude" toward suffering its ultimate reductionism in his famous (infamous) statement, "If we have to start all over again with Adam and Eve, then I want them to be Americans and not Russians, and I want them on this continent and not in Europe" (Lens, 1977, p. 69). Other, more contemporary strategists would suggest that "an intelligent U.S. offensive strategy could reduce U.S. casualties to approximately 20 million" (Colin Gray), thus "Victory is Possible" (Gray and Payne, 1980). Eugene V. Rostow's calculations reflect the pragmatic approach to the holocaust, "10 million dead on one side [U.S.], and 100 million on the other [USSR]" (Scheer, 1983, p. 88). Thus the U.S. wins, and the grotesque numbers of prompt deaths, surgically abstracted from biological reality, are justified by this inhuman accounting scheme for winning nuclear war.

In the last few months, the Reagan administration has deliberately dampened its nuclear warfighting rhetoric, in large measure due to the healthy, active opposition of the American people and concerned parliamentarians.

But rhetoric does not guide "Reagan's Ruling Class," nor is his merely a "reign of error." At its core a real, unrelenting belief in a holy nuclear crusade against the USSR intends to drive the devil from the kingdom of the earth.

While the president had an "optimistic" view of the world of 1984, the authoritative, expert editors of the *Bulletin of the Atomic Scientists* took the drastic step of moving the *Bulletin's* Doomsday Clock from four to three minutes to midnight. How can the public mediate between these visions of the future? From the weight of evidence, it seems the president was less concerned with detailed strategy than with the valuable rhetoric of an election year. But Reagan's rhetoric is guided by his advisers because his own spontaneity has bred so many gaffes and statements of sheer ignorance. We must examine the president's men—those who experienced the exhilarating "victories" of the first term, from the KAL-007 incident to the Soviet walk-out—to know what the real policy of the U.S. is all about.

The members of the Committee on the Present Danger who now occupy the seats of power in defense and foreign policy have not changed their views, their policies, or their plans. The extermination of the Soviet Union still tops their agenda; they are clever, devious, and dangerous. Directing the rhetoric of the president was important, because they needed to return to power in 1984 and maintain the holy nuclear crusade against the USSR. In many ways this president is possibly more a captive of his advisers than any other president has been. Reagan's beliefs, while philosophically simple and strategically simplistic, are held honestly; unfortunately, his beliefs coincide with those of his advisers who wield real power, motivated and reinforced by fanatic hate. In this wedding of the struggle for power and the ideology of virulent anti-Sovietism, we face the danger of a total war system propelled by its own dynamics and independent of the will of the human actors. During the MX debate, President Reagan, in typical "newspeak," said, "A vote against MX production today is a vote against arms control tomorrow" (CBS, "Face the Nation," 1 January 1984). Thus MX, which he calls the "Peacemaker," becomes a vehicle for arms control, and arms control today guarantees nuclear war tomorrow: war is peace. MX, like Pershing II, has only the respective functions of counterforce and decapitation first-strike. Surely they are viewed that way by the Soviets.

This issue is fundamental. We conduct the search for superiority at the expense of the search for security. More weapons have led to less security. The transformation of U.S policy from deterrence to warfighting presents the most dangerous threat to world security we have witnessed. Doubly dangerous is the reinforcing doctrine of "flexible response," a euphemism for "first use." The basing of the new Euromissiles becomes a most serious provocation when accompanied with announced plans to fight and win a nuclear war, and a commitment to destroy the USSR, preferably by a "decapitation" strike.

The Supreme Allied Commander in Europe General Bernard Rogers is dedicated to nuclear warfighting: "Not that we'll ever get to the position where we won't eventually have to rely upon nuclear weapons" (Smith, 1984). The myth that the Warsaw Pact has overwhelming superiority over NATO has been dispelled by experts (Komer, 1984) and even by the Pentagon's own estimates (Mearsheimer, 1982). The linkage of a Soviet attack with superior conventional forces that threaten to overrun Western Europe with NATO's use of so-called theater nuclear weapons to repulse and defeat them contains multiple myths. There is no way to prevent a nuclear war from escalating. Even a "theater" nuclear war in Europe would be suicidal, killing friend and enemy alike. "The closest analogy that comes to mind would be fighting a tactical nuclear war in the New York–Washington urban corridor at rush hour" (Bracken, 1984). General Omar Bradley, former chairman of the Joint Chiefs of Staff, suggested that such a war would end up "killing ten friends for every enemy foe." Such disparate figures as Robert McNamara, Lord Carver, former British chief of staff, and Henry Kissinger have discredited the threat of "first use" in Europe because "it has lost all credibility," "it makes no military sense," and "we cannot possibly mean it." National thinkers have always responded thus to irrationality; unfortunately, today irrationality is policy.

"In June of 1982, Ronald Reagan took the portfolio of national security for himself" (Halloran, 1984). The military doctrine developed from Weinberger's Defense Guidance Document DG FY 1984–1988 (the "five-year plan") became National Security Decision Directive #32 (NSDD-32) when Reagan signed it on its formal adoption. This was a doctrine of military interventionism and confrontation politics that mandated that the U.S. fight and win (prevail) through conventional wars or a limited or protracted nuclear war if deterrence (threat) failed. It aimed at invulnerability and superiority of all legs of the triad and of the C^3I system. Deliberately interventionist, NSDD-32 considers as a viable policy the economic suffocation of the USSR through an arms race. The plan is predicated on the assumption that the USSR, as the "focus of evil" in the world, must be "decapitated."

There is much to abhor in the Soviet system. But this creates a paradox in the context of superpower confrontations in a nuclear age. Soviet aggression and recalcitrance cannot be opposed by force, and therefore, regardless of the relative merit of comparative morality, means other than war must be found to resolve differences between the superpowers. Given the Soviets' siege mentality, intervention and threat are also counterproductive. Thus, the technological and strategic preparation for war is more likely to lead to war. Nuclear weapons represent the ultimate in waste since, at least in theory, they can never be used. But this circle of reasoning leads us back to our paradox and leaves us with the problem. As has been so cleverly observed, "What is everybody's problem tends to be nobody's." In this case, we are dealing with everybody's problem that fortunately has engendered a great global response. Herein lies the hope for a solution.

The Reagan administration has supersecret plans for placing nuclear weapons on allied territory for the U.S. to use without prior consultation with their allies, as described in the annual memorandum signed by Ronald Reagan. It is naive at best to suggest, as Canada has, that the U.S. discuss missile use just prior to actual deployment (*Globe and Mail,* Saturday, 12 January 1985, p. 4, Toronto). In the heat of war there will be no prior consultations and no request for permission. The U.S. military has withheld its real plans and policies from NATO members. The notion that we would have an "advanced readiness state" and that some countries would receive the weapons only in wartime does not consider the speed and consequent disorganization with which war might begin, particularly an accidental nuclear war. (This increasing hazard will be discussed in detail later in the book.) In this respect, the secret agenda has existing options for the president to make a "Launch-on-Warning" (LOW) attack or a "Launch-under-Attack" (LUA) strike, although this has been officially denied. These options will be discussed later.

A SHORT TRANSITION

In the next two chapters, we intend to provide a technical primer on nuclear arsenals and the nuclear arms race so that nontechnical readers may appreciate the sociopolitical, ethical, and environmental implications of nuclear weapons in a deeper and more insightful way. Earlier, we referred to an extremely secret document, Single Integrated Operational Plan #6 (SIOP-6), an elaborate nuclear hit list and the actual battle plan for fighting a protracted nuclear war. We will analyze this document also in the next two chapters, where it can be properly related to the technical issues with which it deals. In addition, the following chapters will address the dynamics of the nuclear arms race that are critical to dispel the notion of superiority, an often-mentioned topic in discussions of the defense budget.

Finally, we repeat our cautionary admonition. While we believe the secret agenda, as we have described it in this chapter, represents the real beliefs, perceptions, and plans of the Reagan administration, the American social system is at once largely open, diverse, and dynamic. Even within government, as we shall see, there are divisions. Thus, we are neither proposing a conspiracy nor making a prophecy. We believe, however, that knowledge of the secret agenda, coupled to an assessment of the key actors, roles, values, organizations, and institutions represented in the administration, provides a basis of considerable insight to an otherwise bewildering set of seemingly contradictory statements and policies. In fact, we intend to elucidate the consistent thread within these apparent contradictions. The secret agenda must be made public and publicly debated. Even in an open society, national security may become a dangerous umbrella for closure.

United States military policies provide the critical dynamic in the arms race. The U.S. acts and the USSR reacts. The USSR seeks a "no first-use" pledge that the U.S. refuses. The USSR supports the freeze while the U.S. disdains it. The USSR acts out of fear at the possible loss of present parity; the U.S. acts out of a compulsion for increased superiority. As we shall see, the dynamics of the arms race makes clear superiority very uncertain, if not impossible.

In *A House Divided,* written in 1962, Melvin Laird, former U.S. secretary of defense, wrote: "In the next few years, conceivably, we could move into the perilous phase of nuclear parity. . . . We must retain and 'increase' our superiority, not lose it. We must have the ability to 'win,' not merely to punish." Melvin Laird's words have become Caspar Weinberger's gospel. And, as we shall see in a later chapter, what Robert Jay Lifton calls "nuclearism," the worship of nuclear weapons as deities capable of simultaneous expressions of destruction and creation, is embedded in Weinberger's "born-again" fundamentalism. There is a religious mission to destroy evil in order to resurrect good, and the instrument for purging the world of evil and fulfilling prophecy is nuclearism.

3

The Dynamics of the Nuclear Arms Race

There are powerful voices around the world who still give credence to the old Roman precept—if you desire peace, prepare for war. This is absolute nuclear nonsense . . . . The world now stands on the brink of the final Abyss. Let us all resolve to take all possible practical steps to ensure that we do not, through our own folly, go over the edge.

Earl Mountbatten, May 1979

The strategic nuclear arms race, now thirty-five years old, is a bipolar offensive-defensive dynamic technological competition, with the word "technological" used in the sense of an "ensemble of techniques" (Ellul, 1965). It is composed of a physical arsenal (forces) of delivery systems, missiles, warheads (or reentry vehicles), supported by an elaborate electronic monitoring, surveillance, and decision-making system (Command, Control, Communications, and Intelligence, or C³I) combined with a complex of strategies. The arsenal of delivery systems has evolved into a triad or three distinct classes or legs: Intercontinental Ballistic Missiles (ICBM's), strategic bombers, and Submarine-Launched Ballistic Missiles (SLBM's). The ICBM's, the most destructive weapons, incorporate the so-called "counterforce" capacity, i.e., the ability to destroy the enemy's ICBM's in their fixed silos. With the addition of Trident II, a new, even more lethal counterforce weapon will have been introduced. Capable of being launched in a depressed trajectory, Trident II can reach targets within ten to fifteen minutes, and possesses the incredible mobility characteristic of submarines. This weapon alters the very definition of counterforce first-strike. There are additional layers of complexity within the triad, such as a broad variety of warheads. Ballistic missiles may have multiple warheads (reentry vehicles or RV's) that are independently targetable or even maneuverable, i.e., MIRV's and MARV's. In general, strategic forces have ranges greater than 5500 kilometers (km.)

Another classification, theater nuclear forces (TNF), is divided in turn into long-range theater nuclear forces (LRTNF), the center of debate in Europe and under negotiation between the U.S. and USSR in Geneva until talks broke off; medium-range theater nuclear forces (MRTNF); and short-range theater nuclear forces (SRTNF), which are also called tactical or battle-

44

field nuclear weapons. These three groups of theater weapons have the following maximum launch ranges: 1000 to 5500 km., LRTNF; 200 to 1000 km., MRTNF; and less than 200 km. for SRTNF tactical weapons. These launch ranges are not entirely meaningful; in distinguishing types of theater nuclear forces, ranges often become arbitrary and ambiguous.

Similar important ambiguities arise to blur the distinction between strategic and theater weapons. LRTNF's can be rightly conceived of as "Eurostrategic" weapons since they can hit Soviet territory, i.e., as cruise missiles. They can be launched from strategic delivery systems such as bombers, submarines, and ships (Stockholm International Peace Institute [SIPRI], 1982, pp. 139, 165). In addition, weapons have targets that are selected according to their significance for either the entire scenario of the war or the limited field of battle. A weapon capable of hitting a unit 5 km. away may not be able to zero in on a seaport 400 km. north. However, the same warhead can incorporate multiple targeting policies and be carried on multiple delivery systems.

Strategic counterforce, i.e., ICBM-destroying nuclear weapons, have a further complex of technical attributes. Essentially, these factors measure the effectiveness and reflect technological sophistication. Among the most important, throw-weight (or payload) of the actual released warhead measured in megatonnage (mt.) equivalent of TNT (excludes radiation, etc.) gives us explosive yield, accuracy or miss distance, defined as the Circular Error of Probability (CEP)—the radius of a circle centered on the targeted area in which half the bombs explode. The factors of yield (Y) and accuracy (CEP) provide an equation for "lethality" (K) as follows: $K = Y^{2/3}/(CEP)^2$ (Aldridge, 1981, p. 23). Note the significance of this equation. Making a warhead twice as accurate has the same result as producing eight times the yield; a warhead of 0.8 mt. (800 kt.) having a CEP two times greater than a warhead of 200 kt. would nevertheless make the latter equally effective in hard-target kill capability (lethality) or silo-kill capability. It is also important to note the effect of using multiple independently targetable reentry vehicles (MIRV's). The equation then becomes Kn where n is the number of warheads per missile. Thus, in our above calculation we would have increased the lethality of the strategic missile with a 3 × 200 kt. to three times the single 0.8 mt. warhead. A more complex but equally significant equation is the probability of kill (Cross-Targeted Probability of Kill [2 on 1]), P_k, which incorporates the further factors of the reliability (g), or percentage of probability that a missile will work properly, and the hardness of the silo target (H), as well as lethality (K) (Aldridge, 1981, p. 24, 25). It would seem, however, that only two new weapons systems have genuine first-strike capacity—MX and Trident II, having P_k's of 87.08 and 90.86, respectively, for silo hardness of 5000 psi, compared to 64.78 for Minuteman III (Robert Aldridge, Pacific Life Research Center, 631 Kiely Boulevard, Santa Cruz, California, 95051,

30 April 1985). But no Soviet missile has a P_k greater than 50 percent of MX, their best being the SS-19, Mod 3, with a P_k of 44.65.

A second category of effectiveness criteria, i.e., cost effectiveness, readiness, availability, response time, etc., also proves significant in assessing the "military balance." All of the above factors apply to offensive systems, but also have some technical and social counterparts, such as "hardening" of targets, ballistic missile defenses (BMD's), civil defense (crisis relocation), and geostrategic factors.

This author has proposed a double-helix model of the dynamics of the nuclear arms race. In the model one spiraling strand represents offensive developments and the other, defensive developments. In general and by nature, defense follows offense. The entire history of the arms race attests to this, including the ultimate defensive "ludicracy"—Reagan's "Star Wars" scenario. The perceived effectiveness of an offensive or defensive development by one side in the bipolar race leads the other side to respond in several ways. It must match, offset, or exceed the offensive increment by both offensive and defensive developments of its own. Thus, offensive or defensive technological developments by either side incite and maintain the arms race. Negotiation from strength or superiority becomes senseless, given this internal dynamic of the arms race. Such attempts at negotiation merely escalate the arms race. Stating one's moral superiority as a basis for becoming militarily superior is a mirror-image phenomena.

The triad of strategic weapons have functional differences. ICBM's are "counterforce" weapons; if successfully launched and targeted they can destroy the enemy's ICBM's in a first or preemptive strike (attack). To a very large degree, the other two legs of the triad have "countervalue"—they can destroy cities, factories, ports, C^3I targets, etc. In fact, ports with military ships and C^3I installations are also strategic first-strike targets. The bomber and SLBM leg of the triad can be used in a combined first-strike but also provide the second-strike or retaliatory capability that is the basis of deterrence. Because SLBM's particularly are presently invulnerable and likely to remain so for decades, they provide real deterrence for any first-strike (counterforce or countervalue) by either side against the other. Thus, the notion that the U.S. has what Reagan called a "window of vulnerability" is meaningless and, as we shall see, untrue as well. It would be proper to classify Trident I and II, advanced Minuteman III, MX, and B-52's equipped with cruise missiles as genuine counterforce weapons. Table 1 provides the numbers of strategic missiles and warheads of the two superpowers based on multiple sources, official and secondary. Table 2 shows the historical trend.

In examining Table 2 it is very important to note the distribution of

TABLE 1
US-USSR Strategic Arms Balance End of 1983

	Number of Missiles	Number of Warheads	Percentage of Total	Megatons	Number MIRVed	Average Warheads/ Missile
			USSR			
ICBM's	1398	6273	71%	4427	421	4-5
SLBM's	941	2317	26%	828	436	3
Bombers	145	290	3%	580	—	2
Totals:	2484	8880	100%	5835	857	
			USA			
ICBM's	1045	2145	22%	1375	550	1-2
LCBM's	568	5152	52%	333	568	9
Bombers	307	2570	26%	2178	—	9
Totals:	1854	9867	100%	3886	1113	—

Sources: Averages compiled from U.S. Department of Defense, *Soviet Military Power* (Washington, D.C.: 1983, 1984); U.S. Department of Defense (DOD), *Annual Reports*, FY 1983, FY 1984; USSR Ministry of Defense, *Whence the Threat to Peace* (Moscow: 1982); Stockholm International Peace Research Institute (SIPRI), *World Armaments and Disarmament Yearbook* and *Arms Control and Disarmament*, 1983, 1984; various issues of the *Defense Monitor* (Center for Defense Information) and the *Bulletin of Atomic Scientists*, 1982, 1983, 1984.

Breakdown: (1) *ICBM's:* U.S.: 45 liquid-fueled Titans, 450 Minuteman II and 550 Minuteman III, all solid-fueled, latter 300 with Mark 12-A warheads (Titans being retired and MX's replacing the Minuteman II's). USSR: 812 SS-17, -18, and 19; 550 SS-11; and 60 SS-13, mainly liquid-fueled.

(2) *SLBM's:* U.S.: 33 submarines with 305 Poseidon C-3 and 214 Trident C-4 missiles. USSR: 64 submarines, latest class Delta II with liquid-fueled SS-N-18 stage missiles; new, larger Typhoon class with advanced SS-NX-20 solid-fueled missile being deployed.

(3) *Bombers:* 341 B-52's and 60 F-111's (medium-range and not SALT-accountable, but capable of strategic functions). USSR: 100 Bear prop-driven bombers; 45 Bisons; 180 Backfire bombers, not included due to nonstrategic range; new Blackjack jet bomber, reported in test.

Analysis: Inclusions and exclusions based on ability to deliver warheads to national territory of each superpower from outside its own continent. Balance is dynamic, due to continuous replacement, retrofit, retirement, modernization, etc. Above tables do not reflect qualitative differences, i.e., force and cost effectiveness, accuracy, reliability, etc. Both superpowers have remained below SALT II limits to date.

TABLE 2
The US-USSR Strategic Arms Race (Missiles)

Date	ICBM's		SLBM's		Bombers		Total Strategic Delivery Vehicles		Total Warheads		Total Deliverable Megatons	
	US	USSR	US	USSR	US	USSR	US	USSR	US	USSR	US	USSR
1960	20	—	32	15	1650	130	1702	150	6500	300	7200	600
1962	80	40	144	20	1650	155	1874	290	7400	400	8000	800
1964	800	200	336	20	1280	155	2416	375	6800	500	7500	1000
1966	1054	250	592	30	750	155	2396	435	5000	550	5600	1200
1968	1054	850	656	40	650	155	2360	1045	4500	850	5100	2300
1970	1054	1300	656	240	520	140	2230	1680	3900	1800	4300	3100
1972	1054	1500	656	450	520	140	2230	2090	5800	2100	4100	4000
1974	1054	1600	656	640	470	140	2180	2380	8400	2400	3800	4200
1976	1054	1500	656	750	390	140	2100	2390	9400	3200	3700	4500
1978	1054	1400	656	810	348	140	2058	2350	9800	5200	3800	5400
1980	1054	1400	640	950	348	140	2042	2490	10,000	6000	4000	5700
1982	1052	1400	632	950	348	140	2032	2490	11,000	8000	4100	7108

Source: Ground Zero, 1982; this corresponds quite well to official sources in the 1982 *Pentagon Annual Report*, DOD *Annual Report*, and sources used for Table 1.

Notes:
1. Until 1974 the U.S. exceeded the USSR significantly in every category except rough equality in deliverable megatonnage.
2. The U.S. reduction in megatonnage from 1970 on reflects increased emphasis on accuracy, Mirving, and modernizing existing systems, i.e., its number of ICBM's has remained relatively constant from 1966 to 1983.
3. The USSR has never matched the U.S. lead in strategic bombers and refueling in flight.
4. Although the U.S. has fewer SLBM's, it has a 2.5:1 advantage in warheads and these are invulnerable.

weapons within each leg of the triad of both superpowers, as well as their relative strengths. The U.S. has a strategic arsenal that is extremely well balanced in distribution among its triad. The U.S. also has a current and continual advantage in total deliverable warheads. The USSR leads in total strategic delivery systems but has a very skewed distribution in the triad. When certain other technical criteria are introduced, the U.S.'s strategic arsenal is undisputably superior, despite consistent statements to the contrary by the Reagan administration. The Nuclear Freeze Initiative's assumption of rough parity nevertheless reflects both superpowers' capacity of massive retaliation, which is the basis of deterrence.

GAMES, STRATEGIES, AND STRATEGISTS: THE "WIN SYNDROME"

The history of the various contending strategies of nuclear war is closely associated with the early post–World War II "think tanks," particularly Rand and, later, the Hudson Institute. The two seminal thinkers, Bernard Brodie and Herman Kahn, represent the dominant contending strategic theories of nuclear war (Brodie, 1946, 1965; Kahn, 1965, 1969; Lens, 1977, p. 64). Each wrote significant works that expressed opposite views of nuclear strategies. Brodie considered assured retaliatory destruction the "absolute weapon": deterrence was based on prompt and massive retaliation and assured by the preservation of second-strike capability. Kahn propounded a limited and winnable nuclear warfighting doctrine. From the beginning his scenario incorporated the concepts of counterforce, escalating graduated (and flexible) response, and damage limitation, supported by civil defense and other measures that fundamentally asserted the view that a nuclear war is winnable, whether limited or protracted.

The theoretical basis of nuclear warfighting and nuclear war prevention rests on game, strategy, and decision theory, all branches of the social sciences that have a powerful bias toward the value of quantitative analysis. They also often involve the tenuous assumption that both opponents share a flawless and omniscient rationality and that neither's actions result from accident, malice, miscalculation, or madness. Fred Iklé, former head of the U.S. Arms Control and Disarmament Agency, put it simply, "What you can't calculate you leave out" (Lens, 1977, p. 140). Given the levels of abstraction required by both sides by these assumptions, and the fact that both sides in the bipolar nuclear conflict have announced publicly many times that they do not intend to play by the same rules, it is surprising that strategic doctrine should again favor first-strike counterforce over mutually assured destruction. But, strategists prefer short war scenarios, because they are inherently more amenable to being calculable, predictable, and "winnable," i.e., they are theoretically self-fulfilling, or incorporate what this author has termed the rule of all complex social-system modeling, PI=PO or "Para-digm-In–Paradigm Out" (Knelman, 1981).

For the period in which Robert McNamara served as Kennedy's secretary of defense, some ambiguity surrounded U.S. nuclear policy, but ultimately Brodie's deterrence by assured retaliatory destruction seemed to win. However, when James Schlesinger, a former Rand director of strategic studies, took office as secretary of defense in 1973, the momentum swung toward Kahn's theories. In the 1970s, powerful forces began to support the Kahn-Schlesinger strategic doctrine (Iklé, 1973; Nitze, 1976; Rostow, 1979). Harold Brown, President Carter's defense secretary, although seemingly ambivalent on the nuclear debate, tended to support the Kahn-Schlesinger views. Brown coined the phrase "countervailing strategy" to describe Kahn's concept. This was codified in Carter's Presidential Directive #59 (U.S. DOD, *Annual Reports FY 1979*, p. 54; *1981*, pp. 66–69). Kahn had made the "unthinkable" thinkable and the unwinnable "winnable"; moreover, he quantified everything from human deaths to chromosome damage.

Herman Kahn was the perfect model for Dr. Strangelove. Since Brodie's deterrence model was not MAD enough for him, Kahn developed a multiplicity of nuclear warfighting scenarios that ranged from "slow motion counter-property war" to "automatic unthinking and uncontrolled war," i.e., protracted war or type-II MAD. Kahn identified forty-four rungs of escalation in his book *On Escalation* (Kahn, 1965, 1969). His major thesis held that a nuclear war did not qualitatively differ from any other war. One side could "cope with all of the effects of a nuclear war" better than the other and, therefore, could end up "saving most people and restoring something close to the previous standard of living in a relatively short time" (Kahn, 1969, pp. 10–11). In *On Thermonuclear War,* Kahn noted that "the limits of the magnitude of the catastrophe seem to be closely dependent on what kinds of preparation have been made, and how the war is started and fought" (Kahn, 1969, p. 78). In this same book, he advocated civil defense, so that "we could evacuate our cities . . . and thus put ourselves in a much better position to strike first and accept the retaliatory blow. We might then present the Soviets with an ultimatum" (Lens, 1977, p. 129). His comments prompted a critic to coin the phrase "Chicken à la Kahn" (Rapoport, 1963).

To sum up, Herman Kahn rejected deterrence theory and instead suggested that any nuclear war was winnable. He advocated damage limitation through the evacuation of cities and, if necessary of course, a first-strike option. By his definition, the "winning" society suffered the fewest losses and recovered the most rapidly. Kahn advocated a counterforce first-strike strategy that could destroy the enemy's retaliatory capacity or limit it to an acceptable level, even though extortion by ultimatum was perhaps preferable.

James Schlesinger, who became defense secretary in 1973, was another "whiz kid" from Rand who continued to represent Kahn's strategic doctrines. But Schlesinger introduced "double-speak" into the debate. He stated to a Senate Foreign Relations Committee, "We have no desire to develop a counterforce capability against the Soviet Union . . . . what we wish to avoid is the Soviet Union having a counterforce capability against the United States, without our being able to have a comparable capability." He promised the U.S. would obtain "the forces to execute a wide range of options in response to particular action by an enemy, including a capability for precise attacks on both soft and hard targets, while at the same time minimizing unintended collateral damage" (Schlesinger, 1974, pp. 86–90). On ABC's "Issues and Answers," 6 July 1975, Schlesinger stated, "America would respond with nuclear bombs wherever aggression is likely to result in defeat in any area of very great importance to the United States . . . . We cannot exclude Korea." In the *New York Times* of Tuesday, 24 June 1976 presidential candidate Jimmy Carter repeated this warning, but included "commitments to the security of Western Europe and Japan . . . . I would be justified in a first-strike."

After his election, President Carter's new defense secretary, Harold Brown, stated, "We cannot make a complete distinction between deterrence forces and what are so awkwardly called warfighting forces" (U.S. DOD, *Annual Report FY 1979*, p. 54). Brown translated Kahn's doctrine into the concept of "countervailing strategy" (U.S. DOD, *Annual Report FY 1981*, p. 66), and this in turn was to evolve into Weinberger's "prevailing strategy," a conversion from response to aggression. An entire generation of nuclear war strategists in the Kahn tradition had emerged and finally attained positions of incredible power in the Reagan administration. Counterforce first-strike strategy eventually became consolidated and integrated into the essential fabric of U.S. policy (Rostow, 1979). The Reagan administration has now fashioned the Kahn-Schlesinger doctrine into policy and posture, formalized by irresponsible rhetoric, misinformation, and messianic fervor. Worse, it is no longer simple deception, but deliberate policy buttressed by blind belief.

The very use of the single word "counterforce" is deceptive: conceptually as well as operationally, the proper term should be "first-strike counterforce." The only way counterforce strategy makes sense is in its prior destruction of the enemy's offense, i.e., ICBM's in fixed silos, particularly so since the USSR has a skewed triad with the greater part of its offense in ICBM's (see Table 1). But counterforce also implies an abstract strategy whereby "surgical strikes" (the sanitized version of first-strike) would be binding on both sides. The value of counterforce-as-surgical-strikes gains reinforcement from assertions that it is more humane than MAD, as it allegedly limits "collateral damage." Counterforce strategy persists, despite numerous official Soviet statements that they would use their remaining offense to maximize "counter-value" targets (urban regions).

Counterforce strategy serves as a deliberate posture to win a "limited war" and overcome "deterrence." This it cannot accomplish. ICBM's are now being programmed/computerized to fire on warning, based on the logic of "launch them or lose them." In addition, no present means exist for effectively destroying the submarine-launched ballistic missiles (SLBM's) of either side. Such missiles could inflict unacceptable damage to the other super-power in a countercity attack, a "holocaust attack," or even an attack on planned evacuation areas, in the unlikely instance that such areas are ever designated. Thus, neither deterrence nor counterforce is stable. An arms race is a race is a race.

The notion of counterforce first-strike capability has still another para-dox. As mentioned, both of the superpowers will likely develop a "launch on warning system" for their ICBM's that will fire missiles on the basis of computer analyses of evidence, without waiting for a political leader's direc-tive (Blair, 1981; Barnaby, 1982). Since the U.S. may already be dedicated to this system, it is puzzling to understand either the "window of vulnerability" idea or the fear of a first-strike knock-out. Moreover, with Trident II fully operational, the U.S. will be able to make a successful first-strike knock-out of ICBM's, and thus Soviet fears are understandable.

In his famous farewell speech of 17 July 1961, former President Eisen-hower offered his famous injunction: "We must guard against the acquisition of unwarranted influence, whether sought or unsought, by the military-in-dustrial complex. The potential for the disastrous use of misplaced power exists and will persist." But, in that same address, Eisenhower gives an equally compelling and prophetic warning, "We must also be alert to the equal and opposite danger that public policy could itself become the captive of a scientific-technological elite" (*Defense Monitor* 10, no. 2, pp. 6–8, 1981). The U.S. has become a national security state, and it appears both prophecies have been fulfilled.

THE ELECTRONIC BATTLEFIELD

More than any other development, electronics and microelectronics in par-ticular, and similar technological offshoots of the race for space have forged a technological revolution in modern warfighting at least as great as nuclear power. A special October 1982 edition of *Spectrum,* the journal of the Insti-tute of Electrical and Electronics Engineers, Inc., reveals the full impact of this revolution. Like all technological revolutions, the combination of new hardware and software has radically altered the techniques and strategies of modern war.

In the lead essay of the above journal edition, Richard De Lauer, former

U.S. undersecretary for research and engineering in the Department of Defense, describes the capabilities of the new technology:

> The ability to obtain strategic and tactical intelligence; to effectively control its resources over a global battlefield; to permit instantaneous communications with its operational forces; to simultaneously identify and track a multitude of targets under and on the sea, on the ground, in the air, or in space; to deliver appropriate munitions with pinpoint accuracy; and finally, to subvert the effort of the opposing forces to do the same. The means for accomplishing this are electronic systems that sense, transmit, compile, analyze, display, compare, store and process information, and then launch, guide, control and trigger the various munitions carriers.

In effect, modern warfare as exemplified by the U.S., which maintains the highest state-of-the-art electronic/space/information technology, has become computerized, digitalized, and controlled from space. At the same time, through information networks, modern warfare has become globalized. As stated many times in the spirit of a "euphoria of gadgetry," electrotechnology is a "force multiplier." War is information attached to nuclear weapons with increasingly less human intervention and interface. The premium placed on time of response or advantage necessitates that the electronic war machine itself renders decisions. In every area "the chips are flying."

The brains of the modern military megamachine are called Command, Control, Communications, and Intelligence or C³I ("C cubed I"). Even this term is outdated: it should read "C⁴I," with the fourth C representing Countermeasures. At the center of the U.S. system is the Worldwide Military Command and Control System (WWMCCS). This giant communications system comprises some thirty-five computers at twenty-five communications centers, with over seventeen million lines of programming code and forty-three radically different communications subsystems that span the electromagnetic spectrum. A single network of 600 computer facilities, five satellite systems, 100 ground satellite terminals, and some thirty million miles of wire extends to all units of the armed forces. It provides automatic secure voice communications (Autosevocom), i.e., encoded telephone services. The networking system integrates strategic air command (SAC), missile silos (ICBM's), missile-carrying submarines, and the other parts of the military force.

Digital signal processing links all the electronic ears and eyes of the system: aboard aircraft in the sky; aboard ships and submarines on and under the sea; and aboard satellites in space. The special issue of *Spectrum* attempts to assess the relative strengths of the U.S. and USSR in electronic battlefield technology and concludes that, in general, the U.S. is significantly more advanced in C³I than the USSR. In particular, the U.S.'s program in Very High-Speed Integrated Circuits (VHSIC) could assure them real superiority in war electronics. (It should be noted again that, as in the case of nuclear "munitions" and carriers, the dynamics of the technological race is bipolar, i.e., a defense/offense race.)

The electronic system of nuclear war makes C^3I targets absolutely critical; they are now as important as first-strike targets. Destroying the brain of a globalized, computerized, and integrated military network renders it inoperable and fragmented. In this context, one must examine the strategic significance of such weapons as the advanced cruise missile (ACM) and air- and sea-launched cruise missiles. A coordinated "first-use" strategy would now direct its attack simultaneously on ICBM's and C^3I targets, while a limited nuclear war strategy would place greater emphasis on the destruction of C^3I targets.

Once operational, the satellite project MILSTAR, with its C^3I system is designed "to provide survivable and enduring command and control . . . through all levels of conflict, including general nuclear war" (Pringle and Arkin, 1983, p. 237). Nine hundred terminals using extremely high frequency (EHF) range will pinpoint nuclear explosions in wartime. A second system of satellites, code-named Forest Green, will be available (Pringle and Arkin, 1983, p. 237). Finally, the NAVSTAR or Global Positioning System has some eighteen satellites linked to every tactical and strategic nuclear weapon in the U.S. arsenal. NAVSTAR's high level of accuracy can convert lower-yield warheads into first-strike weapons, an example being Euromissiles.

The potential of technological means of warfare has an inherent danger in its ability to subvert human will. As the new military electrotechnology moves toward replacing the role of human perception, analysis, and decision, the premiums placed on the new weapons' response time will tend to computerize "intelligence" to the inevitable point of "launch-on-warning" systems. Since these systems can never be infallible, and because they can centralize and coordinate action, they pose the danger of accidental war. In addition, the entire C^3I system itself inevitably tends to become autonomous—in fact, such a capacity would be necessary for a "Star Wars" system. The development of "Star Wars" will convert C^3I into an autonomous system, making it likely that computers will declare World War III.

VERIFICATION: POLITICS AND TECHNOLOGY

When both superpowers tend to view each other with suspicion, verification and verification reliability become reasonable and essential elements of any arms control or arms reduction treaty. Beyond this, the verification issue can be a "red herring" introduced into negotiations to effectivelyobscure or even prevent agreement. Many landmark arms control treaties have been successful and, despite some minor violations or ambiguities, both sides have abided by the letter of these treaties, if not always by the spirit. The Reagan administration has frequently accused the USSR of treaty violations, but in almost every case the accusations are politically motivated and serve the dual purposes of justifying the U.S. arms build-up and discrediting the USSR.

The SALT I treaty provided for three technical means of treaty verification. On-site and "black box" inspection ("cooperative verification") and satellite, radar, and telemetry are "national technical means" verification. Amenability to the latter is subject to the SALT I treaty. The USSR has consistently balked at on-site inspection, but on some occasions it has indicated a limited acceptance of the method. In general, the satellite monitoring and surveillance systems, in conjunction with ground radar and other intelligence systems, have such a degree of sophistication that nothing done to a "macro" level can remain undetected. Production, testing, and deployment of weapons and missiles can all be "seen." Since arms treaties limit the number and kind of existing weapons and the deployment of new weapons, only the deployment stipulation contains a "gray area." Testing sites and the movement of critical materials by rail, road, or other transport can all be verified since the U.S. has totally surrounded the USSR with detection sites, including the use of one in Chinese territory.

The use of "black-box" technology has prompted little public discussion. A "black box" or tamper-free electronic sensing device would serve as a kind of robot inspector whose "messages" could be transmitted to third parties or primary actors. "Black boxes" could replace on-site inspection of more "micro" or smaller-scale activities, including in-plant inspection.

The limits of verification techniques neither hinder nor prevent the successful negotiations of arms limitation, or even of arms elimination. The lack of will and/or the lack of trust between the superpowers inhibits such negotiations. A treaty is an international or bilateral agreement betwen sovereign states. In the case of the superpowers, either side can break or cancel a treaty at will and with impunity. For example, the U.S. appears ready to deploy defensive space weapons in violation of the Anti-Ballistic Missile (ABM) Treaty. In addition, under a Reagan administration dedicated to offensive and defensive nuclear superiority, the U.S. is refusing to proceed with an Anti-Satellite Treaty (ASAT). Therefore the real stumbling block to meaningful arms reduction is not the technical state of verification, but the Reagan administration's dedication to fight and win a nuclear war if the Soviets do not capitulate to U.S. terms.

The present verification systems could adequately oversee a mutual and verifiable freeze on the testing and deployment of *all nuclear weapons*. Such a freeze would be an excellent first step to arms reduction by providing the necessary atmosphere of confidence and trust for further reductions. The verification argument used by the Reagan administration in the freeze issue is either dishonest or paranoid. A violation by the USSR would provide Reagan and his henchmen with the political currency they need to proceed with their build-up. In any case, a mutual, verifiable freeze does not necessarily halt research and development.

All strategic arms control treaties face the essential problem of assymetry between the nuclear arsenals of the two superpowers, particularly in their distribution of missiles and warheads in each leg of the triad. The lowest common denominator approach resolves this difficulty. The side with the greater number of armaments per leg would reduce its weaponry to a level equal to the lower number of the other side. This sensible and meaningful method seems impossible in the present political environment or even in the foreseeable future. The next best approach is a mutual freeze.

An even more pragmatic view is that given the present rough parity (actually, U.S. superiority), neither side would qualitatively benefit by undetected cheating. In fact, not even on-site inspections could prevent deliberate cheating. Ultimately, advantage would only accrue with the actual testing of some new secret weapon that would be immediately detected. Limits on the number, kind, and amenability of tests to detection can be incorporated as safeguards. The SALT II treaty lent itself to this sensible and pragmatic approach. The U.S. even protected its new key weapons—MX and cruise missiles—from being part of this treaty. A Senate Intelligence Committee report concluded that SALT II was "adequately verifiable."

There is a further problem in verification that is semantic. Treaty language is a jungle of dispute. The ambiguities of interpretation allow both sides to accuse the other of violation. There cannot be an absolutely foolproof verification system whose treaty language is absolutely unambiguous. Nor is this the issue for those who genuinely desire arms control. If one side is openly dedicated to achieving superiority, there cannot be a meaningful treaty in any case. This situation has caused suspended negotiations in the past. If either side believes the other is dedicated to superiority and/or cheating, this too provides barriers to agreements. The assumption of moral superiority by one side or the other or, worse, the dedication to the destruction of one side by the other is the most formidable obstacle to peace. Under the present administration the U.S. is responsible for these obstructions. In coupling a "decapitation" doctrine with the installation of Euromissiles capable of carrying out such strikes, the U.S. erects a terrible barrier to nuclear disarmament, and imposes a frightening hazard of a possible accidental nuclear war.

Both sides have mutually accused the other of treaty violations. The U.S. has accused the USSR of seven violations: three in regard to SALT II and one each in regard to the Threshold Test Ban (TTB), the Anti-Ballistic Missile Treaty (ABM), the Conference on Security and Cooperation in Europe (CSCE), and chemical weapons. The USSR has disputed all of these and almost all substantive violations have been disputed by independent assessors. In turn, the USSR has accused the U.S. of violating SALT I, SALT II, ABM, TTB, the Limited Test Treaty (LTB), chemical weapons, CSCE, and the Non-Proliferation Treaty (NPT). In all these incidences, a case can be made for the accusations on both sides, but its validity depends on definition, procedural issues, and hair-splitting interpretation. The U.S. has no doubt violated the intent of SALT II, but its violations are excused on the basis of nonidentification: the U.S. did not ratify SALT II. Since the U.S. is on record as reconsidering the ABM Treaty and may be waiting for SALT II to lapse to undercut it, Reagan accusations against the USSR seem to be both hypocritical and unsubstantive.

In the *Toronto Globe and Mail* of Wednesday, 30 May 1984, a Canadian NATO report revealed the true attitude of the Reagan administration. This report, prepared by Michael Forrestal, quotes the ubiquitous Richard Perle, U.S. assistant defense secretary: "Soviet violations raise questions about the integrity of the arms control process that may be far more significant than the short-term military impact. . . . Arms control without compliance is nothing more than an exercise in unilateral disarmament . . . [and the administration is reviewing its position to see whether it should] . . . *feel liberated from our obligations under these treaties* [Italics mine]." This appears to be part of a real U.S. plan to disavow key treaties, like the ABM Treaty, and to totally disengage the U.S. from its voluntary adherence to SALT II, giving it the go-ahead on all new weapons development and deployment, including "Star Wars." The U.S. maintains an absolutist position on verification that requires the impossible from both, namely, total, 100 percent verification of every aspect of every treaty. This is the only thing colored red in the Reagan administration's policy: it is a "red herring" to justify dumping arms control and accelerating arms build-up. On his June visit to Ireland, President Reagan's "new" offer smelled just the same. We possess overwhelming evidence that the Reagan administration opposes arms control and reduction. On the contrary, the U.S. has committed itself to superiority and to a policy of a nuclear showdown with the USSR, unless the Soviets unilaterally capitulate.

The ideological and philosophical adherents of the Reagan administration's policies exhibit a curious contradiction in that they are international interventionists that still retain the old isolationist tendencies of some of their conservative predecessors. To maintain their paradoxical position, they must reject the United Nations and many of its special agencies and prefer to abandon Europe, if necessary, in order to combat the communist threat elsewhere. The conservative Heritage Foundation, in *A World Without the UN,* recommends that the U.S. reconsider membership in the entire UN system (*Globe and Mail,* Friday, 25 May 1984, Toronto). This book concludes that the UN organization does more harm than good. It attacks WHO, disarmament activities, human rights forums, UN peacekeeping efforts, and FAO, stating about this last organization that in recent years it has become "wedded to the outworn rhetoric of wealth redistribution."

The current U.S. policy of preparing to reject arms control by using verification as an excuse is consistent with the go-it-alone mentality. It is consistent with adopting a global mission to rid the world of what the U.S. considers an "evil empire," and the "focus of evil" in the world. It is consistent with abandoning allies who do not totally share the Reagan world view: NATO will either fall in line or face rejection. Canada, of course, is treated even more crudely, being a vassal state. The consistency was evident from the beginning. It took Reagan eighteen months to even proceed to the negotiating table. Then, each proposal made to the Soviets was patently designed for nonacceptance. This will be expanded in later chapters.

In January 1985 new talks between Andrei Gromyko and George Shultz ended with the agreement to begin a new round of arms negotiations in Geneva in March 1985. Considerable, although not damning, evidence exists that the Reagan administration was manipulating the Soviets for purposes that were mainly designed to sanction the U.S.'s modernization program and the development of other systems such as "Star Wars." Official and unofficial sources sent out a number of conflicting signals, not the least of which was the release of a new list of alleged treaty violations by the General Advisory Committee (GAC) of the Arms Control Disarmament Agency (ACDA) that could lead one to suspect that the new negotiations were designed for non-agreement.

ALLEGATIONS PRECEDE NEGOTIATONS

Some evidence suggests that the Soviets may have violated three treaties: SALT II, the 1971 prohibition on use of chemical and biological weapons (CBW), and the ABM Treaty. In the first case, there is no clear evidence of violation because of ambiguities in the allegations. In the second case, the use of so-called "yellow rain" by the Soviets has been disputed by independent experts, but the claim that the Soviets appear to be developing and storing biological weapons clandestinely is serious. While the charge was sufficient to convince Jack Anderson (*Santa Barbara News-Press,* Tuesday, 1 March 1985, p. A-13), its source, the CIA and a secret report of the National Security Council (NSC), made it suspect. It could be a deliberate distortion by the CIA to justify U.S. intentions to proceed with similar developments because no independent evidence is available. A major radar array near key Soviet ICBM bases in the interior of Soviet Asia at Kiasnoyarsk seems to be the one clear violation, this in the case of the ABM Treaty. One need not doubt the Soviets' capacity to cheat, but one must balance this with the

Soviets' reasonably good record over a long period of numerous treaties with the U.S. The U.S. cheats by falsifying Soviet weapon superiority and military spending. Moreover, the politics of violation accusation, like that of verification demands, throws as much doubt on the Reagan administration's sincerity as on alleged Soviet violations. Since the Reagan administration usually accuses the Soviets of doing exactly what the administration plans to do, we may assume that they intend to abrogate ABM, violate SALT II (by building a second new ICBM), and develop a new CBW capacity, based on accusations in a report of the General Advisory Committee of ACDA (GAC).

Therefore, without doubting the Soviets' capability for violation, there is too much political correlation with these Reagan administration allegations and nuclear policies. The demand for perfect verification and the timing of violation allegations suggest they are both means of fulfilling the secret agenda, a policy not in favor of arms control. On 21 February 1985, Ronald Reagan accused the Soviets of violating a SALT I agreement by converting a ballistic missile submarine to a cruise-carrying one that does not have to be counted in the SALT II agreement. A formal U.S. government report issued on 1 February 1985 stated categorically that this was not a violation. Many independent arms control experts, including Harold Brown, former secretary of defense (*Globe and Mail,* Saturday, 23 February 1985, Toronto), agreed with the report's conclusion, a fact that does not bolster confidence in the administration's allegations. In the same article, arms control expert William Kincaid of the Carnegie Endowment for the Humanities said, "It's another example of the President trying to take advantage of public ignorance." One wonders if this is the public's or Mr. Reagan's ignorance.

While building a very large radar array installation in the Soviet tundra of Siberia would be a clear violation of the ABM Treaty, given known purposes, the accusations involve some strange circumstances. Radar arrays may be perfectly legitimate early-warning systems, but their sites are restricted to border positions according to the ABM Treaty. The huge ten-story structure situated in the bleak, flat tundra could not possibly have been an attempt at deception, since it could not be hidden. On the other hand, such an installation is probably used to direct interceptor missiles, as well as for early warning. Since it had to have been under construction for years, the U.S. must have known about it for years, even though the U.S. claimed to have discovered it only in July 1983. The U.S. blamed cloudy weather over Siberia for its failure to detect the site earlier, but five years of cloudy weather is difficult to swallow. No one claims that the Soviets have developed interceptor ballistic missiles designed to strike incoming U.S. ICBM's. They only claim that at some time in the future the Kiasnoyarsk radar installation could become an ABM "battle management" unit. The Soviets maintain that the array is for space tracking, which is perfectly legitimate: the U.S.'s Cobra Dane is just such a system. The upgrading of the U.S. Ballistic Early Warning Systems in Greenland and Canada may also be questioned in terms of antiballistic missile capabilities.

The U.S., in fact, has accused the USSR of seventeen arms control violations, ranging in credibility from one that is "certain," to sixteen that are ambiguous, probable, possible, or questionable. The U.S. made the charges just before serious negotiations were to resume, but even the one certain violation has not damaged U.S. security. According to Kenneth Adelman, "Our security has not yet suffered because of Soviet noncompliance" (Toth, 1985).

Meanwhile, the authors and promoters of the secret agenda seized on the verification and violation issue to undermine the March 12 talks in Geneva. Colin S. Gray, the member of Reagan's Advisory Committee on Arms Control and Disarmament (GAC) for whom "Victory is Possible," stated, "The U.S. government has no business negotiating new arms control agreements unless it has a responsible policy to deal with Soviet cheating on existing agreements" (Toth, 1985). The Pentagon recommended "offsetting violations" as the proper approach. ACDA wanted to make the clearing up of old charges a prerequisite for new agreements (Toth, 1985).

The ABM Treaty had created a special joint U.S.-USSR body to resolve verification conflicts. This is the Standing Consultative Committee (SCC). This committee has done a good job in the past, considering that consensus is a requirement and there are U.S. members. Now the ubiquitous Richard N. Perle, assistant secretary of defense, claims that the Carter administration resolved its concern over ambiguities "by accepting what was done in violation of the treaties" (Toth, 1985). The SCC has usually clarified alleged ambiguities, always referred to at one time as violations. An alleged violation becomes an ambiguity when it cannot be proved to be a violation. What is obvious is that Weinberger is preparing to scuttle both ABM and SALT II over the alleged violations, and the attack on SCC is part of that preparation. It is also part of the move to abort the new arms talks.

If the Kiasnoyarsk missile array violates the ABM Treaty, then: (1) the U.S. should now declare the ABM Treaty null and void and abrogate it— this is what Weinberger and the Pentagon really want; or (2) the Soviets should dismantle it as a prerequisite for any treaty on missile defenses. A third and best option is to have third-party verification. In fact, a third-party satellite surveillance and monitoring system, with the provision for third-party on-site inspection in special cases, could solve most of the problems of verification. We insist that the U.S. uses alleged violations to subvert arms control and to pursue military superiority, and not to register any genuine concern for the treaty. This also includes their response to Kiasnoyarsk, regardless of the merits of this case. The Soviets could not be more stupid if, in fact, Kiasnoyarsk is what it appears. They could not hide it; they knew it would be a violation. They fear U.S. "Star Wars" development, which requires abrogation of ABM: why give the U.S. the ammunition to do what they most fear? Stupidity? Callousness? Or both? But the U.S. defense gang considers verification techniques too technologically complex, while they affirm "Star Wars" as feasible. This is either a naked expression of deceit or the selectivity that derives from conflict of interest: verification technology in fact is far less complex than "Star Wars." But the political nature of the allegations is virtually proven by the membership of GAC—seven out of twelve are current or former members of the Committee on the Present Danger and all twelve opposed SALT II. And Ronald Reagan claims the GAC is "bipartisan" (Longstreth, 1985)!

The SALT II Treaty stipulates the number of ICBM's and the number that can be MIRVed. But while the USSR is being accused of violation with its SS-24's, the U.S. was planning and procuring to violate the treaty, with its addition of Trident II to its present stockpile. While the Soviet Union is accused of violating the ABM Treaty, the U.S. was officially on record as being in favor of abrogation, and is taking steps with SDI to do so. Now that Gorbachev has come to power, Reagan's "window of vulnerability" has mysteriously been replaced by a new invention, the "window of opportunity." Gorbachev is young enough to be around for at least twenty years, while the reality is that Reagan will be around for no more than three years. This latter fact provides the real window of opportunity. A new U.S. president who is genuinely dedicated to peace could have real opportunities to make progress.

NEGOTIATIONS TO ACHIEVE NONAGREEMENT

Max Kampleman and Paul Nitze, both original members of the Committee on the Present Danger (CPD), are the senior members of the current U.S. arms negotiation team: Kampleman as its chief negotiator, and Nitze as its chief adviser. More than a decade has passed since the last major arms control treaty; more than that will elapse if these two staunch advocates of U.S. superiority have their way. Nitze's long record as a cold warrior indicates his belief in the viability of nuclear warfighting and the policy of negotiating from strength. Despite his apparent concessions in the SALT agreements, Nitze believes in negotiating to win, not to achieve peace or parity. In Nitze's lexicon, "winning" means neutralizing the Soviets and quantifying the losses: counting the dead and measuring the rate of postwar recovery (Pringle and Arkin, 1982). Kampleman—an ideological cohort of the viscerally anti-Soviet Pipes, Podhoretz, and Perle—believes that arms control equals unilateral disarmament.

The CPD continues to uphold the secret agenda both in Washington and abroad. While the Russians send veteran arms negotiators as delegates to the talks, the Reagan administration appoints a chief negotiator who does not believe in negotiations with the Soviets, and a chief adviser whose hard-line, cold-warrior record would be difficult to surpass. Of the entire U.S. delegation, only Nitze may be considered expert in the field of nuclear weapons. While Kampleman has previously dealt with the Russians on human rights issues, both he and Tower need careful briefing in nuclear armaments because of their limited knowledge of the field. Once again, the Reagan administration has sacrificed knowledge and expertise for ideology.

When one analyzes the real views of many of the key advisers who influence and shape policy, one can be reasonably certain that current negotiations are designed to achieve nonagreement. Richard Perle and Colin Gray have seized on the verification issue and seek to make past, alleged violations a basis for preempting future agreements. Kenneth L. Adelman, director of the Arms Control and Disarmament Agency and another key actor in current negotiations, actually favors arms control through an arms race. In "Arms Control With and Without Agreements" (*Foreign Affairs* [Winter 1984-1985]), Adelman argues against signed and ratified arms control treaties. He proposes "arms control without agreement," and, in effect, preempts the possible success of the new talks. Paul Nitze, writing in the same issue of *Foreign Affairs,* devotes most of his article, "Living with the Soviets," to the difficulties inherent in arms negotiations. Like Adelman, Nitze offers a flimsy straw of hope in the guise of "mutually advantageous tradeoffs." Both men clearly show their commitment to superiority: Adelman seeks to achieve it through nonagreements; Nitze desires to accomplish it through "parallel" tradeoffs. In actuality, what they both say is build and let build, and let the bargaining chips fall where they may (Draper, 1985).

This so-called "soft" line represents the Reagan administration's attempt to make political capital out of appearances; but the words of two true hard-liners, Henry S. Rowen and Irving Kristol, indicate the real nuclear military policy of the U.S. In the 14 December 1984 issue of the *Wall Street Journal,* Rowen tells us that "We could do worse than have four more years of palaver, while each side pursues its own program . . . . No U.S. objective is obtainable through any remotely feasible arms-control agreement." Kristol informs us that he wants negotiations to "drag on, tediously and endlessly and pointlessly," so that they "will dispose of the arms-control issue for the rest of this administration's term in office."

At best, therefore, the pessimism from the secretary of state's side counters the "realism" from the side of the secretary of defense. If the U.S. is not acting in bad faith, its negotiation attempts have certainly been designed to achieve nonagreement. Neither the "pessimists" nor the "realists" believe in arms control as parity and mutual reduction; both believe that "Star Wars" will lead to clear U.S. superiority, their operative definition of arms control.

The U.S. must know that it engages in a charade that mocks true arms control and disarmament. The Soviets will not be consigned to an inferior status. Because both sides have different objectives in view—the Soviets seek parity, the U.S. superiority—mutual paranoia based on the flimsy grounds of national mythology will probably cause arms negotiations to fail. The increasing unmanageability of the nuclear arms race enhances the attainable goals of the Nuclear Freeze Initiative, particularly its secondary phases of complimentary reductions.

The writings of such men as Paul Nitze contain smatterings of truth in their recognition of the intrinsic political, technological, and military assymetry between the superpowers. Unfortunately, these men fail to note another crucial difference between the countries: the Soviets negotiate out of desperation; the U.S. bargains in the bad faith of arrogant superiority.

The rapid introduction of high technology into the nuclear weapons systems tends to make the nuclear arsenal autonomously self-destructive. "Star Wars" and cruise missiles are basically destabilizing to both sides. Nonverifiability is now designed, but the absence of trust, coupled with suspicion and hatred, presents the most fundamental hazard. The Gorbachev era may introduce valuable and necessary changes in the internal structure of the USSR; however, it will not alter the fear, anxiety, and paranoia so deeply entrenched in the national Soviet psyche.

THE HUMAN RIGHTS ISSUE

Of all the outstanding issues of alleged treaty violations, those relating to arms control, compliance, and verification are not as serious or fundamental as the abuses of human rights in and by the Soviet Union. While it appears that the USSR has violated SALT II by building two new ICBM's, the SS-X-24 and the PL-S (only one is allowed, so the SS-24 is an alleged violation), and may have violated the ABM Treaty by its large phased-array radar installation at Kiasnoyarsk, neither allegation is certain. Nor is the alleged CBW violation certain. However, the certainty of human rights violations cannot be contested. The Soviet Union has violated the Helsinki Accords, particularly the Final Act and the Madrid Agreement, which were obligations freely undertaken by the USSR, on the basis of Western norms of freedom of speech and assembly.

It is probably true but of little consolation that the absence of improvements in human rights in the Soviet Union is in part due to the poisoning of the atmosphere of superpower relations by Ronald Reagan and his administration. One may also argue that Russian siege mentality, which probably preceded the 1917 revolution, accounts for Soviet paranoia about security and its interpretation of security as a necessary conformity that is confused with consensus. Soviet communism is a centralized, isolated, hierarchal, paternalistic political system integrated with love for Mother Russia. The blundering bureaucracy that operates out of siege paranoia leads the Soviets to help defeat SALT II ratification by intervening in Afghanistan; it assists U.S. weapon procurement by shooting down Korean Air Lines 007, and probably by violating arms control without full knowledge of political consequences. For example, the encryption on Soviet missiles makes their tests difficult to monitor, and access to telemetry is another provision of SALT II that the Soviets also appear to have violated.

A major problem between the superpowers is the political, technological, and military asymmetry of the two systems. Each system interprets very fundamental concepts such as human rights and freedom in radically different ways. In a world of nuclear weapons, conflicts arising from such radically different systems must be resolved, yet they cannot be settled by war. This creates a dilemma, and arms control and disarmament are situated at its heart. It is our contention that the "second cold war" initiated by the Reagan administration makes it more, not less difficult to resolve this dilemma. One can respect firmness when dealing with the Soviets, but one fears that firmness as frozen into a world view of implacable, inflexible hatred will certainly feed the tools of destruction. Modern states, including the superpowers, cannot deal with each other in terms of mirror-image moral judgments that are absolutes!

On the other side, when Ronald Reagan can view the contras as the modern equivalent of the brigades of Lafayette, we have a different distortion of values. Whether it is the primitive anticommunism of Reagan or the more sophisticated variety of a Kampelman or a Kirkpatrick, they all prefer friendly terroristic or corrupt systems like that of Somoza's Nicaragua, Batista's Cuba, and Pinochet's Chile to communism. There is a powerful bias at work that allows the end of defeating communism to be justified by terrorist means. This same bias tends to produce a contradictory judgment of what is morally acceptable. Fortunately, in the U.S. millions of people and many political figures condemn human rights violations even when committed by anticommunists. These people rightfully condemn the Soviet regime and a Pinochet in Chile for the same reasons. However, the record shows that visceral anticommunists do not apply the same criteria: their hatred of communism distorts the consistency of their love of freedom.

We are committed to the belief that peace and justice are indivisible goals, but we are equally committed to the belief that sacrificing one for the other is insane. Peace without justice is better than justice without peace in the nuclear age, a terrible contradiction but a logical consequence of the technology of death outstripping the search for peace. In a world of peace and injustice, the struggle would not cease, but methods other than technological violence would have to be used. We recognize our own contradictions in the circular route we have taken, for a world in which peace and injustice co-existed would not be secure. But in order for civilization to proceed, we must eliminate the threat of nuclear war because there can be no causes when there is no world. We wish to affirm that a U.S. policy that seems to extend human rights everywhere is valid, but that policy must be consistent and coherent. The policy of the Reagan administration is neither. It embodies intrinsic injustice in many of its domestic and foreign programs. The ultimate enemy is war, not the Soviet Union, and peace is the only way to defeat war. Yet many former Democrats have supported Reagan and some, for example, Max Kampelman, have joined him.

Max Kampelman has the reputation of being a liberal humanist. Who else among the founding board members of CPD in 1976 could clearly be considered a liberal humanist? There was Saul Bellow, who won the Nobel Peace Prize for Literature in 1976. There was James T. Farrell, the well-known novelist but still a questionable choice on our basic criteria. There were two or three trade unionists, the most notable being Lane Kirkland of the AFL-CIO, who probably regrets the early affiliation. Then, out of a total of some one hundred founding board members, we find Max Kampelman who, together with Bellow, is a genuine liberal humanist. But one would have to raise a fundamental issue with both of them. Look at the company they keep. Kampelman is the chief negotiator at Geneva. He believes in the myth of alleged Soviet nuclear superiority. We know he believes in the myth of "Star Wars." We know he is skeptical of achieving a meaningful arms treaty with the Soviets, despite public assurances to the contrary. The great majority of the founding board members of CPD could never be considered liberal and rarely humanistic. They are hard-line conservatives.

Max Kampelman's stance probably reflects a mix of two elements—visceral anti-Soviet feelings and technological ignorance of the dynamics of the arms race and the military balance. This makes him an ideal selection for the Reagan administration, with an obvious element of clever cooptation involved: Kampelman was recalled from Geneva to help sell the House on the MX. Kampelman is a long-standing liberal Democrat who has sold out without being obvious about it: an excellent choice to serve the purposes of Reagan's secret agenda.

As for Ronald Reagan's record on human rights, any man who could have said "America has never known slavery" is ignorant of both history and human rights. To liken the contras to "freedom fighters" or, worse, as equivalent to America's "founding fathers" is yet another example of the same myopia. He compounded this historical ignorance with an obviously racist remark when he appeared to justify the shooting and killing of South African demonstrators by stating that some of those who did the shooting were black. Blacks violating the human rights of blacks is fine for WASP Reagan. Jimmy Carter tied human rights to aid whether the violators were communistic or terroristic; Reagan's reversal of Carter's policy again illustrates his insensitivity to the issue. It is perfectly acceptable to Reagan, Kirkpatrick, and the rest of the present administration to support anticommunist regimes, even when they violate human rights. Kirkpatrick's conversion to the Republican party was long overdue. Now it is Kampleman's time to play turncoat.

Reagan probably has the worst record on human rights of any modern president. His administration is characterized by a flagrant lack of caring for the large numbers of poor, elderly, and otherwise disfranchised minorities. Here is a man who, on his May 1985 visit to West Germany in commemoration of the end of World War II, originally refused to visit a concentration camp, on the grounds that it would reopen old scars. To this he added the allegation that practically no one alive remembers the holocaust. Compounding his ignorance and insensitivity, Reagan then agreed to visit a German military cemetery in the name of reconciliation, commemoration, and the healing of old wounds, despite the fact that former SS officers were buried there. Not satisfied with this, Reagan then suggested that even the SS were victims of the Nazi regime, thus equating the persecutors with their victims. We can be reasonably sure that Reagan has forgotten the holocaust; the issue for Ronnie is who is more important to him—the Kohl government, or those who fought for freedom in World War II or were the target of Nazi genocide. In the end, Reagan divided his trip between the Germany military cemetery at Bitburg and the Nazi concentration camp at Bergen-Belsen, but he yielded only because of the enormous pressure and publicity generated by his intended visit.

Every arms control treaty has intrinsic loopholes. For example, the ABM Treaty does not cover antisatellite weapons (ASAT's), but ASAT's may be used as antiballistic missiles. The U.S. has done just that with its homing devices. ABM does not prohibit interceptors for short-range missiles, but these could be upgraded to genuine antistrategic ballistic missiles. The U.S. homing vehicle launched from F-15's can do this. SALT II prohibits more than one new ICBM, but does not prevent upgrading or modernizing an existing system. Such upgrading can be equivalent to a totally new ICBM. SALT II does not limit throw-weight, and this loophole has been exploited by the USSR.

If one examines all the military treaties existing between the U.S. and the USSR, the compliance record on both sides is fair, not perfect, and about equal in the record of violations. The continual allegations that the Soviets violated the Threshold Test Ban Treaty (TTBT) have been revealed as outright lies. Dr. Dewitt of Lawrence Livermore attested to this in a radio talk on 1 April 1985 that affirmed lack of violations.

4

The Sense and Nonsense of Superiority

What in the name of God is strategic superiority? What is the significance of it, politically, militarily, operationally, at these levels of numbers? What do you do with it?

Henry Kissinger, July 1974

In the next few years, conceivably, we could move into the perilous phase of nuclear parity. . . . We must retain and increase our superiority, not lose it. We must have the ability to "win," not merely to punish.

Melvin R. Laird, former secretary of defense, *A House Divided*

The U.S.'s long history of attributing nuclear superiority to the USSR probably began as early as 1950 with the famous landmark document, National Security Council Report NSC-68, drafted under the direction of Paul Nitze (thirty years later, one of President Reagan's two original chief arms negotiators). This document emerged during the period of debate over the development of thermonuclear weapons or H-bombs (Ford et al., 1982). The concern was that the USSR would develop these weapons rapidly and then seek a means of delivering them to the U.S. Moscow provided the information sought by intelligence advisers: it displayed two long-range bombers (the Bear and the Bison) in May Day parades of 1954 and 1955 (Ford et al., 1982, p. 18). This was not the first time that Soviet threats, implied or implicit, were to assist the U.S. rationale for its build-up. The "bomber gap" led to the rapid development of strategic intercontinental bombers supported by refueling tankers, so that by 1959 the U.S. led the USSR by seven to one, and it continues that lead to this day by about three to one.

By 1959, the "bomber gap" had been laid to rest. We witnessed the emergence of a "missile gap," prompted in large part by the USSR's successful August 1957 launch of Sputnik, the world's first orbital satellite. In each of these fictitious gaps, the U.S. estimates for massive Soviet superiority were short term. In the case of missiles, for example, the USSR was to have had one thousand ICBM's by 1961 and three thousand by 1962. "Let that be the record," said Senator Stuart Symington, a protagonist for U.S. missile build-up (Hanson Baldwin, *New York Times,* Monday, 25 March 1959). Yet by 1962, the USSR had a mere forty (see Table 2). Eventually Senator Symington blamed the CIA for its constant error in preparing the "national intelligence estimate" (NIE). He kindly suggested the CIA used "intent" as a basis of their estimate, rather than "capability" (Bottome, 1971, pp. 54–55). The error was colossal, about 96.5 percent. The consistency of such "errors" made by the CIA and official documents and statements of the U.S. Department of Defense covers a period of some twenty-five years. Once, in 1977, the CIA admitted that it had been 100 percent wrong in its estimates of Soviet defense equipment for ten years (Holzman, 1980, p. 26). Even Henry Kissinger in his period of ascendancy shared the remarkable and unlikely hypothesis of a rationally limited nuclear war: "A war which began as a limited war would have the advantage that its limitation could have been established—and what is more important—understood—well in advance of hostilities" (Lens, 1977, p. 114). (Eventually Kissinger repudiated this stance and returned to deterrence theory. "What in the name of God is superiority?" he asked in 1974 [Ford, et al., 1982, pp. 11, 12]). But Schlesinger, following Kahn, went the furthest, "I think we have to make the underlying calculation about nuclear war intellectually acceptable" (Lens, 1977, p. 116). Kahn had earlier defined "the hallmark of the expert professional [is] that he doesn't care where he is going as long as he proceeds competently" (Lens, 1977, p. 46). A winnable limited nuclear war was now clearly defined as the plans of competent professionals having intellectual acceptability. The last element to complete this posture of the planned destruction of our planet was to make it morally acceptable, and that was the element advanced by the Reagan administration. Reagan surrounds himself with a highly selective and biased group of advisers whose complex of views incorporates an ideological anti-Soviet mission: the destruction of the USSR communist state by force, blackmail, or economic suffocation; absolute belief in the "win syndrome" in a nuclear war; and a religious zeal in support of their goals. It is difficult to separate elements of deception, ignorance, malice, and belief in this complex of views. In some ways, they follow an old American tradition of downgrading their own forces and exaggerating those of the USSR. In other ways they follow what has been called "the tragic enshrinement of toughness"—a very apt phrase—most likely reinforced by the humiliation of the Iranian affair and the need to reassert "the greatness of America" as the leader in the cause of freedom and the Free World. The new posture certainly involves a fear of the USSR to the irrational point of attributing irrationality to it, i.e., an attack on the U.S. Much of this represents a homogeneous collective social paradigm that infects the Reagan administration. At the same time, the military is effectively allowed technological autonomy. Technocratic experts who remove the social, environmental, and ethical constraints from their technological goals operate weapons research and development as they see fit. Thus Charles Kupperman of ACDA can say, "Nuclear war is a destructive thing but still in large part a physics problem" (Scheer, 1982, p. 6). Or Fred Iklé, former head of ACDA and now in a more senior position in the U.S. defense establishment, could occasionally be candid, "The useability of nuclear weapons is built into them" (Lens, 1977, p. 103). Former Pentagon director of research and engineering John S. Foster, notorious for such statements, said, "We are moving ahead to make sure that whatever they do, or the possible things we imagine they might do, we will be prepared . . . . We see possible threats on the horizon, usually not something the enemy has done, but something we have thought that he might do, and that we must be prepared for" (Lens, 1977, p. 63). U.S. Admiral Moorer described this technological momentum very clearly in answer to a 1969 question by Senator Brooks regarding the arms race, "Well, I think it is a function of technology, Senator, and I do not think it ever ends. I mean, this has been going on since the Stone Age" (Ford et al., 1982, p. 16).

Before proceeding to the current status of the debate concerning "who's on first," it is necessary to return to Kissinger's 1974 statement on "superiority." He added, "What is the significance of it, politically, militarily, operationally, at these levels of numbers? What do you do with it?" (Smith, 1982, p. 32). The very notion of "superiority" at the present level of nuclear warfighting forces is mythic. Given the dynamic nature of the nuclear arms race, that superiority will likely remain mythic indefinitely, notwithstanding Reagan's altered image from cowboy to "Buck Rogers in the Twenty-first Century." A large number of independent experts have, at various times, estimated that deterrence is served by something between 200 and 400 deliverable warheads or a total megatonnage of 200 to 400 mts. hitting each side (Wiesner, 1982). Two hundred mts. at the critical targets of each would effectively destroy the life-support systems of modern civilization, and kill some 50 percent of the populations of each of the superpowers, without accounting for long-term environmental and ecological effects. There is no credible defense to the triad arsenals. What both sides now have is an obscene overkill and overskill. It is no longer a matter of how high the rubble will bounce but of converting the rubble to fine sand. The entire basis of the military balance debate rests on the fallacious U.S. assumptions that a nuclear war can be limited, or if protracted can be "won" in any case; and that a "first-strike counterforce" strategy can so paralyze the USSR that their second-strike or retaliation could be made acceptable through various damage limitation measures, such as crisis relocation (civil defense), bomber defenses, antisubmarine warfare, etc. There is also a curious myopia to the intrinsic dynamics of the nuclear arms race. This is the static view that real superiority is possible, i.e., one side makes critical and significant developments while the other side stands still. Finally, of course, superiority on the U.S. side is morally justified because superiority is necessary to keep the peace, and also because the U.S., being morally superior, would not attack the USSR. This latter point is contradicted by numerous official policy statements, as we have noted already and will further document later.

In examining all sources, official and secondary, it is clear that there is a distinct difference between the public media statements of politicians and their surprising on-the-record agreement (convergence) that there is a rough parity between the two superpowers. In fact, most high-ranking officials, when in situations of formal committees, make the same admissions. A large number of former U.S. Chiefs of Staff and numerous high-ranking former Western military officers also dismiss any superiority for either side. Officials of both the government and the military admit to U.S. superiority (*Defense Monitor* 13, no. 6, 1984 [Washington: The Center for Defense Information]). Also, the issue in the military balance debate has to do with "trends" rather than current or economically and technologically feasible expectations. Uncertainties are used for maximum advantage in soliciting support. The debate includes comparisons of both nuclear and conventional forces, of defense spending, "theater" balances, vulnerability, etc. These, of course, involve a numbers game, whereby inclusions and exclusions and the use of ill-defined numbers (such as comparing operational and inventory arsenals and their accompanying megatonnages) can confuse the outcome. Moreover, as we have illustrated, the thirty-year history of fictitious gaps (bomber "gaps" [1953– 1957]; missile "gaps" [1959–1962]; antiballistic missile or ABM "gaps" [1963–1967]; security "gaps" [1972–1973]; civil defense "gaps" [in the sixties, seventies, and again currently]; spending "gaps" [intensified by the Reagan administration]; and Reagan's "window of vulnerability") are in the same tradition (News conference, 31 March 1982; Johnson, 1982; "ABC News," 1981; numerous other publications). The myth of alleged Soviet superiority seems independent of the party or president in power, since the above "gaps" occurred in the Eisenhower, Kennedy, Johnson, and Nixon periods, with continuing overlaps and repeated falsehoods. The purpose of these mythical gaps was, in fact, the basis for continuing U.S. superiority in every area, with the exception of an accord reached on ABM's. In time, each prediction of Soviet superiority in each of the areas turned out to be false. Table 2 illustrates this for the period from 1960 to 1974. Secretaries of defense from John Foster Dulles to Melvin Laird and James Schlesinger were directly implicated in deceiving the U.S. public. While the Sputnik event in 1957 was the political basis for the U.S. programs to outstrip the Soviets in bombers, missiles, and SLBM's, the momentum already existed at the time of Sputnik (York, 1970). From 1954 to 1970 the impetus for accelerating missile development was aided by Soviet boasting and threats, which seem to be the most intense when they are most vulnerable. (Excellent sources documenting the fiction of gaps or the alleged Soviet superiority are available: Ford et al., 1982; *Defense Monitor,* 1982; Lens, 1977; Bottome, 1971; York, 1970; and numerous issues of the *Bulletin* of Atomic Scientists.)

In the five years since the Reagan administration has been in power, exaggerating the strength of Soviet nuclear forces has reached the point where it would be difficult not to conclude that deliberate deception was involved. The orchestrated chorus of misinformation is now more intense than ever before, partly because of the homogeneous world view and belief system of key actors in this administration. Key members of the defense establishment, including Weinberger, make categorical statements of Soviet superiority. Also typical is the view of former undersecretary of defense for research Richard De Lauer, who said, "The Soviets don't have to pull the trigger. They have the superiority. They've got a deterrent and we don't and that's the 'window of vulnerability'" (Smith, 1982). This is not mere nonsense but a compound of lies.

It is our contention that contrary to the assumption of rough parity (the position of the Nuclear Freeze Initiative), it is the U.S. that has been and remains superior to the USSR in nuclear warfighting forces, and that NATO is superior to Warsaw Pact. While we question the meaningfulness of the idea of superiority, it is important to assemble and document the facts on the military balance debate. We need to establish criteria for assessing the credibility and validity of methodologies used for comparisons. The new plans of the Reagan administration to consolidate and expand superiority therefore present the most dangerous threat to any hope of stabilizing and reducing nuclear arsenals.

AN ASSESSEMENT OF CREDIBILITY

Making judgments about the relative credibility of opposing sides in the nuclear debate poses a real problem. Both civil and military experts disagree about technically complex issues. Fortunately, credibility assessment criteria can be of great assistance in solving this problem, if not in totally resolving the issues. The debate over public use of nuclear energy is virtually over, to the almost total discredit of its proponents. What was too cheap to meter is now too expensive to build or even operate after construction. Horizontal proliferation is an almost universally acknowledged problem with no solution: as yet, there is no technically and commercially feasible method for the safe disposal of nuclear wastes (a problem even greater in the military). The first criterion of credibility is the historical record, or the history of failed predictions and forced retractions.

In the case of civil nuclear power, the former U.S. Atomic Energy Commission (AEC) became so enmeshed by the failure of its credibility that it was eventually terminated because of its record of noncredibility (Ford, 1982); there is also the short history of the Environmental Protection Agency (EPA) during the Reagan administration. A very similar situation applies to many aspects of the nuclear arms debate. We have already revealed the history of fictitious gaps in U.S.-USSR military balance; but the issue of NATO's alleged inferiority also exists: "NATO continues a tradition of nearly thirty years of denigrating its own military capabilities and exaggerating the Soviets'" (Leitenberg, 1982). The author goes on to state that "without such exaggeration the political leaders of its member states would not be able to muster a consensus in their own parliaments to support defense expenditure it considers necessary." The author deplores the overestimates, stating, "It also has an unfortunate consequence in that the process is not innocuous, and the emphasis on weakness has complicating political effects in Western nations." This is a rather mild censure of a policy of deception and misinformation to justify goals based on that very misinformation. But the situation is worse, since global military budgets and the U.S.'s monstrous $1.9 trillion to be spent in the next five years inevitably distort domestic and global social priorities. Bad money not only drives out good, but drives out good social policy. Based on the dismal historical record of assessing the military balance, one can have or should have grave doubts about the very same current assessment. The repeated public statements by Reagan and Weinberger and the supporting official documentation by the CIA and the Department of Defense are no different, except for intensity, consistency, repetition, and, most of all, the attempt to execute a policy based on false assessment. Although one could fill this book with documentation, we will cite a few examples. After the defeat of the MX in the House of Representatives, Reagan claimed: (1) the facts on the "Peacekeeper missile" were clear and straightforward—the U.S. has kept the world peace because "we maintained a margin of safety"; (2) the United States "hasn't built a new land-based missile in fifteen years" or, a few weeks later, at his 14 December 1982 news conference, "we have stayed static and have not improved in the last fifteen years in any of our missiles" and "we do not match them in accuracy" (Paine, 1983b). Now what are the facts? In the last fifteen years the U.S. has deployed three new types of ballistic missiles—Poseidon, Minuteman III, and Trident I and II—and two new types of bomber-launched missiles—the short-range attack missile (SRAM) and the air-launched cruise missile (ALCM)—in fact, a total of 2900 new missiles, all of which are more accurate than any missile in the Soviet arsenal. "It would be difficult to find any knowledgeable technical authority to substantiate the President's assertion" (Paine, 1983b, p. 6). The record continues to be contaminated, if anything, more grossly.

A second and obvious criterion is the question of conflict of interest. In fact, it is linked to the historical record. Obviously the definition of conflict of interest is provided by the institutional affiliation of the person making a declaration or judgment. Even when the public is confronted by scientific peers of equal credibility, for example, Nobel laureates, who publicly disagree on these issues, conflict of interest defined as above provides a first cut on whom to trust. When one examines the official sources of information of either the U.S. or USSR, one must be skeptical. When one listens to experts employed by these governments or to parties, private or public, that benefit from a particular governmental policy, one should retain doubt. Thus, for example, a very large number of retired senior military persons now deny and oppose the official position of the U.S. government or NATO-member governments.

A third criterion of credibility is evidence of internal contradictions or even anomalies in policy and rationale. These often appear in differences between the same person's public media statements and responses in committee sessions under interrogation, or between pronouncements and admissions. They can also arise in totally conflicting statements made by representatives of different branches of government. A recent example occurred on the same day, Sunday, 27 March 1983. General John Vessey on "This Week," an ABC news broadcast, responded to the question of superiority by stating clearly and categorically, "Neither side is superior." That day, Secretary of Defense Caspar Weinberger, the guest on NBC's "Meet the Press," stated, "The Soviets support the freeze because they have a significant superiority." To add to this confusion, when Senator Percy, at a Senate Foreign Relations Committee meeting, 29 April 1982, asked if Defense Secretary Weinberger would exchange U.S. nuclear forces for those of "the Soviet nuclear arsenal," Weinberger stated, "I would not for a moment exchange anything, because we have an immense edge in technology" (*Defense Monitor* 11, no. 6, 1982, p. 1). Former Defense Secretary Harold Brown echoed this response on 31 April 1982 (*Defense Monitor* 11, no. 6, 1982, p. 2). On 24 March 1981, John Lehman, Navy secretary, stated the U.S. Navy forces were "far superior in both numbers and quality" (*Defense Monitor* 11, no. 6, 1982, p. 6). On the other hand, on occasions too numerous to document, President Reagan has stated categorically that (*a*) the Soviet Union is superior, and (*b*) the Soviet Union is outspending the U.S. two to one on defense.

Perhaps the ultimate example of internal contradiction was a little-noticed document prepared by a group of U.S. agencies—DOD, Joint Chiefs of Staff, State Department, Central Intelligence Agency (CIA), Arms Control and Disarmament Agency (ACDA), and the National Security Council (reprinted by the *Defense Monitor* 9, no. 8A, 1981). An ultraright conservative group known as the American Security Council had made a film, "The SALT Syndrome," that contained a broad variety of allegations of U.S. weakness, so grossly inaccurate as to require the above official response. Obviously, this astounding response, which asserted U.S. supremacy in almost every area of the nuclear arms race, had a most surprising conclusion: "The combination of carefully negotiated arms control agreements . . . and sound military programs . . . give us far more security than either a diplomacy unbacked by strength or an unending arms build-up unsupported by diplomacy." Unfortunately, these events occurred toward the end of the Carter administration, and the new Reagan administration returned to groups like the American Security Council for its source of policy. All of the immediately previous U.S. Joint Chiefs of Staff except one have supported the thesis of rough parity. Five of seven former U.K. chiefs have taken this position.

The examples of anomaly, internal contradiction, opposite statements on or off the record, candid admissions, whistle blowing or leaked documents, hedging followed by reluctant admission during hearings, differences between covert and overt statements, etc., abound: to document them would require at least another book. They cover every technical, strategic, and socioeconomic aspect of the nuclear arms race, from civil defense to defense budgets. The major conclusion from all of these is the past, existing, and future maintenance of U.S. superiority will continue, coupled, as we shall see, with a policy to fight and win a nuclear war. Sometimes anomaly becomes apparent only by comparing different areas of the debate. An interesting anomaly arises, for example, in comparisons of various studies of civil nuclear-reactor accidents with the military estimates of radiation effects from fallout in various scenarios of nuclear war. A worst-case civil nuclear reactor incident or core meltdown, according to "The SANDIA Study" (*Nucleus* 5, no. 1, 1983), provides vastly greater radiation damage estimates to humans than any military estimate, which tends to downgrade this so-called "collateral damage" or—an even more sinister euphemism—"bonus kills." Yet the neutron bomb is predicated on enhanced damage from exposure to neutrons, which is derived directly from recent studies in radiation health physics. Actually the history of reactor safety studies, like its parallel history of fatality estimates in nuclear war, shares a common history of apologetics for nuclear power, consistently revealed to be gross underestimations and naked accommodation by the elite of nuclear proponents, public and private (Knelman, 1976).

There is, however, above all the criteria for credibility we have discussed, a more fundamental and theoretical consideration that involves the methodologies used for comparisons of the military balance. Intrinsic flaws and biases in these methodologies, when corrected, lay to rest the contention of Soviet supremacy.

METHODOLOGY AND MYTH:
THE INTERNAL DIALECTICS OF DECEPTION

Estimating the relative strengths of the two superpowers and their allies is a complex, restricted, and often tenuous task, and structural aspects of the USSR make it doubly so. The Soviet Union publishes an annual undefined military budget, but unlike all other major industrial nations, it fails to provide any specific details. Undoubtedly, it is incomplete and deceptive. Even if it were comprehensive, it would still pose the problem of converting rubles to dollars to provide comparisons with U.S. expenditures that are complete and virtually open for scrutiny and debate. Nevertheless, the CIA estimates Soviet annual military spending. This detailed estimate proves very significant for policymaking and, of course, for justifying U.S. military expenditures proposed and pushed by the DOD and the government. These CIA estimates provided the basis for Reagan's $1.9 trillion defense expenditure over the next five years. But, the claims made by the Reagan administration are based on alleged Soviet superiority now, i.e., on the premises that the USSR is outspending the U.S. by a factor of two to one, had technical superiority as of 1983, and has made the U.S. vulnerable to a first-strike attack through the "window of vulnerability."

The U.S. views its own superiority as nuclear equity. There is no question that what Reagan is saying is, if you give us this budget, we will regain our lost superiority and can then negotiate properly, from strength, since peace always comes from strength. One cannot exaggerate the importance of this policy debate. If, contrary to Reagan's assertions, there is now rough parity or, as this author has contended, U.S. supremacy, then the thrust of the entire Reagan program is not mere supremacy, but clearly and officially involves the notion of fighting and winning a nuclear war, or winning by blackmail, coercion, or economic suffocation of the USSR. Thus the world faces a huge new arms race in an atmosphere of extreme tension coupled to the distorting influence of its huge cost. If the methodology used by the CIA has provided false estimates, then there is madness in its methodology.

There are several components to military balance estimates. The first concerns expenditures and is a matter of economic methods of cost assessment. A second technical element involves the relative effectiveness of the hardware and intelligence systems (C^3I). A third technical-strategic category provides effectiveness criteria, measures flexibility, availability, response time, size of operation areas, i.e., geostrategic differences, distribution of targets, etc., (see Tables 1 and 2). It is our intention to deal with each of these separately. Unfortunately, magic numbers can become tragic numbers.

COMPARATIVE MILITARY EXPENDITURES

The first problem that arises in comparing military budgets is sometimes called the "index number effect." The Soviets base their currency, the ruble, on an almost exclusively domestic monetary system that cannot accurately reflect comparative internal prices or the relationship between internal and foreign prices. Therefore, filling the gaps in knowledge requires a host of unproven assumptions. Uncertainties such as these invite, if not compel, "worst-case" or "upper-limit" estimates of Soviet expenditures when dollar-to-ruble comparisons are used. Likewise, a ruble-to-dollar comparison would exaggerate U.S. defense expenditures (Holzman, 1980; Sivard, 1983).

Structural differences between the two superpowers also affect comparisons. The USSR defense system is labor-intensive while the U.S.'s is capital-intensive, because of the relative cost of each being more effective. Manpower is cheaper than hardware in the USSR. While the CIA admits these factors introduce biases and makes some attempt to correct for them, it still continues to provide, in general, dollar comparisons that exaggerate Soviet expenditures. When applied to Soviet costs, U.S. pay schedules for personnel and costs of equipment lead to an inevitable exaggeration of the latter's expenditures. In fact it has been shown that even the CIA's unofficial ruble comparisons contain serious methodological errors (Holzman, 1980), in part because the CIA uses "building-block" analysis. The Soviets break expenditures down into roughly ten groups or building blocks, such as manpower, equipment, construction, operating costs, research, training, and services, etc. Merely discounting Soviet military pay rates by the same percentage the CIA uses elsewhere for doctors and teachers (20 percent, due to the lower standards in the USSR) removes almost 25 percent of the dollar comparisons of military expenditures between the two countries (Holzman, 1980).

The use of U.S. analogs for equipment/hardware evaluations introduces very significant biases. While the CIA attempts to adjust for the generally inferior quality of equivalent Soviet hardware, it admits that "our estimates tend to overstate the costs of producing Soviet design. This is probably the general case" (U.S. Congress, Joint Economic Committee, 1978; Select Committee on Intelligence, U.S. Congress Hearings, 3 September 1980; Holzman, U.S. Armed Services Committee, March 1982). The general level of sophistication, digitalization, accuracy, availability, readiness, etc., of the U.S. forces are far greater than those of the USSR.

Even estimating manpower costs presents methodological problems admitted by the CIA (Sivard, 1982). Not many Soviet divisions are at full strength, and many so-called military personnel are really paramilitary, i.e., civilians in uniform. In addition, the CIA does not take into account the Soviets' use of the military for industrial and agricultural work. The tendency again is to assume a "worst case" and thus to incorporate significant upward bias (Sivard, 1983).

The so-called "spending gap" is yet another of the fictitious myths that have been deliberately spawned to justify an arms build-up and/or development. This standard ploy for selling the defense budget is used over and over again by the highest public officials of the U.S. government, including the president and secretary of defense. The assertion that the USSR's military budget is increasing at an annual rate of about 5 percent per year has persisted since 1977, repeated by Defense Secretary Donald Rumsfeld in 1977, his successor Harold Brown in 1979, and, of course, Caspar Weinberger in 1982 and 1983. In fact Harold Brown spoke of the "steady increase in Soviet defense efforts each year for more than fifteen years" and that such an increase was "clear and dramatic" (Garthoff, 1984, p. 5). This meant that the Soviet rate of increase of some 5 percent had begun in 1964!

Now, revised CIA and NATO estimates prepared since the middle of 1983 acknowledge that Soviet military spending has increased at a rate of just 2 percent since 1976 (Garthoff, 1984, p. 6), and that rate has continued through 1983! Thus the so-called "relentless and disquieting index" of Soviet intentions and build-up has been exposed as the real relentless and disquieting excuse for the U.S. build-up. After 1979 the Carter defense budget increased at an annual rate of 10 percent; under Reagan, beginning with fiscal year 1984, the request was for a 13 percent real increase! The difference between the U.S. and the USSR in the rate of military spending became 11 percent per year—so much for the myth of the "spending gap."

The CIA study cited above, contrary to every deceitful public statement by Caspar Weinberger, has acknowledged that Soviet military expenditures from 1976 through 1984 have increased at an average rate of 2 percent per year real growth. Comparing this for four years of Reagan budgets, 1981–1984, the U.S. increased its military spending by 4.63, 7.51, 7.66, and 4.05 percent real growth, respectively, not including the huge, accumulating "backlog" in the pipeline (*Defense Monitor* 14, no. 4, 1985, p. 6). The important fact is that 95.7 percent of the top-secret 1984–1988 FY Defense Guidance Document's budget has been approved through 1981–1985! In reality, the U.S. leads a real "spending gap" by an overwhelming margin. As for the credibility of U.S. secretaries of defense, we can only hope history and the record will catch up to their consistent deceptions before it is too late. In the meantime, the anatomy of ths deception should be revealed, as well as the methodological flaws in analysis.

We have argued elsewhere that such methodological flaws result from the hidden assumptions or even the deliberate intents of the study. U.S. policy has consistently demonstrated this in its search for nuclear superiority. However, deception reinforced by implacable belief is endemic to the

Reagan administration. Unfortunately, the public has not yet been fully informed of this process.

By attempting to introduce corrective methods to overcome the CIA's methodological flaws, such as assigning a "zero price" to significant technological superiority, the World Priorities Institute's (World Military and Social Expenditures, WMSE) conservative assessment of expenditures is revealing (Sivard, 1982). The methodology is complex and beyond the scope of this book; however, the following table reveals a new fictional gap—the "expenditures gap":

TABLE 3

Military Expenditures (Billions $) 1980

SOURCE	WARSAW PACT			NATO		
	USSR	OTHER	TOTAL	US	OTHER	TOTAL
1. U.S. GOVT.	200	30	230	110	120	230
2. IISS	N/A	20	N/A	135	125	260
3. SIPRI	125	10	135	140	130	270
4. WMSE	130	15	145	140	140	280

(1) ACDA; (2) International Institute of Strategic Studies; (3) Stockholm International Peace Research Institute; (4) World Military and Social Expenditures. (The latest figures indicate NATO is outspending Warsaw almost 2:1.)

It should be noted that IISS (London) has been severely attacked for parroting CIA and other U.S. official estimates and for committing serious errors of exaggerating Soviet expenditures (Leitenberg, 1982; *Defense Monitor,* 1982; Holzman, 1982; Sivard, 1983). Table 3 shows a major discrepancy between U.S. government figures and those from other sources. U.S. official documents on the military balance characteristically reflect such a major disparity (Leitenberg, 1982), but the power of their exaggeration is extremely significant. The U.S.'s publication of *Soviet Military Power* in September 1982, and its presentation to NATO, created a new level of anxiety in Europe and, in effect, for the world (Leitenberg, 1982).

Table 3 indicates that both SIPRI and WMSE show the U.S. outspending the USSR by 10+ percent, but NATO outspending the Warsaw Pact by over 90 percent. The U.S. government shows NATO and the Warsaw Pact spending about the same, but the distortion arises from the relatively large amount attributed to the USSR, 33 percent greater than the U.S. The spread between the first group and the U.S. estimate is over 40 percent, which has also been arrived at by other independent assessors (Holzman, 1982; *Defense Monitor* 11, no. 6, 1982, p. 4; Sivard, 1983). In the *Defense Monitor's U.S.-Soviet Military Facts* (1982), CDI provides figures comparing NATO and the Warsaw Pact in twelve military categories. Except for tanks, armored vehicles, and heavy artillery, NATO is significantly superior as of 1982, outspending the Warsaw Pact by $256 billion to $202 billion, maintaining manpower of 5.8 million to 4.8 million, and rating very superior in every category of strategic nuclear weapons. (A number of official U.S. sources document the nuclear superiority.)

In conclusion, there seems to be abundant evidence of a systematic upward bias in the evaluation of Soviet military expenditures. Such unreliable reporting has an extremely significant impact on U.S. policy, as we have suggested. It not only affects economic policies but also accelerates an arms race already out of control. Thus a policy based on misinformation becomes self-fulfilling, especially when we are dealing with simple deceptions and paradigms of true believers. The issue was put decisively when reference to figures released on Soviet strength elicited the response, "They are just plain inaccurate . . . . they are nonsense, balderdash, phony, fake, and I might add untrue" (Proxmire, 1980).

TECHNICAL FACTORS IN METHODOLOGICAL ASSESSMENT

We have already provided the theoretical bases of technological comparisons of the superpowers' nuclear warfighting systems. The critical criteria of strategic missile effectiveness, "lethality" and "probability of kill," illustrate U.S. superiority in unequivocal terms (Aldridge, private communication, 30 April 1985). This same source also points out that only MX and Trident II, of all the strategic missiles in both camps, are true first-strike weapons, having incredibly high values for lethality and probability of kill. Despite the propaganda to the contrary, the United States has kept pace with the USSR in the actual growth of strategic warheads between 1969 and 1983, i.e., 4000 to 10,000 for the U.S. and 1660 to 7800 for the USSR.

As another propaganda trick, the U.S. asserts that it has not developed a new ICBM since the 1970 Minuteman III (a modification of Minuteman II [1966], which is a modification of Minuteman I [1962]). However, the retrofit is so qualitatively significant that to judge by numbers alone is deceiving. The 550 Minuteman III's in the U.S. arsenal represent a huge, qualitative technological leap in such matters as accuracy, new guidance software, warhead advances, MIRVing, etc., that almost triples each warhead's kill capacity while improving its cost effectiveness. In fact, Minuteman III equipped with its new guidance system and the Mark 12-A warhead will provide the same silo kills per warhead (about 0.83) as the most updated version of the USSR's SS-18's and SS-19's expected by 1985 (Aspin, 1980; Paine 1981).

The size of Soviet missiles or "throw-weight" of the last stage has often led to the contention of a so-called "throw-weight" gap. Actually, Soviet missiles, a generation behind the U.S.'s in design efficiency, still use predominantly liquid fuels that reduce readiness and introduce a host of problems. The Mark 12-A warhead, while just 2 percent heavier than its predecessor the Mark 12, can produce 100 percent greater blast. Throw-weight is thus an inaccurate and deceiving measure of effectiveness. The cost effectiveness of the Mark 12-A is remarkable, about $0.9 million per silo killed for the U.S. to $5.8 million for the USSR, or a 6.4:1 advantage in cost effectiveness (Aspin, 1980, p. 29). The same cost effectiveness applies to silo upgrading through increased "hardness" whereby the U.S. has delayed Minuteman III obsolescence until 1986 (Aspin, 1980, p. 30).

In terms of technological comparisons, the development of air-launched cruise missiles (ALCM's) marks the single, most significant advance in the entire nuclear arms race. It in effect nullifies the Soviet bomber defenses that represent as much as 15 percent of their defense budget (Perry, 1978), so that B-52's can remain operational. By modification in weapons and avionics the ACLM's will increase penetration capacity (actually negating Soviet bomber defenses) and increase silo kill capacity to 0.97. The USSR will spend more than $50 billion to attempt to find a defense for ACLM's. By the time they do, "stealth" techniques ("electronic countermeasures" or ECM) will allow CM's to "elude or spook Soviet radar" at high cost effectiveness (Perry, 1978; Aspin, 1980; Aldridge, 1983). Morover, expert opinion suggests ALCM's or CM's in general would be immune to "Star Wars" weapons.

Time constraints do not allow a more detailed analysis of technological comparisons. In the area of naval capacities, the U.S.'s SLBM's as well as general naval forces are far superior, both in conventional and nuclear capabilities. In general, the USSR's nuclear weapons and delivery systems are at least one generation behind the U.S. The U.S., for example, introduced solid fuels in the 1960s. Finally, when comparing electrotechnology C^3I, "the United States leads in most areas" (*Spectrum*, 1982). The journal *Spectrum* devoted an entire issue to "Technology in War and Peace" (October, 1982). Despite the journal's conservative approach and its major sources being official government documents, the net superiority of the U.S. emerges with extreme clarity. In a commissioned paper on remote sensing satellites (RSS), this author concluded that U.S. superiority in the space field was even greater than *Spectrum*'s analysis (Knelman, 1983c).

GEOSTRATEGIC AND SECONDARY TECHNICAL FACTORS

Among geostrategic factors, the USSR's highly concentrated population and industrial centers significantly reduce their number of targets compared to the U.S. (Cockburn, 1982). There are only 258 cities over 100,000 in population, only thirty-four major refineries, twenty-five major chemical plants, and 1398 missile silos. There are thus no more than 1800 significant strategic targets including cities. But for a retaliatory stance, i.e., deterrence, there are only about 400 targets. With almost 10,000 warheads in the U.S. arsenal, this factor is significant. In contrast, distribution of population and industry in the U.S. is far less concentrated. Just one advanced, and as yet invulnerable, Trident I submarine can destory 128 Soviet cities, while Trident II will be able to destroy 192 "hard" targets, the equivalent of one thousand Hiroshimas. Trident II warheads of 475 kt. are now designated W-88.

The U.S. has other geostrategic and technological advantages. The Soviet Union is effectively confined to its own land mass and surrounding waters. The U.S. has a global network of strategic facilities, including naval bases, that surround the Soviet Union at all points of its perimeter. This geostrategic difference gives the U.S. a vast twenty-to-one edge in ocean use. Moreover, it bottles up Soviet naval forces by closing off or restricting movements from one theater to another. The U.S. has over 600 long-range air-refueling tankers, compared to 30 for the USSR (*Defense Monitor* 11, no. 6, 1982), thus compounding their geostrategic advantage. The U.S. also maintains over 55 percent of its thirty-two ballistic missile submarines at sea at all times, compared to about 11 percent of the Soviet Union's sixty-two strategic submarines, which more than doubles the effective U.S. force at any one time, and with superiority in accuracy, etc., (*Defense Monitor*, 1981, 1982; Sivard, 1982, 1983).

In general, the U.S. has significant advantages over the USSR in sociotechnical factors, such as readiness or alert time, availability, flexibility, etc. It has over twice the availability operational use of navy ships, almost five times for submarines, and, even with comparison of Air Force pilots, three times the availability (Sivard, 1982; Paine, 1982a). Thus "the forces ready for instantaneous launch" on a "day-to-day alert" or "generated alert forces" in the U.S. are superior, even as admitted by official sources (Paine, 1982a). Response times of ICBM's are also much better for the U.S.

We can conclude that while much of the above is not quantified or quantifiable in general, force effectiveness, cost effectiveness, and strategic effectiveness are all in favor of the U.S. In comparing the values of the products of civil technology, i.e., what discount to apply to Soviet goods, from automobiles to TVs, as compared to U.S., a general figure of about 40 percent is used (Holzman, 1980). There is every reason to believe that a similar quality discount should be applied to military comparisons to measure the high-technology gap and the geostrategic gap. Thus, being fully aware of the methodological pitfalls, we can only conclude that at the present time the U.S. leads the USSR in the nuclear arms race.

We have tried to assess the issue of superiority in rational terms, both direct and indirect. The arithmetic of superiority has both a political and a credibility aspect as well as a technical content. Ultimately superiority is nonsense: both sides have sufficient "second-strike" capacity to inflict terrible damage to the other. The submarine leg of the triad provides this deterrence. But deterrence is not stable, particularly if denied and replaced by a warfighting strategy. The "launch-on-warning" strategy would likely mean that the ICBM's of both sides would be used in an all-out nuclear war, leading to a "holocaust effect." However, given the Reagan program to develop all weapon systems, B-1, MX, stealth, neutron bomb, advanced cruise missiles, Trident II, and "Star Wars" weapons (supply-side militarism), the perception of U.S. superiority by both sides could be extremely dangerous and will certainly accelerate the arms race, with all its ensuing costs.

Reference to Table 2 coupled with our analysis suggests that the U.S. has had real superiority in the nuclear military balance from the beginning of the arms race to the present. This is reflected in the entire history of arms limitation/reduction negotiations and treaties. From SALT I through SALT II, for example, the U.S., negotiating from strength, managed to eliminate the strategic-bomber leg from SALT-accountable systems. U.S. superiority in this leg, coupled with the evolution of air-launched cruise missiles (ALCM) to be carried by strategic bombers, maintains U.S. superiority. In fact, if one adds all prospective cruise missiles (not negotiable in SALT, START, or BUILD-DOWN) to the total U.S. strategic warheads being negotiated, the U.S. will have more than a two-to-one lead in warheads in the next five years or so. In SALT I and even SALT II the Soviets made concessions from relative weakness. The U.S., having failed to ratify SALT II, will not accomplish any increase in security unless the nuclear freeze becomes a treaty. The dangerous period will be between now and 1990 since the U.S. will have attained a margin of perceived superiority. Now that the Reagan administration will remain in power until 1988, the danger of nuclear war will be very great in the next few years.

The placing of Euromissiles with short delivery times to key targets in the USSR makes the "launch-on-warning" scenario much more plausible. Should the Soviets detect, through false alert, what they believe is a "decapitation" strike from West Germany, we could conceivably have World War III. The U.S. has "won" the battle over the definition of "strategic" in previous treaties. Soviet SS-20's cannot strike targets in the U.S.; Pershing II's can strike targets in the USSR. Thus the continuing advantage of the U.S. in negotiation persists. Since the Reagan administration apparently (and all the evidence supports this) believes a nuclear war is winnable and survivable, and also believes the USSR is the "focus of evil," the above scenario is further complicated.

THE BATTLE OF THE BUDGET

A basic test for the authenticity of the supersecret warfighting plans of the Reagan administration would certainly lie in the defense budget. To accomplish the simultaneous and redundant goals of defeating the Soviet Union in peace and war requires a huge budget. Since part of that budget is an investment in deceit, designated to lure the Soviets into costly and unproductive military expenditures, cutting back on such an important investment, whose paycheck could be "victory," would be difficult to deny. We have suggested that "Star Wars" may be the key. "Star Wars" might seem to be the answer for those who believe in technological infallibility and are blind to the dynamism of the arms race, i.e., those who seek unilateral advantage. This group would include the space lobby, the advocates of the technological fixes, the myopic believers in the omniscient power of science and technology, and, perhaps, a complementary and large group in the Soviet Union, as well as most of the Politburo. Thus Reagan and Gorbachev and the technical and commercial high-frontier lobby of both countries share this collective ideology of progress and technological infallibility. In his second debate with Walter Mondale Ronald Reagan admitted he did not understand the science of "Star Wars"; he has chosen to believe his "kitchen" science adviser, Edward Teller, and his formal science adviser, George Keyworth. Teller was denying the possibility of "nuclear winter" even while the National Academy of Sciences was validating it. Teller—the master of denial of anything negative to nuclear power—most often has to indulge in myths to sustain his reasons. His record is so bad that one would expect him to be more careful, but he never relents and rarely is right.

By early December, barely three weeks after the election, the battlelines were drawn over the defense budget. Reagan had declared he would never raise taxes except "over his dead body." He simultaneously promised to reduce the budget to under $100 billion by 1988. This combination typifies the very definition of voodoo economics (perhaps some witch doctor is sticking pins into a Reagan doll).

Meanwhile, David Stockman, then budget director, was doing his job and trying to cut spending as instructed. Stockman's proposal had to include defense spending cuts totaling $58 billion over the period ($8 billion in 1986, $20 billion in 1987, and $30 billion in 1988).

Reagan, for his part, had decided to cut $33.6 billion from domestic programs for FY 1986 (beginning October 1, 1985). The arithmetic reality is based on the unrelenting logic of numbers and the politics and mythology of war and peace. Caspar Weinberger, secretary of defense and champion of the Pentagon, is ill informed on numbers if they denote weapons but is passionately devoted to them if they denote military expenditures. He is not interested in budget cuts but in defense spending. At least, he is consistent in defending his government's own secret military plans, policies, and programs. But while the State Department continued its historical conflict with the Defense Department, and Stockman pursued his mandate, and a seeming majority of Congress agreed that defense could not be spared the cuts, the issue simmered until Reagan had to choose. Reagan predictably chose supply-side military economics. Procure everything, every weapon system you can imagine, and hope the output is peace or victory.

In the first three weeks of December 1984 the battle of the budget raged. The divisions within the executive branch were clear, and so were the divisions between elements of the executive and Congress. Weinberger took his stand firmly, arrogantly, and clearly. He denied he had agreed to the cuts proposed by Stockman. He made his own devious proposals for cuts that were not cuts.

A State Department official described the Weinberger proposal for defense spending "cuts" as "silly." "It's so, so little as to be worth laughing at" (*Arizona Republic,* Friday, 14 December 1984). Weinberger had proposed two military pay raises, one in FY 1985, and a pay freeze in FY 1985, thus effectively adding zero to the cuts. In effect, the military would get one pay raise in January 1985 and a second in September 1985, but none after 1 October 1985 when FY 1986 begins. Even in David Stockman's budget projections, defense spending is to grow from $250 billion in 1985 to $330 billion in FY 1988! Weinberger's position is clear. Cuts are to be tied to "progress" in arms negotiations with the Soviets. But such "progress" is, of course, to be controlled; it is assured that there will be no progress. Thus there will be no defense cuts.

In the wake of the hijacking of a Kuwaiti airliner to Iran, the debate took other forms that again illustrated the conflict between State and Defense. Their public response to the hijacking hinted at divisiveness. The media fervently issued reports of the rift, but generally they lacked perspective. State had won a victory over Defense with the appointment of Paul Nitze as chief arms negotiator in the next round of superpower talks. Paul Nitze may be an endangered hawk, but actually it is the doves who are most endangered. The current generation of healthy hawks cannot forgive Nitze for negotiating SALT I, a seeming diversion from his consistent position on arms control. Nor can they forgive him for his Geneva walk-in-the-woods agreement with the Soviets over Euromissiles that limited NATO to 300 cruises of one warhead, and the Soviet side to 75 SS-20's with three warheads each. Keep in mind Nitze's record in his writing key articles on nuclear war winnability, his role in the "B-team" exercise, and his activities in CPD. Barbara Tuchman likened Nitze's appointment as chief INF negotiator to "putting Pope John Paul II in charge of abortion rights." The public "disagreement" between Weinberger and Shultz included all these elements as well, but the media did not air them.

Instead, the electronic media, all three networks and some independents, consistently painted the Weinberger-Shultz "controversy" in terms that suggested a role reversal had occurred between them. But Weinberger's speech to the National Press Club delivered a clear, hard message: the next time the U.S. gets into a war, it will fight to win, even if that means using nuclear weapons. Like Reagan, Weinberger has clearly threatened the use of force, but unlike Reagan, Weinberger has set the conditions, namely, when the U.S.'s vital interests are at stake and when the U.S. had clearly defined its objectives. When one couples this with Weinberger's own pet Defense Guidance Document FY 1984-1988, we know he has already defined the U.S.'s most vital interest—the destruction of the Soviet Union by pretext or design. Weinberger doesn't want another Vietnam or Lebanon. Even if it involves millions of deaths, the next time the U.S. attacks, it attacks to win. (How the media could possibly interpret this as a "soft" stance compared to the relatively mild and controlled position of George P. Shultz is amazing and a source of constant surprise.) Clearly Weinberger did not intend to lose the defense budget debate.

In the middle of the debate Reagan made a characteristic slip of the tongue. At his Friday, 14 December 1984, White House ceremony celebrating the attaching of license plate "No. 1" to his limousine, Reagan responded with considerable irritation to reporters' questions, ". . . those leaks are without solid foundation . . . We are still in the basis of negotiating . . . or not negotiating, that's the wrong term to use." Of course negotiating is not the right term, but close enough. Infighting, soliciting, pressuring, etc., would be even more correct terms. Reagan's support for Weinberger's position authenticates the "five-year plan" (*Arizona Republic,* Saturday, 15 December 1984, p. 20). In fact, when the military budget cut of $8.7 billion for 1986 was finally announced, a large part of it came from a 5 percent pay cut for civilian workers in military establishments; uniformed personnel actually received a pay increase of 7 percent.

It is ironic that the defense budget "debate" is over whether to spend $292.9 billion in 1986 (House and Senate agreement), or $313 billion (Reagan proposal), or $299 billion (Reagan's other proposal, after internal pressure from congressional Republicans). Reagan's $299 billion still represents a 6 percent increase over 1985. This is more than the entire world spent on armaments only a few years ago. Senator and former Navy secretary John H. Chafee (R-R.I.), said, "All senators in the room [at a meeting of Senate Republicans and members of the executive] wanted defense to take its fair share . . . most senators feel defense should be frozen [at its present level] as an initial suggestion" (*Arizona Republican,* Saturday, 15 December 1984, p. 20). Senator Simpson (R-Wyo.) said that Pentagon spending had increased by an average of 13 to 14 percent a year during Reagan's first term. In 1985 the military budget had doubled since Reagan took office. According to the CIA, the USSR's defense budget has grown at an average of 2 percent (after inflation) over the same period. Moreover, the U.S. defense budget was larger than that of the USSR when Reagan took office.

Earlier in this chapter, we illustrated in detail the process of deception that goes into the accounting systems of the Pentagon, whether it reports weapons or dollars. Giving substance to this claim, Senator Simpson, interviewed on Thursday, 13 December 1984, accused the Pentagon of "playing the game of cooked figures and real growth and inflators and deflators" and "Anybody who can tell us that we haven't charged up the defense budget in the four years of the Reagan administration is smoking something" (*Arizona Republic,* Saturday, 15 December 1984, p. 20). The image of Weinberger and pot is the ultimate insult.

By 17 December 1984, it was official: Weinberger had won the first round. Ronald Reagan announced that he had agreed to $28 billion in defense spending cuts over the FY 1986–1988, less than half the amount proposed by David Stockman. Weinberger declared himself the winner, as reported on "CBS News" of 18 December 1984. He was quoted as referring to the cuts as a "very satisfactory budget result decision" that would allow the U.S. to regain its "necessary deterrent strength" and would not involve cancelling any military programs. Now Ronald Reagan has to find huge, extra cuts to meet his commitment of deficit reduction to below $100 billion by 1988. Let us examine the arithmetic. Reagan has agreed to cut domestic programs by $33.6 billion in 1986. If we add the three-year cut of $28.1 billion to this, we have a total of $61.7 billion. The remaining cuts will have to come from domestic programs. What will the real deficit be in 1988? The $200 billion estimate could be highly underestimated. Also, both the White House and Caspar Weinberger have referred to the budget as a continuing process that is revised each year. One could predict with considerable accuracy that the promised $9.2 billion, 1987 and $10.2 billion, 1988 defense spending cuts ($19.4 billion) are not firm commitments but stalling tactics.

The first round in the battle of the budget (or bulge) did not settle the whole fight. Reagan's announcement drew an almost universally negative response from members of Congress, Republican and Democrat alike. The battlelines were clearly drawn. Aside from voodoo economics we shall undoubtedly witness voodoo politics. To battle Congress, Reagan and Weinberger will need pretext and protest. Their pretext could come from the "failure" of the next round of arms talks, which will be blamed on Soviet intransigence. Reagan will protest by going to the people with a platform designed to win the midterm elections, a replica of his "peace through strength," "evil empire," and perfect verification demands of the past.

A side effect of the budget battle could have seen the demise of the MX program. Congresspersons who had supported development, such as Les Aspin (D-Wis.), had already indicated withdrawals of support. Senator Barry Goldwater (R-Ariz.), chairman designate of the powerful Armed Services Committee, had supported MX also, but he has recently announced, "My heart has never been in it" and "I think we have had enough. I think they [the Soviets] have more than enough and I don't see any big sense in going ahead building" (*Arizona Republic,* Friday, 14 December 1984). Both these senators capitulated in the crunch. The most recent developments in the battle of the budget represented a serious defeat for Reagan and Weinberger. Originally, they had requested an 8 percent real increase for 1986, then 6.7 percent, and finally they presented a new package that requested a 3 percent increase. Recognizing the imminent defeat of this, Reagan finally capitulated and agreed to a one-year freeze. Credibility is outraged by all this, since at every stage the need for the military budget increase was said to be absolute, with no possibility of accepting anything else. On 2 May 1985, after the Republican-controlled Senate had placed the defense budget on the chopping block, Reagan, speaking to reporters in Bonn, stated, "It is an irresponsible act" ("NBC National News," 4 May 1985). Yet he was forced to concede a freeze by 9 May, proving that he must be irresponsible by his own definition. The fallout from the series of policy blunders, gaffes, and patent deceit connected with the Bitburg event would continue to haunt Reagan. In Europe he got nothing. In fact, his Nicaraguan policy was universally rejected and his importuning for "Star Wars" was abandoned rather than face rejection. Meanwhile, Reagan demonstrated his ignorance when he charged that the Soviets plan to make their SS-24's mobile and that this constitutes first-strike intent (*San Francisco Chronicle,* Thursday, 9 May 1985). In fact an expert, Spurgeon Keeny, Jr., was quoted as stating this was an invalid conclusion. Worse, Reagan's conclusion made no sense. The SALT II treaty that the U.S. never ratified is now being discussed and the propaganda preparations, i.e., rationalization by accusation, have begun.

SECOND TERM: LAME DUCK OR HURT HAWK

Interestingly enough, no commentator, to the knowledge of this author, attributed any part of Reagan's motive in pursuing new arms talks with the Soviets to the deadlock in Congress. The House adopted a mutual moratorium on ASAT testing and enacted a large cut in the "Star Wars" budget, but the Senate was more supportive. In the end, the House and Senate finally agreed to place riders on the appropriations for not only ASAT's and SDI, but also for the MX. While the Defense Appropriations Bill allowed for the production of twenty-one MX missiles, actually supplying production funds is prohibited until two separate resolutions on authorization and appropriation were passed. Votes on these resolutions were to be taken fifteen days after the presidential report on MX, due 1 March 1985. These resolutions had been designed to be finite without amendment, and to take effect on 16 March 1985. The superpowers have now agreed to reconvene in Geneva on 12 March 1985.

The two riders/restrictions on the ASAT's require that no ASAT be tested against an object in space until 1 March 1985. After that date, and before testing an ASAT in space, the president was to submit four reports that in effect certify that an anti-ASAT treaty is being negotiated, and that the proposed testing would neither violate the ABM Treaty nor threaten later negotiations. After submission of the reports, testing must wait an additional fifteen calendar days. The Air Force will be allowed two "successful" tests of an ASAT, but are restricted to three tests in all. Of course, another rider allows the U.S. to test "to avert clear and irrevocable harm to the national security." The USSR, following a self-proclaimed moratorium, has not tested an ASAT since August 1983.

Although Congress placed severe restrictions on the Strategic Defense Initiative (SDI or "Star Wars") in both the Defense Authorization and Appropriations Acts, the authorization agreement detailed above was not as strong as the House had wished. The U.S. had not declared a moratorium on testing. On the contrary, the U.S. has tested its ASAT system—a two-stage missile that utilizes a homing device for targeting carried aboard an F-15 jet. The tests to this date, however, are against "points" in space, not actual targets. On 15 January 1985 it was announced that President Reagan would file the "certification" necessary to begin testing by 1 March 1985.

It would appear to this author, at least, that there is no substantive compliance with the congressional restrictions on the resumption of ASAT tests. The Soviets, of course, agreed to a date for the beginning of talks on space and the other two areas. It appears obvious that the timing of the Shultz-Gromyko talks was designed to meet the congressional restrictions. But what signals, if any, did the U.S. secretly send to the USSR to bring them back to negotiations? We believe this must have occurred. This hypothesis accounts for the conflicting signals that came from the White House before and after the congressional meetings of 7 and 8 January 1985. It also accounts for the difference in interpretation of these sessions given by Caspar Weinberger and George Shultz. Weinberger is obviously going through what, to him, is a mere formality of compliance to Congress without substance. Everything Weinberger has said in public illustrates he is closely following the top-secret defense guidance and accompanying security documents' directives. What Weinberger and Company are going to do to fulfill their fantasies of "Star Wars" capability, and incidentally force the Soviets to respond to such a costly pursuit, is intriguing. With the House clearly opposed to SDI and the Senate somewhat reluctant to support it, and with the problems inherent in declaring a budget, defining the goals, and analyzing the consequences of militarizing space, the Ninety-ninth Congress could be a critical factor in the cause of peace. That 1986 is a midterm election year strengthens opposition to the secret agenda of the Reagan administration.

It will be of great interest to see how the New Right fares in 1986 and, in general, whether it can continue to influence a second-term Reagan. The new arms negotiators named on 18 January 1985 do not clearly resolve this question. The chief negotiator, Max L. Kampelman, is certainly fringe New Right, although he is a nominal Democrat. Former Texas senator John Tower, named as strategic arms negotiator, represents the Old Right; he is hardly superior to Edward Rowny, being less knowledgeable and committed to the doctrine of "peace through strength." Less is known about Maynard Glitman who was named as negotiator for intermediate-range nuclear weapons (Euromissiles), but one may assume that he is also a hard-liner.

The ides of March could well have foretold matters of great significance to arms negotiation and to the great issues of peace and war. The president has an apparent mandate from the people, but he also faces substantial opposition to his policies. He must solve the budget problem without raising taxes and without cutting defense. He cannot resolve these impossible contradictions within a congressional context. Thus he must go to the people and appeal to them directly, in hopes of pressuring Congress to comply. But he will have to go to the people not only with broken promises, but possibly a renewal of the Soviet threat myth. Is this an omen that the new arms talks, like START, ZERO-ZERO, and BUILD-DOWN, will be deliberately designed so that the Soviets withdraw and once again appear as the clear "enemy"? It will be much more difficult the next time. He may well end up as lame duck or hurt hawk.

The top-secret Defense Guidance FY 1984–1988, SIOP-6, and NSDD-32 in effect spell out the proposed budget. The present budget proposals of Caspar Weinberger conform to the dictates of the secret agenda to a remarkable degree. Further, the secret agenda also determines the kinds of weapon systems being proposed and their purposes (see chapter 2). It would appear, therefore, that the Reagan administration is on target for its second term.

Even if the president receives congressional opposition from members of his own party, he is prepared to go to the people to defend the defense budget in the name of peace, arms reductions, and American security. The current debate in Congress would indicate that both houses are determined to cut the defense budget.

The battle of the budget war came with "Budget Monday," 4 February 1985, the opening shot. The new budget calls for federal spending of $973.7 billion in FY 1986, beginning 1 October 1985. The president has put his money where his mouth is, and his mouth is reading the text of the secret agenda. Nothing substantiates our claim that the top-secret guidance and planning documents discussed in chapter 2 represent the real policies of the Reagan administration more than the proposed defense budget. The proposal for FY 1986 increases the defense budget by over $30 billion to the staggering figure of $313.7 billion. Every weapon system on the open and closed books, including "Star Wars," is being proposed for procurement. Obviously, Reagan and Company intend to go to the people in this battle, since they cannot win in Congress. They will trot out the old arguments again and parade them before the American people: "Cutting any of the proposed weapon systems will send the wrong signal to the Soviets"; "You can only bargain with the Soviets from strength"; "The Soviets have cheated and will continue to do so"; "Cutting the budget now will subvert the March 12 arms talks"; "The Soviets are outspending us in their search for superiority"; etc., etc. Even as patent a lie as Weinberger's claim that the Soviets can shoot down cruise missiles is not above declaring. Meanwhile, the voodoo economics of Reagan continues to deter the inevitable judgment day of deficit budgeting, assuring that when the crash occurs it will be bigger than ever. Since hardly anyone can defer gratification, there is broad, general satisfaction with the current economy, and therefore with Reagan. But those of us who can defer gratification, political as well as economic, know that the contradictions will climax, possibly sooner than later.

Ronald Reagan is a sort of reverse Robin Hood. Given the present nuclear-arms overkill, Reagan's plan to reduce domestic spending in order to increase the military spending represents a total distortion of priorities. We can predict that when the inevitable economic downturn occurs and interest rates climb once again, the poor will continue to pay the price. Taxes will have to go up, despite all the promises of never. Already, promises of a deficit target of $100 billion in 1988 have collapsed. The war of the budget began on 4 February 1985. One way or another the American people will be the losers. The last phase of the war entered its critical stage in April 1985, but the mood of Congress has changed, and Reagan may be in trouble.

By the end of May, the U.S. appeared to be accomplishing its mission to abort the arms talks in Geneva. As reported in the *New York Times* of

Monday, 27 May 1985, p. 1, the USSR charged the U.S. with sabotaging the talks. In fact, Mikhail S. Gorbachev, the Soviet leader, had stated categorically on 23 April 1985, "Washington does not seek agreement with the Soviet Union" (*New York Times,* Monday, 27 May 1985, p. 6). *Pravda* was quoted as using the phrase "overt sabotage." Thus the Soviets are playing to the U.S. script.

In May, T. S. Eliot's "cruelest month," Ronald Reagan and Caspar Weinberger became members of a new species, "hurt hawk." Reagan's Teflon surface became seriously chipped as the Senate and House both revolted against the obscene defense budget. By 23 May 1985, the House had reduced the defense budget from an original high request of a 9 percent increase above inflation for 1986, to a net decrease of -3 to -4 percent, a reduction of 12.5 percent from the initial proposal. The freeze on spending that Reagan and Weinberger so desperately accepted became a "build-down" as the inflation increase was removed by the House (i.e., reduced the budget from $302.5 billion to $292.6 billion, the 1985 figure).

The one-year freeze proposed by the White House and the Republican leaders was still a deception. A carry-over of unspent billions would remain in the pipeline, creating a huge backlog of $280 billion. This is how a freeze is not a freeze: the spending of that backlog has already been authorized (Gordon Adams, 1985), but Weinberger, like the character in the story who is given a limited time to spend a huge amount of money in order to obtain a greater reward, could not spend it. Weinberger's arrogant defense of defense and his eroding credibility and Reagan's rapid image loss contributed to the budget revolt in which Republicans and Democrats joined forces to express their displeasure.

The build-up in strategic weapons drives the defense budget and the deficit and "locks in" the budget authority. Since spending these amounts authorized for projects tends to be delayed due to the long lead time necessary for research, development, and production, budget submissions with "cuts" in 1986 could be recaptured in later years as "budget authority" already authorized. In effect, the budget proposed in the "secret agenda" and specified in the "five-year defense plan" will be virtually achieved by FY 1988 (Defense Budget Project, Center on Budget and Priorities, Washington, D.C.). While the total defense budget has doubled since 1980, spending on strategic systems is up 305 percent! The worst offender will be the Strategic Defense Initiative (SDI) or "Star Wars." In the period 1981-1985, the Reagan administration received $2.1 billion in defense "budget authority," with "backlog" surpluses now at $280 billion. These surpluses, mainly due to lower inflation and fuel costs, are *"locked-in" to the Pentagon's account unlike any other departmental savings,* which revert to the general pool of federal funds. The politics of military spending takes a natural course of overselling leading to overspending. Excessive budgets invite excesses of "overselling the threat" to accomplish "overselling the remedy" (Lowe, 1967).

Columnist Carl T. Rowan expressed his outrage at Reagan's budget appeal as follows: "Who else would go on nation-wide television to promote a budget that would break his promises to old people, take food from young people, cripple public education, deny bright teen-agers the chance to fully develop their potential by going to a first-rate college, and further enrich the military-industrial complex . . . and try to sell it as the taxpayers' protection act?"—and even worse, to then defend his budget by stating that "what is at stake is nothing less than democracy itself" (*Washington Spectator* 2, no. 13, 1 July 1985, p. 1).

The series of setbacks for the Reagan administration seems to be attributable to multiple causes. The deficit issue has remained strong on the public agenda, possibly stronger than anticipated. The defense budgets of the past five years have been so large and so all-encompassing that even some of those who thought the U.S. was not strong enough have now become convinced of its clear military and technological superiority. The game of gaps has broken down; so has Caspar Weinberger's credibility, in importuning for bigger budgets with increasingly weaker arguments. The revelations of the orgy of overruns in defense contracting has caused public dismay. As well, the disclosure of huge rip-offs by defense contractors strips any veneer of corporate morality. The largest corporations in America have committed criminal fraud.

In a more subtle way, Reagan's mask of amiable invulnerability has slipped, revealing much ignorance, some weaknesses, and political ineptitude. As a net effect the White House defense budgets collapsed from their original 9 percent to 6 percent to 3 percent to 0 percent to -3.5 percent for 1986. These are the real, hoped-for, and emergent constraints and obstacles to the "secret agenda." After giving Reagan everything he requested for five years, Congress is rebelling in the sixth. The 1986 defense budget will represent a wounding loss for Reagan and the New Right.

MX: THE MISSILE OF UNCERTAIN GENDER

Congress applied special conditions to MX, and one required that it survive four legislative votes. Both the Senate and House had to vote on the $1.5 billon for twenty-one additional MX's (for FY 1985), and in addition each had to vote for the actual appropriation. In fact, both Armed Services Committees had to vote also. In return for its support of MX, Congress demanded that the president engage in serious arms negotiations.

In January 1985, Reagan maneuvered the Soviets back to the bargaining table by some sort of secret inducement. If one were to examine all the varied official and unofficial signals that were made or leaked, the Soviets had to have been offered something tangible. Then the Reagan luck took over when Chernenko died. Vice President Bush, who attended Chernenko's funeral, transmitted Reagan's letter of invitation that sought a meeting with the new Soviet Premier Mikhail Gorbachev. At the time of writing, a response on principle seems to have been made, but no date was set. It may be that Gorbachev is less paranoid than Reagan. This could mean serious trouble for present U.S. policy. We are left with several possibilities. Either the Soviets are naive or desperate or both, or they may be playing a more subtle game. We can see ample evidence that Reagan has done everything to torpedo any possible agreement, but both superpowers may actually desire to subvert negotiations in order to make the other side appear responsible. The Soviets may be playing for time, recognizing the ongoing battle of the budget and Reagan's lame-duck term after 1986. Gorbachev has announced that there will be no further SS-20's deployed until November, when the Netherlands has to decide on cruise deployment. This is a clever tactic, but the U.S. is playing a well-defined script, spelled out by the secret agenda described in chapter 2. Perhaps the Soviets recognize that "Star Wars" could suffocate the U.S. economy, and they may settle for the less costly and more feasible system of countermeasures. What is most likely is that each side will act out its mutually assured paranoia. The tragedy of any of these scenarios is that peace and security are the victims.

On the occasion of the "Shamrock Conference" on 17 March 1985 in Quebec City, Reagan explained that his summit-meeting invitation to Gorbachev, the new Soviet premier, was "sincere, eager and cordial." He then belied these adjectives by stating at a luncheon meeting, "Let us always remain idealistic but never blind to history . . . . We cannot look the other way when treaties are violated, human beings persecuted, religions banned and entire democracies crushed." He went on to say that the "Soviet record of compliance with past agreements has been poor" (Skelton, 1985). Keep in mind that one of the conditions Congress spelled out for the MX votes was that the U.S. actively pursue negotiations. How anybody could conceive that Ronald Reagan, whom an entire conference of U.S. historians had voted as the president most ignorant of history, could invoke historical arguments with accuracy is surprising. Evenmore astonishing is how anybody could believe that Reagan's invitation to Gorbachev and the current negotiations are genuine.

As the MX issue wound down to decision time, Reagan used every piece of ammunition in his political arsenal to win the Senate vote on funding the second twenty-one missiles with their $1.5 billion price tag. He used obvious erroneous but politically powerful arguments; for example, he tied support of the MX to the ability of the U.S. team to negotiate effectively in Geneva, and thus to ilustrate "strength, will and unity" to the Russians. This same president had argued that the MX was necessary to help close a U.S. "window of vulnerability"; when that myth was dispelled by his own Scowcroft Commission, the MX was mysteriously transformed into a necessary "bargaining chip." According to Gary Hart (D-Colo.) Paul Nitze had said, "We have no intention, if we build these MX's, to give them up" (*Washington Times,* Tuesday, 19 March 1985, p. B-1). The MX is either a "sitting duck" or a first-strike weapon. Is this the kind of signal to send to the Russians in the middle of negotiations? MX, alleged violations, and "Star Wars" are the three components of what could be interpreted as a conspiracy to scuttle the talks and blame it on the USSR.

While Reagan and others talked of "bargaining chips," the American Security Council spoke of dire need. "Essentially, the choice now before Congress is between replacing some of our aging ICBM's or unilateral disarmament by obsolescence" (John M. Fisher, *Washington Times,* Tuesday, 19 March 1985, p. B-1).

With the MX vote and the debate that surrounded it, March became a critical time for the U.S. The issue involved more than a mere division of hawks and doves, more than the procurement of funds for the military; it became a confrontation between conscience and politics. The spectacle of a house divided could hardly have been interpreted by the world as an expression of unity and will.

On Tuesday, 19 March 1985, the Senate voted fifty-five to forty-five to release $1.5 billion to produce the twenty-one additional MX missiles. Ten Democrats voted with forty-five Republicans for the MX, while eight courageous Republicans voted with thirty-seven Democrats against. Reagan had used undue pressure to secure his hollow victory. He had suggested that it was unpatriotic to vote against MX. He stated that the Senate vote would "send a message of American resolve to the world." He had argued that a "no" vote would undermine the U.S. negotiating team in Geneva. He had warned undecided Republicans that he would not support them in their bid for reelection. He had also said that a "no" vote would gravely weaken U.S. defenses. Senator Gary Hart (D-Colo.) put it best when he said "An awful lot of people were out there today holding their noses" (Fritz, 1985). Yet there was no real victory for Reagan.

Reagan had scheduled the MX vote to follow the start of the Geneva talks, which were themselves scheduled to influence the vote. Even Senate Majority Leader Robert Dole (R-Kan.) agreed that the Geneva talks had won Reagan "a vote or two." Both Senator Robert C. Byrd (D-W.Va.) and Senator Robert Packwood (R-Ore.) used the adjective "agonizing" to describe their decision to vote for MX. Senators Mathias (R-Pa.), Specter (R-Pa.), and Grassley (R-Iowa) had their arms twisted; only Grassley had the courage to sustain his negative vote. Senators Byrd (D-W. Va.), Fore

(D-Tenn.), and Nunn (D-Ga.) will not be voting for MX the next time around when forty-eight more MX's will be requested. Former senator John Tower (R-Tex.), now the negotiator for strategic weapons at Geneva, had described the MX as a "sitting duck," while Senator Tom Haskin (D-Iowa) called it the "glass-jaw missile" (Fritz, March 1985). Senator Dale Bumpers (D-Ark.) put the lie to the notion that the MX was an important bargaining chip by pointing out that the last Soviet offer on strategic weapons would have permitted the U.S. to deploy 680 large MIRVed ICBM's! All of this contributes to the emptiness of Reagan's so-called victory. Winning approval of a missile variously described as a "sitting duck" with a "glass-jaw" and a "bargaining chip" on its shoulder is, by definition, not a victory. And Senator Hart is so correct: the vote and the pressure to secure it have a bad odor. It will reinforce the strong Soviet conviction that Reagan will not bargain in good faith.

Senator Robert Packwood (R-Ore.), who normally would have voted against MX, made a strange remark that attributed his "agonizingly difficult" vote on MX to the persuasion of Max Kampelman, U.S. chief negotiator at Geneva. Packwood stated, "Today's vote is attributable to the humanity, decency and judgment of Max Kampelman" (Sector and Nauth, 1985). One need not doubt Kampelman's decency nor his humanity, limited, of course, by the jaundiced perspective of any member of CPD. However, ascribing "judgment" to a man who believes in "Star Wars" and is cynical about arms control is hardly appropriate.

Kampelman had negotiated the Madrid Agreement of the Helsinki Accords on human rights and had a reputation for being "progressive." However, one suspects that like his colleague, long-time Democrat Jeane Kirkpatrick, former United Nations representative now converted to the Republican Party, Kampelman is more anti-Soviet than pro-human rights. These so-called freedom lovers prefer Somoza to Ortega or Pinochet to Allende. This same Kampelman helped create the Committee on the Present Danger and said, "If there is a present danger—as we all agreed there was—there's no sense pussyfooting about it," as he swung CPD to an alarmist line in 1976 (Sanders, 1983, p. 153).

Both the Senate Armed Services Committee and the Senate Appropriations Committee had approved MX. The committee votes of both houses are recommendations only and do not have legislative force. Still, the House Armed Services Committee, under the "liberal" leadership of Representative Les Aspin (D-Wis.), voted overwhelmingly for MX, despite a Democratic majority. In the first hitch, the House Appropriations Committee, in a close vote of twenty-eight to twenty-six (some members were absent), voted against MX. The Senate's turn came again on Wednesday, 30 March 1985. This time, on appropriations on the $1.5 billion requested, the Senate voted for MX.

Max Kampelman revealed his true colors in Washington on Monday, 25 March 1985—his one-day lobbing blitz in favor of MX. Kampelman, a former Humphrey Democrat, has long lost his progressive views and has become part of Washington's lobbying game. Kampelman categorically stated that voting for MX would protect negotiations in Geneva. Like Reagan, he was having it both ways: an expensive "bargaining chip" was also needed to close a "window of vulnerability." Kampelman and Reagan and the Committee on the Present Danger now shared a single purpose. They directed all their pressure against the House, where the Democrats enjoy a large majority. Democrat Kampelman was there to get them to sell their vote to Reagan.

The House votes went the way of greatest political pressure, unable to withstand the combination of threats, promises, and outright bullying. The tactics of Donald Regan are more direct than his predecessor: you either vote for the president or you are put on a "hit list." Thus it was predictable that the House's first vote was 219 to 213 for MX, with some sixty Democrats persuaded to join the majority of Republicans. Nevertheless, twenty-four courageous Republicans voted "no."

Typical of one group of House Democrats persuaded to vote for MX was Representative Les Aspin (D-Wis.), chairman of the House Armed Services Committee and nominally a "liberal." While Aspin admitted MX was "a marginal system," he felt he had to support it as a "bargaining chip" at Geneva, since to vote against it would weaken the U.S. negotiating position (NBC, "Meet the Press," 17 March 1985). Aspin also reiterated that his support was contingent on continued good-faith negotiations by the Reagan team. He pointed out that since MX was an FY 1983 budget issue, the impending House vote, by agreement, could only be an unconditional "yes" or "no" on the twenty-one additional MX's. Aspin expressed belief that the next request for forty-eight additional MX's might not be supported. However, he also said that negotiations at Geneva could continue for a long time. The tragic flaw in Aspin's reasoning is that in protracted negotiations, Reagan will continue to make the same incremental demands for further MX's, using the same argument of strengthening the U.S. bargaining position. This is incremental destruction of arms control by protracted negotiation designed for nonagreement.

Reagan predictably called the House vote "a vote for peace, for a safer future and for success in Geneva" (Gerstenzang, 1985). This intimated that the 213 House members and forty-five senators who voted against MX were in favor of war, an unsafe future, and a failure of the negotiations. Representative Bill Alexander (D-Ark.) said, "The White House will give you anything you want. Some members felt they got a commitment that Republicans wouldn't be so hard on them, [that] they wouldn't spend so much money to defeat them." House Speaker Thomas P. (Tip) O'Neill, Jr. (D-Mass.) said,

"There is $9.9 billion out there the President has the right to spend. His people have the power to say where it is going to go. That's a little carrot they can throw out there" (Gerstenzang, 1985). Representative Frank Horton (R-N.Y.) said he received a call from Max Kampelman who told him rejecting or postponing the weapon would seriously damage the negotiations. Kampelman's influence plus the Soviets' clumsy shooting of Major Nicholson in East Germany (the Soviets are notorious for committing brutal acts at times favorable to Ronald Reagan) certainly captured marginal votes. On 28 March 1985, the House voted a second time, 217 to 210 in favor, with six abstentions.

Remarkably some congresspersons, such as MX opponent Representative Norman Dicks (D-Wash.), voted yes because they believe Reagan is negotiating in good faith. Kenneth L. Adelman directs the Arms Control and Disarmament Agency (ACDA) because he is clearly not in favor of negotiated arms control treaties. He reminded the U.S. that "the Soviet Union is a totalitarian country domestically and an expansionist country internationally . . . . We should understand what we have to contend with in arms control and around the world" (*Santa Cruz Sentinel,* Thursday, 28 March 1985, p. 1). We know what we have to contend with in arms control as far as Adelman, Kampelman, and the other planners of nonagreement are concerned.

The tactics of the Kampelman team cannot lose the real game being played, as defined by the secret agenda (see chapter 2). If negotiations are extended, more "bargaining chips" as well as entire new, advanced weapon systems will be requested, and these will be more difficult to oppose than MX. If negotiations break off, then the Soviets will be blamed and procurement will be unopposed. The worst that could happen for the Reagan team is that negotiations would be successful, but one can be assured that could only occur through major Soviet concessions to U.S. superiority.

In fact, the future of the MX is still uncertain. Reagan and Kampelman will surely not be able to use the same trump card from the same old deck in the next vote on MX. It already appears that the additional forty-eight first-strike weapons will not be produced. The Republican-dominated Senate Armed Services Committee under its chairman Barry Goldwater has approved a subcommittee recommendation to slash the request under the 1986 FY budget in the fall (*San Francisco Chronicle,* Wednesday, 3 April 1985). This same news story also reported that the House would be inclined to limit the total MX procurement to fifty. Moreover, more bad news for the Reagan defense budget came from Senator Barry Goldwater (D-Ariz.). He had revealed a three-option plan for the defense budget that reduced it to less than the 6 percent increase above inflation Reagan requested. In the meantime, the administration had come up with a Republican consensus budget that would reduce defense spending to a 3 percent increase. This was designed to be defeated, as it was almost certain to be unpalatable to Democrats.

MX is a straw missile, a bargaining chip, or even a chip of fools. The Scowcroft Commission admitted it was "political" and made no strategic sense (Paine, 1983a). It can only be used in a first-strike posture. In fact, the U.S. is moving away from large MIRVed ICBM's to concentrate on a maneuverable single warhead, Midgetman, and to build up the firepower and invulnerability of the other two legs of the triad. By the 1990s the U.S. plans to have a totally new look in its nuclear arsenal, with enormous numbers of cruise missiles, mainly sea launched, plus 2600 advanced-type missiles that can elude radar, all weapons of extreme accuracy. They are planning to build some 272 strategic Pershing II's. With a new SLBM fleet of Tridents, a new bomber fleet of B-1B's and "stealth" and 1000 Midgetman, virtually invulnerable, their present arsenal of warheads will have doubled. Even if the entire current arsenal is retired and replaced, the accuracy and relative invulnerability of the new strategic combination would represent an enormous increase in delivered lethality (SIPRI, 1984).

MX may well be a bargaining chip, not in the talks with the Soviets, but in the battle of the budget. While the Senate and House have voted the money for the second 21 missiles, Congress seems sure to balk at the 48 more in FY 1986. (The Pentagon would like 200.) The budget squeeze could ultimately determine U.S. nuclear policy. Or, giving up the MX may be a deliberate ploy to induce the Soviets to cut their ICBM force. The terrible aspect of this game of pretending to want arms control is the multiple deceptions endemic to it. They are not merely applied to the Soviets, but to Congress and the American people. Reagan is possibly a willing dupe, but more likely an ignorant instrument of these deceptions. There is no "window of vulnerabilty." Launch-on-attack prohibits a Soviet first-strike. The time to verify such an attack is sufficient. The present submarine leg of the U.S. triad is more than sufficient for deterrence. The entire masquerade is obscene.

In May the Reagan administration received a severe blow with respect to MX. The Senate, voting on the 1986 defense budget authorization bill, limited the total number of MX's to fifty rather than the one hundred requested. Of the forty of those weapons to be built in 1986, only twelve were authorized. Moreover, there is a clear warning that this new total of fifty-four (four are spares) could well cap MX production if the current basing mode in Minuteman silos is not altered. The "window of vulnerability" has now been disclosed for what it was, a wall of superiority. And Cap the Gap Weinberger has been revealed as an arrogant dealer of marked cards rather than an honest broker of defense.

THE ZERO-SUM EQUATION FOR ARMAGEDDON: NSDD-32 AND SIOP-6

The "five-year war plan" is projected to cost $1.6 trillion over FY 1984–1988. If 1983 is included, the actual National Defense Budget 1983–1988 is $2 trillion. Of this, 22 percent, about $450 billion, is designated for fifteen major nuclear weapons systems. The rate at which nuclear weapon spending is projected to increase is about 25 percent per year (actual increase 1983–84), higher than total military spending or any other sector of the budget. While the rhetoric of the Reagan administration has been forcibly altered, the plans and programs remain. They are to fight and win a nuclear war, limited or protracted. At present projections, by early 1990 the U.S. will have almost 17,000 new nuclear weapons (*Defense Monitor* 12, no. 7, 1983). In 1986, by DOD's own numbers, the Pentagon will be spending $1 billion per day—$32 million per hour, or $533 thousand per minute. This budget also conceals an entire list of other nuclear-related acquisitions, a broad range of military programs, research and development, , DOE's warheads and bombs, FEMA's preparation for survival, ASAT development, SDI, etc.

Among the major new strategic nuclear weapons are the following:

TABLE 4

MISSILES	DOE Designation	NUMBER	NOTES
Pershing II	W-85	380	First-strike potential
GLCM	W-84	560	
Bomb-1984	B-83 (bomb)	2500	1 mt. yield (for B-1 bomber)
SLCM	W-80-0	758	Strategic Reserve for protracted war
ALCM (2 versions)*	W-80-1	3500	C^3I targets
Trident I (C-4 SLBM)	W-76	1536	MIRV x 8
MX (ICBM)	W-87	1000	First-strike potential
Trident II (SLBM)	W-87	960	MIRV x 10, first-strike potential
	TOTAL	11,194	

OTHERS: Theater, tactical, antisubmarine, ABM, etc.   5,598

GRAND TOTAL   16,792

---

*The Advanced Cruise Missile is a highly classified project, but should be operational by 1987/88 within the Weapon Testing Agreement period between Canada and the U.S. (Source: CDI and Pacific Life Research Center);*Defense Monitor,* 12, no. 7, 1983 (Washington: Center for Defense Information).

Nuclear weapons firing procedures have safeguards in their multiple and redundant pre-launch and launch procedures. The principle of "two-man rule" governs every launcher—ICBM, bomber, or SLBM. It is physically impossible for only one person to "aim" the missile so that a turn of the "firing key" will cause a launch within the "missile launch control capsule" (a sealed space). Both operators must turn their keys simultaneously, after performing several sequential procedures.

The SLBM's are a special case and use a secret "four-man rule" procedure. Rumored "special procedures" in effect constitute a "launch on negative warning" system: if all C^3I are "knocked out" and there is a total failure in communications, contingency plans provide launch guidance (Calder, 1979). Also, any leg of the triad remaining after nuclear war begins has contingency plans for launch without presidential directive.

The entire nuclear war machine lacks the capability of missile recall or missile "self-destruct." This is extremely dangerous in that accidental war seems inevitable. Much more effort should be made to develop systems that can "abort" missiles in flight.

It is important to understand the Ellulian nature of military nuclear technology (Ellul, 1965). In effect, the ensemble of nuclear technical means, including hardware and software, determines the ends for which it is designed. The system tends to become technologically autonomous. The decisions which we make today in the field of science and technology determine the tactics, then the strategy, and finally the politics of tomorrow. This technological autonomy subtly tends to usurp the role of human decision (will) in transferring C^3I systems to electronic decision-making devices. The increased premium placed on time reinforces the move towards autonomous and omniscient technologies. The nuclear arsenals tend to focus more and more on hair-trigger launch responses and, ultimately, to "launch-on-warning" systems, two dueling nuclear robots, armed with hair-trigger arsenals and programmed to respond by nonhuman command. "Moving the arms race into space will merely make the esoteric cause of war become progressively more plausible" (Calder, 1979, p. 118). The role of accident in inducing a nuclear war tends to become a certainty, given the inherent impossibility of creating infallible and perfectible systems.

The pervasive influence of the military nuclear arsenal has still another significant element. Its technology directly violates all the principles of sound design. In reality ours is a "baroque arsenal" (Kaldor, 1982) with endemic cost overruns. Due to the intrinsic mission orientation of weapon acquisitions, the cost-plus accounting determines the inevitable waste and unreliability. Immense military budgets drain the economies of the superpowers and preclude funds necessary for advancing social welfare, closing the social gaps between rich and poor, and protecting the environment.

Originally, the U.S. had planned to build 4348 ALCM's. As the FY 1984 budget was being prepared, the number was cut back to 1739, so the U.S. decided to proceed directly and immediately to the Advanced Cruise Missile (ACM). There is some indication that the future totals will be approximately the same, with some 2600 ACM's being projected. The estimation is that this weapon will be operational in 1987/88. The "umbrella agreement" for weapon testing between Canada and the U.S. expires in 1988, and one can be certain that the ACM will be tested in Canada. The ACM is more clearly a potential first-strike rather than a deterring or "first-use" weapon such as the ALCM (*Defense Monitor* 12, no. 4, 1983, p. 11). Nevertheless, "the role of the ALCM's in penetrating Soviet bomber defenses and striking C^3I targets is highly acknowledged. Command, control, communications and intelligence and ability to kill mobile targets will be critical during the protracted phase of conflict" (USAF Study, *Air Force 2000: Air Power Entering the 21st Century,* June 1982).

FROM MAD TO NUTS

As we have observed, strategic nuclear strategies have evolved over time into contending systems. The two dominant strategies have polarized into (*a*) deterrence and (*b*) warfighting doctrine. At various times in different administrations, one or the other or a combination of both have been dominant. In fact, deterrent strategies have even had a consistent rider—"if deterrence fails"—that converts them to warfighting strategies. In the 1960s deterrence was ironically described by the acronym MAD, or "mutually assured destruction." Until the present, this was thought to be the basis for the prevention of nuclear war, hopefully, forever.

However, the advent of the Reagan administration has consolidated and confirmed a nuclear warfighting doctrine made operational by guidance and decision documents, such as NSDD-32 and a new, single integrated operational plan (SIOP-6). This warwinning *and* surviving plan also involves programs for massive civil defense.

SIOP's are nuclear "hit" lists or target allocations. From historical analysis, it would seem that the number of targets and the degree of redundancy—overkill—are a function of technology rather than policy; in other words, the number of targets has increased with the number of deliverable warheads. Some authors have developed a new acronym to describe these new nuclear warfighting plans that contrasts to the literal interpretation of MAD—NUTS, Nuclear Utilization Target Selection (Keeny, Jr., and Panofsky, 1981/82). This author prefers to use the concept of Nuclear Utilization Tactics and Strategies for the acronym NUTS. The preference is due to the fact that beneath and beyond rhetoric, the hard core of present U.S. policy is a warfighting and warwinning belief system entrenched in real operational plans. While common sense would insist we are obliged to live in a MAD world, the rebuttal of Reagan is NUTS.

Two elements make this situation uniquely dangerous. First, we are not dealing with mere rhetoric. NUTS is a real policy translated into real plans and programs. The people behind it have a long, consistent, and highly documented belief in these plans and programs. NUTS has been legitimated by their belief and armed by their conviction. These people, earlier identified, have captured U.S. defense and foreign policy. One must not be deceived by the occasional public demurrals, or the present policy of Reagan's speechwriters who vainly attempt to alter his image of cold warrior to peacemaker—"peace through strength," of course.

The second element is even more disturbing. The probability of a nuclear war through "accident, malice, or madness" increases with the growth of the arms race and of international tensions; in fact, it tends towards 100 percent. Existential terrorism, such as the October 1983 bombing of Marine headquarters in Beirut, simply awaits a nuclear device.

SIOP-6

One of the top-secret planning documents mentioned in our chapter on the secret agenda is the Single Integrated Operational Plan #6 (SIOP-6). This document comprises a nuclear hit list of all enemy targets, and defines the number and types of weapons to be used on each target. But it is more: it is a plan to fight and win a nuclear war, even if protracted. General Bernard Davis, chief of U.S. forces in Europe, provided a clear statement of Reagan nuclear policy. To the question "What is our policy called, in place of mutually assured destruction?" General Davis replied, "Counterforce, or 'warfighting,' the two are synonymous" (Arkin, 1983a). Caspar Weinberger told the Senate Foreign Relations Committee in November 1981 that the new twist was to "prevail" (Arkin, 1983a, p. 9).

This is the heart of the new Single Integrated Operational Plan (SIOP-6). It explicitly states that the policy of "prevailing" has replaced the policy of deterrence by using the words "protracted," "enduring," and "flexible" to describe its elements. "The intent is to implement a nuclear war policy that ensures limitation and control" (Arkin, 1983a, p. 9). The key to such a policy is a survivable C^3I system that will persist "throughout crisis situations up to and including *protracted nuclear war* [Italics mine]" (Arkin, 1983a, p. 10). The estimated cost of this system is now $31.5 billion.

The supersecret SIOP-6 has its own security classification—Extremely Sensitive Information or ESI (Pringle and Arkin, 1983). It might seem strange that a Canadian author who is certainly not privy to any national secrets except through reported "whistle-blowing" or "leaks" should have the temerity to deal with the current nuclear warfighting plan. In many ways I am indebted to the work of Peter Pringle and William Arkin, who, like other superb investigative reporters, have managed to put together pieces of a puzzle. Each piece, whether information or experience, is declassified, unclassified, or merely the result of some naive exponent or proponent. Moreover, "keys" to the puzzle are often leaked. By being good detectives and using inference, it is possible to gain access to secret information because it is supported by nonsecret information that, in fact, indirectly measures what one seeks. In some cases the medium is the message. For example, the Pentagon publishes its own unclassified signals handbook. SIOP-6 is a hit list that activates all the weapons in the U.S. arsenal—tactical, intermediate, and strategic. In addition there are target lists for the Warsaw Pact countries, China, Cuba, and Vietnam. Thus every conceivable "enemy" target inside and outside the Soviet Union is on this nuclear hit list, amounting to more than 40,000 in number. In fact targets have grown exponentially in time, even faster than the weapons available to strike them. The Soviet Union only has 900 cities larger than 25,000. There are only 3,500 key military targets and 300 major industrial targets.

The designated warfighting operational plan of SIOP calls for the "escalatory exchanges of thermonuclear weapons . . . culminating in a major strategic nuclear exchange" (Pringle and Arkin, 1983). SIOP-6 as a strategy document consists of a variety of "selected attack options" and suboptions to carry out "multiple exchange campaigns," including nuclear strikes such as Launch-on-Warning (LOW) or emergency responses, and Launch-under-Attack (LUA), although these contingencies have been officially denied. LOW or LUA could be the result of a false alert. SIOP-6 (and the rest of the secret-agenda documents) explicitly denies the distinction between conventional and nuclear weapons; it eliminates "any arbitrary division between categories of nuclear weapons systems" (Arkin, 1983a, p. 12). The planned use of Pershing II's for decapitation strikes against the Soviet leadership is also made explicit, thus effectively destroying the political arguments of the "dual-track" NATO decision; moreover, it has been learned that Pershing II's are to be given "reload" capacity (Arkin, 1983b)—all making it clear that Pershing II's have been assigned a strategic role, and supporting Soviet charges. SIOP-6 places great emphasis on an enduring C^3I system in order to "redirect our surviving assets." The Integrated Operational Nuclear Detection System provides part of that system. Aboard some twenty satellites to "detect, locate and report" nuclear detonations worldwide "within 100 meters," it allows real-time "transattack and postattack damage assessment capability." The C^3I system must "provide the capability to execute ad hoc plans" (Arkin, 1983a, p. 10). The myths of warfighting, warwinning, and war surviving have been operationalized on "terms favorable . . . to the United States." The plan calls for "survivable and enduring command and control. . . through all levels of conflict, including general nuclear war" (Pringle and Arkin, 1983, p. 237), or put even more bluntly, "The victor [in a nuclear war] . . . devising systems which will be resistant to enemy attack and which will degrade gracefully . . . after the initial clash" (Principal Undersecretary of Defense for Research and Engineering James Wade, April 1982). The same James Wade said, "We must not fear war" (Pringle and Arkin, 1983, p. 244).

Both implicit and explicit parts of the secret agenda are designed to either bypass existing treaties or violate them deliberately, using the excuse, of course, that the Soviets had committed the violations already. This is true of the Strategic Arms Limitations Treaty (SALT II) and the Anti-Ballistic Missile Treaty (ABM). Cruise missile deployment bypassed SALT since cruises and antisatellite weapons (ASAT's) were excluded. "Star Wars"/SDI typifies the second approach, treaty violation. But, in a general search for superiority, modernization is the name of the game.

MODERNIZATION IS THE NAME OF THE GAME

One current euphemism for the nuclear arms race is modernization. Modernization in the U.S. is leading us in definite technological directions: into space-based exotic weapon defenses ("Star Wars"); into small, accurate mobile ICBM's like Midgetman (reverse "missile envy"); into hardened C^3I systems; into increasingly hardened ICBM silos; into the "global positioning system"; and generally into superior first-strike capability. Such first-strike capability is particularly dangerous since it sacrifices crisis stability for war-fighting ability. The full development of the next generation of SLBM's such as Trident II converts this retaliatory force into an attack system. ICBM duels are essentially mythic. There is sufficient advance warning time, about thirty minutes, for each side to launch them rather than lose them. The mutual destruction of empty silos with an incredible amount of "collateral damage," mainly radiation, mocks the dueling principle and is pure military nonsense. The superaccurate SLBM's, with their much shorter flight times, constitute a genuine threat to ICBM's, including Midgetman. The development of the technique known as depressed-trajectory SLBM's reduces flight times to a degree where the bomber leg of the triad becomes extremely vulnerable. A simultaneous launch of accurate SLBM's in normal trajectory, but with flight times under twenty minutes, threatens the ICBM leg.

The Soviet response to U.S. modernization will ultimately be just as we have indicated above, i.e., increasingly accurate SLBM's with the depressed-trajectory option. Moreover, the Soviets might not wait indefinitely for a U.S. first-strike capability to mature, enriched by the "global positioning system" (GPS) together with defensive and offensive space systems. They might decide that a preemptive strike of their own is their only hope. In fact, it is more likely to be a catalytic strike in a crisis situation prompted either by a false alert or delegation of authority in the Soviet political-military hierarchy. KAL-007 may have been an intelligence bonanza for the U.S., but it must also have revealed to the Soviets their decision-making inefficiency.

A freeze would prevent modernization, the rapid updating of destabilizing weapon systems. Since the security of both the U.S. and the USSR has been and will continue to be inversely proportional to the qualitative and quantitative expansion of the arms race, then the freeze truly serves stability. In fact, the superpower that first "freezes" and once again concentrates on simple, old-fashioned deterrence could have the best weapon of all. Moreover since basic deterrence is a form of military conservation and efficiency, it has very large economical and political benefits. As a spin-off benefit of the freeze, chemical deterioration of the components of thermonuclear warheads and neutron bombs renders such weapons inoperable after several years, thus the freeze becomes reduction. With a freeze the relatively superiority of the U.S. will remain intact. Genuine defense systems like silo hardening can continue to be improved without the danger of modernization. Without a freeze, Soviet capability will undoubtedly increase. Their relatively backward nuclear military technology will unquestionably develop very accurate SLBM's equipped with the depressed-trajectory option. If those who believe in a policy of nuclear warfighting, winning, and surviving do not intend to launch a first-strike, then their policy is not served by a continual arms race. Higher levels of arms coupled to higher levels of tension could instigate a preemptive strike.

The entire history of the arms race illustrates the evolution of insecurity; for example, the current vogue of hardening ICBM silos merely invites larger and larger warheads. Nevertheless, policymakers would extend the arms race to space, activate "stealth" and the advanced cruise, and generally enhance accuracy as security measures. Continuing the modernization trend in effect assures the ultimate catastrophe. Thus, the Reagan administration's policy becomes self-defeating.

The basic questions remain. How long can the military technological revolution remain separated from the political and economic forces leading to war? How long can such technology remain in advance of its own accidental use?

With the reelection of Reagan and the return of his hawkish advisers, there seems little question that the pursuit of superiority, modernization, will continue unabated on the earth, under the seas, and in space. The margin for error in computerized systems such as "Star Wars" will decrease, thus raising the probability of accidental war.

Our contention is that the arms race has decreased, rather than increased, global security and the security of the two superpowers. While the USSR played "catch-up" in the decade that preceded Reagan's election in 1980, the U.S. has maintained its superiority throughout the decade, despite Reagan's continual claim of Soviet superiority. The submarine leg of the U.S. triad probably will remain invulnerable to a first-strike. This is particularly true for the U.S., but more hypothetical for the Soviets. This situation will remain for many decades, providing a deadly retaliatory capacity.

Some incredible distortions of reason become necessary to justify the arms race. "Star Wars" is perfectible "against all incoming missiles" because technology is omniscient; yet verification, even when based on the same technology, is imperfectible. As one can see, credibility is very imperfect. The MX is required because of the policy of deterrence, but the policy of deterrence has been officially abandoned. The U.S. claims it wants deep cuts in nuclear arsenals as it builds up its arsenal. Reagan and others claim that the U.S. cannot deal with an "evil empire," but they seek to resume arms talks. Reagan supporters have attacked SALT from the beginning. Reagan campaigned against SALT, and Congress did not ratify it. The U.S. insists that both sides should abide by SALT, while the U.S. military pursues offensive and defensive weapons systems that either bypass SALT II or are omitted from it. The U.S. decries Soviet military intervention but invades Grenada and intervenes in Central America. The Reagan administration pronounces the preservation of freedom and democracy to be its special domain while it deals with, subsidizes, and supports dictatorships all over the world. The U.S. leads the arms race and pleads catch-up. The risks of such deceptions and distortions, particularly in regard to arms control, are much more dangerous.

THE SEARCH FOR A SALT-FREE WORLD

Ronald Reagan provides evidence of his ignorance on the nuclear arms race in his continual assertion that the nuclear arsenal of the USSR had surpassed that of the U.S., particularly in the seventies. True, the U.S. actually decreased the total number of its launchers while the USSR increased theirs by a significant count:

	1970		1980	
	TOTAL LAUNCHERS	TOTAL WARHEADS	TOTAL LAUNCHERS	TOTAL WARHEADS
U.S.	2222	4000	1980	10,312
USSR	1890	1890	2600	6846

Source: SIPRI, 1981, p. 21.

However, while the U.S. decreased its total number of launchers by several hundred in that decade, it increased the total number of warheads by 250 percent. The introduction of MIRVs, multiple warheads capable of being independently targeted, provided each launcher with the far-greater accuracy needed for increased hard-target kill. Obviously, this is not a simple deterrence policy but a warfighting strategy that preceded the Reagan administration. Counterforce targeting had its roots even earlier in the plans of the military of both the U.S. and the USSR.

In the early days of nuclear strategic debate, the world was relatively simple. Nuclear war could be avoided if the superpower representing morality had second-strike capacity: if the other side launched a first-strike, the attacked side would retaliate. Since both first-strike and retaliation (second-strike) imposed an intolerable cost, the superpowers maintained a stand-off position of MAD (mutually assured destruction). Theoretically at least, in the absence of other factors, this should have made nuclear war unthinkable and, as Jonathan Schell proposed, "undoable." Even so, MAD as a deterrent presents manifold problems: it assumes shared rationality; it ignores escalation dynamics; it discounts the possibility of nuclear wars initiated by "madness, miscalculation or malice." Most tragically, the deterrent of MAD vanishes when those espousing contending doctrines rationally believe nuclear wars can be fought and won, and zealously conceive of a winnable nuclear war as a holy mission.

Even in the beginning of the nuclear weapons age, the military of both sides had plans to use nuclear weapons. For many military strategists, nuclear warfare represented an extension of conventional means of warfare, not a radical departure from it. Theoretical doctrine, which included thinking about the unthinkable and being prepared to do the undoable, became a respectable activity for ultrarational theorists. Nuclear warfighting and deterrence became companion pieces in strategic studies. A clear political statement of this twinned policy emerged in President Carter's Presidential Directive #59 (PD-59) of July 1980. The explicit notion that a nuclear war need not be catastrophic became embedded in policy. Denial that nuclear war involved the "fate of the earth" became the rationale of this new rationality. With the Single Integrated Operational Plan #6 (SIOP-6), nuclear warfighting became firmly entrenched as the official but secret doctrine (Pringle and Arkin, 1983). To bolster its claims for the survivability of nuclear war, this doctrine specifically disavowed distinctions between tactical and strategic nuclear weapons and distinctions between nuclear and conventional weapons.

There are semantic riders to this strategy of winnability. Its claims are generally qualified by the phrase "should deterrence fail." But the euphemistic notions of controlled warfare, escalation dominance, flexible response, target selectivity, and surgical or sanitary strikes all qualified the rejection of MAD and the acceptance of NUTS. To deter or not to deter does not seem to be the question. Presidential Directive #59 (PD-59), signed by Carter on 25 July 1980, merely confirmed what Defense Secretary James Schlesinger had admitted in 1974. Selectivity and comprehensibility of targeting, Schlesinger's "counterforce" or Harold Brown's "countervailing" strikes, affirm warfighting doctrines, not the old deterrent threats of eradicating your opponent's cities. Today's phrase is "prevailing with pride."

Further, counterforce contains a logical contradiction. If your doctrinal aim is to knock out the enemy's retaliatory force—their unlaunched weapons systems—you must strike first; therefore, you have willy-nilly introduced a first-strike, first-use doctrine. This is the dangerous hair-trigger situation we face today. Each side must be prepared to strike first. This is a failure of deterrence, and "should deterrence fail" we have nuclear war.

The U.S. has not publicly admitted having a "first-strike doctrine." It has rejected the notion of "no first-use" in the name of credibility and flexible response. It has also maintained that "first-use" is for tactical weapons only. SIOP-6 throws the lie to this by specifically defining all weapons as strategic.

The USSR understandably considers Euromissiles, particularly the Pershing II's, as strategic. The 1800 km. version stationed in West Germany or Alaska can strike critical targets such as Leningrad and Kiev, as well as those in East Germany, Poland, etc. The 4000 km. version could strike Moscow.

Pershing II is a key decapitation weapon that could kill "time-urgent" targets such as C^3I, airfields, and ports. Its special radar guidance system (RADAG), developed by the Goodyear Corporation, makes Pershing II the most accurate ballistic missile in the U.S. arsenal to date. Its circular error of probability hit is 40 yards, compared to 400 yards for the Soviet SS-20. Like the SS-20, Pershing II has a two-stage rocket, but Pershing rockets have mobile launchers and can travel at over 8000 km. per hour. Unlike the SS-20 with its three 150-kiloton warheads, Pershing II has only the single W-85 selectable yield warhead manufactured by the Martin-Marietta Corporation. This warhead is believed to be capable of a yield of 50 kt., but can provide yields as low as 10 kt. The Pershing II is a first-strike and a counterforce weapon, being capable of silo kills and hard-target kills.

Originally, the U.S. intended to place 108 Pershing II's in West Germany as a replacement for the Pershing I's. The Pentagon now reveals that 311 Pershing II's are on order. We do not know why the Pentagon increased the number of ordered units: 203 more units than necessary for replacement seems a very large excess.

The entire Euromissile debate exemplifies a possibly deliberate "failure to communicate" on the part of the U.S. Ever since the SALT I treaty of 1970, the U.S. has searched for a "SALT-free" weapon, and cruise development seemed to answer this need. The INF talks counted Soviet SS-4's, SS-5's, and

SS-20's as the intermediate tactical weapons that they are; however, the 400 MIRVed warheads from Poseidon C-3 missiles assigned to NATO are defined as Eurostrategic weapons. Under the SALT II treaty, they are "SALT-counted" and not included in INF reckoning. Therefore, the U.S./NATO Poseidon, the British/NATO Polaris SLBM's, and French missiles are omitted when establishing the European military balance, even though the European NATO forces are controlled by the Supreme Allied Commander, Europe (SACEUR). Clearly the U.S., which never ratified SALT II but lives by its word for now, is really interested in a SALT-free world, where they have definitive superiority. It is predictable that Weinberger will use the new arms talks as an excuse to demand every new weapon system in the "secret agenda." As we have already witnessed, this was the argument used to support the MX.

In these last two chapters we have attempted to provide the readers with a technical threshold of information sufficient to deepen their understanding of the sociopolitical and strategic issues of nuclear warfare. The Korean airline disaster has both technical and political implications. In a volatile world best characterized as a gigantic tinderbox, any incident, any tragedy could serve as the match that would ignite the globe. Moreover, the Korean airline incident casts a more sinister shadow on the secret agenda that the Soviets accommodated through stupidity and paranoia.

THE JAMES BOND 747

When the Soviets admitted, after an unforgivable six-day delay, that a Su-15 Soviet fighter interceptor had shot down South Korean Air Lines Flight #007 (KAL-007) on 1 September 1983, the world responded with genuine moral outrage. Puzzling residual questions lend all the qualities of a spy thriller to the whole affair. The very number of the flight connotes the crude but typical irony of U.S. military intelligence (the notorious Fiscal Year 1984–1988 Defense Guidance document was dubbed the "Five-Year Plan"). The U.S. strangely delayed reporting the incident for many hours. Because super-conservative Georgia Representative Lawrence P. McDonald was aboard flight #007, the John Birch Society charged that McDonald was the principal target of the shooting. The counteraccounts by the superpowers contained contradictions and misinformation.

The behavior of KAL-007 remains inexplicable. Experts have insisted that the Inertial Navigational System's (INS) three redundant computers are effectively fail-safe. In addition, two other systems were in operation— weather radar and the eyes of the pilot, Captain Chun Byong In. The plane was equipped with the normal high-frequency radio and a hidden hijack-alert signal. Two KAL sky marshals were on board. The plane flew a particular route so thick with a mix of civilian and military spy aircraft that it lends itself to screening activities by U.S. intelligence. A U.S. RC-135 spy plane was present in the flight area of KAL-007, and the U.S. originally castigated the Soviet fighter pilot for not having radio communications with the civil aircraft; yet on 6 October 1983, the U.S. admitted its military aircraft were also unable to contact KAL-007. The U.S. claimed that the clearness of the night made visual recognition of the plane a certainty. Authoritative Japanese sources state such recognition would have been impossible, given the night's relatively poor visibility and the Soviet interceptor's distance from the civil aircraft.

Such questions of recognition and warning are important. Did pilot 805 of the Soviet fighter plane recognize KAL-007 as a commercial plane? Did he give warnings or signals in advance of shooting it down? The radio transcripts turned over to the U.S. by Japanese ground control give no indication of either. The Soviet Su-15 came within 1.2 miles (2000 meters) of KAL-007, but at one time flight #007 veered as much as 1200 km. off course. Why didn't Japanese controllers or U.S. intelligence services warn KAL-007 that it was way off course?

The CIA was responsible for the official Korean foreign ministry report that the plane "had not exploded or crashed, but was known to have been forced to land" on Sakhalin Island (Quinn et al., 1983, p. 21). George Shultz finally broke the news to Washington: surely U.S. spy satellites were directed to observe the site. The USSR made a bureaucratic blunder in its six-day delay in admission, but it seems that the importance of U.S. postevent intelligence justified the U.S. delay and obfuscation, such as its puzzling on-again, off-again statements regarding recovery of KAL-007's "black box."

Some experts have claimed that the probability of failure of all redundant navigational systems is about 1 in 40 million. Information obtained through radio contact with flight #007 seems strangely contradictory. Japanese controllers received a short message from pilot Chun concerning a change in flight altitude, but much of the communications appeared garbled. A fellow KAL pilot on flight #008 that crossed paths with flight #007 stated he was unable to make radio contact (Quinn et al., 1983). Captain Chun's behavior seemed as erratic as the flight itself.

The supersophisticated electronic intelligence center in Fort George Meade in Maryland, operated by the National Security Agency, knew a great deal about the entire event. They have groundposts throughout Japan and China and monitored all the messages. It has been reliably reported that a "decoded English translation of the Soviet pilot's conversation with his ground control was on the duty officer's desk at NSA within ten minutes of the pilot speaking" (Quinn et al., 1983). Why then did the U.S. not intervene and why did NSA delay going public?

According to many analysts, interpretation of the tapes played in the emotive context of the special UN Security Council session supported the opinions that (*a*) the Soviet pilot confused KAL-007 with the RC-135 spy plane seen earlier; and (*b*) the Soviet fighter planes did try to catch the KAL-007 captain's attention (Westlake, 1983). The fifty-minute transcript never indicated any knowledge of the type of aircraft. Military expert pilots do not believe the aircraft could have been recognized (Westlake, 1983).

The argument about invalid preprogramming of the redundant inertial navigation system (INS) is not deemed credible when the experience of Captain Chun Byong is considered (Westlake, 1983). There were three independent Litton Industries LTN-72R INS units on the plane. A postulated possible source of the error involves the incorrect positioning of a five-position switch that sets the automatic pilot into various operational modes. The plane undoubtedly had a radio problem; attempts to correct this could have sufficiently distracted the flight crew so that they did not turn the five-way switch to the INS mode. There is a low probability that this irresponsible lapse could have occurred. The 747 is equipped with a weather radar picture that should have alerted them to any wind or magnetic variation effects that could take them off course. This should have led them to make certain the five-way switch was on the INS mode. The radio beacon directional station and radar station at the U.S. Air Force base on Shemya Island should have given the KAL-007 its correct bearing and distance information when it passed. Several days after the shoot-down, the U.S. reluctantly admitted that the KAL-007 had passed the RC-135 returning to Shemya Island after flight #007 had passed KAL-008 and a United Airlines aircraft heading to Anchorage. If the RC-135 crew did not recognize KAL-007 as a civil aircraft, then it is easy to understand how the Soviets also did not.

Once the aircraft had penetrated Soviet airspace and flown over a top-secret Soviet military area, the Soviets had reason to shoot it down, given their perspective: regardless of its identification, the plane's flight pattern revealed a serious weakness in Soviet radar coverage and in their air defense system.

As the KAL flight crew realized the serious error in their flight path, their increased concern with correcting their course could have meant that the Soviet fighter plane's flashing lights and cannon-fire warnings went unnoticed.

One must not excuse Soviet behavior or culpability in the tragedy of KAL-007. But the deplorable and dangerous response of those self-righteous zealots of the vitriolic right who screamed for revenge and alleged the cruel, deliberate, and premeditated murder of 269 persons hindered serious arms negotiations and reduction. It intensified global tensions and led to a new and dangerous increment in the arms race. One suspects this reaction to have been the calculated design of those in the Reagan administration who still believe in winning an inevitable nuclear war.

To return to the actual incident, the Japanese high command has contradicted official U.S. assertions that clear weather enabled certain identification of KAL-007. General Goro Takeda, retired chairman of the Japanese Joint Staff, stated categorically that the Soviet fighters faced the difficult task of identifying the aircraft *in the dark with very little moonlight* (italics mine), and "you would have to get within 200 to 300 meters of the aircraft to identify the characteristic bulge of the 747" (*Gazette,* Thursday, 15 September 1983, Montreal). The closest Soviet fighters got to KAL-007 was about 2000 meters. It is also now agreed that the Soviet pilot fired warning shots that were neither seen or heeded by KAL-007. General Takeda, and many other reputable sources, stated that the "methods that [the Soviets] employed in their interception were not good." Henry Kissinger attributed the downing of the jetliner to confusion and misunderstanding among the Soviet air defenses (Gazette News Services, Friday, 15 September 1983, Montreal). The USSR itself officially acknowledged it had made an error in identification (Greve, 1983), even though U.S. intelligence sources now admit that there was no identification of KAL-007 as a civilian plane (Greve, 1983). The Soviet radar operators bungled the entire intercept operation; moreover, their interceptor fighter planes were also extremely inefficient in locating KAL-007. In a *New York Times* interview, General Charles A. Gabriel gloatingly stated that the Soviet handling of the incident "gives us a little more confidence" that our bombers can penetrate Soviet defenses (Greve, 1983). Su-15's have a very short combat radius of only about 700 km. In addition, Soviet pilots and their radar ground control do not work well together in tracking intruders. The KAL incident is reported to have provided U.S. intelligence with a "bonanza" of valuable information on Soviet radar gaps, communications problems, and chain of command (Greve, 1983). Even the U.S., with its superior record, makes errors in locating and tracking unexpected intruders. One high-level USSR source has admitted that some of the confusion came from Moscow, and not the local commander. Although three radar stations on the Kamchatka peninsula were out of order (*Gazette,* Tuesday, 10 October 1983, Montreal), top regional air defense commanders have since been fired.

The area where the KAL-007 crashed is a nerve center for any Asian outbreak of hostilities. Many Soviet submarines, including the most advanced Delta-class ballistic missile–type, are based in Petropavlosk, where they require assured sanctuary. In addition, many Soviet missile tests take place in the area, and the Soviets harbor their Pacific fleet there. Thus, U.S. intelligence has intense interest in the area.

The U.S. uses RC-135's, nicknamed "ferrets" (Kahn, 1983), to "tickle" Soviet radar installations. The ferrets force the Soviets to turn on their radar systems to "identify" the spy planes. The spy planes in turn carry electronic intelligence equipment (ELINT) that monitors and records the radar signals. From these transmissions, the U.S. garners specific information on all the physical properties of the radar site. In the event of a future bombing attack, this information would allow attacking bombers to elude, "spoof," or jam Soviet radar. The USSR also uses such aircraft in their intelligence program.

Dozens of incidents involving alleged spy planes have been publicly acknowledged. During the 1950s the USSR shot down three U.S. planes, killing all on board. The Soviet shooting down and capture of U.S. pilot Gary Powers and his fully equipped U-2 spy plane drew widespread attention during the Eisenhower administration. South Korea, to underscore the sacredness of some targets, forbids any flight over the presidential Blue House in Seoul—it fired at a civil U.S. 747 when the plane strayed over the official residence. On 15 April 1969, the North Koreans shot down a U.S. Navy EC-121, and the entire crew of thirty perished (Kahn, 1983). In April 1978, the USSR forced down a KAL 707 jet after it had flown over 1600 kilometers of Soviet airspace. In the last ten months seventy-seven Soviet "ferrets," converted bombers, have violated U.S. territory, but none of the intercepted has been shot down (Kahn, 1983).

After all the rhetorical accusations, counteraccusations, and explanations given by the various parties involved, a fairly clear account of the KAL-007 incident has emerged. Both superpowers now admit that the USSR defense command on Kamchatka peninsula confused the civilian Boeing 747 with the U.S. RC-135 that it had identified earlier. The "mystery" plane had an erratic flight path. First, it headed toward the extremely sensitive Soviet installation at Petropavlosk; then, it veered back over international waters. When it flew back into Soviet airspace, it appeared to be on a flight path to the supersensitive Soviet base at Sakhalin. Article 36 of the Soviet border law states that force may be used against intruders "in cases when violations cannot be *achieved* by other means." The general of Soviet Air Defense Forces (PVO) in Moscow probably ordered the commander at Kamchatka to shoot down KAL-007. The Su-15 Soviet fighter pilot, an interceptor from the Sakhalin Island base, obeyed the command and reprehensibly shot down the aircraft: it fell just before it left Soviet airspace, on its way southward through Japanese air-defense installations.

It is unlikely that KAL-007 carried any special "spy equipment," since any service ground crews would notice cameras and radar detection devices and thus breach the security of a "spy mission." However, KAL-007 could have been used as a "ferret" to draw information for the RC-135 or a U.S. intelligence-gathering satellite. The Soviets may have been about to conduct a missile test in this strategically significant area. Soviet SS-20 missiles sited here can strike western U.S. targets if the Soviets should retaliate against Pershing II's in West Germany. The U.S. is also greatly interested in the Delta

Class III Soviet submarine. Equipped with SLBM's and MIRV liquid fuels, the SS-N-18 can hit most U.S. targets from Soviet home waters. With a range of from 8000 to 9000 kilometers, these vessels can escape U.S. antisubmarine warfare systems. In addition, the Soviets have developed a new class of submarine, the Typhoon, that is larger than any of those in the U.S. nuclear field and is designed to carry eighty large warheads. Twelve of these new submarines, equipped with very advanced solid-fueled missiles, will operate from a secret base in the Kuril Islands. The Soviets produced the Typhoons in direct response to the Euromissiles, and have offered them as a bargaining chip in the IRNTF talks. With all this strategic military information available, U.S. intelligence activity in the area would be great.

The shooting down of flight KAL-007 undoubtedly was an accident. Former Canadian prime minister Pierre Trudeau became the first Western leader to categorically state this in a debate in the House of Commons on Tuesday, 4 October 1983. Henry Kissinger and James Schlesinger agree with Japan's high command in calling it an accident.

The National Pilots' Association also accepted this interpretation and dropped its boycott of Soviet airlines. Despite the availability of all this information, then Progressive Conservative leader, now Prime Minister Brian Mulroney, the poor person's clone of Ronald Reagan, still accused the Canadian government of being "soft" in their response to the KAL-007 incident, and demanded further condemnations. Gilbert Brunet, assistant editor-in-chief of the influential Montreal newspaper *Le Devoir,* wrote that Trudeau had given Mulroney "a lesson in political courage and international experience . . . well-informed, the government leader had no difficulty tripping up his neophyte adversary on these questions which will still be troubling Canadians when Mr. Mulroney's hopes to have taken Mr. Trudeau's place. . . . the harmonizing of action of the Western countries behind the Reagans and the Thatchers is not desirable in its very essence" (Stewart, 1983). In following the lead of these cold warriors, Mulroney hopes to cast doubts on Trudeau's anticommunism. The former Canadian prime minister enhanced his image as statesman by recognizing the danger inherent in the vicious anti-Soviet propaganda of the Reagans and the Thatchers. Unfortunately, Mr. Trudeau damaged his credibility somewhat by stating that Reagan had made "a pretty admirable response to the Soviet attack" (Stewart, 1983). With few exceptions, the U.S. media also tended to interpret Reagan's response as moderate, even as Reagan milked the event for its propaganda value. His reaction was patently contrived to drum up support for his military budget and policy.

Television may be self-limiting in regards to news and news analysis: this would be one explanation—albeit a poor one—for its "hands-off" attitude toward the present president. Although the press attempts to uphold its traditional toughness, fairness, and obligation to seek and print the truth, newspapers and journals also show biases. In general, the majority of the media have treated this president gently, despite Reagan's notorious gaffes, blunders, and intemperate anti-Sovietism. Reagan clearly used the KAL-007 incident to buttress his nuclear military policy. The *New York Times* recognizes the Reagan tactic and notes that "using the Korean airliner incident to intensify anti-Soviet rhetoric . . . has proved bankrupt" (Lewis, 1983).

George Kennan, former U.S. ambassador to and expert on the Soviet Union, had warned earlier that the statements of Mr. Reagan and some of his administrators created a "dangerous march to war." To support their views, "they would point to an image of that regime . . . an image largely of their creation. It is an image of unmitigated darkness. . . . As applied to the Soviet leadership of the year 1983 it is grotesquely overdrawn, a caricature" (*Globe and Mail*, Wednesday, 18 May, 1983, Toronto). In the May *New Yorker*, George Kennan further castigated the Reagan administration: "This view is . . . inexcusably childish, unworthy of people charged with conducting the affairs of a great power in an endangered world." Kennan maintained that despite its conspiratorial nature, the Soviet regime has a deep interest in avoiding war.

Even James Schlesinger, a hawk who has served Democratic and Republican administrations alike and an arms expert, has criticized Reagan's response to the KAL-007 event. "I doubt that the Soviets knew at the time it was a civilian aircraft." He went on to state that Reagan's overreaction was both counterproductive and dangerous.

While the U.S. and other countries make political claims that ascribe responsibility for KAL-007 to the USSR, the real issue of culpability will be decided in the court as suits against Korean Air Lines come to trial. One class-action suit taken in San Francisco seeks damages of more than $99 billion from KAL for its "willful misconduct" (Dentzer et al., 1983). The president of KAL has admitted, "We are criminals because we are responsible."

It would appear then that all three parties to this tragic event—KAL, the USSR, and the U.S.—bear some responsibility for the incident. No matter what security principles apply, the USSR remains guilty of at least "manslaughter" in its shooting down of an unarmed civilian aircraft. On the other hand, deliberate intrusions into the sovereign airspace of a country are criminal acts. Even the U.S. would shoot down a Soviet plane flying over U.S. territory on a path to the White House, Colorado Springs, or Fort Meade. An internationally acceptable system of elaborate communications between all planes—civil and military—accompanied by agreed-upon reasonable and humane norms of conduct in case of intrusions would minimize loss of life.

It is helpful to view this entire incident in the context of the political situation in South Korea. From the time of the Park Chung-Lee administration in 1972 through the present regime, South Korea has continually violated human rights. Emergency Regulation #9 of 13 May 1975 legitimated the use of arbitrary arrest and imprisonment. In early February 1981 General Chun Doo Hwan of South Korea became the first foreign president to visit the White House after Ronald Reagan's inauguration. In toasting Hwan, Reagan noted, "If I have one message to give to the Korean people today, it is that we share your commitment to freedom"—a toast almost identical to the one Vice President Bush made to General Marcos on a visit to the Philippines in 1981. The Chun Hwan and Marcos regimes are among the worst in the world in terms of their records on human rights violations. Amnesty International (and the U.S. State Department annual reports on human rights) documents hundreds of imperial arrests, tortures, official murders, and vicious restraints. Thousands of victims of these brutal regimes have paid the ultimate price. Instead of reacting with indignation, Reagan and Bush praise the Hwan and Marcos governments. Selectivity of response in opposing repression is an unacceptable policy for a democratic country. Favoring regressive military juntas because they are anticommunist is equally unacceptable. Despite all of the above, the shooting-down of KAL-007 was reprehensible.

KAL-OO7: IN RETROSPECT

A British scholar has developed a much more elaborate theory of U.S. espionage (Johnson, 1984). While it does not contain radically new information, this analysis indicates that U.S. espionage utilized KAL-007. "It is only possible to say that it fits all the known facts while the U.S. version fits almost none of them. That we have been lied to seems indisputable" (Johnson, 1984, p. 6).

The espionage conspiracy theory sets the scene in the highly secret Soviet naval complex in the Sea of Okhotsk and the port of Petropavlosk on the Kamchatka peninsula. This particularly sensitive port harbors about half the Soviet fleet of nuclear weapon submarines and also serves as a missile site. Because of its many strategic and political advantages, the North Pacific theater is gradually replacing Europe as a major nuclear war region. The U.S. has maintained intense surveillance of this region for over two years. In April 1983, the media almost completely ignored the "largest exercise conducted by the [U.S.] Pacific Fleet since World War II" that took place in international waters off the coastline of Kamchatka (Johnson, 1984, p. 24.). One can judge the impact of this exercise on the Soviets by imagining a huge Soviet flotilla conducting invasion maneuvers 250 miles from San Diego.

Satellite reconnaissance has not replaced inspection by "slow-moving" aircraft equipped with high-resolution cameras and supplemented by electronic surveillance equipment. Could a Korean civilian aircraft be deliberately equipped with such devices and deliberately involved in a provocation that would violate Soviet airspace over a highly sensitive military area? The Korean CIA shields the activities of the U.S. CIA, and there is a high level of integration between the two. KAL-007's pilot had formerly served as an officer in the Korean air force. Since South Korea is a "pliant client state," the pilot could have been controlled by the CIA. The problem of loading surveillance equipment aboard without detection could be easily overcome if the conspiracy theory is true. A CIA officer, formerly stationed in Korea, said that "senior KCIA officials used KAL for personal international drug smuggling operations" (Johnson, 1984, p. 25). Later disclosures acknowledged that "carriers owned by [friendly] governments are fitted with devices for intelligence collection" (Johnson, 1984, p. 26). As an editor of *Defence Science* admitted, KAL airlines "regularly overfly Russian airspace to gather military intelligence" (Johnson, 1984, p. 20). In addition, a Lufthansa pilot, quoted in a West German newspaper, said, "Pilots who have flown international routes for two decades often notice U.S. military planes using civilian air routes and behaving like civilian planes—the mixing of military and civilian planes was provoked by the military" (Johnson, 1984, p. 24). Several days after KAL-007's downing, President Reagan inadvertently explained the RC-135's role in the incident, but his explanation has been discounted. In Reagan's version, the RC-135 was on the scene in an attempt to head off the Korean plane. Two veterans of the RC-135 characterized Reagan's statement as "unbelievable" and a "major effort . . . to bewilder the public . . . . it was grotesque to imagine that an RC-135 could not have headed off the KAL-007, if it wanted to" (Johnson, 1984, p. 24).

The crux of the conspiracy theory, however, assumes that the U.S. deliberately placed the USSR in a Catch-22 dilemma. As a spy plane, the KAL-007 could provide the U.S. with significant intelligence. If the Soviets shot it down, their action would confirm Soviet barbarism ("an act of barbarism born of a society that wantonly disregards individual rights and the value of a human life"—President Reagan) and provide a real propaganda plum that would enable the U.S. to counter opposition to Euromissiles. As a result, Reagan's MX proposals would receive congressional approval.

The above scenario, if correct, indicates the extreme clumsiness of Soviet diplomacy. The Soviets behaved as predicted, entering and embracing the snare the U.S. had laid for them. Despite this, if the scenario is correct, the U.S. remains responsible for the death of the innocent victims of KAL-007.

An article in the *Nation* of 18 and 25 August 1984 proves that the U.S. government deliberately distorted aspects of the affair; and worse, that it purposefully followed a policy of nonintervention that resulted in the deaths of the 269 persons aboard KAL-007 (Pearson, 1984). Pearson presents the following facts: (1) Various U.S. military and intelligence agencies knew well in advance that KAL-007 flew off course; (2) These same groups knew that the territorial incursion of KAL-007 was extremely sensitive—a major missile test was being prepared there; (3) These same agencies could have warned KAL-007 to correct its course in time to prevent the tragedy; (4) The U.S. probably had jammed Soviet radar systems on Kamchatka and possibly Sakhalin Island; (5) The White House, the Pentagon, and the secretary of defense also knew the above facts well in advance of the actual shoot-down. The fundamental question of why the U.S. allowed the incident to occur remains unanswered. President Reagan's statement concerning the inability of the RC-135 to communicate with KAL-007 and head it off has been refuted. In this case, there is little question that the RC-135 was on a flight path that would have enabled it to do both.

The KAL-007 incident continues to raise new evidence of indiscretion, ineptitude, and even conspiracy. Yutana Hata, a member of the Japanese Diet (parliament), released reliable new reports from Japanese ground controllers that the South Korean aircraft had transmitted false altitude readings. This revelation proved the major discrepancies in the government's accounts. "This will be the start of the real truth-finding" (*San Francisco Chronicle,* Friday, 17 May 1985, p. 32).

The above analysis has added merit in that KAL-007 "turned out" to be an intelligence bonanza for the U.S. It could not have turned out that way if the U.S. had warned the pilot. We are thus left with another conspiracy hypothesis: that the pilot was not a party to the incursion, but that the U.S. profited from an incident they could have prevented.

5

Myths, Gaps, and Gaffes

The United States has much to offer the Third World War.
Ronald Reagan, "Trivial Pursuit"

(On nuclear war) *It would be a terrible mess, but it wouldn't be un-manageable.*
Louis Guiffrida, FEMA

Nuclear war is a destructive thing but in large part a physics problem.
Charles Kupperman, ACDA, 1981

If there are enough shovels to go around everybody's going to make it. . . . It's the dirt that does it.
T. K. Thompson, Reagan's undersecretary for defense

In the previous sections we have provided the background of a set of persistent myths that have, unfortunately, tended to guide, if not to deliberately influence, U.S. nuclear arms policy. The political process gives a logical sequence to the creation and solidification of these myths. A numbers game involves the use of captive experts who provide the magic numbers that all too often become tragic numbers. Experts justify and sanctify establishment decisions that were made beforehand: decisions become the beginning of a process, not its outcome.

"Gapology" is the act of securing a military development and defense budget by alleging a fictitious lag in the nuclear arms race. Myths have become established through so-called "gaps" (or "windows") that purportedly represent the difference in defensive or offensive arms development between the U.S. and the USSR. Some comparisons are more odious than others. An excellent source of these fictitious lags is *Stop Nuclear War* (Barash and Lipton, 1982). It identifies the subject as "The World According to Gap" and the process as "gapping," even though Reagan's off-the-record responses might well be titled "The World According to Gaffe." Ronald Reagan's legendary propensity for the gaffe spawned a book entitled *Ronald Reagan's Reign of Error* (Green and MacColl, 1983). The media, with considerable discipline, has avoided repeating his gaffes; in fact they rarely find him categorically wrong. Representative Udall (D-Ariz.) has said Reagan "has an immunity, as if he's not judged in the same courtroom" (Green and MacColl, 1983, p. 17). Is this the triumph of charm over truth? Has the superficial American boy–hero image of the president won over genuine knowledge and leadership of the statesman?

Reagan is recognized as the worst-informed political leader in the West, but somehow in the U.S. political arena, his ignorance, coupled with a powerful ideological thrust, is the source of his power and appeal. Ronald Reagan has publicly stated as truth every nuclear myth described in this book, from his repeated assertions of Soviet nuclear superiority to his wildly exaggerated accounts of Soviet civil defense ("in one summer alone, they [the Soviet Union] took over 20 million young people out of the cities to the country to give them training in just living off the countryside" [Green and MacColl, 1983, p. 38]). The CIA denied many of Reagan's assertions, such as his statement that the USSR has "hardened" its industry against a nuclear attack.

Reagan's ignorance of the nuclear weapons systems of both superpowers is even more dangerous. For example, he thought that SLBM's could be recalled after launch (Green and MacColl, 1983, p. 46). In a more sinister fashion, he has stated, "There is no question about foreign agents that were sent to help instigate and help create and keep such a movement [the nuclear freeze movement] going" (Green and MacColl, 1983, p. 47). A House Select Committee investigated this charge and officially declared it untrue. Reagan was unaware that the large majority of Soviet warheads were in the ICBM leg of the triad; in fact, he is so unaware he almost seems a charming puppet, less concerned with credibility than with posture, rhetoric, and even deliberate provocation. Since he appears to be manipulated by a sinister puppeteer, his advisers are obviously responsible. Yet Anthony Lewis of the *New York Times,* adopting an unusually harsh but totally understandable appropriate tone, blasted Reagan's Lebanon policy: "To the complicated problem, Reagan has brought ignorance, ineptitude, self-delusion and purposeless militarism. . . . there can be no reasonable American policy while the United States has a rigid, ignorant, irresponsible president" (reprinted in the *Gazette,* Saturday, 11 February 1984, p. B-3, Montreal). While Lewis's characterization of Reagan seems correct, there is a contradiction. Does Reagan make these decisions himself or does he merely rubber-stamp advice that seems in broad accord with his world view? The influential West German *Der Spiegel* responded to the invasion of Grenada with a view similar to Lewis's, "Ronald Reagan . . . probably considers the world is a movie . . . . Grenada is no accident. . . . it has the old, tested B-movie motives . . . on the right, the cavalry on the hilltop; left in the bush, the enemies of civilization, the Reds. So simple, so old, is Ronald Reagan's California cosomology" (*Washington Spectator,* 15 December 1983). The same issue of the *Washington Spectator* carried an editorial from the French daily *Le Monde* that referred to Grenada as representing Reagan's "power in the service of peace . . . today it would rather seem to be power in the service of the ridiculous." The British journal *The Economist* featured a cover picture showing Reagan as James Bond, captioned "Is Reagan Licensed to Kill?" (*Washington Spectator,* 15 December 1983). All of these commentators correctly attribute responsibility to Reagan, but do so apart from the real political context in which he operates.

Despite all the sharp foreign and domestic criticism, Reagan rose in the polls. Reagan has appealed to the deep psyche of a core of the U.S. public who think and feel as he does. A strange amalgam of conservatism, pseudo-romanticism, fundamentalism, and arrogance works to support the Reagan mystique. By election analysis, some 27 percent of the electorate endorsed this ideological agglomeration and supported Reagan. Of course, Reagan's timing was miraculous: American humiliation over Iran and American guilt over Vietnam required expunging. American Firstism, global assertiveness, and simplistic faith in God, country, and strength needed a revival. No one was going to kick the U.S. around again. The economic and political policies of the U.S. were to be forged together into a dangerous oversimplification, a return to an impossible dream: a nineteenth-century vision, armed with the weapons of the twenty-first century and inspired by the powerful mission of destroying Soviet communism.

A powerful group of ultraconservative defense and strategic analysts have captured U.S. foreign and military policy. They share only the heart of their world view with Reagan. They have filled the body of their world view with sophisticated and often sinister games. In their scenarios Grenada is a pawn. Arms control and reduction talks are pawns. Central America is a pawn. Lebanon is yet another. They are after the king; the rest is contrivance. They provide Reagan with mere details. They are cynical. They do not protect Reagan from the impact of his gaffes and contradictory, false statements, because they do not believe it diminishes his strength. They think politics is a trivial pursuit for the masses who can be manipulated, and they play on that part of the U.S. psyche, capitalizing on the cowboy hero, the good and bad absolutes, the shoot-out, and the ride into the sunset with the golden girl of the West. The "peddlers of crises" really run the show. When one places the ideological spectrum on a circle, the extreme right and the extreme left come together at a single point, and one can recognize their style and the form and content of their approach in the official "defense" policy documents. They are Drs. Strangelove who have learned to love the bomb. They believe in winning, but they have found willing allies in the fundamentalist believers in apocalypse. In Caspar Weinberger and Ronald Reagan they have found the perfect vehicle to speed their chosen path.

Real semantic gaps exist between alleged arms race claims and the reality of that race. The factual gap between guarded statements made in public and candid responses given in confidence indicates another way of playing politics. Gaffes, on the other hand, are a product of ignorance rather than intention, and gaffes seem to be the special product of the Reagan administration, with the president being the leading gaffe-maker.

"Gapology" becomes more pernicious than ignorance when it forms the mythical base for real policy. The following list represents the long, if not comprehensive, history of these fictitous gaps (Bottome, 1971; Lens, 1977).

1. The Thermonuclear Gap	1949–1951	
2. The Bomber Gap	1953–1957	
3. The Missile Gap	1959–1962	
4. The ABM Gap	1963–1968	
5. The Civil Defense Gap	(renewed in the 1960s, 1970s, and 1980s)	
6. The ICBM Gap		
7. The Missile Gap		
8. The Expenditures Gap		
9. The Deterrence Gap	(Although numbers five to	
10. The Warwinning Doctrine Gap	eighteen did not originate in	
11. The Counterforce Gap	the Reagan administration,	
12. The Throw-weight Gap	this regime has invoked, re-	
13. The International Political Success Gap	newed, and intensified them.)	
14. The NATO Conventional Forces Gap		
15. The "Crisis Relocation" Gap		
16. The Anti-Satellite Weapon Gap (ASAT)		
17. The Cruise Missile Gap		
18. The Space-Based Defenses Gap		

Each of these alleged gaps served as a motivation or pretext for developing new weapons and systems or for modernizing existing weapons and systems. In virtually every case, the U.S. has preceded and exceeded the USSR in technological sophistication and broad effectiveness. In some cases the USSR prompted the U.S. to invoke a "gap" by "showing off" new Soviet developments that the U.S. had considered unfeasible or beyond Soviet capability. In a few other cases the USSR bluffed the U.S. into pronouncing a gap. However, in general, the rationale for weapons development and military budgets has been an alleged Soviet threat rarely substantiated by reality. No administration prior to Reagan's has committed itself to superiority in every area of nuclear weapons, offensive or defensive. No previous administration has sought a budget—now estimated to be well over $1 trillion for the next four years—of this size for such a broad shopping list of developments. The 1985 budget is the largest projected expenditure on the military in U.S. history. It is highly unlikely that the USSR, with half the GNP of the U.S., will be able to match this outlay even with great economic sacrifice. This, of course, is a fundamental aspect of the plan.

The sum of the Reagan gaps has led to maximization of new weapon development accompanied by a nuclear warfighting capacity, will, and doctrine. These gaps, while fictitious, have now become enshrined myths, and these myths have become the basis of policy. "Linkage" and "domino" theories have led to a new focus on Central America, where a new Vietnamese-type "exercise" may await.

From an analysis of Soviet and U.S. military and political writings, both sides seem to adhere to a nuclear military strategy of warfighting, a strategy of how to fight and win a nuclear war (Kaplan, 1982). Both assume that war is independent of technology and thus both blur the distinctions between conventional and nuclear war. But when one turns to political statements made by the leaders of the two superpowers in the last few years, there does seem to be a difference. Soviet leaders are on record as offering unconditional "no first-use" statements, and admitting that there can be no winners in a nuclear war (Kaplan, 1982), even though some Sovietologists dismiss these statements as mere propaganda. On the other hand, many U.S. political leaders, from Melvin Laird to Caspar Weinberger, have expounded a warfighting, warwinning doctrine by official document or statement. "If deterrence fails, we must have the capability both to fight and win a war. . . . we must have the ability to win, not merely to punish. . . . to keep the peace today and tomorrow depends . . . [on making] it credible to the enemy that we will take the initiative and strike" (Laird, 1962). The Reagan administration has intensified this warfighting and warwinning doctrine by making it a cornerstone of official defense policy, as NSDD-32 and SIOP-6 clearly illustrate. Despite occasional public disclaimers, a new convergence between the philosophical, political, and religious views of the majority of the Reagan cabinet and their leading advisers tends to make them the most dangerous factor in leading the world to a nuclear holocaust. They have created a permanent global missile crisis and initiated a new nuclear arms race that will dwarf the arms status of 1980.

A paper in the *Bulletin* in 1983 reveals some of the more basic myths that appear in a *Reader's Digest* article by Edward Teller. The *Bulletin* author exposes the irrationality and mythic quality of Teller's paranoia (von Hippel, 1983).

The major myths concerning the nuclear arms race cluster around the general myth that a nuclear war is both winnable and survivable. The following list attempts to identify these myths more comprehensively.

1. The notion of fighting and winning a nuclear war, the "win syndrome," has a long and vulnerable history. Its myths include the professed policies of (*a*) winning a "limited" nuclear war or limiting a nuclear war once it has begun; (*b*) winning a "protracted" nuclear war by limiting damage, i.e., by suffering less damage than the other side; (*c*) attaining meaningful but mythic "superiority" to fight and win a nuclear war or what Reagan has termed the "margin of safety."

2. As a derivative myth of seeking "superiority," it is consistently alleged that the USSR's strategic "superiority" in numbers, throw-weight, and accuracy results in the U.S.'s "window of vulnerability" that precludes deterrence. The president's blue-ribbon panel on nuclear strategic forces, the Scowcroft Commission, negated this myth.

3. Soviet civil defense is highly effective and vastly superior to U.S. efforts.

4. The effects of a limited or protracted nuclear war could be easily mitigated through civil defense or "crisis relocation"—a nuclear war is survivable.

5. The biological, social, and physical impact of a nuclear war will not disrupt U.S. society, and its industries would quickly recover—nuclear war is neither qualitatively nor quantitatively different from conventional war.

6. Defensive nuclear systems such as "Star Wars" weapons could protect us from attack—nuclear systems are perfectible and infallible.

7. The USSR has consistently exceeded the U.S. in military spending, particularly nuclear expenditures, and their outlays have increased in the past few years.

8. Because the USSR is untrustworthy, negotiations or treaties are unreliable; only strength, "superiority," provides a "margin of safety." Arms development, not reduction, presents the path to peace: only real intimidation can convince the Soviets to negotiate.

9. The Nuclear Freeze Initiative favors the Soviets, while START, Reagan's pet, is superior.

10. The U.S. nuclear warfighting doctrine, strategy, and weapon systems are more humane than those of the USSR.

11. The nuclear arms race is static: real superiority can be attained and preserved, and the USSR can only be contained by threats and power.

12. Nuclear war can be conventionalized. (This is a form of "biopolitics"—the art of converting what is biologically unacceptable to what is politically desirable.)

The Nuclear Freeze Initiative (NFI) seems to be the most hopeful and acceptable proposal for arms control and reduction; yet for reasons that cast doubt on the integrity of the media, it has interpreted the initiative as a unilateral action that provides the Soviets with a distinct advantage. In part, the media derives its perspective from the myth that the USSR is at present ahead of the U.S. in the arms race. Both the *Bulletin* of Atomic Scientists and the Union of Concerned Scientists published excellent articles explaining NFI and debunking Reagan's START proposal (Paine, 1982, 1983; Jackson, 1982; Halperin, 1983).

A *Toronto Globe and Mail* article presents new evidence that debunks another myth: the alleged superiority of Soviet ICBM's. Information from "top-secret" U.S. test data on Soviet ICBM's states: "Their accuracy isn't even within the ballpark of being able to launch a first-strike against our Minuteman missile silos, not even with their large, powerful warheads"; and "All tests on SS-18 and SS-19 missiles, the most advanced Soviet ICBM's, have been gathered by U.S. satellites which tracked the missiles. . . . intelligence monitoring of their radio missile guidance systems showed the missiles wobbled" (*Globe and Mail,* Tuesday, 1 March 1983, p. 9, Toronto). In the same article, Professor Kosta Tsipis of MIT, an acknowledged expert in the field, noted that from his findings, "The Pentagon has stated Soviet missile accuracy to be six times greater than it actually is." Moreover, this test data derived from Siberia would overstate missile accuracy because Arctic conditions, such as gravitational fields, snow, ice, wind, etc., "bias" missiles fired over the North Pole. Soviet missiles also use an extremely corrosive fuel that contributes to electrical failure. Soviet primitiveness does have its virtues. Very large, inaccurate warheads can make craters larger than their CEP's, thus exposing naked silos with useless "hardened" lids. Thus MX has its myths, since all "basing" modes are self-debasing and vulnerable to the "pulsed" firing that avoids the fratricide of incoming missiles. The political decision to proceed with 100 MX's in existing silos again rests on the politics of the "big stick." U.S. missiles are also apt to be far less accurate than planned until the new NAVSTAR Global Positioning Systems and terminal homing devices become operational. Despite the fact that operational failures are endemic to both sides, the U.S. continues to escalate its threats and proceed with its immense technological development of nuclear weapons. Reagan policy continues to serve the myth that the USSR will crawl to the peace negotiating table in terror, and so agree to permanent U.S. superiority.

The techniques of credibility assessment can neatly explode many of the myths. "Proof of the pudding" or "putting your money where your mouth is" arguments expose the lies behind the myths. For example, if civil defense were a viable option, providing the population with "100 million shovels" would be by far the cheapest means of attaining it. If ALCM's were not so significant, they would not have been ordered off the "bargaining-chip" list in SALT talks. Would Western Europe expand trade with the USSR and develop a joint project to deliver Soviet gas to West Germany if it believed the threat of nuclear attack?

Consistent propaganda from official and unofficial sources supports the myth that the USSR violates strategic arms control treaties. Because verification of nuclear tests is important, the U.S. has focused on alleged Soviet violations of the Threshold Test Ban Treaty, and their tests of two new ICBM's—one missile more than those existing prior to 1 May 1979, and so a violation of SALT II. Senator James McLure, an ultraconservative Republican, is the main advocate of publicly attacking the USSR for violation of these treaties. Independent experts writing in *Science* put this propaganda to rest once again (Smith, 1983). They agree that there is no conclusive evidence of Soviet cheating. Such propaganda justifies the recommendation of the President's Commission on Strategic Weapons: that the U.S. should develop and test the Midgetman in violation of SALT II. The U.S. supports SALT II but refuses to ratify or uphold it.

Retired high-ranking figures of the Pentagon present views on nuclear warfare that qualitatively differ from the rhetorical opinions of their active counterparts. Rear-Admirals Eugene Carroll, Jr., Gene La Rocque, and John Marshall Lee, Generals David C. Jones and Richard Ellis, and Brigadier General B. K. Gorwitz all stand on record as critical of the current policies of the Reagan administration. Even retired Admiral Stansfield Turner, former head of the CIA, raps the MX decision and the justification of support by the Scowcroft Commission. The commission admitted that the decision to proceed with the MX was political, not military, and nevertheless recommended it. For Turner, it was good money thrown at bad politics.

Former NATO commanders and top-ranking officers from many NATO countries also criticized U.S. policies. In some cases, these critics have become activists in the organization Generals for Peace and Disarmament. Admiral Robert Falls, Canadian past-chairman of NATO's military committee, has even recommended a unilateral reduction by the West (*Gazette,* Tuesday, 28 June 1983, p. B-2, Montreal). Since political independence implies credibility, Admiral Falls's trustworthy observations reinforce the views of so many retired high-ranking military officers.

A cluster of myths surrounds the concept of survivability. These myths deny or underestimate the short- and long-term effects of radiation damage on humans, animals, and the biosphere, and assert the effectiveness of civil defense, now euphemistically termed "crisis relocation," in reducing casualties and injuries. Many organizations and agencies have dealt thoroughly with these myths and offered highly documented evidence to explode them (OTA, 1979; Physicians for Social Responsibility, 639 Massachusetts Avenue, Cambridge, Mass. 02139; a special report of the United Nations, "Nuclear Weapons," 1980; Adams and Cullen, 1981; the Union of Concerned Scientists, Cambridge, Mass., and numerous articles in the *New England Journal of Medicine* and the *Bulletin* of the Atomic Scientists). In particular, their excellent scenarios depicting the effects of a single, large thermonuclear explosion on various cities in the United States and Canada provide an ample refutation of the myth of survivability. Other studies dealing with the delayed, global effects of a nuclear war present a picture of "unimaginable holocaust" (NAS, 1975; OTA, 1979; *Scientific American* 241, no. 1, July 1979 [on "nuclear winter"]; TTAPS, *Science,* 1983). A worldwide nuclear war would murder civilization by "killing even time and memory." While studies of the after-effects and survivors of Hiroshima and Nagasaki provide some insight into these problems, these cities were struck by small atomic weapons and thus represent minimum effect.

At their current levels, existing medical, communication, and transportation services could not deal with the number of people suffering the various aftereffects of a nuclear war. The incredible, inevitable devasation of a nuclear explosion would destroy such systems and render the idea of crisis relocation quite ridiculous. U.S. cities, including San Francisco, have shown a heartening resistance to designing and testing such a relocation plan. These cities quite correctly point out that not only are these plans hopeless, but worse, they also suggest a preparation for nuclear war. The resistance of various hospitals to suggestions that they cooperate in such crisis preparations is also a testimony to their good sense.

Many independent experts have thoroughly discredited and debunked the twelve myths. Despite their lack of credibility these myths have still become the official policy of the Reagan administration. A policy formed in thrall to myth is dangerous; even more subtly dangerous is the policy developed by true believers, unencumbered by doubt or reason and buttressed by ignorance, simplistic analysis, and narrow religious dogma.

The report of the "blue-ribbon" panel designated to review the U.S. strategic position (the Scowcroft Commission) clearly denied Reagan's "window of vulnerability" without damaging Reagan's credibility. Perhaps his credibility is so low that it cannot be reduced. But too many people still believe the official lies about the relative strengths of the U.S. and USSR. The media, particularly television, seems strangely reluctant to attack Ronald Reagan for his grotesque gaffes and goofs; yet it misunderstands, misinterprets, and misrepresents the Nuclear Freeze Initiative. Despite whatever pressures are brought to bear on them, one suspects that the media must know better.

SURVIVABILITY: THE MYTH THAT WILL NOT DIE

One of the more pernicious myths discussed posits that a society can survive a nuclear war by means of civil defense. Survivability is a necessary twin concept of winnability: winning has no meaning other than victory, and victory must involve the survival of your society (or civilization) and the defeat of the enemy. Yet the concept of survival itself has levels of meaning. Merely surviving in a world bereft of culture, time, and amenities, and laden with the hazards of a poisoned environment seems intolerable existence, inconsistent with winning. The survivors who continue to witness the unbelievable pain and torment of the dying cannot judge winning by the comparative statistics of destruction, by the enemy's greater losses and suffering. The enemy, after all, is largely innocent. They are we. The calculators of nuclear war have coined their language to deceive us: damage limitation and rapid recovery of society and industrialization can be achieved by "crisis relocation," by moving out of target areas, utilizing primitive shelters, and eventually returning to a livable and recoverable society. This is the world of T. K. Jones and the Federal Emergency Measures Agency (FEMA).

Political leaders and their expert advisers, armed with conventional wisdom and true belief in infallible techniques and the virtues of their system, do not recognize the problems created by their false calculations. They plan to win nuclear wars and survive attack. To quote Louis Guiffrida, head of FEMA, "It would be a terrible mess but it wouldn't be unmanageable" (Scheer, 1983, p. 1).

Civil defense in the U.S. began with the Gaither panel that recommended a massive shelter program to President Eisenhower in 1957. After much debate and several reviews, including one by the National Security Council, the program was judged as not cost-effective—it would not save enough lives to justify the cost. In recent times, the Federal Emergency Management Agency (FEMA), formed in 1979 and currently headed by L. Guiffrida, has resuscitated the feasibility of crisis relocation planning or CRP by shifting the civil defense emphasis from shelters to evacuation. FEMA has solicited the support of various social and physical scientists and a number of think-tanks to justify its claims for CRP in the test case, a 6559-megaton attack on the U.S. The Reagan administration supports CRP because, having committed itself to a nuclear warfighting and winning strategy, it cannot admit that such a war would cost the deaths of tens of millions of Americans, nor can it admit to the environmental and biological damage that would persist long after. CRP is an essential element in the preparation for nuclear war: its effectiveness measures the survivability of nuclear war. The admission that CRP would not be effective would make intentional nuclear war totally unacceptable. CRP is essential to the doctrine of fighting a nuclear war and prevailing, i.e., in the end, suffering less damage than the enemy.

A society has a critical need for civil defense and crisis relocation plans to protect its people in case of all kinds of disasters, from floods to fires. FEMA and the administration assume that a nuclear war does not essentially differ from these other disasters (McConnell, 1981). Following this unwarranted assumption with equally invalid assumptions, FEMA has concluded that 80 percent of the civilian population at risk could be saved by crisis relocation planning. It obtained this magic number not from an operational or percursor event analysis, but from an input assumption, confirming the "garbage in–garbage out" law of computer modeling (Estes, 1981).

The assumptions that justify CRP programs are all self-fulfilling: they support a conclusion that has been decided in advance. This is the ultimate methodological flaw in science. The conclusion has been transformed into the assumption and the assumptions have been selected to justify the conclusion. A superb book *The Counterfeit Ark* exposes all of this flawed analysis (Leaning and Keyes, 1984).

The assumptions that justify CRP effectiveness in a 6559-megaton war (a force equivalent to 4 million Hiroshima bombs!) affront common sense, let alone illustrate a bankrupt methodology.

1. Lead warning times of five to seven days prior to an attack.
2. Successful evacuation of some 120 million people from high-risk areas to join approximately 15 million in areas of low risk, resulting in a sheltered population of 135 million.
3. These 135 million are expected to spend one to four weeks in improved shelters in the evacuation area.
4. Whether relocated by the government's CRP or their own volition, the 150 million (80 percent or 120 million will make it) who leave high-risk areas (including large cities such as New York, Chicago, and Los Angeles, with their legendary traffic jams) are expected to travel between 50 and 300 miles to designated relocation areas.
5. A subset of 30 million persons, the so-called "essential workers," will be asked to commute daily into major urban areas to maintain infrastructure.

Proponents of CRP effectiveness utilize an inherent reductionist argument. Using the effects of natural accidents, nuclear power-plant accidents, the single nuclear explosions on Hiroshima and Nagasaki, or nonnuclear wars, they extrapolate effects of large-scale nuclear war that are mere extensions of their precedents. By reducing all long-term biological effects to short term, they reduce biology to physics. Thus, the unprecedented nature of nuclear war is simply discounted. The possible disruption of all services, including highways and transport; the psychological ramifications of widespread panic, the supposed discipline of the population; the presumed immunity to radiation of the essential workers; the conjectured viability of improvised shelters (sometimes trenches dug in the earth, to be occupied by one person for as long as twenty-eight days); the potential communications failure, and Soviet accommodation in choice of targeting—all the "ifs" are either ignored or countered with "best-case" examples.

Even more questionable assumptions postulate that the 120 million survivors of this nuclear war can continue to survive in the postattack period, and can obtain for themselves the necessities of food, shelter, and clothing that will enable them to reconstruct their society and eventually restore their civilization. These assumptions simply discount the thorough research on the long-term medical, environmental, ecological, and biological effects of nuclear war. They ignore evidence of a vast increase in infectious diseases and epidemics, the loss of immunity, the loss of medical personnel and medical services to treat the survivors.

The FEMA doctrine of CRP and survival also discounts the full impact of radioactivity on population and fertility, the impact of "nuclear winter" on agriculture, and the necessary impact of chaos and horror. Reductionism is so absurd that some researchers actually discount "worst-case" scenarios because there would be nothing to study (Leaning and Keyes, 1984, p. 35). Remove the unprecedented and you have the precedented. The nuclear power plant is a major Trojan Horse: targeting nuclear power plants in a nuclear exchange would multiply the effects of radiation, leading to an unprecedented hazard of huge proportions.

"Survivalists" and "cataclysmists" engage in more than academic debate. Survival has genuine moral value. But if the only basis of survival is the avoidance of nuclear war, and if CRP, at best, is a cruel hoax and, at worst, is an essential element in preparing to fight and win a nuclear war, then the only apparent morality is to deny any support to CRP or any civil defense against nuclear war and concentrate one's efforts on waging peace.

A final argument for CRP proposes that in the event of a limited nuclear war, whether the U.S. is the victim of a first-strike or the two superpowers have a limited exchange, it would be better to protect some people at any cost. The preparation for crisis relocation in event of nuclear war must be predicated on the exposure of large populations, thus the 6559-megaton attack scenario. One cannot preselect limited strikes and identify the targets, so we either have massive CRP or none. The very act of preparing for massive CRP involving 135 million persons is an act in the preparation for nuclear war. Both sides would interpret it as such, if either side perceived the other indulging in such preparation. That such a massive CRP program would be ineffective in any case does not alter its intrinsic meaning as a preparation for war. The assertion that the USSR is engaging in such preparations adds no merit to the argument. Even if the assertion were true, which it is not, the basic argument of ineffectiveness would hold. From the U.S. point of view, it might be better to let the Soviets waste their resources in this exercise in futility.

The various studies funded by FEMA to justify its CRP program have a more fundamental distortion than those involved in its methodological flaws. A general law of social modeling prescribes that the modeler, or, more often, the funding agency, incorporates his/her belief system and views as a set of implicit assumptions or "givens" that are taken as true in a study. Taken together, these beliefs comprise a social paradigm, in this case, the winnability and survivability of nuclear war. The general law governing this type of analysis becomes PI-PO, "Paradigm In–Paradigm Out" (Knelman, 1981). The assembly of beliefs that constitutes, the world view then becomes a self-fulfilling prophecy. Social scientists often find this tragedy endemic to their roles as advisers, since in effect their scientific methodology is corrupted to provide the advice that is being sought, or they too fall victims to PI-PO.

Massive CRP for the surviving population would reduce society to a survivalist anarchy. A critic responding to the civil defense movement of the early sixties commented on its consequences, "The social cost of going underground would not fall short of the total transformation of our way of life, the suspension of our civil institutions, the habituation of our people to violence and the ultimate militarization of our society" (Piel, 1963).

The notion of surviving a nuclear war becomes even more grotesque when one examines the kind of world that would remain. Nothing illustrates the counterproductiveness of survival measures more than an analysis of the physical and psychological environment in which the survivors would find themselves. In an eloquent denial of crisis management, the Brown University student association passed a motion asking the university to stock cyanide pills and make them available in the event of a nuclear war. We cannot manage this crisis except by avoidance. In the next chapter we will detail the various social and environmental consequences of nuclear war, but a preliminary analysis is appropriate here to help dispel the notion of the feasibility of nuclear warfighting, winning, and surviving. The consequences of nuclear war are beyond our imagination, since nothing in our present or past history, not even the single bombs dropped on Hiroshima and Nagasaki, compare with it.

Nuclear war confronts us with a semantic vacuum. To describe it we must commit linguistic surgery if we have any hope of achieving true meaning. The language we must use departs from experience to indulge in unreal abstraction. Language becomes the sanitation system for dealing with nuclear war. Nuclear sanitary engineers like Herman Kahn, Paul Nitze, and Eugene Rostow reduce the calculus of holocaust to abstract numbers that present meaningless concepts such as victory, loss, and recovery. Linguistic rape is the only way to deal clinically with the unspeakable and unthinkable; this is the only way the strategy scholars can break a "necessary silence." Extinction can never be made meaningful because it is, by definition, the end of meaning. Knowledge dies. "By imagining extinction we gaze past everything human to a dead time that falls outside the human tenses of past, present and future" (Schell, 1982, p. 140). The death of time has no grammatical tense.

We are lured into the false context of organized illusion. "The impact of technologicalized and apocalyptic violence [is] made increasingly routine" (Gardiner, 1974). Desensitized or apathetic, we are sealed "into a context of systematic illusion," leaving the experts to solve the problem they created. And they are part of the problem. The human response to extinction is psychological closure or numbness—denial, repression, and distraction—a galaxy of methods to close the mind to the unthinkable, or to lessen its impact in a Kahn-like way, for example, by changing it into actuarial calculation. Individual death is ecologically sound, if not attractive, for it involves recycling to infinity. It gives a sense of continuity to human life that provides a perspective of time and history. For some, this ecological wisdom allows the grace of accepting death as a part of life; for many, organized religion or traditional folkways provide the support for coping with death. The threat of species extinction shatters this necessary sense of continuity. For the U.S. Catholic bishops nothing can justify nuclear extermination. For the fundamentalists species extinction merely offers an opportunity for transcendence, for "intrapsychic purity at the expense of extrapsychic reality"—an organized form of numbness. Psychological security is thus purchased at the expense of involvement and commitment.

There is a new selling of the nuclear age by converting it to an abstract system set into motion by a depersonalized agent pushing a button. Each actor in the system is psychologically removed from both consciousness and responsibility—the grounds for impersonal ecocide. The new "cold warriors" work with computerized scenarios. The new combatants are "silo sitters," computer attendants and instrument watchers, all removed from the horror by physical and psychological distance. Nuclear warplanning is the ultimate nihilism because it can only destroy the knower and the knowledge. But "in the service of greater awareness—even just its beginnings, lies our hope" (Lifton and Falk, 1982, p. 110). Awareness becomes bewareness and hope becomes engagement. That is all any of us has, and the sum of all our hopes is all the world has.

Nuclear wars are now fought as simulated computer games known as scenarios. Calculations from some of these studies indicate that environmental impacts would be as damaging as the medical effects (Holden, 1983). According to studies by Carl Sagan and others, 5000 megatons released in a large counterforce first-strike would reduce sunlight by 95 percent in the midlatitudes of the Northern Hemisphere. Temperatures would drop as low as -23°C and remain below freezing for months. High radiation levels of up to 250 rads would cover 30 percent of the affected area. Toxic pollution would result from the huge fires. Ozone depletion would raise the intensity of ultraviolet radiation, causing great damage to humans, plants, animals, and helpful microorganisms (Holden, 1983, p. 822). These aftereffects would last for months or longer.

These effects would not be confined to the Northern Hemisphere. They would affect the entire global atmospheric system due to the interhemispheric transport of thousands of tons of nuclear debris and dust. Relatively small megatonnage wars would trigger negative climatic changes.

These new assessments of the environmental impacts compound the horror of the medical effects. Another dimension is not yet publicly discussed. Some fifty materials are critical to modern civilization in the industrialized world. With few exceptions, the bulk of these resources have already been used. Dynamic reserves of many of these critical materials are insufficient to re-create civilization as we know it. Even if everyone were not killed in a nuclear holocaust, and certainly everyone would not be, replacing the existing levels of the capital/physical stock of "civilization" would be impossible. In this sense, both time and history would end. The human (social), physical, biological, psychological, and cultural environments would be radically altered, if not permanently damaged. Very likely they would be incapable of returning to their former levels.

Several psychiatrists have analyzed the psychological phenomena associated with the imagery of destruction and extinction connected with nuclear war. Such professionals note the increasing incidence of a kind of nuclear neurosis, particularly in young persons, and this phenomenon is evident to anyone who has the opportunity to encounter and communicate with them. The psychological profiles of the survivors of the Hiroshima and Nagasaki bombings provide another insight into the psychic impact of nuclear war. The Nazi death-camps illuminate some aspects of the holocaust syndrome.

Some psychiatrists believe the "imagery of extinction" has impact on five existing modes of biological and social continuity: the family and procreation; the theological; the eternal nature of creativity; the continuity of Nature itself; and finally, what is termed "experiential transcendence," a mystic state where time and death disappear (Lifton, 1982). All of these provide some sense of human immortality and continuity. They give us our sense of the present and of the future. Some psychiatrists now think that the threats of technological extinction, a kind of global suicide pact of nations, and ecocide, the murder of the environment, powerfully affect all five modes. The destructiveness of their impact on our collective psyche and, in particular, on the agents of the future, our children, could be devastating. It could reinforce our alienation from Nature. It could reinforce personal closure by subsuming the questioning and searching necessary to deal with the problem. It reinforces the apocalyptic vision of the fundamentalists who literally believe in the imminent end of the world. Yet this unprecedented danger has also spawned hope, perhaps in a measure equal to hopelessness. It has certainly polarized the forces of life and those of death.

Robert Jay Lifton has described the doctrine of winnability and survivability in a nuclear war as the "logic of madness." We have used a less dramatic word, mythology. There is madness in their mythology. Lifton has written, "Civil defense is part of the fundamental illusions about a nuclear war: The illusion of surviving. The illusion of recovery. It's massive denial" (Goodman, 1983). Thus we have a doctrine of massive assured denial (MAD). Lifton also said, "In itself [civil defense] seems like a natural and appropriate thing to do. But it increases the possibility of nuclear war by making it more acceptable. That's why it's immoral" (Goodman, 1983). Aside from the immorality of deluding the public, civil defense or defensive measures generally are a critical component of the arms race. Civil defense can be perceived by the other side as preparation for nuclear war. When analyzed in the context of NSDD-32 and SIOP-6, it is preparation for nuclear war.

T. K. Jones, the undersecretary of defense responsible for the Federal Emergency Management Agency (FEMA), is the Dr. Strangelove of civil defense. FEMA has assured that U.S. agriculture and food supplies would survive a nuclear war: "Sufficient production seems assured to meet survivor needs" (Goodman, 1983). This is remarkable and dangerous nonsense in the light of Sagan and Ehrlich's environmental impact assessment. The long "nuclear winter" following a nuclear war will be particularly hostile to food production. A group of Soviet scientists have met with their U.S. counterparts and agreed on the scientific authenticity of these findings (Shabecoff, 1983). At this meeting, they agreed that a nuclear freeze was a necessary first step in avoiding the ultimate holocaust. In fact, the great majority of independent experts agree that a nuclear war is neither winnable nor survivable. The nuclear warfighting policies of the Reagan administration receive a solid negation from both the world of the church and the world of science.

Both sides plan nuclear wars as if they were games. Various official agencies and other institutions have simulated nuclear wars in the past twenty years. There have been some ten major studies in the U.S. and the U.K. since Robert McNamara served in the Kennedy administration. Simulated nuclear war is an exceedingly complex game involving a multiplicity of factors, a variety of scenarios, and a host of uncertainties; but these unknowns do not constitute methodological deterrence for devoted game players with their technological toys. The level of abstraction is necessarily great, and the complex war system involves the uncertainty of human behavior in crisis conditions. Under these conditions the best one can do is make what appear to be credible assumptions, be certain these are overt, and then draw what appear to be reasonable conclusions.

One of the myths involved in these "credible" assumptions is the myth of the obliging enemy. This adversary limits the quantity and kind of targets struck; never launches a "surprise" or short-warning attack; attacks military targets and not cities; possesses missiles accurate enough to launch "surgical strikes against strategic hamlets" so that those who suffer second-degree burns, radiation damage, and assorted wounds have all the medical and transport services intact and available to them. That the other side may not act as predicted by simulation; that a disparity exists between the capabilities of medical facilities, and the number of projected casualties and injuries— these facts do not prevent the program of civil defense from being planned by both the superpowers. Nor do the other myths deter this cruel illusion of survivability.

The controversy over the hazards of radiation, part of the nuclear power debate, is relevant to the issue of survivability. Current evidence would certainly indicate that this hazard has been underestimated. The potential for cancer and genetic disorders from nonlethal or even low-level exposures to ionizing radiation from fallout is very large. Radioactive decay of fallout is an extremely complex inverse function of a power of time. Fallout levels are calculated in "rems," an acronym for "radiation equivalent man"—a measure of the biological impact of ionizing radiation. An initial level of 1000 rem per hour reduces to about 100 rem per hour in about 7 hours, to 10 rem/hr. in 49 hours, to 1 rem/hr. in 343 hours (about 15 days), and to 0.1 rem/hr. in 100 days. The cumulative dose is significant, not the rapidity of decay. For example, at an average integrated exposure of only 1 rem/hr., you would receive a dose of 24 rem/day, 168 rem/week and over 672 rem/month. Exposure to amounts of radiation between 500 and 1000 rem integrated dose would cause lethal effects. Thus, anyone leaving a bomb shelter after one week would still receive a lethal cumulative dose within a few weeks. A one-megaton explosive yield spreads lethal amounts of radiation over 22 square kilometers. A one-megaton bomb hitting a 1000-megowatt nuclear power plant will lead to a 100-rem exposure over an area of 34,000 square kilometers; the same bomb striking an ordinary target will cause that exposure over only 2000 square kilometers (Rotblat, 1981).

It is important to distinguish between prompt and delayed radiation effects. Doses are also measured in Radiation Absorbed Dose, or rads, approximately equal to rems. Although people differ in their natural susceptibility to radiation, younger people tend to be more susceptible to it. An exposure of about 350 to 450 rad within sixty days of exposure is usually considered as lethal to 50 percent of the people exposed. However, uncertainty exists about the effects of low radiation levels received as a cumulative dose over time. The consensus (FEMA excepted) is that lower doses, received as a single exposure or cumulatively over time, will have the same health impacts. At doses between 450 and 1000 rads, a high risk of death from infection and hemorrhage occurs about three weeks after exposure (Rotblat, 1981). Blood abnormalities predominate. At doses between 1000 and 3000 rads, gastrointestinal symptoms predominate and death from infection or hemorrhage results in about two weeks. At exposures over 3000 rads, neurovascular symptoms appear within the first hour of exposure, and death is certain for all within four days (Leaning, 1984, p. 203). With the best treatment available, only those in the 400 to 700 rad exposure would have a 50 percent chance of survival. With the major disruption of medical services and the death of a majority of doctors, it is altogether reasonable to assume that a majority of all persons exposed to prompt or cumulative doses greater than 350 rads would die. Exposures as low as 6 rads per day or 0.25 rads per hour would cause 90 percent of those exposed to die within one year (Lushbaugh, 1974). Society would suffer its "final epidemic."

In a large-scale nuclear war, not the immediate target area alone would be exposed to eventual lethal doses: the entire area of the United States would be so exposed (von Hippel, 1983). Living in a small, dark, confined earth-covered shelter with the necessary life-support materials for one or two weeks presents its own horrors. One could drown or suffocate in one's own waste, die from lack of oxygen or the effects of heat and overpressure. If one had suffered a nonlethal exposure prior to reaching the shelter, one would be infected by the ionizing radiation and neutron exposure that cause a kind of nuclear AIDS. "Survivors" leaving the shelters after a week or so would exhibit symptoms of immunity deficiency. If avoiding prompt death is winning and surviving, awaiting a lingering death is an intolerable biological indignity. It is a cruel hoax to hold out the false hope of survival with dignity and a vision of rapid recovery.

The theoretical amount of fission required to create enough fallout to destroy every living species, except cockroaches, on this planet is 1 million megatons or 1 trillion tons, i.e., a teraton, based on the numbers of prompt deaths by early radiation exposure (Adams and Cullen, 1981, p. 116). By combining all the prompt and delayed effects on species, ecosystems, the ozone layers, climate, etc., global holocaust would occur as a result of an explosion of less than 1 teraton of fissionable material. For the 750 million people involved in a war between the superpowers, 10,000 megatons, about 13 tons per person, would constitute the holocaust—an obscene overkill.

The two superpowers have about 10,000 megatons in their combined strategic arsenals (see Table 1). Writers of nuclear war scenarios customarily use between 5000 and 10,000 delivered megatons to assess the prompt and delayed social and environmental damage. If cities are included in the major targets of an all-out nuclear war, it is safe to assume the prompt death of some 80 percent of all the peoples of North America and Europe. Because of delayed social and biological effects, these regions would be effectively eliminated from the living world. This unprecedented catastrophe would murder the present and foreclose the future. Citizens have to decide which path would better eliminate this risk: preparing for war or waging peace.

Myths are transformed into policy by a subtle process that blurs the the first hour of exposure, and death is certain for all within four days (Leaning, 1984, p. 203). With the best treatment available, only those in the 400 to 700 rad exposure would have a 50 percent chance of survival. With the major disruption of medical services and the death of a majority of doctors, it is altogether reasonable to assume that a majority of all persons exposed to prompt or cumulative doses greater than 350 rads would die. Exposures as low as 6 rads per day or 0.25 rads per hour would cause 90 percent of those exposed to die within one year (Lushbaugh, 1974). Society would suffer its "final epidemic."

In a large-scale nuclear war, not the immediate target area alone would be exposed to eventual lethal doses: the entire area of the United States would be so exposed (von Hippel, 1983). Living in a small, dark, confined earth-covered shelter with the necessary life-support materials for one or two weeks presents its own horrors. One could drown or suffocate in one's own waste, die from lack of oxygen or the effects of heat and overpressure. If one had suffered a nonlethal exposure prior to reaching the shelter, one would be infected by the ionizing radiation and neutron exposure that cause a kind of nuclear AIDS. "Survivors" leaving the shelters after a week or so would exhibit symptoms of immunity deficiency. If avoiding prompt death is winning and surviving, awaiting a lingering death is an intolerable biological indignity. It is a cruel hoax to hold out the false hope of survival with dignity and a vision of rapid recovery.

The theoretical amount of fission required to create enough fallout to destroy every living species, except cockroaches, on this planet is 1 million megatons or 1 trillion tons, i.e., a teraton, based on the numbers of prompt deaths by early radiation exposure (Adams and Cullen, 1981, p. 116). By combining all the prompt and delayed effects on species, ecosystems, the ozone layers, climate, etc., global holocaust would occur as a result of an explosion of less than 1 teraton of fissionable material. For the 750 million people involved in a war between the superpowers, 10,000 megatons, about 13 tons per person, would constitute the holocaust—an obscene overkill.

The two superpowers have about 10,000 megatons in their combined strategic arsenals (see Table 1). Writers of nuclear war scenarios customarily use between 5000 and 10,000 delivered megatons to assess the prompt and delayed social and environmental damage. If cities are included in the major targets of an all-out nuclear war, it is safe to assume the prompt death of some 80 percent of all the peoples of North America and Europe. Because of delayed social and biological effects, these regions would be effectively eliminated from the living world. This unprecedented catastrophe would murder the present and foreclose the future. Citizens have to decide which path would better eliminate this risk: preparing for war or waging peace.

Myths are transformed into policy by a subtle process that blurs the significance of assumptions by absorbing them into belief. The model becomes the message. The universal law of system modeling becomes PI-PO, "Paradigm In–Paradigm Out." The conclusions bury the assumptions and the analysis becomes self-fulfilling. Nuclear war and its biological impacts are reduced to physics. It is reductionism ad absurdum. Many key members of the Reagan administration ascribe to this reductionism. Suffused by the rationalization "better dead than Red," and propelled by the notion that we must fight communism, this reductionism means we must plan to win the war. Identical mirror-image beliefs probably pervade on the communist side, so the false beliefs of two world systems hold the planet captive. Each side calculates the "fate of the earth," while it plans to win and survive a nuclear holocaust. The result of every credible study is roughly the same. One hundred million casualties—the majority of the population of both sides—would result from a war abstracted to include only the two superpowers. Given the arsenals existing today, bringing Europe into an all-out, "total use," "insensate" nuclear war could cause casualties of more than 500 million (*Gazette,* Saturday, 27 August 1983, Montreal). A group at Saint Anselm College in Concord, New Hampshire, reported the results of their computer "war game": if the U.S. and the USSR unleashed their combined arsenals of 17,965 warheads on 700 U.S. and Soviet cities with a population of 350 million, both sides would lose 75 percent of their populations. Yet, believe it or not, the researchers say "the Soviet Union does win and does have superior nuclear power." This is an inhumane level of abstraction. The potential biological impact on the natural environment, on the ozone layer, and the biosphere; the long-term poisoning of the earth and its waters by fallout; all aspects of the "holocaust" are seemingly ignored. The real possibility that unleashing ten gigatons of nuclear fission products would render the earth incapable of supporting life is part of the abstracted "facts."

All people lose in a nuclear war; even generals, presidents, and strategists lose their families and their future. The "holocaust effect" murders the future as it kills the present. The avoidance of nuclear war becomes the most urgent, human, and worthy goal in the entire social agenda. The black activist Dick Gregory perceives the issues correctly: "If I demonstrate for black rights in the morning and they drop the bomb at noon, there won't be any rights to demonstrate for in the evening."

On 27 August 1984—the anniversary of the great "I Have a Dream" speech of Martin Luther King, Jr.,—people once again marched in Washington in the most hopeful consensus of our time, fusing the issues of peace, jobs, and human rights together into the ecological cause of history. The demonstration targeted the the Reagan administration and its policies of war, unemployment, and the denial of human rights in America and the world.

Reagan's deceptive arms control and reduction "initiatives" also victimize Americans and others. The deception of START and "build-down" is simple to reveal. Like Zero-Option, these ploys intend to disarm the USSR while retaining U.S. superiority (the "margin of safety"). By reducing ICBM's alone, the Soviet arsenal will be dramatically reduced while the U.S.'s will remain relatively intact. Cutting both ICBM's and bombers will produce an even better "margin of safety" if the cruise missile program is included. Table 1 shows the reason for this. A one-third reduction in ICBM's would reduce Soviet warheads by 1800, U.S.'s by 700. This would leave the U.S. with some 9000 warheads and the USSR with 5900. Cutting bombers by a third but equipping the remaining U.S. B-52's with ALCM's would lead to a Soviet reduction of 100 warheads, but would equip 200 U.S. B-52G and H class bombers with 4000 ALCM's. The USSR will then have 5800 warheads and the U.S., some 12,000. START is in effect a plan to reduce the USSR to a lower level than the U.S., and "build-down" is really build-up. Zero-Option would leave 162 British and French missiles intact while reducing the USSR to zero.

Reagan's numbers game takes on more sinister overtones when one considers that the U.S. intends to "build-down" technologically inferior systems and to "build-up" vastly superior ones, with the net effect being a military technological build-up. Phasing out 52 Titan II's and many of the 450 Minuteman II's and replacing these with MX at a rate of 1 for 2 phased out will considerably increase the number of ICBM warheads. One hundred MX missiles carry 1000 warheads—half as many warheads as are in the total existing 1052 ICBM missiles in the U.S. arsenal. The qualitative and quantitative superiority of B-type and stealth bombers armed with stealth cruise missiles will far outweigh a mere build-down in existing bomber stock. While the USSR is modernizing also, it is very questionable that they could come close to matching the U.S. in this nuclear numbers/quality game.

There is a kind of prescience in the little-known fact that in 1958 Ronald Reagan and Nancy Davis starred in a "G.E. Theater" production, "A Turkey for the President." Trivial Pursuit, the game, not the presidency, is the source of this and other trivia on the former ambassador of General Electric, such as "The solution to Viet Nam is to pave it over." Reagan's "foot in mouth disease" is perhaps most dangerous when the rhetoric is threatening. In 1983 alone he threatened to intervene in the Middle East and Central America. His response to the KAL-007 incident chilled the entire world. He cannot have it both ways. Either you can never negotiate with the "evil empire" or you must accept some measure of coexistence far short of war. In a dynamic arms race the attempt to negotiate from strength is extremely dangerous because it enlists the potential of a preemptive strike from both sides.

BUILD-DOWN IS BUILD-UP

The Reagan administration has introduced a series of so-called arms reduction plans, START, Zero-Zero, and "build-down," all of which are barely concealed efforts to maintain U.S. superiority. To understand this assertion, one must reexamine the existing military balance, as we have done with considerable elaboration in chapter 4. Our conclusion was that the U.S. had superiority in the following ways:

1. A more flexible system with a greater number of deliverable warheads.
2. A better balanced triad of weapons.
3. General technical advantages in its arsenal accuracy.
4. Geostrategic advantages.
5. A superior C^3I system.

We noted an even more meaningful superiority in the U.S.'s rate of "force modernization" and development and deployment of new and more effective weapons such as B-1, stealth, Trident II, ACM, MX, and with other advanced warheads and ballistic reentry missiles (ABRV's). "Build-down" refers to total numbers and has no real reference to quality or effectiveness or balance. In actuality, build-down is an arms race of modernization and effectiveness. By proposing a reduction in throw-weight and missile volume, then silo-kill ("hard targets") probability (P_k) strongly favors the U.S. (see chapter 3). So does rocket fuel technology.

In the SALT II-accountable inventory, each side has about 8500 ballistic missile warheads. It is proposed to reduce these to 5000 on each side. The U.S. would wish to do this anyway if it were modernizing its present arsenal. It would replace Poseidon (as Poseidon has replaced Polaris) with Trident I and Trident II. There would be fewer Trident II's but their firepower and accuracy would be much greater. It would eventually replace all Titan and Minuteman ICBM's with MX and then with Midgetman armed with ABRV's and very likely mobile. The net result would be a significant increase in counterforce first-strike capacity with fewer warheads and launchers. Obviously the USSR would have to make deep cuts in its ICBM leg to meet the 5000 ceiling, due to its skewed distribution of its warheads, approximately 74 percent as ICBM's.

In another essential deception of this proposal, the U.S. has already undertaken force modernization in the ICBM leg, in the SLBM leg, and with advanced cruise missiles (ACM). The dynamics of the race favor the U.S. in momentum, initial advantage, and economic capability. To match this modernization, the USSR would have to rebuild almost all its arsenal, because the USSR has a massive investment in inefficient, liquid-fueled weapons.

A second stage of "build-down" would include bomber forces and their missiles. Here the U.S. proposes a total reduction of 8500 "standard weapons stations" (a curious technical concoction of factors favoring accuracy and reliability). Since the bomber leg of the Soviet triad is negligible, this would either force deep cuts in the other two legs or a massive bomber weapon development. One suspects that, as with all Reagan proposals, "build-down" is designed to be one the USSR must refuse. Thus, one can suspect that the Reagan administration continues to be motivated by the goal of superiority rather than arms control and reduction. Unfortunately a group of "bipartisan" congressmen—Les Aspin, Albert Gore, Norman Dicks, William Cohen, Sam Nunn, and Charles Percy—have entertained and supported this act of duplicity in the name of "compulsory double build-down." All of these reasonable men have been induced to support the administration on the basis of future arms reductions, i.e., build-down by build-up. "Placing every new weapon into an agreement is the price Congress and the U.S. taxpayer are being told they must pay to induce the Reagan administration to agree to reductions" (Paine, 1983b). The movement to clear first-strike capacity by the U.S. provides a double bind. In a period of great tension, it encourages a preemptive strike by the stronger and also a preemptive strike by the weaker. The greatest state of destabilization possible would exist while such an imbalance in capability was in force. "It may be a secret agenda for side-tracking disarmament while the U.S. gets on with rearmament," stated Senator E. S. Muskie about START (Scheer, 1983, p. 7).

Leaving rhetoric and true belief aside, ignorance in a president is possibly more dangerous than any other quality. Mr. Reagan was, for example, under the impression that a ballistic missile could be recalled after having been launched. More recently he stated to a group of congressmen that he had not realized that most of the Soviets' strategic weapons are in land-based systems (*New York Times,* Sunday, 16 October 1983). He then added that this might be the reason so many considered his arms proposals one-sided! Mr. Reagan has even given new meaning to retreat. He calls this redeployment. This would be like General Custer referring to Little Big Horn as redeployment.

Several "liberal" senators and representatives, among them Representative Les Aspin, a long-standing critic of Reagan policies, supported the Scowcroft Commission's recommendation to deploy 100 new MX missiles in Minuteman sites. The Scowcroft approach won approval in the House by 239 to 186 in May 1983 (House Democrats voted against it). This was surprising because of the assumptions involved:

1. The USSR's 600+ SS-18 and SS-19's are so highly accurate and powerful that they are effectively MX missiles.
2. These Soviet missiles can make an effective strike and destroy U.S. missile silos; therefore, as Reagan proclaimed, there is a "window of vulnerability."
3. The USSR would accept the three-part Scowcroft package of (a) 100 MX's "only," (b) arms control "promises" by the Reagan administration, and (c) a "promise" to move away from MIRVed to small single-warhead Midgetman missiles.
4. The Soviets would be driven to bargain because of MX.

The contradictions, if not actual invalidities, in these assumptions are remarkable. The Scowcroft Commission flatly denied the "window of vulnerability" proposition. In the modern period, the USSR has never been forced to negotiate because of U.S. superiority; on the contrary, such attempts have intensified the arms race. If there is rough parity without MX then there is less than parity with it, because MX adds 1000 warheads to the ICBM leg. The silence of right-wing defense advocates on the 100-MX victory indicated their satisfaction. Reagan has made no serious arms control overtures since the House vote.

Even though putting 100 MX's in fixed silos represents the administration's thirty-fifth basing scheme, it still fails fundamental tests of arms control and serious defense. It is counterproductive as arms control: technically, MX is the most accurate silo-killing weapon in either superpower arsenal. Thus the 100 MX missiles invite the highest priority preemptive strike because they are the most threatening weapon in the U.S. arsenal. Furthermore, Trident II, the only weapon comparable to MX, will come on line about the same time, thus adding to the first-strike threat. The liberal Democrats (and Republicans) have acted expediently, clinging to promises they know will not be kept, and standing firm in their conviction that they can reverse themselves later. Les Aspin and others have fallen into the trap of incrementalism, contributing to the thin edge of the superiority wedge.

RONALD REAGAN: A SUMMARY PORTRAIT

It is said that Ronald Reagan is lucky. He seems to miraculously escape the worst consequences of his unending blunders, partially because of coincidental and unrelated news-catching events. As Rep. Pat Schroeder (D-Colo.) noted, "He's the Teflon-coated President; the blame doesn't seem to stick" (*Energy News Digest,* April 1984, p. 2, Allendale, N.J.). With very few exceptions, the dominant electronic media has a "hands-off" policy in regard to Reagan's notorious gaffes. Anthony Lewis of the *New York Times* is almost alone in the ferocity of his attacks on Reagan's political blunders. However, because of the fiascoes of U.S. policy in Lebanon and in the mining of harbors in Nicaragua, Americans are beginning to hit back with timing that Reagan's luck cannot evade. In Anthony Lewis's column in the *New York Times,* Thursday, 12 April 1984, a letter by Sen. Barry Goldwater to William Casey, director of the CIA, states, "Mine the harbors in Nicaragua? This is an act violating international law. It is an act of war. For the life of me, I don't see how we are going to explain it." Lewis deplores Reagan's apparent contempt for domestic law as well, viz., Reagan's intervention on tax exemptions for segregated schools and the attempt "to install a massive new censorship system in government without any basis in law." In reviewing *Ronald Reagan: The Politics of Symbolism* by Robert Dallek, the reviewer states: "It is so difficult for liberals to get a fix on Mr. Reagan that they are tempted to comfort themselves with contemptuous stereotypes; a simpleton, an ex-movie actor, carefully programmed by others, who has succeeded politically by putting a friendly face on greed and anti-Soviet paranoia" (*Energy News Digest,* April 1984, p. 2, Allendale, N.J.). These stereotypes present an irresistible temptation because in large part they are true. But Reagan also appeals to a genuine yearning for a powerful political symbol in the psyche of a large number of Americans. Anthony Lewis says, "But Ronald Reagan is not a conservative—not in the sense of Barry Goldwater. He is a radical who wants to enlarge the power of the executive, including the power to wage secret wars, regardless of law and tradition" (*New York Times,* Thursday, 12 April 1984). But Lewis only describes a symptom: the diagnosis of the disease is deeper and more complex. Reagan is atune with a hard core—possibly a many as 20 percent—of the American electorate. He is both symbol and servant of their own views and beliefs, their frustrations, and their ignorance. At the same time, Reagan is the instrument of a power core, the right wing of the "military-industrial complex" who wait in the wings (right only) to seize real power. They are the isolationist/interventionists who believe in "containment militarism." Reagan represents a great backward revolution, one giant step backward for America and the rest of humanity.

What can one think of a president of the world's most powerful country whose lack of knowledge has disgraced his office, whose language of homily has degraded the art of poltics, and whose capacity for gaffes, bloopers, and plain erorrs has never been exceeded by any other world leader, now or in the past? One wonders if Reagan attended the School of Immaculate Misconception. One could excuse the absence of bravura and eloquence; one could even excuse falling asleep at key briefings. But Reagan's statements like "Now we are trying to get unemployment to go up, and I think we're going to succeed" (Green and MacColl, 1983, p. 9), or "The United States has much to offer the Third World War" (Trivial Pursuit) become less excusable. Ralph Nader once said, "Reagan is the first president to own more horses than books." Even

George Bush realized that the president is not an intellectual. In the heat of his battle against Reagan for Republican leadership, Bush commented on Reagan's proposals: "I think there's a factual gap and I have to home in on it" (*New York Times*, Thursday, 4 December 1980). Reagan uses "obvious exaggerations, material omissions or half-truths, contrived anecdotes, voodoo statistics, denials of unpleasant facts and flat untruths" (Green and MacColl, 1983, p. 9). These six types of error still miss the essence of Reagan-think, a form of Orwellian double-think that is effective, ominous, and incorporates a very simplistic but total world view.

In fact, Reagan's statements embody a coherent ideology: unyielding, adamant anticommunism that is confused about fine distinctions; a belief that perfectly free enterprise can take care of the poor, the sick, and the old without government welfare programs, and can also protect the environment without government controls; a belief in a fairy-tale America stripped of all ugliness and inequity, an America painted by Norman Rockwell; and a strong fundamentalist religious belief. By placing his ideological values above all else, Reagan can ignore or distort facts, pursue "larger truths" through small errors, and, above all, ascribe to his enemies the thoughts and actions that are in his own mind. Reagan-think has three elements: (1) asserting as true what is known to be false; (2) pursuing policies that he has previously opposed; (3) attributing to others what he intends to do (the "turn-the-tables" technique). Thus Reagan is permitted to have his way, while he justifies his actions by accusing his opponents of provocations. Doubt and dissent are identified at best as weakness; at worst, as subversion. In pursuit of his ideological compulsions, Ronald Reagan has reserved the right to treat the truth with more disdain than any U.S. president in history. Representative M. Udall (D-Ariz.) has said that Reagan "has an immunity, as if he's not judged in the same courtroom" (Green and MacColl, 1983, p. 17). But a large number of Americans relate to Reagan, to his ordinariness, to his misinformation, and certainly to his appeal to resurrect American supremacy in the world, by playing policeman, bully, or Western cowboy hero, if necessary. One need not be surprised by the rumor that Reagan has a stand of redwood trees on his ranch with only one tree standing. After all, if you have seen one . . .

Europeans and Canadians cannot understand all this: "The Americans will shortly proceed to re-elect this lazy old ignoramus by a landslide" (Gwynne Dyer, *Gazette*, Saturday, 13 October 1984, Montreal). Gwynne Dyer, who writes from Europe for the *Gazette*, goes on to suggest that "There are millions of people better qualified to be president than Ronald Reagan, but nobody who would make a better king." The *Manchester Guardian* calls him an "amiable old buffer" and explains that "what goes wrong can't really be his fault because he didn't understand what was happening in the first place" (*Energy News Digest*, August 1984, Allendale, N.J.). In late October

1984 in the *New York Times,* James Reston wrote that in his forty years of covering Washington, he could not remember a time when official Washington thought so little of a president's talents, but the country at large thought so much of them. The Teflon president, wrapped in the Stars and Stripes and wearing a Stetson hat and cowboy boots, appeals to the lowest common denominator in American culture. This, of course, is the key to his success. That lowest common denominator is large enough to elect presidents. "The President is such a plausible manipulator of fraudulent statistics, such an inveterate garbler of history . . . a listener just gulps and blinks like a toad" (Lars-Erik Nelson, *New York Daily News,* Tuesday, 19 June 1984). But Reagan's appeal is real. As Nicholas von Hoffman wrote in *Harpers,* "Age and his ideological arteriosclerosis rob Reagan of nimbleness and subtlety. And he is abetted and egged on by the myriads of capitalist youth marching and chanting societies, the Jousters for Jesus, the Young Americans for Freedom, the Helms Helpers . . . refining the unalloyed abstract values so dear to demented idealism" (*Energy News Digest,* no. 281, September 1984, p. 2, Allendale, N.J.). Reagan appeals to more than just idealism; he heralds the pay-off of good economic times. Even this is a blinkered vision: those good times are almost exclusively good to the rich, to the privileged, and to the "haves" in general. Students want a piece of the pie, and they see Reagan providing a bigger pie while offering hope and exuding amiable confidence with a firm handshake, steady eye contact, and a winning smile. "Life is basically simple: Pledge allegiance, salute flag, revere John Wayne, watch out for foreigners. . . . When you have acquired a loving wife, big car and a house on the hill, you have made it and enter the Kingdom of Heaven, where well-off Americans get the best tables" (Herb Caen, quoted in *Citizens Energy Digest,* no. 283, November 1984, p. 2, Allendale, N.J.). In what I. F. Stone called "America's most fateful election," the people elected a TV image through TV information, the ultimate trivialization of knowledge. Mr. Clean, pure in heart, mind uncluttered with facts, and ready to draw his six-shooter, is the perfect TV image.

The myths, gaps, and gaffes analyzed in this chapter constitute the substantive material of Reagan's world view and belief system. Reagan's virulent, moralistic anticommunism; his crusader zeal in service to anticommunism; his ignorance of foreign affairs; his suspicion of all things foreign; his intrinsic go-it-alone, "tall-in-the-saddle" isolationism/containment attitude; his religious fundamentalism; his intellectual laziness; and his great skills at reading teleprompters unite in the ideal, symbolic macho man to lead America into World War III.

Do not underestimate Ronald Reagan. His power lies in his ability to reduce the world to a struggle between good and evil, to justify good doing what evil does to defeat evil, to attribute to evil what good does in defense of good—all this is a powerful cosmology. Those who oppose Reagan become dupes or worse, because there are only two sides. Those who oppose school prayer oppose religion. Those who oppose MX oppose the U.S. In Reagan's simplistic world view, facts, conceptual coherence, and the rules of traditional evidence are dispensable and are abandoned for the sake of ideological mission.

The American Historical Association devoted a meeting to ranking U.S. presidents in regards to their knowledge of history (*Los Angeles Times,* 1981). Several historians who ranked Reagan last commented on Reagan's incredible ignorance of history. They cited famous Reagan observations: "America has never known slavery"; that New Dealers had supported the model of Mussolini's fascism; and "we have driven God out of the classroom." Professor Hoff-Wilson of Indiana University said, "It is easier to declare a revolution when you are historically illiterate," and noted that Reagan substituted "crowd-pleasing nostalgia" for history. Professor David Montgomery of Yale described the Reagan administration as "the careful cultivation of mean-spiritedness," while a Professor Burns said, "conservative Republicans . . . have finally found Mr. Right." These comments describe the essential social policy of the Reagan administration: the crudity of Reaganomics, the falsity of the "trickle-down" theory, the disaster of deregulation, the support of a "free market" for the poor and a CARE program for the rich, the open invitation to destroy the environment, and the expansion of the "industrial-military complex." After more than two years of Reagan's administration, the Harris index of alienation indicated that the "U.S. hit records for sad, bitter alienation" (*Toronto Star,* 1983). Other polls indicate that a majority of Americans reject the massive arms build-up. The Congress remains divided on the nuclear freeze issue, but a majority support arms cutbacks. The regulatory agencies, their mandates totally reversed, are in a state of crisis.

THE LAST GAP

Throughout all the formal and informal, official and unofficial accounting of the military balance, the U.S. has consistently led in the number of warheads. While it has been conceded that the USSR's nuclear arsenal exceeds that of the U.S. in megatonnage (total throw-weight), the U.S. has compensated for this excess by amassing more warheads with more accurate delivery systems. Statistics can lie. For example, the population of Ireland exceeds that of mainland China if only redheads are counted. Nuclear weapons accounting can do this by including both tactical and strategic weapons or separating them; by counting operational ready-to-launch warheads or stockpiled weapons; by considering the reload issue; by excluding one leg of the triad; by including or excluding some theater weapons because of their ownership, or because they can reach a superpowers' sovereign territory. This type of accounting destroyed INF talks in Europe.

The U.S. Department of Defense, in an obvious ploy to support its massive budget, has now invented the warhead gap, the latest myth. According to DOD, the USSR has about 8000 warheads more than the U.S., mainly in the tactical and theater class, 34,000 to 26,000 (a complete total of all types) (Scott, 1984).

The DOD now claims that it has warned about the "warhead gap" since 1978 when it began. This is incredible, since until now, every government agency from the Pentagon to the CIA has issued official estimates showing the U.S. leads in total warheads. To support this startling and patently false "warhead gap," DOD manufactured "worse-case" assumptions, e.g., that the Soviets have reloads available for every weapon in their arsenal; that every delivery vehicle, even when clearly designated as conventional in armament, counts as either a nuclear or a "dual-capable" system.

Using this latest fictitious gap, DOD is planning weapons procurement that would add 16,000 new warheads of all kinds to the U.S. arsenal. Thus "the motives for inflating the warhead gap seem more real than the gap itself" (Scott, 1984, p. 44). The public must see this in its proper historical context. Every previous gap has been not mere fiction but a reverse gap. The U.S. has always led, if not in mere numbers, then in the superior accuracy, reliability, maintenance, speed of activation, C^3I systems, geostrategic factors, economic and technological capacity, etc., that make the difference. As in all other bids for the budget, every increase in the size of the nuclear arsenals has increased insecurity, making the arms race a race for greater insecurity.

CONCLUSIONS

The concept of nuclear warfighting rests on a complex set of myths that distill to two: (1) the notion of winning; (2) the notion of surviving. In some direct ways, the deliberate creation of fictitious gaps that establish and/or maintain U.S. superiority fueled the arms race, and the Reagan administration has intensified it. The secret agenda continues to dictate the defense budget. However, nothing destroys the mythology of fighting and winning a nuclear war more than revealing the dramatic climate changes that would likely occur after such a war—the subject of the next chapter.

6

This Is the Way the World Ends:
First with a Bang, Then with a Whimper

There are, as I began, cumbersome ways to kill a man. Simpler, direct and much more neat is to see that he is living somewhere in the middle of the twentieth century and leave him there.

Edwin Brock

Someday, science may have the existence of mankind in its power and the human race commit suicide by blowing up the world.

Henry Adams

THIS IS THE WAY THE WORLD ENDS

The myths that suggest that limited or protracted nuclear wars can be won, and that societies that "win" can survive, have recently been challenged by accumulating information on the consequences of nuclear war for the Day Before, the Day After, and One Year Later. The Day Before deals with unintentional nuclear war initiated by a variety of means, a problem that becomes inevitable as tensions persist and worsen and weapons systems become more complex and computerized. The Day After depicts the prompt effects of nuclear attack. One Year Later refers to the "nuclear winter" of the postattack period, in which the entire world suffers a lowering of temperature severe enough to induce winter in the Northern Hemisphere. This biological disaster of unprecedented dimensions would destroy all social systems, agricultural systems, and ecosystems. Ironically, even in a unilateral, all-out nuclear attack that met with no response, both the attacked *and* the attacker would suffer the biological disasters of radical climate change, deadly global radioactive fallout, and severe ozone depletion.

THE DAY BEFORE: UNINTENTIONAL NUCLEAR WAR

The world nuclear weapons system has evolved into a hair-trigger explosive due, in part, to the complexity of the system, the high state of international tension, and the premium placed on time by the increased technological sophistication of these weapons systems. The dynamics of the nuclear arms race is itself continually destabilizing. Each increment of either offensive or defensive capability triggers a matching and overcoming response. Mutually Assured Destruction (MAD) or deterrence strategy is based on terror (the words "deterrence" and "terror" have the same root), which seems to have led to mutually assured delusions and mutually reinforced misconceptions. Because of mutual suspicion, the dynamics of the nuclear arms race makes the search for guaranteed invulnerability—"Star Wars" defenses—a powerful destabilizing source. If deterrence were to be really effective, it would require trust, understanding, and communication, all presently lacking. In fact, strategic and doctrinal contradictions are themselves a source of destabilization and crisis.

The lack of communication in the very broadest sense is the major source of crisis. Assumptions of intent, credibility problems, contradictory doctrines, coercive bargaining, the use of nuclear alerts, and demonstrations of resolve—threats of all kinds, from low-key probes to bluff calling—all are examples of failures to communicate. They can lead to catalytic events and catalytic war. When one side views stability as superiority and the other side views it as parity, then the problem of noncommunication is fundamental. The division of the world into two primary antagonists increasingly dominated by group-think, whereby good is assumed by one and evil ascribed to the other, is itself a stage for crisis.

In an environment of distrust and noncommunication, the autonomy of a world weapon system already subject to inherent technological problems of speed, size, and complexity increases the probability of an accidental nuclear war. Some may argue that the probability of an accidental nuclear war is very small, but the risk is unacceptable because the consequences are so great. This zero-infinity risk problem has a low probability of accidental occurrence but an unacceptably high cost. A nuclear war would represent the highest possible cost for the entire world. Every effort must be made to avoid it.

Confidence-Building Measures or CBM's (1975) have not mitigated tension and distrust. The Hot-Line Agreement (1963), the Agreement to Reduce the Risk of Nuclear War (1971), and the Prevention of Nuclear War Agreement (1973) were all designed to increase communication and avoid war. At the first UN Special Session on Disarmament, UNSSOD I, the General Assembly proposed steps to insure "the prevention of attacks which take place by accident, miscalculation, or communication failure." The real paths chosen have led in the opposite direction.

Serious credibility problems underlie much of the present NATO strategy: Would conventional war lead to nuclear use? Would limited nuclear war be extended to general nuclear war? Does a first-use or flexible response strategy deter conventional attack? Nuclear war has no conventions, no workable systems of crisis management for its prevention.

The UNSSOD I declaration on the prevention of accidental nuclear war has both technological and political feasibility. It is not in the interest of either of the superpowers to be drawn into an act of mutual annihilation; neither NATO nor the Warsaw Pact adopts a doctrine of mutual suicide. While it is in nobody's interest to have an unintentional nuclear war, the mutual confidence that might emerge from attempts to circumvent accidental war could contribute to achieving a significant reduction, if not elimination, of nuclear and conventional weapons, and, ultimately, to a weapons-free world and a state of world peace.

The danger of nuclear war has radically increased due to a combination of political and technological factors. In particular, an accidental or unintentional nuclear war is now much more plausible. Three main assumptions underlie our concern:

1. Unintentional, accident-initiated nuclear war or nuclear war initiated as a result of accidents or incidents that lead to military escalation is more likely than intentional war; yet, it should be preventable.

2. It is in everyone's interest to prevent unintentional nuclear war; therefore, it is not a conflictual international issue.

3. The possibility of unintentional war increases over time as a product of the numbers, complexity, and the nature of the nuclear weapons system itself, including the C^3I component. Computer software failure has increasing significance. The history of "false alerts" sufficiently emphasizes the danger.

Three main classes of accidents and incidents could trigger nuclear war:

1. Accidents in the information system.

2. Accidents involving human error, deviant behavior, miscalculation, or terrorism.

3. Accidents and incidents involving nuclear and/or conventional and chemical/biological weapons.

The classes of accidents may, in turn, be broken down to a number of modes, sequences, and scenarios. Much analysis has been done (Newcombe, 1983; Frei, 1983; Bereanu, 1983; Aldridge, 1983; Roderick and Magnussun, 1983). Some analysts have computed probabilities for various scenarios (Newcombe, 1983; Frei, 1983). As we have noted, "accidental nuclear war" may result not only from a pure accident but also from an escalation of a local conflict, third-party conflict, natural accident, acts of malice or madness, etc.

The following types of accidents or incidents could initiate an accidental or unintentional nuclear war:

A. *Accidents Involving Information:*
1. False alerts and alarms with decreasing response time (U.P.I., U.S. Congressional Report, Tuesday, 26 May 1981).
   a) Response time is decreasing, leading to "launch-on-warning" postures.
   b) Validation times are increasing due to complexity of system.
2. C^3I network complexity leads to virtual inevitability of "link" failure in the web or chain.
3. EMP chaos (electromagnetic pulse) could collapse nerve centers of C^3I.
4. Self-activation due to failure in software for early warning systems (EWS) triggers "false alerts." (The probability of failure is in fact an inherent characteristic of the total computer system [Bereanu, 1983]. It is a natural example of complexity entropy or information "noise.")

B. *Accidents/Incidents Involving People:*
1. Psychological failure of national leaders.
2. Psychological failure of weapons handlers.
3. Proliferation of nuclear weapons/devices.
4. Escalation of conventional, local, or small wars.
5. Terrorist acts of malice.
6. Predelegation of authority to launch or a conspiracy to usurp authority.

C. *Accidents Involving Weapons:*
1. Increased development of first-strike weapons. (Both the leader and the loser in this race become more prone to preemptive action.)
2. Nuclear weapons accidents. (There is a long history of such "broken arrows" [Lapp, 1962; Dumas, 1980].)
3. Nuclear and conventional weapons unreliability (Tsipis and Bunn, 1983; Aldridge, 1983).
4. Increased power and precision of conventional weapons (verification problem).
5. Increased use of missiles designed for both conventional and nuclear warheads, such as cruise missiles (verification problem).
6. Stockpiling and development of chemical and biological weapons (CBW); rapid development of DNA laboratories, including small commercial units.
7. Militarization of space; development of space-based weapons and/or ballistic missile defenses.
8. Nuclear proliferation and fuel-cycle vulnerability.

Much analysis has been done on these sixteen scenarios or modes for the induction of accidental nuclear war. It now appears that Class A is highly amenable to prevention/control technologies, as is Class C, numbers 1, 2, 3, and 8. Some sort of "third-party" initiative, perhaps the use of "black-box" detection devices, might prevent accidental nuclear war in the above cases. The other classes illustrate more difficult cases that must also concern us.

The various unintentional war scenarios involve the extreme complexities of human behavior, machine behavior—hardware and software—and human-machine interface behavior. Beyond this, they present subtle but extremely hazardous dangers inherent to the potential use of modern nuclear weapons systems by persons motivated by extreme malice and engaged in acts of existential terrorism or sabotage. Moreover, the scenario that could lead to nuclear war may not be triggered by an accidental use of nuclear devices, but by situations arising within conventional civil and military activities. Given a very low psychological threshold of anxiety during a period of great international tension, a major accident created by a failure in or sabotage of a nuclear power plant could lead to nuclear war. The deliberate release of a large quantity of radioactive waste or the physical dispersal of plutonium acquired by clandestine means could precipitate the use of nuclear weapons. Using missiles designed for nuclear warheads with conventional warheads could also lead to nuclear war, as could an inability to verify cruise missiles. Exocet and cruise missiles in the "smart" class could lock on to the wrong target.

Some new conventional weapons have such increased power and precision that their devastation effects appear very similar to those of tactical or theater nuclear weapons, without the radiation. A local conventional war in areas of great tension—the Middle East, India-Pakistan, South and North Korea, etc.—could escalate into a global nuclear war. We do not fully understand the linkages in catalytic war or the problem of common-mode failure in risk assumption in social or physical systems.

Very large civilian and military losses could induce escalation to a nuclear weapons response. New, extremely potent biological weapons whose initial dispersal is not verifiable, or natural outbreaks of an epidemic that could be interpreted as an attack represent such types of unintentional nuclear war. Terrorist activities and use of biogenetic agents become an increasingly plausible trigger for unintentional war.

Excellent opportunities for initiatives in the area of avoidance of unintentional nuclear war exist. Radiation affords relatively simple detection systems. The rate of throughput of a process from the original signal through verification and validation to communication could be monitored/verified through the use of tamper-proof black-box devices. Use of an international system such as NAVSTAR (some 17,300 terminals for a global navigation system by the U.S. military) could be extremely valuable. Methodologies such as event/fault tree analysis used in nuclear reactor safety studies could be adapted to both social and technical systems as an assessment technique. Environmental monitoring of social and technical milieus in search of problematic precursor events is yet another valuable technique. The multi-lingual international communication center recently created in New Zealand serves as a positive example of a general hot-line system.

Another method of safeguarding against unintentional nuclear war would equip all strategic missiles with "on-board" electronic devices that could activate a conventional explosion to abort missiles in flight. This would negate an accidental launching made in haste or in error. All missiles, including SLBM's, should be completely safeguarded against local commanders and activated only by heads of state. This would necessitate "override" devices under the control of heads of state. A treaty should prohibit "launch-on-warning" postures by removing short–flight-time "strategic" weapons that can hit the territory of either superpower. This would of course include "decapitation" weapons such as Pershing II's and cruise missiles. Forward-based strategic systems should be moved back by mutual verifiable agreement so as to increase launch and validation times. Crisis control management should be in the hands of third parties or joint superpower teams.

The idea of a joint U.S.-USSR information and crisis center was first proposed by Senator Sam Nunn of Georgia and the late Senator Henry Jackson of Washington. This kind of crisis control and management would access a global surveillance and monitoring system and make "hot lines" available to both heads of state. Such a system could not only mediate "accidents" but also could help prevent third-party/terrorist attacks.

Another device for the control of missiles is the so-called "permissive action link" or PAL, electromechanical locks that require a valid code to release warheads. These devices make it impossible for anyone to detonate a warhead without a specific electrical input from the head of state. By agreement both sides could equip their missiles with PAL's, as Robert McNamara recommended in his eighteen confidence-building steps toward disarmament (McNamara, 1983). The U.S. now has PAL's on all air- and ground-based missiles, but not on SLBM's.

The problem of horizontal proliferation could also be solved through a high level of cooperation in safeguarding methods by all nuclear reactor vendors. The USSR has the best record among such vendors by demanding ratification of the Non-Proliferation Treaty (NPT) prior to a sale and recovering and auditing waste. West Germany and France have been most irresponsible.

LAUNCH ON WARNING: A HAZARDOUS MYTH

After several years' debate and a review of thirty different basing modes—all designed to make the MX more invulnerable to a Soviet counterforce strike —the decision to proceed with 100 MX missiles in existing Minuteman silos makes no strategic sense. General Scowcroft, chairman of the President's Commission on Strategic Forces, seems to agree with this and has admitted the basing decision is political. This is the politics of the nuclear bully who has set out to force the other side to capitulate in the military balance. With their improved accuracy and the number of warheads per MX, these 100 new missiles will be equivalent to about 1000 Minuteman III missiles (Steinbrunner, 1984). Combining this with the existing 550 Minuteman III ICBM's gives the U.S. a total force of 1550 equivalent missiles. These figures, taken together with the decision to place Pershing II missiles in West Germany (and probably Alaska) and the revelations of the "decapitation" doctrine in NSDD-32, represent an exceedingly destabilizing factor. Perceptions of increased vulnerability by the USSR, together with decreased times for verification and validation, will inevitably lead the USSR to a "launch-on-warning" or "launch-on-attack" posture. In turn, the U.S., by placing its major new weapon in a fixed silo mode, has also increased its own vulnerability to a preemptive strike. The ratio of warhead to silo for an assured kill (given advanced accuracies) is about 2.5; taking only silos that house advanced missiles, both countries have now reached this ratio (Steinbrunner, 1984).

There is little doubt that both sides are considering "launch-on-warning" systems. Both believe in the vulnerability of their ICBM's despite large uncertainties that a preemptive strike would be successful (Tsipis and Bunn, 1983). Therefore it would appear that we are once again dealing with myths—the myth of ICBM vulnerability and the myth of "launch-on-warning" infallibility. The real problems and uncertainties of attack and response in these two modes of preemption and "launch on warning" have increased the risks of unintentional nuclear war. In strategic doctrine an unauthorized or accidental launch is termed a Type I Error, while failure to launch on predetermined targets is a Type II Error. Both require a different set of controls, chain of command, and opposite information flows. It would seem impossible to maximize the avoidance of both types of error simultaneously. The greater the number of negative controls or redundant information/decision procedures necessary before launch, the slower the response to orders to launch.

In the case of fixed silo missiles, there is the problem of attack timing. This combined with pinpoint accuracy is absolutely necessary to avoid the problem of fratricide, so the attack sequence is timed to avoid destruction of new incoming missiles by exploding ones. Small timing errors would actually benefit the recipient of a "launch-on-warning" attack in a mutual "launch-on-warning" war because ICBM's are more vulnerable in boost phase out of their silos, than in them. Later they would be subjected to high winds and debris from ground-level explosions. The time of launch is twenty-five to thirty minutes for both sides. Because the two minutes necessary to make a "launch-on-warning" decision would allow the other side the tactic of communications disruption by EMP, the command systems could be seriously disabled. The necessary measures of assessment, identification, retaliation decision, and launch could fail. SLBM's could disrupt C^3I by exploding large nuclear weapons in the stratosphere creating electromagnetic pulses (EMP) that would disrupt or destroy a great deal of electric and electronic equipment; a second pulse resulting from a short disruption of the earth's magnetic field would disrupt land communications. The effect of such an explosion would be much like a highly accelerated lightning bolt.

Theoretically, in the absence of EMP, the existing U.S. C^3I system, supplemented by infrared sensors on geosynchrous satellites, could sense such an attack with some precision within minutes. Further evidence of attack would be provided within fifteen minutes by the Ballistic Missile Early Warning System (BMEWS) radars in Alaska, Greenland, and Britain. U.S. antiballistic radar in Grand Forks, North Dakota, would detect the attack five minutes later. False alerts from these systems seem endemic (Bereanu, 1983). Twenty minutes of an available time of twenty-five to thirty minutes would have elapsed, providing just enough time to launch a retaliatory attack of U.S. ICBM's. Without EMP disruption, both sides would have time to launch their ICBM's at the empty silos of the other, assuming the case of a preemptive attack and existing redundant communications systems. EMP itself would constitute a preemptive attack and SLBM's could be launched, compounding the nonsense.

In a large-scale prior-EMP "attack" the missiles of the country attacked could conceivably be destroyed in their boost phase. This would render "launch on warning" impractical. There are provisions to "harden" and protect all the key components of the U.S. C^3I system, including the important emergency ultrahigh frequency equipment on aircraft used for airborne command, but even this effort will not provide a reliable launch-on-attack system (Steinbrunner, 1984). Even without EMP, the command systems of both superpowers are vulnerable to direct attack by a minimal number of weapons, which is probably the preferred strategy.

The superpowers' military commanders inevitably tend toward preemptive use under the tension of a prolonged crisis. A clear "no first-use" policy or treaty by both would help eliminate this, particularly if supported by a "third-party" validation system. Nevertheless the vulnerability of overall command systems has very dangerous implications. One of its results might be to give more autonomy to individual commanders, greatly compounding the risk of a "false" launch. This already appears to have been done in the case of SLBM commanders. Once again, the conflict between Type I and Type II error tends to favor the latter; the prevention of "accidental" unauthorized use will be sacrificed for "efficiency" of response.

The Brookings Institute has developed a complex mathematical model that attempts to assign scores for the effectiveness of negative and positive controls of a command post of an ICBM squadron. The model tends to reinforce the conclusion that some disruption sufficient to pressure the military commanders to launch with insufficient negative information will occur. Preemptive strikes on strategic command systems are thus the major opportunity strategy. It seems to be forgotten that SIOP-6 recognizes this priority and "decapitation" includes it. Pershing II's are almost ideal for this function. Scientists from the Brookings Institute fail to make the connection between real existing plans and their abstract analyses, i.e., between politics and science. However, they have made a contribution in noting that once a nuclear war has begun (after the first fifty to one hundred explosions), strategic command coherence and coordination will probably fail; thus individual military commanders will pressure their political leaders for more autonomy or for a quick decision to launch. The risk is to "lose." All of this increases the dangers of the escalation of a limited to a protracted war, and the vain attempt to build "launch-on-warning" systems, despite their impracticality. The latter is merely another form of the arms race, as are "Star Wars" developments. It seems inevitable that both sides might provide autonomy to SLBM commanders because of their "second-strike" and anticommand system functions. Thus instead of two ultimate decisionmakers, we will have one hundred, each powerful enough to destroy the entire U.S. or USSR.

In the previous analysis of the KAL-007 incident, we have suggested that the evidence supports a conspiracy theory on the part of the U.S. We have not concluded that this is true; however, if our analysis of Reagan policies and programs for fighting and winning a nuclear war to destroy the Soviet Union is true, then this and other conspiracies are possible. If the belief that such a war is winnable, survivable, and necessary is combined with the capacity for conspiracy, then could an "accident" become intentional? With Soviet submarines equipped with cruise missiles deployed near the U.S., and Pershing II's and other short-flight "decapitation" weapons near the USSR, one "false alert" could launch a nuclear war.

The televised news of 20 May 1984 contained references to a speech by former Defense Minister Marshal Ustinov that threatened to station Soviet SLBM's, with eight- to ten-minute flight times to critical targets, off the American coast. The Soviets justified their actions as a quid pro quo for Pershing II missiles. "Missile Conferences Called to Evaluate Possible Threats" require a threshold time of seven minutes to resolve false alerts. (This threshold time has been derived from data acquired through the U.S.

Freedom of Information Act [Crissey, 1984]). Two of the most serious false alerts, one caused by a microchip failure and the other by a mislabeled computer tape, occurred in 1979 and 1980 (Wallace, 1984). In 1983 alone, "false alerts" or alarms occurred every two days out of three, for a total of about 250. During a political crisis involving the superpowers or their surrogates, obviously the most dangerous period, such false alerts took between six and eight minutes to resolve. The collection, processing, and transmission of the initial signal takes about two to three minutes (Steinbrunner, 1984). If we assume that it takes at least that time to validate this signal, then we again have a threshold of about seven minutes, below which a "launch-on-warning" or "launch-them-or-lose-them" posture is adopted. Statistical analysis has calculated that a simulated event, a false alert leading to a "launch-on-warning" response, has a 95 percent chance of occurring on or before the eighth day of a crisis (Wallace, 1984).

This calculation is optimistic. A very complex system operating during a crisis would most likely experience an enhanced rate of false alerts that would increase throughout the entire period of the crisis. The most comprehensive study of false alerts verified this by using statistics derived only from NORAD. If we assume that the Soviets also experience false alerts during a crisis, and that their system approximates the monitoring capability of the U.S.'s, then the probability of an accidental nuclear war occurring during a crisis when a "launch-on-attack" posture is in effect becomes very high. The uncertainties of these analyses do not alter the extreme hazard of unintentional nuclear war, particularly during a crisis.

A permanent state of crisis now exists between the superpowers due, in large part, to the policies of the Reagan administration. Both sides feel pressure to move to a "launch-on-warning" and "launch-them-or-lose-them" posture. The conflicts in the Middle East, in particular, the Iran-Iraq war and the bombing of tankers, are gradually bringing the superpowers into confrontation in that region where they both have vital interests, and thus intensify the danger.

Both Pershing II's and Soviet SLBM's positioned off U.S. coastal waters have flight times of eight to ten minutes—just outside the threshold time for a "launch-on-warning" response. Arguing from a general comparison of U.S. and Soviet early warning systems, the USSR may be placed in a "launch-on-warning" posture by times longer than seven minutes. Cruise missiles, particularly the advanced type equipped with "stealth," have long flight times because of their slow speed, but they can remain undetected and, therefore, unverified until they are very close to targets. Our argument thus remains unchanged. Euromissiles, coupled with warfighting plans and decapitation strikes, are excessively destabilizing and will tend to force the USSR into a "launch-on-warning" posture.

TWO WORST-CASE SCENARIOS

The U.S. and/or the USSR suffers an alarm in its detection system. This alarm indicates that a missile may be on a flight path to Washington and/or Moscow, with a calculated flight time of five minutes. "Conferences Called to Evaluate Possible Threats" currently require seven minutes to validate this alarm. False or real, this particular alarm occurs at a time of heightened superpower tension, possibly due to some international incident. What happens next?

The "hot line" would probably be used to request verification; however its use would be a dangerous gamble for either side. Since a "decapitation" strike might well be the preferred first use of nuclear weapons, why would either side admit that it had indeed launched such an attack? The attack could also result from a "false alarm," or it could be a real attack, launched by a malicious third party. It could be a mock missile designed to initiate a nuclear war. What would the president of the U.S or the premier of the USSR do in the above event?

Because of the seriousness and increasing likelihood of such a dilemma, a means to avoid such a grave misunderstanding must be found and implemented quickly. A necessary first step is pull-back. All launchers capable of hitting strategic targets must be moved back well beyond the seven-minute launch time. All launchers that can defy detection should not be deployed or tested. The deployment and testing of cruise missiles, particularly the sea-launched, air-launched, and advanced "stealth" types, should be frozen. While these weapons are relatively slow, they are difficult to detect and verify.

According to New York Congressman Tom Weiss's letter to Bill Wickersham, executive director of the World Federalist Association, Washington, D.C., dated 15 July 1984, "An officer of the Navy Department informed me that with the support of as few as three other officers, the Commander of a Trident submarine *could launch an unauthorized attack against Soviet targets* [Italics mine]." The commander must enlist the support of the radio operator and communications officer to announce that he has received an official, coded transmission to launch from the president. Two other officers must authenticate this coded message by checking a special code locked in a two-man control safe. Thus, a conspiracy would involve a total of four officers and a radio operator, but the latter need not be party to it. It only takes about fifteen minutes to launch the missiles by command of three officers, the commander and two other executives. On a "CBS Reports" show in 1981, Rear Admiral Powell Carter, director of the Navy's Warfare Division, admitted that such a scenario could occur (*Defense Monitor*, 1985a, p. 6). According to the authors of SIOP-6, the crew, in theory, could refuse to take orders for an authorized launch without later charges of mutiny

(Pringle and Arkin, 1983); however, this is not likely.

Given this scenario, the commander of a U.S. SLBM submarine is the third most powerful person in the world, as Norman Cousins once observed. Under certain conditions, a Trident submarine commander has the right to launch full firepower: twenty-four missiles, each equipped with eight MIRV's that have 475 kilotons of yield per warhead and hard-target kill probabilities of 91 percent against a 5000 psi silo. This represents 192 deliverable warheads, each capable of a force about thirty-five times as powerful as the Hiroshima bomb. Targeted on cities of over 100,000 and major political, military, and industrial sites, the total deliverable 91.2 megatons would destroy the USSR as a modern state. Depending on warning time, the Soviets would probably launch their entire arsenal at the U.S. World War III would be over in thirty minutes; civilization would end thirty minutes after a "false alarm."

The history of official recognition of the danger of accidental nuclear war extends from former President Kennedy's warning that nuclear war might begin through "accident, miscalculation or madness," through UN declarations, and, more recently, to the U.S. National Academy of Sciences resolution. The academy's unanimous resolution, passed in 1983, specifically resolved "to reduce the risk of nuclear war by accident miscalculation." At the first UN Special Session on Disarmament (UNSSOD I), a General Assembly resolution unanimously urged "the prevention of attacks which take place, by accident, miscalculation or communications failure." These major resolutions cover the various modes of accidental war initiation.

INITIATIVES FOR CRISIS CONTROL

In addition to the existing Hot-Line Agreement and the "Accidents Measures" agreement of 1971, France proposed a crisis mediation and control system that could assist in avoiding accidental nuclear war at UNSSOD I in 1978. A UN-operated agency, the International Satellite Monitoring Agency (ISMA), would use satellites and receiving stations to monitor disarmament and security agreements, investigate specific incidents, and assist in treaty verification and violation. U.S. Defense Secretary Caspar Weinberger also made proposals to update and improve communications between the superpowers, and some were agreed upon 17 July 1984. Other aspects of Weinberger's proposals have yet to be adopted.

At a speech at Washington State University on 22 October 1982, the late Senator Henry Jackson proposed the establishment of a much more ambitious, permanent Joint U.S.-USSR Crisis Consultation Center. On 15 June 1984, a proposal by Senators Nunn and Warner to create centers in Washington and Moscow to maintain constant communication received a vote of eighty-two to zero as a nonbinding amendment to the defense authorization bill.

Several other imaginative proposals, such as the Nuclear Age Peace Foundation's Accidental War Assessment Center, emerged in congressional hearings in 1984. Genevieve Nowlin, in a letter to the Nuclear Peace Foundation of Santa Barbara, California, proposed an unarmed, multinational space patrol similar to ISMA, but with some organizational and functional improvements.

CONCLUSIONS

Command, Control, Communications, and Intelligence (C^3I) involve computer linkages between various sensing systems on the ground and in space. The information mode of accidental nuclear war has been associated with computer hardware, software, or operator error. All three types of errors have caused serious false alerts. Of the three types of missile conferences used to alert response—display conference for routine errors, missile threat assessment for serious alerts, and attack conference—missile threat conferences, the second level, have occurred on seven known occasions (Bereanu, 1983; also see unpublished paper, "Computer System Reliability and Nuclear War" by Alan Borning of Computer Sciences, University of Washington, Seattle, 22 October 1984, for details).

Despite redundancy and other reliability improvements, computer error seems unavoidable. Recent disclosures about faulty microchips, supplied to the Pentagon by Texas Instruments and placed in multiple systems, only hint at the extent of possible technological problems. The premium placed on time, accuracy, and perhaps first-strike requires even greater reliance on our C^3I system. Space-based defense systems ("Star Wars") utilizing exotic weapons will have to be launched about ninety seconds after sensors observe Soviet missile launches. This decision will have to be made by computers. The possibility of common-mode and system failure during a period of international crisis, possibly accompanied by mutually reinforcing alerts by the two sides, will allow little leeway for computer error. In addition, the Strategic Computing Initiative (SCI) being developed by DARPA proposes to research and design total robotic war, at least at battlefield levels.

A purely technological peace fix does not seem credible because solutions require altered policies and perceptions and must embody trust, reinforced by communication and good will. Technology can, at best, only serve policy directions. Current technological development aims almost totally at increasing effective kill by shortening response speed to command, improving accuracy of hit, and safeguarding integrity of strategy. The Global Positioning System (GPS), with its eighteen Navstar satellites, will apparently make every weapon in the U.S. nuclear arsenal so accurate that even low-yield battlefield weapons could have high hard-target kill capacity (to eventually allow a CEP of 10 meters). Time-urgent targets will become seductive.

WHO'S IN CHARGE?

The competing requirements governing the use of nuclear arms present essential contradictions. Missile readiness to fire and speed of release conflict with the control necessary to prevent an inadvertent nuclear launch. The chain of command in the European theater emanates from the president of the U.S. In a period of crisis, it is virtually certain that this hierarchy of control would break down, leading to a delegation of authority in a "launch-them-or-lose-them" case. We suspect that General Bernard Rogers, commander-in-chief of U.S. forces in Europe, already has predelegated authority.

The entire issue of who has the authority to initiate a nuclear war remains a matter of concern because of the ambiguities in the procedure. Presumably, the president and the secretary of defense, as the National Command Authority (NAM), have official control over nuclear weapons. At all times, the president carries with him a secret code card that identifies him to the military and enables him to order an attack. However, when the president fell victim to an assassination attempt in early 1981, he discovered that not only had the FBI retrieved his code, but also that the Joint Chiefs of Staff (JCS) had an exact duplicate (*Defense Monitor*, 1985, p. 2). Should the president become incapacitated, Vice President George Bush, chairman of the JCS General John Vessey, Secretary of Defense Caspar Weinberger, and Deputy Secretary of Defense William Taft IV all have these codes that would become authoritative, as they did during the president's cancer operation.

In the event of a decision to launch, the president issues an Emergency Action Message (EAM) that allows the secretary of defense to carry out a specific attack plan. His directives then proceed to those officers or officials who hold the codes necessary to arm air- and land-based nuclear weapons, and those weapon commanders who can carry out the arm and launch orders.

The EAM also passes through the JCS to the Strategic Air Command (SAC), which, in turn, communicates the message to an airborne command center, the National Emergency Airborne Command Post (NEACP) or "kneecap." There are four NEACP aircraft in the U.S. and similar aircraft in all military theaters of the world.

All bomber weapons and land-based missiles, whether intermediate or intercontinental, have permissive action links (PAL's), electromechanical locks that require a proper code to arm the nuclear warheads; sea-launched weapons do not. It seems likely that at the earliest signs of possible conflict, the PAL codes would be released to launch crews. PAL codes operate under a "two-man rule": the ten ICBM's controlled by each underground Launch Control Center (LCC) cannot be fired unless two officers sitting twelve feet apart receive the "enabling" PAL codes and launch order. Should they receive such an order, the officers would remove codes from a red metal box, verify the message, and simultaneously insert keys into locks above their desks. Actual launch requires two valid launch commands and thus involves a total of four officers. A second vote by an LCC, in effect, orders launch.

As weapons systems proliferate in an atmosphere of enhanced tension, such complexity itself becomes a potential source of unintentional nuclear war. While the process involved in launching a strike predates the Reagan administration, new factors such as the technological hair-trigger in the context of the "secret agenda" render the present situation more dangerous than at any time before. Active preparation for nuclear war began as a response to the cold war and so predates the Reagan administration, but now the Reagan administration has reinvented the cold war.

Since February of 1961, modified civilian jets known as EC-135's have conducted ongoing secret missions under the code name "Looking Glass." Every eight hours, one of these planes takes off from Offutt or Ellsworth Air Force Base, carrying aboard a U.S. Air Force general, a battle staff, and operations and communications officers. The jet flies a top-secret pattern and always lands at an undisclosed airfield.

Although never stated, it is strongly suspected that the general aboard the "Looking Glass" flight can independently authorize a strike if communications fail. The EC-135 has all the attack authentication codes on board. Hypothetically at least, the "Looking Glass" operation could order the launch of all Minuteman missiles. Only the general's inability to issue an "emergency action message," and the military's adherence to the "two-man rule" stand as the major safeguards against such an action.

The "Looking Glass" operation provides the single command post designed to survive a nuclear attack; yet experts do not believe it to be invulnerable. Because it is guided by civil air traffic control, its location could be discovered. Under certain accidental circumstances, "Looking Glass" could become the prime decisionmaker, but its vulnerability might allow only a fifteen-minute period in which to make the decision to launch after a real or alleged enemy attack. While the U.S. has complex and redundant operational plans that initiate a war, its capacity to quickly call off or end a war is limited. "Controlled escalation" requires perfectible and invulnerable communications between the superpowers—an unrealistic expectation.

Accidental initiation and escalation of nuclear war are much more probable than intentional and controlled war scenarios. In reality, SIOP-6 is not a plan for limited war, the euphemistic "controlled escalation"; instead, it is an immutable set of plans for all-out nuclear war. Nevertheless, the president and the Pentagon live in an Alice-in-Wonderland nuclear world, secure in their mythology of strategy and technological infallibility. They cannot have it both ways. Placing a premium on warfighting cannot be reconciled with war prevention and "controlled escalation." Fortunately, positive initiatives that enhance rather than threaten security are available.

At the very minimum, a pull-back treaty would accommodate resolution of alerts by providing adequate response time. A mutual and verifiable treaty must prohibit weapons developments that destabilize alert resolution.

THE DAY AFTER

A nuclear explosion has three distinct, direct or immediate effects—blast, heat, and radiation. The explosion itself lasts for only one-millionth of a second. After a small delay, the incredible fireball is engulfed by a mushroom-shaped cloud. Each nuclear explosion creates a specific range of effects depending on its explosive yield and its height above ground zero. Many calculations and studies have examined the effects of heat, blast, and radiation by utilizing simulation war scenarios or pictures that delineate the type and number of weapons, their targets, and the spatial factors—surface or airborne—of actual nuclear attacks (NAS, 1975; Glasstone and Dolan, 1977; ACDA, 1979; Lewis, 1979; OTA, 1979; Rotblat, 1981; Ambio Advisory Group, 1982; Woodwell, 1982; Bergstrom et al., 1983).

These analyses deal with what is termed the lethal area, i.e., the radius in which a certain percentage of the inhabitants will be killed or injured (termed Lethal Dose Percentage or LD%), based on the population data or numbers and density of people exposed. Using population data obtained from the U.S. Bureau of Census, one can derive percentages that address the impact of a nuclear attack on the ten largest cities, which represent over 57 million people in 1980, or on all cities according to the Standard Metropolitan Statistical Areas (SMSA's). While the physics that transforms the nuclear energy into the multiple effects of blast, heat, and radiation is complex, with all this information one can calculate the number of deaths from pressure shock, literal incineration, and deadly radiation—a grisly picture, despite the cool quantification of physicists and engineers. Many deaths and injuries result indirectly from the collapse of buildings and the shattering of glass in an environment of violent winds and raging fires. Table 5 gives the numbers and totals of persons killed and injured by each of the effects for all the major cities in the U.S. Estimates for each effect are separate so there is no double counting.

In Table 5, the figures given under blast effects include not only all those killed within an area in which the overpressure is five pounds per

TABLE 5

EFFECT	FATALITIES	INJURIES	COMBINED CASUALTIES
	(MILLIONS)	(MILLIONS)	
Blast	50–80	30	80–110
Thermal Radiation (Heat)	0.4–14	0.3–12	0.7–26
Fires	0.7–7	0.7–7	1.3–13
Ionizing Radiation			
(Early)	12–18	—	12–18
(Local Fallout)			
(Delayed)	39–55	—	39–55
Totals (Millions)	102–174	31–50	133–222

Source: Derived from data in *Nuclear Winter* by Mark Harwell (New York: Springer Verlag, 1984).

square inch (5 psi), but also include people killed by indirect effects; the figures for the effects of thermal radiation only include those outside this area. In general, about 50 percent of the total casualties are people killed and injured due to direct and indirect effects of blast. Casualties from thermal radiation and fires are not included under blast or ionizing radiation effects. You can only die or be killed once.

Casualties in this anticities scenario (countervalue attack) range between 133 and 222 million persons, in effect nearly the entire U.S. population. Table 5's nuclear war scenario is derived from a Swedish Academy of Sciences study (Ambio Advisory Group, 1982; Peterson, 1983) in which a total of 14,750 warheads were exploded with a combined yield of 5650 megatons worldwide. Mark Harwell refined the Ambio scenario to reflect the precise number of warheads and their yield on a specific number and kind of targets.

The Day After creates a world of nuclear arson, nuclear fragmentation, and nuclear storms and fires, followed by massive outbreaks of infectious diseases. The social service systems of health, sanitation, transportation, and energy are destroyed. To dare to speak of survival or of winning under such circumstances is the ultimate obscenity and the supreme inhumanity.

The short-term effects of nuclear explosions, blast, fire, and radiation, have received considerable study. After all, we have two "experiments" on human beings—Hiroshima and Nagasaki—together with numerous atmospheric and ground-level tests of different weapons. A new study focuses on the longer-term effects on climate. Large quantities of particles thrown into the atmosphere from volcanic eruptions have yielded fairly reliable models that researchers used to study regional and global climatic effects of nuclear war. Other work suggested that nuclear explosions could cause massive fires that generated huge quantities of sooty smoke (Crutzen and Birks, 1982). The combustion of widely used synthetic organics would release exceedingly toxic chemicals (Esposito et al., 1980).

ONE YEAR LATER: THE NUCLEAR WINTER OF OUR DISCONTENT

The phenomenon known as "nuclear winter" describes the radical change in climate and cooling effects that last for up to one year following a large nuclear exchange. Vast areas of our planet Earth would endure prolonged darkness, freezing conditions even in summer, violent winds, toxic smog, large increases in ultraviolet radiation due to ozone depletion, and persistent, deadly radioactive fallout. This phenomenon connotes a vision of biblical apocalypse, specifically, the ecological holocaust to follow the final battle of Armageddon. The total effect embraces the combined collapse of social services—food, health, transportation, power, and sanitation—with the consequences of very large numbers of cases of hypothermia, radiation and other poisonings, and epidemics of infectious diseases known only to history. The Four Horsemen of the Apocalypse would ride rampant. Human deaths would number in the hundreds of millions and some species would become extinct. A serious question persists whether civilization and the biosphere itself would survive. Geological theory moves in full circle, from catastrophism through uniformism and back to the theory of a catastrophic change. Nuclear war has a catastrophic impact on climate.

A SHORT HISTORY OF THE CONCEPT OF NUCLEAR WINTER

The concept of "nuclear winter" derives from theories of climate change, particularly rapid climate change. Most scientists who have studied the nuclear winter phenomenon have largely ignored, or denied recognition to, the major contribution made by climatologists: a rich literature on the history and science of climate change (Bryson, 1984).

Climatologists study the natural and unnatural mechanisms underlying climate change. Their research has indicated that human societies have made major impacts on climate by: (1) changing the carbon dioxide (CO_2) levels of the atmosphere through the large-scale combustion of fossil fuels; (2) decreasing the ozone level of the stratosphere through the use of ozone-destroying chemicals that diffuse ten to fifteen miles above the earth's surface, thus increasing the amount of ultraviolet radiation reaching the earth; and (3) releasing dust into the atmosphere through mechanical actions and large-scale soil erosions. Nuclear explosions affect climate in all three ways at once.

To study the effects of large quantities of dust in the atmosphere, climatologists use data from a "natural" producer of particle pollution—volcanic eruptions (Lamb, 1971). The study of the correlation between large volcanic eruptions and pervasive climate change, and the evolution of deserts into "climates of hunger" combine with ecosystem stress theory to become the heart of the nuclear winter analysis.

Carbon dioxide has a warming effect on the atmosphere—the "greenhouse effect"—but it redistributes the total energy received by the atmosphere and the earth instead of changing it. Dusts, however, can cool the earth and the atmosphere by deflecting a significant portion of solar energy that otherwise would be received.

Volcanic eruptions provide a natural simulation of nuclear war by emitting huge quantities of dust (ash) into the atmosphere. All the historic, enormous volcanic eruptions, from Tambora (1815) and Krakatoa (1883) in Indonesia, to Mount St. Helens and El Chichon (1982), Mexico, in the Western Hemisphere, had observable effects on climate. Tambora's eruption produced the famous "year without a summer" in 1816. Throughout the middle latitudes of the Northern Hemisphere, temperatures averaged about 1.8° F colder than normal. In England, the average summer temperature fell to 5° colder than normal. Certain regions experienced virtual continual rain from May to October, 1816. New England and eastern Canada had snow in June and frosts in all twelve months of 1816. Crops died or failed to ripen and rotted in the fields. Northern Ireland and Wales suffered serious food shortages that led to food riots. Lord Byron, in a poem about Tambora, gives a remarkable prophecy of "nuclear winter":

DARKNESS

by Lord Byron

(This was written in June 1816, following the eruption of the volcano Tambora in Indonesia in 1815. The eruption had the greatest atmospheric effects ever to be recorded. Though Tambora is in the Southern Hemisphere, Europe had its coldest known summer the following year and there were worldwide crop failures.)

I had a dream, which was not all a dream.
The bright sun was extinguish'd, and the stars
Did wander darkling in the eternal space,
Rayless, and pathless, and the icy earth
Swung blind and blackening in the moonless air;
Morn came and went—and came, and brought no day,
And men forgot their passions in the dread
Of this their desolation; and all hearts
Were chill'd into a selfish prayer for light.
And they did live by watch fires—and the thrones,

The palaces of crowned kings—the huts
The habitations of all things which dwell,
Were burnt for beacons; cities were consumed;
And men were gather'd round their blazing homes
To look once more into each other's face.
Happy were those who dwelt within the eye
Of the volcanos, and their mountain-torch:
A fearful hope was all the world contain'd;
Forests were set on fire—but hour by hour
They fell and faded—and the crackling trunks.

Our planet Earth retains its capacity to sustain life through its life-supporting atmosphere, its environmental resources, and its ultimate, life-nourishing source of energy, the sun. An intricate web of self-regulating processes controls the exchange of matter and energy to maintain the dynamic equilibrium necessary for viability. The atmosphere serves as a window to light, a blanket to heat, and a supplier of oxygen. The earth is a greenhouse, and the fundamental process that is the source of all its life is photosynthesis. Anything that seriously interferes with this almost miraculous combination of sunlight, green plants or plankton, and carbon dioxide that produces biomass— the vast complex order of living things, from plants to animals, in the biosphere—can threaten the basis and continuity of life. Particulates in the atmosphere produce an antigreenhouse effect.

Many other natural and humanly induced "catastrophic" events beyond volcanic eruptions yielded data that elucidated the "nuclear winter" concept. The very large H-bomb tests, such as those on Bikini Atoll, 1 March 1953, as well as hundreds of other atmospheric nuclear tests of groundbursts and airbursts provided information on the quantity of dust, the nature and dimensions of cratering, and the pattern, nature, and dimensions of radioactive fallout. The atomic bombings of Hiroshima and Nagasaki and the mass fire-bombings of German and Japanese cities in World War II furnished data on firestorm and incineration patterns. Detailed study of dust production and distribution from the Mount St. Helens and El Chichon eruptions provided facts on residence time and global distribution of particles. Ozone depletion due to stratospheric testing of H-bombs in the early 1960s buttressed the general theory of ozone depletion due to manmade chemicals reaching the stratosphere. Global radiation from the large Chinese bomb tests over the past twenty years proved very valuable in analyzing global fallout patterns. Large forest fire, earthquakes, and huge urban fires such as the great Chicago fire were still another source of data.

The modern development of the "nuclear winter" hypothesis probably began in 1971, as Carl Sagan, noted Cornell University astronomer, studied the atmosphere of the planet Mars through monitors aboard the satellite

Mariner 9. The satellite carried an infrared interpherometric spectrometer, an instrument designed to sense temperatures at various levels above the planet's surface. This instrument (and others) recorded the surface cooling of Mars over a period of three months. This cooling could be attributed to violent global dust storms that quickly spread over the entire planetary surface. Sagan connected the planetary or at least hemispheric climate change with the presence of widespread dust, possibly derived from huge storms.

Sagan enlisted the assistance of two of his students, James B. Pollack and O. Brian Toon, who worked for NASA at the Ames Research Laboratories. They developed computer models to measure temperature changes following volcanic eruptions. In 1982 they were joined by a brilliant atmospheric scientist, Richard P. Turco, from a Los Angeles think-tank, R and D Associates. With the addition of a fourth participant, Thomas P. Ackerman of Ames, the group of Turco, Toon, Ackerman, Pollack, and Sagan became known as TTAPS.

The climate change study derived further impetus from the revival of the catastrophic geological theory. Geologic evidence indicates the mass extinction of many species about sixty-five million years ago. In 1980 a group of scientists suggested that a very large asteroid may have struck the earth at about that time in the Cretaceous period (Alvarez et al., *Science* 108, 1980, pp. 1095-1108). The National Academy of Sciences (NAS) and the Office of Technological Assessment (OTA) had studied the effects of large-scale nuclear war in 1975 and 1979, respectively; however, Alvarez's asteroid hit theory formulated the hypothesis that the creation of huge quantities of dust and their ensuing dust clouds would affect weather. (Alvarez et al., 1980).

In a parallel and significant development, the Swedish environmental journal *Ambio* commissioned Paul Crutzen, a Dutch scientist at the Mainz Institute of Chemistry and the Max Planck University in Berlin, to do a study on the ecological consequences of nuclear war. Crutzen, a famous atmospheric scientist who had unraveled the chemistry of ozone vulnerability, enlisted the assistance of a visiting colleague, John Birks of the University of Colorado. The *Ambio* nuclear war scenario presumed that some 14,747 nuclear warheads would release 5742 megatons of explosives—about half the world's total strategic nuclear arsenals—over most Northern Hemisphere cities with populations over 100,000.

Crutzen and Birks made a critical and revolutionary contribution to the nuclear winter theory when they shifted their attention from dust to smoke (soot). This emphasis had eluded all the earlier analyses, including those of Sagan and the TTAPS team. When Sagan observed the huge dust storms' effect on Mars, the cooling he noted was not that significant. The giant volcanoes of Tambora and Krakatoa had only reduced average temperatures about 1° C; yet they produced a total quantity of dust that almost equaled the amount produced by a very large nuclear war. Smoke/soot has a far greater capacity to absorb sunlight than dust, particularly volcanic dust. Crutzen and Birks had not computed the climate impacts of smoke and soot with any degree of accuracy, but Richard Turco used their research in developing the much more sophisticated model used by the TTAPS team. Introducing smoke into the calculations altered the conclusions derived from a very complex, if one-dimensional (using only vertical, not lateral, movement), model with a great number of nuclear war scenarios. Using the variables of a large or small attack directed mainly at weapons, cities, or both, the team monitored the effects of each case to study the climate changes. Essentially, they studied the production of dusts and smoke from multiple sources, the particle size distribution, the residence time movement, and position in the atmosphere (troposphere and stratosphere). These particulate properties enabled them to compute the amount of attenuated (reduced) sunlight reaching the earth, how long this reduction persisted, and the degree of cooling caused by the reduced sunlight. The optical properties of the particulates and the physics of absorption, reflection, scattering, etc., are well established, if simplifying assumptions are made. Soot from urban fires proves particularly effective in blocking sunlight.

A second team of scientists, led by biologist Paul Ehrlich of Stanford, had studied the long-term biological and ecological consequences of nuclear war for some time. A third group planned a conference on the biological consequences of nuclear war in late 1983 (Ehrlich et al., 1983). The three groups decided to collaborate.

In conclusion, the analysis involves three separate but later integrated models:

1. A Nuclear War Scenario model.
2. A Particle Microphysical model.
3. A Radiative-Convective Optical model.

These analyses measured the quantities of dust and smoke produced, their dynamics, and their optical effects. *Science* published the results of TTAPS's studies and their implied biological consequences (23 December 1983, pp. 1283–1300), after NAS received the original 120-page document. A more sophisticated three-dimensional model reduced many of the uncertainties, refined the analysis, and considered more factors than the earlier TTAPS model (*Scientific American,* August 1984). Anne Ehrlich also published an excellent summary article of both climatic and biological effects of nuclear war in the *Bulletin* of the Atomic Scientists, April 1984. Many other independent studies—from the Soviet Academy of Sciences, the Swedish Academy of Sciences, the U.S.'s National Center for Atmospheric Research, the Royal Society of Canada, the federal Department of Environment, Canada—have confirmed these findings. The U.S. DOD commissioned the National Academy of Sciences to conduct a study. After eighteen months,

NAS's 190-page report, issued 11 December 1984, supported the findings of TTAPS, but predictably suggested further studies to narrow residual uncertainties. The process of peer review is open ended, particularly where it carries political implications. One can be certain that as with the acid rain issue, further studies will probably be the only action taken. Critics of nuclear winter theory, such as Edward Teller of Lawrence Livermore Laboratories, have seized on the uncertainties and discovered "loopholes," such as a nuclear war in which no cities would be attacked, forest fires almost eliminated, and only "surgical strikes" involved. Those who have a stake in nuclear power deny its negative aspects; their credibility on the issue reflects their record and their conflicts of interest. Teller fails on both counts. Teller's own phrase, a zero-infinity risk, would justify our total rejection of nuclear war. In this case, the probability is not zero; instead it is very high, and the inherent risk remains infinite. It is a risk we should never take.

A Conference on The World After Nuclear War, held at the Sheraton Washington on 31 October 1983, drew seven hundred diverse persons. Scientists from the Audubon Society, Woods Hole, the National Center for Atmospheric Research, and one Soviet scientist, Vladimir V. Aleksandrov of the Soviet Academy of Sciences, attended, as well as people from foundations, publishing houses, universities, public interest and environmental organizations, and the general public. The "Moscow Link," a closed-circuit satellite connecting the U.S. and the Soviet Union, enabled American and Soviet audiences and participants to view each other on large screens, and to exchange views across some four thousand miles. While minor differences occurred in the independent Soviet Academy studies, their basic results were similar to those of the Americans. Scientists on both sides declared that these new findings made nuclear war totally untenable, nuclear superiority a delusion, and nuclear weapons a "cancerous growth which threatens" the whole earth.

By disseminating this new knowledge of "nuclear winter" to millions of citizens all over the world, people transmit the genuine hope that peace can influence policy. The atmospheric test ban (ATB) prohibiting the testing of nuclear weapons in the atmosphere resulted partly from the broad dissemination of the dangers of fallout. Scientists like the Pugwash group and citizens groups all over the world contributed to this meaningful treaty. The entire history of environmental protection illustrates how people armed with information can change the direction of government. Even in closed societies like the Soviet Union, the international community of scientists and world public opinion can influence policy. The "nuclear winter" discovery has already been a minipeace initiative because scientific teams from the U.S. and USSR have exchanged their discoveries and agreed that a nuclear war has no winner. We would now recommend a national teach-in on the policy implications of "nuclear winter."

THE PHYSICS AND BIOLOGY OF "NUCLEAR WINTER"

In the "nuclear winter" phenomenon smoke, soot, or dust reflects/absorbs sunlight, the source of the earth's light and heat, preventing its entry and impact on the earth's atmosphere, its waters, and lands. Smoke actually blocks sunlight more effectively than dust, so the vast number of fires following a nuclear attack/war causes the "twilight at noon" phenomenon. This critical interception of sunlight takes place in the stratosphere, over seven miles up.

The stratosphere is more stable than the atmosphere, particularly its lower part or troposphere. Fine dust and smoke in the stratosphere persist for long periods and avoid the cleansing and dispersing processes of rain, wind, and thermal circulation that take place in the lower atmosphere. The almost continuous stable clouds of very fine dust and smoke would trap sunlight in the stratosphere.

The evidence for the "nuclear winter" phenomenon derived from data from bomb tests in the atmosphere and stratosphere as well as ground bursts, the limited experience of Hiroshima and Nagasaki, the mass bombing of Dresden, Tokyo, etc., in World War II, the impact of volcanic eruptions, large-scale forest and brush fires, the Chicago fire, and massive dust storms on Mars. The induction of rapid and persistent cooling of large regions of the earth seems to have a low threshold; as little as a 100-megaton attack could have an appreciable effect. Above this threshold, the depth and persistence of cold is proportional to the size of the attack. Very large megatonnage attacks would not only cool the Northern Hemisphere, the war region, but would also spill over to the Southern Hemisphere.

TTAPS also made some new predictions about radiation effects. Radiation has been downplayed, mainly because those exposed to prompt lethal doses would die quickly from blast and incineration. It was thought that radioactive particle retention and decay in the stratosphere would mediate long-term global fallout. However, a new phenomenon, medium-term or intermediate-term fallout derived from both rain and gravitation in the troposphere, could increase the danger of radioactive exposures to very large populations by a factor of ten (one order of magnitude). Radiation-induced disease could be much greater than previously expected.

The major biological impact of nuclear war derives from its drastic blow to the environmental processes and resources that Nature supplies to all living things as absolutely necessary for life and the continuity of life. Without these we would not have breathable air, potable water, or fertile soil. Nuclear war would primarily affect photosynthesis by green plants and marine phytoplankton, the driving force behind and major energy source for all plant growth activity in natural and agricultural systems. The loss of oxygen, light, and heat would devastate low-tolerance species, destroy most annual plants and crops that require a season of sun and warmth, and starve large numbers of domesticated and wild herbivores and carnivores. Other vital environmental goods and services—quality and temperature control of our atmosphere, land, and water; the supply and sanitation of water (the hydrological cycle); the cycling of nutrients (fertilization of soil); pollination and the vast genetic library that is the source of evolution, adaptation, and survival of species—all these would be severely damaged.

The environmental effects of nuclear war would have a physical, biological, and psychological impact on human populations. Massive trauma, starvation, and disease would join together in a "final epidemic." The large quantities of pyrotoxins produced by the combustion of synthetics and organics would undoubtedly contribute to the spread of disease. There is no way to repair the broken circle: social systems cannot escape their dependency on ecosystems. The connection between the biosphere and the sociosphere, once severed, would be difficult, if not impossible, to repair. If civilization is in part measured by the total inventory of hardware (machines, materials, devices, transportations—the "built environmment"), then the destruction of our civilization could be permanent. Dynamic reserves of critical materials lost in the greatest entropy trap of all time could break the lines of continuity. We would, in effect, have a global meltdown, a "China Syndrome" for the world. The studies on nuclear winter did not take into account the possible release of radioactive debris from the destruction of the world's nuclear reactors, or the release of weapons-grade plutonium from nuclear wastes, storage facilities, and stored weapons—the most toxic substance in the world when inhaled in particulate form.

The "nuclear winter" or "twilight at noon" scenario dramatically confirms that a nuclear war is without winners, but it also alters the meaning of deterrence. Previously, the doctrine of deterrence presumed the capacity to launch a "second-strike" or retaliatory attack after suffering a "first-strike" or preemptive strike. If the "nuclear winter" hypothesis has a high degree of certainty, then the superpower that launches a major megatonnage attack on the other also suffers the consequences of the environmental and ecological damage. Even a "no first-use" declaration would no longer make sense, despite its apparent reasonableness. A second-strike would only compound the disaster. The present level of nuclear delivery yield by either side is not usable by either, except as an act of suicide. Assuming the validity of the "nuclear winter" analysis, the case for a radical reduction, even unilaterally by either side, would begin to look plausible.

One Trident submarine, armed with 192 independently targetable warheads, would serve the purpose of deterrence if targeted in a counter-value attack. If each warhead had a one-half megaton yield, this would amount to

91.2 megatons. Two to three warheads targeted on every city with a population of 100,000 on either side would place much of the population of each side in jeopardy, and the total megatonnage involved would remain less than the minimum amount needed to trigger radical climate changes as described in the "nuclear winter" study. The huge combined strategic arsenals of some 10,000 megatons and some 20,000 warheads could be reduced by some 80 percent. Even if one superpower were to reduce its arms by 50 percent it would be an act of sanity, security, and economic advantage.

With a ban on antisubmarine warfare (ASW), both sides could reduce their strategic triad to only SLBM's and eliminate ICBM's and strategic bombers. The delivery megatonnage and the number of warheads in the submarine leg would be more than sufficient for mutual deterrence. An editorial in *Science* made this general point: "We must proceed at once to an examination of the scientific reality of the nuclear winter and of the implications of this reality for our policies of arming for suicide and our fears that a suicidal weapon might be used against us" (Simon, 1984).

This kind of initiative would, in itself, build confidence. If it were not for "Strangelove mentalities [who] become fascinated again with the possibilities of a 'surgical' pre-emptive strike" (Simon, 1984), a joint study of nuclear winter would be the only sane response.

THE PREDICTABLE PENTAGON

The nuclear winter studies drew considerable response (TTAPS, 1983). The generally supportive National Academy of Sciences report of December 1984 recommended further study to reduce the persistent uncertainties. Representative Tim Worth (D-Colo.) has revealed the contents of a recent seventeen-page Pentagon report on "nuclear winter." In it, the Pentagon neatly side-steps the issue: it accepts the possibility of serious climate changes after a nuclear exchange, but denies that this has any policy implications. It offers brazen distortions and, at times, clear falsehoods as reasons for its denials. The Pentagon report claims its current policy would "reduce the probability of severe climate effects" because of the trend to develop highly accurate weapons with lower yields and a policy of "surgical strikes," combined with a "no cities" strike. SIOP-6 is an absolute denial of this; it proposes incredible attack redundancy on all possible targets. The Pentagon report "pushes" "Star Wars" by claiming that "[it] would serve to remove any potential for environmental disaster." This is not true: "Star Wars" are neither perfectible nor effective against a multitude of countermeasures. The U.S. plans to double its strategic arsenal in the next decade, compounding the distortion that the U.S. is "moving away from the concept of deterring nuclear war by threat of retaliation." Finally, in seizing on the uncertainties, "We are faced with [a] high degree of uncertainty, which will persist for some time." Thus the Pentagon issues a statement of hope as well as denial.

In the *Atlantic Monthly* of November 1985, Thomas Powers discusses his conversations with Pentagon officials on the nuclear winter issue. Powers claims to have picked up "interesting nuances," namely, "a wistful hope that 'more study' will make the nuclear winter problem go away." As Powers correctly suggests, if the uncertainties never go away, "more study" can go on forever. This typical tactic of denial and delay characterizes many of the Reagan administration's responses to persistent environmental problems such as acid rain and toxic wastes. To have the temerity to state that current policy is designed to obviate "nuclear winter" is obscene and obscure. The Russians have moved to larger, high-yield weapons. Now nuclear winter can be initiated by one side attacking the other without retaliation. The uncertainties will disappear only after a nuclear war. This is the real policy of the Reagan administration.

At a Washington conference on "nuclear winter" on 27 March 1985, long-time cold warrior Fred Iklé stated that current U.S. nuclear policy was best suited to offset the nuclear winter phenomenon in a nuclear war. SIOP-6, the detailed nuclear hit list, puts the lie to this shameless assertion. KGB headquarters and the Kremlin are "decapitation targets." Redundant multiple-weapons strikes against each target, including major Soviet industrial sites, form part of the "secret agenda." The more accurate weapons to be developed in the next five years—like Trident II—will still have multiple warheads each having a yield of ten to twenty Hiroshima bombs. The Pentagon is lying to the American people.

7

The Unholy Alliance:
Reagan and the Wrongs of the Right

Jerry, I sometimes believe we're heading very fast for Armageddon, right now.
Quoted in James L. Franklin,
"The Religious Right and the New Apocalypse"

We are living in a pre-war, not a post-war world.
Eugene V. Rostow

I hope we never get into another war. . . . If we do, I want us to come out of it No. 1, not No. 2.
Energy Secretary James B. Edwards

If we have to start all over again with Adam and Eve, then I want them to be Americans and not Russians, and I want them on this continent, not in Europe.
Senator Richard Russell

REAGAN, GOD, AND THE BOMB

The strange amalgam of forces that brought and returned Ronald Reagan to power has sometimes been collectively referred to as the New Right. This umbrella term is appropriate in some senses, but the various groups subsumed under the term are far from homogeneous. Their membership ranges widely, from the small group of influential security intellectuals, to veterans of the Old Right, to the Moral Majority of the fundamentalist evangelicals or electronic pastors. This "congregation" has played a particularly crucial role in the political action movements of the right. Their literal and often liberal interpretation of the Bible, coupled to a blind and absolute belief in the Word, directly relates to the issue of nuclear war.

Reagan is not the first president to claim God as his personal and national ally; but he is probably the first president to openly write religion into politics, to cater to religious fanatics, to declare that "we have driven God from the classroom," and to support the "pro-lifers" in their aim to overturn the 22 January 1973 Supreme Court decision on abortion. The ecology behind that tragic trinity of Reagan, God, and the bomb is possibly more sinister than the doctrines of the scholars of apocalypse in the defense establishment. The Reagan cosmology with its utter simplicity and depth of belief—uncluttered by any rational process of judgment, never confused by the facts, never obliged to follow the dictates of evidence—incorporates the more dangerous quality of the apostles of the New Right. The politics of the sophisticated "Wizards of Armageddon" who wrote the script for the secret agenda merges with the world view of the fundamentalist true believers who anticipate the "Final Days." Reagan supporters share their dedication to destroy the "evil empire," if necessary through the battle of the final days on this earth. This binding dedication is strong enough to overcome their differences, be they religious, intellectual, or economic, and create the hard-line, undifferentiated, ultraconservative perception of the Soviet threat.

Reagan-think propounds a world view of simple dichotomies, distilled into the ultimate struggle between good and evil. Reagan is the piper who plays the seductive tune. The nuclear arsenal provides the instrument for a self-fulfilling vision of destruction.

RELIGION AND NUCLEAR WAR

The position that fundamentalist/born-again religious organizations have taken on nuclear war stands in stark contrast to that of other churches in the West. In the vanguard of peace, the World Council of Churches and the Catholic Church have both condemned nuclear war. The Lutheran Churches of the Netherlands and the two Germanys have also played a prominent role in the peace movement. The Catholic Church and other religious bodies in Central and Latin America and the Third World have more often placed human justice on the top of their agenda and provided martyrs for this cause. People facing the continual torments of hunger, poverty, deprivation, and dispossession find it difficult, if not impossible, to relate to any larger issue of mass destruction or extinction. Still, many groups and individuals in the Third World have shown their concern and become part of the global peace network. Some Third-World leaders, such as Gandhi and Nyere, have gained prominence in the search for justice *and* peace.

Roman Catholic bishops of the U.S. took a surprising, courageous, and incisive position and have spoken out against nuclear war with vigor and clarity. This provides hope that moral vitality still persists in American life. It stands in sharp contrast to the moral position of the Moral Majority and their electronic churches.

There is little precedent for the direct association of religion and politics in the U.S. because the Constitution has mandated the separation of church and state. But, presidents from Truman to Reagan have invoked God, good, and evil in the name of the U.S.'s mission to be superior in nuclear arms, remain superior, and, if necessary, fight and win a nuclear war. Even citizen Richard Nixon said in 1980, "It may seem melodramatic to say that the U.S. and Russia represent Good and Evil, Light and Darkness, God and the Devil. But if we think of it that way, it helps to clarify our perspective of the world struggle" (Ford et al., 1983, p. 13). Nixon's statement indicates his pragmatism. But in the voices of Ronald Reagan, Caspar Weinberger, and the unholy alliance of the New Right—the Born-Again movement, the "Moral Majority," and their psychotically anti-Soviet advisers—any hint of pragmatism or politics disappears, drowned out by the shrill, clear voices of true believers, the nuclear holy crusaders. This alliance of the ultra-conservatives, fundamentalists, and scholars of apocalypse links nuclear armament to moral rearmament and crusades for a holy Christian war against "godless communism," Reagan's favorite phrase. They have buttressed their preaching with plans for a huge arms build-up to fight and win any nuclear war or to destroy Soviet communism by blackmail, coercion, or economic suffocation. Their cliche- and slogan-filled rhetoric tragically reflects a simplistic world view untainted by the complexity of reality. The danger lies in the sincerity of their belief. When Reagan said, "It is time for us to start a [military] build-up and it is time for us to build to the point that no other nation on this earth will ever dare raise a hand against us, and in this way we will preserve the peace" ("CBS Evening News," 14 June 1981), he really meant it. It is necessary to make this link between Reagan's and Weinberger's fundamentalist beliefs, the organized campaign against secularism, ultraconservatism, and the military and other policies of the administration.

When Reagan spoke at the National Association of Evangelicals in Orlando, Florida, he deliberately linked the belief in God to opposition to a nuclear freeze, and to support of a massive build-up in U.S. arms. He said, "There is sin and evil in the world and we are enjoined by Scripture and the Lord Jesus to oppose it, should deterrence fail." Reagan went on to say that "Soviet communism is the force of evil in the modern world. . . . [they] possess the aggressive instincts of an evil empire" (Lewis, 1983). Lewis comments, "But it is not funny. What is the world to think when the greatest of powers is led by a man who applies to the most difficult human problem a simplistic theology, one in fact rejected by most theologians?" Can the concept of good and evil be applied "to the contentious technical particulars of arms programs . . . or whether 10,000 nuclear warheads are enough, whether the United States needs a first-strike weapon against the Soviet Union. . . [or] whether a nuclear freeze is likely to make the world more or less safe"?

To be fair, the U.S. has long rejected deterrence in favor of a warfighting doctrine. At various times, Robert McNamara, James Schlesinger, Donald

Rumsfeld, and Harold Brown preferred the "strategic doctrine" of a limited nuclear war. Former President Jimmy Carter gave this doctrine substance in his presidential directive (PD-59). Harold Brown, secretary of defense under Carter, used the expression "countervailing" strategy, which really meant that the U.S. must develop the capacity to "prevail" at any level of escalation in a nuclear conflict. Supporters of Brown's strategy argued that it had merit for deterrence, although the more sane, in their moments of candor, expressed doubt that a nuclear war could be "surgically controlled." No such doubts cloud the official policy of the Reagan administration. Armed with the primitive belief that God is not only on their side but also guiding their mission, they have developed policies and plans to fight and win a limited, protracted, or all-out nuclear war.

In its most frightening aspect, the Reagan administration couples its warfighting policy with a fundamentalist, religious world view. The end of the world is engrained in the minds of the reborn. Armageddon is not a mere tenuous prophecy, but an absolute prediction. For key members of the administration, Armageddon is the basis of policy. In a radio interview on "Washington Talk" on 23 August 1982, Defense Secretary Caspar Weinberger was asked if he believed the world was going to end and, if so, "Will it be by an act of God or an act of man?" Weinberger replied, "I have read the book of Revelation and, yes, I believe the world is going to end—by an act of God, I hope. . . . I worry that we will not have time to get strong enough . . . . I fear we will not be ready. I think time is running out . . . but I have faith" (Scheer, 1982, preface). Former Interior Secretary James Watt stands on record with the same belief, and thus his policies were designed to make the environment expendable. One hundred religious leaders accused the Reagan administration of taking the position that "reconciliation with America's adversaries is ultimately futile" (*New York Times,* Thursday, 24 October 1984). At a conference of religious leaders in the Washington Hotel on 23 October 1984, the Christic Institute claimed to have collected eleven statements by Reagan that suggested the imminence of Armageddon. In the second Mondale-Reagan debate, Ronnie characteristically brushed this charge aside, but Rabbi Brickner claimed Mr. Reagan had "talked about it [Armageddon] in a serious, frightening way." The internal logic is terrifying; if the world is going to end and if God is on your side, then "an act of man" becomes "an act of God."

In the USSR, one can find a mirror-image rhetoric that replaces God with communism and a mirror-image paranoia about the U.S. However, the USSR leaders declared a "no first-use" commitment on 15 June 1982 (Weiler, 1983).

THE BATTLE OF ARMAGEDDON

The current fundamentalist theology of Armageddon is convoluted and complicated. The "born-again" group expressly believes that at present the world is in an age of satanic control (the "evil empire"). Shortly, Soviet, European, Iranian, Arabian, African, and Chinese armies will invade Israel and be totally destroyed, possibly by a nuclear war. A remnant of Israelites will be saved to accept Jesus as their messiah. Christ and an army of saints will then return to earth to punish the unbelievers and destroy the forces of anti-Christ in the "big one," the battle of Armageddon. Caspar Weinberger believes in the "end of the world" (Scheer, 1983, preface). Reagan has been quoted as saying "Never has there been a time in which so many [biblical] prophecies are coming together. There have been times in the past when people thought the end of the world was coming, and so forth, but never anything like this" (*New York Times,* Thursday, 24 October 1984); and "Jerry, I sometimes believe we're heading very fast for Armageddon" (*Boston Globe,* Sunday, 2 May 1982).

Jerry Falwell, head of the Moral Majority, predicted the Russians would have come from across the Mexican border by 1981, "if Reagan had not been elected in 1980" (Fitzgerald, 1981). In an interview with Robert Scheer, Falwell stated, "We believe that Russia, because of her need of oil—and she's running out now—is going to move in on the Middle East, and particularly Israel, because of their hatred of the Jew, and that it is at that time that all hell will break out. And it is at that time when I believe there will be some nuclear holocaust on this earth" (Scheer, 1981). Falwell, like Reagan, denied all this on behalf of most evangelicals; however, the statement of one hundred religious leaders at the Christic Institute's conference correctly identified the Religious Right as proclaiming, through some of its leaders, "an ideology of nuclear Armageddon." The images of the "Last Days" present in sketches of the "Day After" and "nuclear winter" link the holocaust and the final battle of Armageddon to the devastation of nuclear war. The way out for true Christians is based on the Rapture concept.

The arrival of the anti-Christ heralds the biblical end of the world. Napoleon seemed to be this anti-Christ to believers at the start of the nineteenth century. Since the 1950s American fundamentalists have applied the anti-Christ mantle to Soviet leaders and the entire communist system.

The early transference of the Rapture concept to the U.S. was used to enforce the view that fundamentalists keep their distance from politics. Fundamentalists believed that only God could bring them to salvation; it could not be won through their own interventions. Ronald Reagan first recruited evangelical conservatives to the cause of sectarian politics and an anticommunist world view. With his assertions that the Soviets were the force and "focus of evil" in this world, and that "God has been driven out of the schools," Reagan sought the active support of Jerry Falwell and company. In overlaying politics and national interest with "Christian" dogma, Reagan broke with two of America's greatest democratic traditions, the separation of church and state and the rule of law. The new conservative agenda seeks unreasonable restrictions on travel and speech, on trade union rights, and on civil rights in general. The 1984 election and the vain boasting of Jerry Falwell all attest to this. Justice itself seems seized with the same conservative, sectarian dogma as politics. In campaigning for the seat of Jewish Representative Howard Wolpe (D-Mich.), opposing Republican candidate Mark Siljander sent a letter to local ministers urging them to help "send another Christian to Congress" (Lewis, 1984).

This is the thrust of Falwell's registration campaign that claims to have enlisted some eight million new, registered voters. Postelection analysis supports the view that Reagan drew votes from white males from the South, Midwest, and West. Not only the rich, but also the poor voted for Reagan, even though the lower economic classes have traditionally remained Democrat. Evangelical ministers use the Scofield "Rapture" bible for massive conversion, both religious and political. Their success has won hundreds of thousands of converts among the poor Catholic refugees of Central America, and the fundamentalists have become a major factor in the politics of El Salvador.

Four hundred television stations and 500 radio stations across North America transmit Jerry Falwell's "Old Time Gospel Hour" once a week. He runs a multimillion-dollar evangelical empire that includes a thirty-five building complex in Lynchburg, Virginia. In one of his cassette tape sets, the Rapture concept enables Falwell to say, "Hey! It's great being a Christian. We have a wonderful future ahead . . . so we don't need to go to bed at night wondering if someone's going to push the button and destroy the planet between now and sunrise" (Kowolowski, July 1984, p. 31).

The Falwell enterprise's overt political wing, the Moral Majority—not really a majority and, to many other Christians, not really moral—assembled in 1979, dedicated to "born-again" religion and politics. James Watt and Caspar Weinberger are "born-again" Christians, and so is Ronald Reagan, if his political actions reflect his belief. The New Right and the Old Right, combined in the Moral Majority, played a key role in the presidential elections of 1980 and 1984. Like their nonsectarian cousins from the Committee on the Present Danger, the fundamentalists elected their man to the White House in 1980 and kept him there in 1984.

The "exact" prophecy of the Bible tells the fundamentalists that their God, who created a fully equpped, fully inhabited universe *exactly* 5,988 years ago, is about to bring it to an end. Independent fundamentalist ministries such as Second Coming Incorporated produce an unappetizing array of television productions and magazine publications—*It's Happening Now, Bible Prophecy News,* and the *Endtime Messenger*—that prophesy the final days. Hal Lindsey's book *The Late Great Planet Earth* has sold over fifteen million copies and won him the title of *New York Times*'s bestselling nonfiction writer. Falwell's television specials, his booklet *Nuclear War and the Second Coming of Jesus Christ,* and his book *Armageddon and the Coming War with Russia* have sold millions, and give the lie to Falwell's later attempts to deny that he associated nuclear war and religious prophecy (*New York Times,* Monday, 29 October 1984). In effect, he has marketed the end of the world.

Today, the world has approached the end of the "Church Age," epitomized by the rise to power of Reaganism, and the signs of the beginning of the Tribulation period appear everywhere: the rise of feminism, the sexual revolution, the divorce rate, legalized abortion, the absence of school prayer, herpes, AIDS, and, most of all, communism. This Armageddon doctrine inserted into the nation's political arena "seems to justify nuclear war as a divine instrument to punish the wicked and complete God's plan for history . . . . In the Armageddon world view, this final era [the battle of Armageddon] is foretold in Holy Scripture, constitutes God's plan for humanity, and cannot be prevented" (*New York Times,* Thursday, 24 October 1984).

The two most powerful political figures in the U.S., Reagan and Weinberger, may be performing their official duties according to their interpretation of Scripture. This could account for the five-year warfighting plan and the U.S. position on the Middle East. Reagan is the instrument of prophecy, commander-in-chief of the forces of good in the battle of Armageddon that takes place in Israel. The debacle in Lebanon was merely a mini-Armageddon. Reagan is the instrument "to punish the wicked and complete God's plan for history." Deterrence will fail because the Bible tells us so. The policies of nuclear warfighting and warwinning become self-fulfilling prophecies. But how does the administration's myth of survivability accord with the Moral Majority's biblical and prophetic reality?

Fundamentalists assure their survival through a concept termed the "Rapture." The development of this notion began in Scotland, after a young Glaswegian woman claimed to have had a "vision." Darbyites, members of a Scottish fundamentalist Protestant group, produced the major version of the Rapture in the Scofield Reference Bible in the 1820s. According to it, exactly seven years before the final battle, the great nuclear war, the period known as the "Tribulation" begins. During the Tribulation, God will take "true Christians" bodily away from earth and into heaven.

Many cultures and religions share an "end of the world" notion. The Koran refers to it: "Have faith in Allah and the Last Day—these shall be rewarded" (Koran 4:60). The Bible says, "Gather yourselves together, that I may tell you that which shall befall you in the last days" (Gen. 49:1); and "This know also, that in the last days perilous times shall come" (2 Tim. 3:1). The Rapture is not in the Bible, but Jerry Falwell actually distributes a bumper sticker with the words, "If the driver disappears, grab the wheel!" Jerry Falwell, Ronald Reagan, Caspar Weinberger, and the rest of the "good" will suddenly vanish. The Soviets will invade Israel. According to Reverend J. Falwell, wood will replace metal through a superadvanced technology of instant transmutation. How could the Bible be wrong! According to Writ, Russia will lose exactly 83 percent of her soldiers and be repulsed in Falwell's version of the "Russians are Coming." The remaining seven years of Tribulation will be occupied entirely with burying Soviet soldiers and burning wooden shafts.

Next, according to Falwell, "the Antichrist will move into the Middle East, place a statue of himself in the Jewish temple holy of holies and demand that the whole world worship him as God" (Kowolowski, July 1984, p. 32). The "nonraptured" world—all Jews, Mohammedans, Hindus, atheists, primitives, homosexuals, feminists, proabortionists, communists, etc.—will flock to worship anti-Christ. Then the "hero" (Ronald Reagan) will return and, in a nuclear duel in which Armageddon, a city near Jerusalem, becomes ground zero, will destroy all the followers of anti-Christ. At the Second Coming, Jesus, floating on a white (mushroom-shaped?) cloud, will return to bring the Millenium. After one thousand years of a world of Falwell, Reagan, and Weinberger clones, eternity brings "eternal bliss and joy for those in Heaven, eternal suffering and torment for those in hell," the non-Christians, homosexuals, feminists, communists, etc.

The crux of this issue is whether the most powerful man in the world, the president of the United States, Ronald Reagan, believes all this. Falwell told Robert Scheer of the *Los Angeles Times* on 4 March 1981 that he and Reagan have discussed biblical prophecy and "that Reagan agrees with him" (Kowolowski, July 1984, p. 32). Reagan led the battle to return prayer to the schools and declared 1983 to be "The Year of the Bible." He has addressed the National Religious Broadcasters convention during each year of his presidency. Reagan invited Jerry Falwell to a private briefing by the National Security Council. Ronald Goodwin, Falwell's second in command, wrote to their followers, "He [Falwell] met with President Reagan in the White House and the President personally instructed him to thank every member of the Moral Majority for defending the President's program to save America from Soviet nuclear blackmail" (Kowolowski, July 1984, p. 33). In April 1983, Falwell informed his followers, "Well, nuclear war and the Second Coming of Christ, Armageddon, and the coming war with Russia, what does this have to do and say to me? . . . none of this should bring fear to your hearts, because we are all going up in the Rapture before any of it occurs" (Kowolowski, July 1984, p. 33). But Reagan has even more direct linkages with the Moral Majority. Morton Blackwell, special assistant to the president in the Office of Public Liaison, and Paul Weyrich, of the Heritage Foundation, masterminded the successful fundraising campaigns for Reagan sponsored by the political action committees of the New Right. Their activity has extended to the campaigns of the British Conservative Party, and created the Coalition for Peace through Security in opposition to the Campaign for Nuclear Disarmament movement in Britain. The trans-Atlantic linkages of the Old and New Right converge in policy and accommodation that infect NATO and subvert attempts for nuclear disarmament and arms control.

The Moral Majority asserts its moral superiority but offers no intellectual analysis of nuclear war. No questions are asked about the notions of justice or whether war can ever be just. No questions are raised about the strategy or doctrine of nuclear warfighting. The bankrupt assumption of morality based on the oversimplified virtues of family and faith has neither form nor content. Their church has become the town meeting place for propounding a red-neck theology, tainted by elements of racism and chauvinism. Images of fire and brimstone instill fear and blind adherence. God and evil are *de facto* concepts, presented without analysis or justification. In contrast, U.S. Catholic bishops have written and preached one of the finest moral analyses of nuclear war ever elucidated, in an often hostile atmosphere. Their courage matches the depth and honesty of their questions and answers.

VATICAN II AND THE U.S. BISHOPS' "PASTORAL LETTER ON WAR AND PEACE"

Vatican II's *The Pastoral Constitution on the Church in the Modern World* (Abbott and Gallagher, 1966) is a Catholic charter of collegiality investing national conferences of bishops with the responsibility to address the moral problems of particular concerns to various nations. In particular Vatican II noted that we are forced today "to undertake a completely fresh appraisal of war" and soundly condemned the bombing of Hiroshima and Nagasaki as an "unspeakable crime against God and man." Despite this, Vatican II subscribed to the policy of deterrence.

In 1979 Cardinal Joseph Krul, archbishop of Philadelphia, altered the position of American bishops on nuclear war and nuclear strategy. In his testimony before a Senate Committee regarding SALT II, Cardinal Krul went beyond the notions of a "just war" and strictures on the use of weapons "permitted" by Vatican II (Hearings on EX Y, 96-1, 96th Cong. 1st sess. 1979, Part IV, pp. 116–130). Cardinal Krul and a majority of American bishops rejected *all use,* even threatened use, of strategic nuclear weapons, even against military targets, and questioned the controllability of nuclear exchanges.

In June 1982 a group of Catholic bishops began meeting to draft a comprehensive statement on nuclear war. By the time of the revised third draft, the bishops' "Pastoral Letter on War and Peace" had enunciated the following points:

1. Condemnation of *any use* of the U.S. strategic nuclear arsenal against civilian or military targets located near cities.

2. Prohibition of first-use of weapons against *any targets*.

3. Prohibition of any nuclear weapon likely to be released by accident.

4. Recommendation of immediate, bilateral verifiable agreements to halt the testing, production, and deployment of new strategic systems, followed by negotiated bilateral "deepcuts" in the arsenals of both superpowers.

5. Rejection of any attempt to achieve superiority in the nuclear balance (Winters, 1983).

The Reagan administration made an active attempt to influence the bishops. The public voiced vigorous objections. Two letters from Judge William Clark, former National Security Adviser, to the Vatican protested against the bishops' letter, and retired General Vernon Walters visited the Vatican to register his opposition.

If we examine the pastoral letter in detail, we see that it opposes every feature of the Reagan administration's plans and policies regarding nuclear war. It supports the Nuclear Freeze Initiative. It rejects the doctrine that a nuclear war is winnable and survivable. It rejects the notion of limited nuclear war. It opposes "decapitation" (Steinbrunner, 1981–1982). It supports U.S. initiatives and a categorical policy of "no first-use."

The pastoral letter issues a profound moral challenge: "In this document, for example, we have spoken clearly against the deliberate use of weapons against civilian populations. *Catholic military personnel must observe these prohibitions* [Italics mine]" (Origins, 1982).

True Catholics in the military have to choose between loyalty to the state and loyalty to the church, or between loyalty to Reagan and loyalty to God. As one important Catholic has written, "There is hope that a bold Presidential candidate in 1984 (or at least, in 1988) will adopt the 'no first-use' platform" (Winters, 1983).

"No first-use" is an important initiative proposed by many prominent Americans (Bundy et al, 1982; UCS, 1983). On 10 February 1983 the synod of the Church of England also endorsed "no first-use." Leonid Brezhnev, former premier of the USSR, had pledged a unilateral "no first-use" doctrine. "No first-use" would obviously include "no first-strike," but no first-strike as a doctrine excludes "first-use." "First-strike" is normally meant to be a pre-emptive counterforce attack. The Reagan administration has refused to dis-avow either "first-strike" or "first-use"; on the contrary, it has reasserted the right to both.

As an advantage, both sides declaring a "no first-use" policy would in-crease the threshold of trust required for serious arms reduction. Such a declaration by the U.S. would be morally, psychologically, and diplomatic-ally encouraging. The pastoral letter of the U.S. bishops asks that "the United States be prepared, in our view, to take some independent initiatives." Thomas Merton has warned that "As long as you see your fellow man to be feared, mistrusted, hated, and destroyed, there cannot be peace on earth" (Paradise, 1983, p. 34). But Reagan's rhetoric about the Soviets contains such hate that it goes beyond mere rhetoric: it is a deep, un-Christian belief. That belief is "the seed of destruction." Reagan, in support of school prayer, once said, "We have driven God out of the classroom." In fact, Reagan, Weinberger, and company have driven God from the Department of De-fense. The U.S. Catholic bishops have had the courage to expose this in regard to nuclear war.

Archbishop Hunthausen of Seattle further argued that if it was not morally right to use nuclear weapons, it is not right to threaten to use them, and thus not right to possess them, not right to even manufacture them. Those who do, act immorally (Hoyt, 1982). The unilateralists propound a secular equivalent to this religious morality. For life to be sustained we require an existential "secular faith" that is independent of the actions of any other, but imposes a commitment on ourselves to act. The U.S. Catholic bishops' response is an inspiration. This intrinsically implies a faith that other people too will act independently but inevitably governed by existential commitment. This author has termed this an ethic without accounting. In effect, one acts as if winning or losing, influencing events or not, changing the world, or any other accountable goal did not matter. One acts only be-cause one's heart and brain compel one, with no accounting except to one's own private morality; yet, one is compelled to act.

The political leaders of the superpowers act in direct violation of the principles enunciated by the pastoral latter; thus, neither side can claim superior morality. The Moral Majority is neither a majority nor moral, yet the habitual voting patterns of Americans have allowed them to influence, if not decide, the choice of governmental policy. What is the connection between the sophistication of a Jeane Kirkpatrick or a Max Kampelman and the primitiveness of a Jerry Falwell or Pat Robertson? Divided as they are by radical differences in religious background, education, and even nominal political affiliation, they are still allies, wittingly and unwittingly bonded together in common cause. Like all designations, the New Right is imprecise, fuzzy at the edges, and possibly not all-inclusive. The strategy intellectuals and special interest groups like the Committee on the Present Danger almost stand apart. Perhaps their bond lies in the social context of the new politics. As culture becomes increasingly militarized, the transformation of a peace economy to a war economy profoundly influences all aspects of life.

THE NEW RIGHT: ECHOES OF THE PAST

A strange amalgam of political conservatism from the Old and New Right came and stayed in power with Ronald Reagan as their standard-bearer. Behind the front of predictable groups—the fundamentalist, born-again Moral Majority, the Committee for the Survival of a Free Congress, The Committee on the Present Danger, the Heritage Foundation, Helm's Helpers, the National Conservative Political Action Committee, the Conservative Caucus, the antiabortion zealots, and an ultraright group of mainly Western millionaires—are the most faceless managers of the political right, such as Paul Weyrich, Terry Dolan, and Richard Viguerie of the New Right. Viguerie has multiplied political power by tapping new resources through direct mail. Viguerie has admitted that he and fellow political strategists developed the strategy of direct mail approaches, questionnaires, and solicitations to target groups of the right. They aimed their appeals at the forty-five million followers of fundamentalist preachers, then planned the process for selecting a presidential candidate who would appeal to the New-Right constituency. In an interview reported in the 2 July 1976 issue of *Christianity Today,* Reagan declared he was "born again" and would "seek God" before deciding to run. He spoke of the "need for the nation to turn back to God, on personal spirituality . . . and the divine inspiration of the Bible" (*Washington Spectator,* 1 December 1984, p. 2).

Viguerie did more than develop a technique for mapping a new political resource or for making a president. Viguerie understood a dominant feature of the American psyche. In having a hand on the pulse of the times, Viguerie sensed the mood and psychological needs of millions of Americans. His personalized approach lured thousands of voters, previously not Republican, into the fold. The net effect of his technique was mass conversion.

The New Right is a supersuccessful network composed of several distinct groups:

1. Conservative think tanks such as the Hoover Institution, American Enterprise Institute (AEI), The Georgetown Center for Strategic and International Studies, the Heritage Foundation, and the Institute for Contemporary Studies (ICS) do counterintelligence in the army of ideas.

2. These think tanks of the right are supported by individual "angels" and millionaires, but more often receive funds from special-right foundations:

the Bechtel Foundation, the Adolph Coors Foundation, the Lelly Foundation, the Fred C. Koch Foundation, the John M. Olin Foundation, the J. Howard Pew Freedom Trust, the Smith Richardson Foundation, and the Sarah Mellon Scaife Foundation, representing construction, brewing, energy, pharmaceuticals, oil and drilling, chemicals, oil, Vicks Vaporub, and Gulf oil, respectively. Richard Scaife has supported nearly all the rightist think tanks and centers, and has given them some $144 million in the past twenty years. Scaife, Joseph Coors (brewer), and Paul Weyrich launched the Heritage Foundation in 1974. In fact, Scaife money has gone into 110 rightist ideological organizations. Billionaire David Packard, Stephen Bechtel, Sr. and Jr., and a handful of private, ultraconservative corporations such as Koch Industries, Amway, Reader's Digest, Chicago Tribune Company, Deering Milliken, and Hunt Oil have bankrolled the New Right network. They employ some 300 economists to peddle supply-side Reaganomics. They are directly and indirectly connected to the Reagan administration, and they have direct connections to the CIA through the London-based Forum World Features Ltd. (Saloma, 1984, p. 31).

3. The New Right network also includes the political action committees (PACs). Among these are Phyllis Schlafly's Eagle Forum, the anti-ERA campaign, the National Right to Work Committee, the American Security Council, The Conservative Caucus, Terry Dolan's The National Conservative Political Action Committee (NCPAC), Christian Crusade, Korean Cultural Freedom Foundation, Pink Sheet on the Left, Gun Owners of America, Young Americans for Freedom, Committee for the Survival of a Free Congress, Helm's Helpers, and many others. The Viguerie Company (TVC) accomplished brilliant political feats through direct-mail techniques: they not only raised an estimated $40 million for the 1980 presidential election (Saloma, 1984, p. 46), but also recruited/converted voters to their cause, effectively making Reagan president.

Howard Phillips, national director of the Conservative Caucus, openly boasts "we organize discontent, and must prove our ability to get revenge on people who go against us" (Saloma, 1984, p. 46). We can understand the implications of this revolution of the right.

4. The significant group of the New Right is the Moral Majority, the born-again and fundamentalists Christians, with their electronic ministries that reach and control millions of voters. Viguerie estimates that there may be as many as "100 million Americans—50 million born-again Protestants, 30 million conservative Catholics, 3 million Mormons and 3 million Orthodox Jews—from which to draw members of a pro-family Bible-believing coalition" (*Conservative Digest,* August 1979). The evangelical Christians have a powerful tool geared for strength in the age of opinion control: their giant communications networks now rival the major broadcasting networks in

size. The PTL (People that Love) club, the Christian Broadcast Network (CBN), and Jerry Falwell's network, which includes James Robinson, Pat Robertson, and Dr. Bill Bright of Campus Crusade for Christ International, are the core of the Moral Majority, the religious wing of the New Right. They created four new organizations—the Christian Right, the Moral Majority, the Religious Roundtable, and America for Jesus—to help bring Reagan to power by 1980. They are also part of the network of prolife political action committees. They also maintain extensive direct and indirect connections to the White House. The New Right and the Religious Right formed a coalition to bring and return Reagan to power; they accomplished that goal with remarkable efficiency.

5. The fifth group in the New Right Coalition is the powerful corporate sector, the bankrollers and bagmen who supply the real resources necessary for political action. In many cases, those corporations with irresponsible business practices are the very ones behind the New Right. Predictably, among them are Johns Manville, Sears Roebuck, the Buckleys and their oil fortune, Edward Dillard, Welch, Amway, G.E., Reader's Digest, Hewlett Packard, Bechtel, Coors, Argosy, Dart Industries. W. R. Grace, Mobil, and Gulf.

In 1974 superbig business created the Business Roundtable, a huge corporate PAC designed to re-create U.S. greatness lost through the disillusionment of Watergate and the later humiliations of Iran. The Business Roundtable is linked to the official New Right "think tank," the American Enterprise Institute. By 1983 there were 1512 corporate PACs in the U.S. These PACs spent huge sums during the elections of 1980, 1981, 1982, and 1984. They extended their influence through the development of grass-roots political activity, often in support of antiunionism, lower corporate taxes, and big trade deals, particularly in armaments. The National Right to Work Committee (NRTWC), The Americans Against Union Control of Government (AAUCG), the Public Service Research Council (PSRC), and three other New Right PAC's have large direct-mail operations. The U.S. Chamber of Commerce has become an ultraconservative PAC that spent $65 million in 1983 alone.

6. A sixth group in the New Right network comprises the congresspersons who directly represent New Right ideology. This group, together with the Republican Party Organization, has captured policy, dictating their conservative manifesto at Dallas. Finally, a group of conservative-interest law firms copies the techniques of public-interest law, while fighting the legal battles of the right. Among these are the Pacific Legal Foundation, the Mountain States Legal Foundation, and the National Legal Center for the Public Interest (NLCPI), that protect the rights of industry in violation of the rights of consumers, in resistance to such measures as the control of toxic

chemicals. They are lawyers acting in the corporate interest against the public interest, the reverse of Nader's "Raiders."

This is a "conspiracy of the like-minded," a New Right network composed of a strange amalgam of ultraconservative forces that operate inside and outside of government, dedicated to capturing control of economic, political, and military policy. They have effectively done so, with little resistance from the administration, but, the world hopes, large opposition from the outside. Ironically the New Right network has successfully translated the techniques of networking and political activation long used by the liberals, reformers, and public-interest organizations dedicated to supporting the consumer, defending the environment, and protecting justice and human rights. The visceral and psychological appeal of the New Right will be difficult to defeat.

Our list comprising the various elements of the New Right would not be complete without the inclusion of the Committee on the Present Danger, a self-defined nonpolitical organization that also serves as a PAC in the semantic community.

This is not a return to the old conservatism but a radical turn to the right, unprecedented in U.S. history. Paul Weyrich of the Committee for the Survival of a Free Congress and the Heritage Foundation tells it like it is: "We are no longer working to preserve the status quo. We are radicals, working to overturn the present power structure of this country"; as does Rep. Newt Gingrich of Georgia, "We are compelled by the driving force of ideological vision" (*Washington Spectator*, 1 December 1984, p. 1). When God is on your side, "it is axiomatic that individual liberties are secondary to the requirement of national security and internal civil order." A manifesto of the Kremlin? Not at all; it appears in a report by the Heritage Foundation. These people controlled the platform in Dallas with their "deliberate manipulation of fear and suspicion," and their self-righteous claim to represent the will of God and to define the nature of Western civilization. In this cosmology, Sovietism, the "evil empire," is everything from the actual policies of the Kremlin, to abortion and welfare, to all liberal causes. All must be destroyed in the name of a holy crusade of Christians against an unholy pagan enemy, the beast. These new rightists are not above book burning and thought control: they attack curricula, demand to choose books for libraries, and even try to control the content of lectures. The Moral Majority has an "Index Prohibitorium" of banned books and provides a Citizen's Request Form to be sent to state public instruction departments for seeking the removal of some titles. In North Carolina, the Moral Majority demanded that Aldous Huxley's *Brave New World* be banned and suggested, in hand lettering, that "IT WOULD MAKE A NICE BONFIRE" (*Washington Spectator*, 1 December 1984, p. 3). The New Right has in effect claimed total authority over what is "right" or "wrong." The Dallas platform made that translation. They targeted the Supreme Court for take-over and arms control for subversion in the name of asserting their moral majority. The $64 billion question is, do they own Reagan as claimed by the Committee on the Present Danger? The next four years, if we have four years of future, will tell.

But America has a marvelous history and tradition of dedication to democratic principles, with a level of public participation unequalled anywhere, and with an irradicable and irrepressible vitality. In the most open society in the world, there are millions in the constituency, citizens, scientists, businesspersons and congresspersons, who seek sanity and peace. It is they who must deny the New Right its goals and the fulfillment of its apocalyptic vision; it is they who must demilitarize the American political economy and culture.

The forces behind Reagan are formidable. The New Right and its allies, the political managers and the strategy intellectuals and their functional integration with the military-industrial complex, provide a powerful and reinforcing stimulant for war. They have captured the decision- and policy-making functions of government. Together, in effect, they form a war system whose constant message is more weapons in the cause of defeating "evil." Fortunately, outside this system are Congress and the people—part of a larger system that may mediate and even negate the unified goal of the Armageddon gang.

THE MILITARIZATION OF AMERICA

The "security intellectuals" work inside and outside of government to form the "strategic," political, or economic judgments of current events and scenarios that assess the consequences of policies, decisions, and events.

As these security intellectuals engage in a "massive rationalization of the war system," they act as prime movers of policy. They work in government establishments to reinforce and determine policies of their superiors through elite accommodation and inordinate influence (Talbott, 1984). Like many other scientists imbued with an ideology of omniscient rationality and a theology of infallibility, their linear, reductionist mode of thinking and quantification imperatives encourage an actuarial approach to the human condition. As has been aptly said, "The security intellectual's moral universe is peculiarly flat" (Luckham, 1984, p. 12). This may be a case of the mutual reinforcement of personality and profession, but the security intellectuals' attitude also derives from the alleged moral neutrality and objectivity of science. In a subtle way, they are the other face of the fundamentalists who deal with apocalypse as prophecy; the strategy scholars deal with apocalypse as prophecy denied. Denial is needed to make the destruction implied by a theory of winning and surviving relative. The enemy suffers relative defeat, counted in terms of tens of millions of casualties. Like the fundamentalists, the strategy scholars have a religious belief—scientism. Scientism requires infallible methods, systems, and people. Nuclear war is reduced to a game; all the quality of life is reduced to quantity. "Thinking about the unthinkable" is a proper assertion of scientism, since reductionism accounts for everything but human suffering, love, caring, reverence, wonder, and creation. Like the technical-support establishment behind civil nuclear power, the strategy scholars make Faustian bargains with nuclear numbers games.

The evolution of the full-scale military-industrial complex into a predominantly military culture reached a new stage in Reagan's first term. Defense spending gained influence over and became integrated with the American political economy. Increased defense spending had become a surrogate industrial strategy, an apparently successful tactic if measured in terms of aggregated conventional economic indicators. The supply-siders had a windfall of success. The political fallout led to Reagan's uprecedented victory in forty-nine states. Caspar Weinberger recognized the economic effects of defense spending when he said, "What we spend is designed entirely to preserve the peace. Some of it just happens to help American industry" (*Fortune*, 30 April 1984, p. 49). In fact, the largest defense spending in U.S. history softened the impact of the 1980 and 1982 recessions. The defense industry provides its largest amount of dollars to the high-tech industries of America. Military demand for semiconductors, microchips, and computers threatens their civil supply. The Pentagon is now racing to develop artificial intelligence, the fifth-generation computer, and a Very High Speed Integrated Circuit (VHSIC) that will be generations ahead of current chip technology. These new "brains" of "smart" weapons will have the reaction time, accuracy, and invulnerability that will allow first-strike dominance.

Military research and design now accounts for almost 35 percent of all the research and design done in the U.S. The majority of scientists and engineers graduated in high-tech fields are now recruited into military development. The DOD runs the world's largest training school system, at a cost of $13.4 billion in 1984. The fastest-growing sector in defense spending, weapons procurement, now draws more of the total budget, $107 billion in 1987, than at the height of the Vietnam War (Adams, 1985). In Reagan's proposed budget, defense spending will account for 7.6 percent of the budget by 1987, about $290 billion. Despite the barrage of propaganda during Reagan's first three-and-a-half years in office, the CIA officially discounted the Reagan administration's claims of excessive Soviet military spending. The CIA estimates that the Soviets spent only 2 percent per year since 1976, rather than the administration's claim of 4–6 percent. Only putting a percentage on high technology that the Soviets do not have and cannot build can help inflate the figures on Soviet spending. The myth of Soviet spending, once the basis of U.S. response, is not needed once momentum takes over.

Robert McNamara once wrote, "There is a kind of mad momentum to the development of nuclear weaponry." The Ellulian "ensemble of technical means" now seems the prime mover of military development, but the dynamics and momentum of armaments technology is reinforced by political, economic, and ideological factors. The militarization of culture plays a powerful role.

High-tech war has the video star-wars game as its model. Artificial intelligence will guide smart weapons with devastating accuracy. Robots will become generals. The computer will become emperor. Which is the independent variable in the rapid evolution of a military-industrial state: the existence of technical means; the technical support group; the industrial corporate machine; or the mutual convergence and reinforcement of all three? Lord Zuckerman, in his book *Nuclear Reality and Illusion,* places great blame on the scientists and engineers in the military establishment and on their development of strategic policy and doctrine (Zuckerman, 1982). This recalls President Eisenhower's earlier admonition "that public policy could itself become the captive of a scientific-technological elite." Earlier this year, Jerome Wiesner, former scientific adviser to Presidents Eisenhower and Kennedy, wrote in the *Boston Globe* magazine, "The United States has been running an arms race with itself . . . and in the process became a military culture—a society in which an arms race is accepted as a way of life. . . . We seem absolutely trapped in a delusional system that grips us more year by year." Wiesner extends Jacques Ellul's view that the ensemble of technical means has subverted human ends by speaking of an entire systemic disorder that affects technology, politics, economics, and culture.

Historically and empirically, the preparation for war leads to war. Power's self-fulfilling potential leads to its own exercise. The determination to fight seems always stronger than deterrence by fear of defeat. Power seems resistant to anything but the temptation to be used. Reagan has gone beyond the nineteenth-century dictum of "talking softly and carrying a big stick," and returned to the ancient Roman "if you desire peace, prepare for war." The Soviets mirror this policy, so each acts out its fear of the other. Deterrence works until it doesn't; then it becomes the unwritten history of the end of the world. The Reagan administration's new National Security Decision Directives #13, 32, and 85 officially plan for limited or protracted nuclear war. Reagan and Weinberger, supported by the "holocaust lobby" and the "peddlers of crisis," challenge the continuation of history.

The reinforcing and convergent concepts of a "weapons culture" (Ralph Lapp) or an "armaments culture" (Robin Luckham), the "military-industrial complex" (Dwight D. Eisenhower), the "technological order" (James Ellul), and the supporting cast of scientists, engineers, technologists, and strategists (Knelman, 1971; 1976; 1981) represent a quantum change in the sociopolitical, economic, and cultural states of a society. At the evolution of such a weapons culture, the social dynamics of an entire society become militarized and affect its culture and, therefore, its values and beliefs. Indicators of the evolution of a new social system can be found in its political, economic, technological, and cultural subsystems. In effect we have a political economy of war.

Radical shifts in economic sectors indicate the evolution of social systems. In Daniel Bell's "post-industrial society," a radical shift from the production of goods to the purveying of services had led to the rise of the "information society" (Porat, 1977). Neither analyst foresaw the growth of military demands for goods (hardware) and services (software) within our political economy. The proliferation of military goods and services in the global economy represents a radical shift in the sociopolitical nature of society. What was once termed the "iron triangle" (Adams, G., 1981) has now become a "steel triangle" (Prins, 1983), a three-pointed "military-academic-industrial complex."

The "steel triangle" describes a social system whose internal dynamics flow through weapons acquisition (technology), justification (politics), escalation programs (official policies), to implementation (decisions for procurement and development of weapons systems). This social system operates in a closed circle that constantly feeds on itself and reinforces its own dynamics. The most powerful component of the triangle is, of course, the industrial component.

In 1980, the DOD awarded 203 U.S. higher-education contracts worth $652 million annually to the "academic" leg of the triangle. Table 6 presents data on the top twenty universities involved in U.S. military research in FY 1979 and 1980. As this table indicates, the three most advanced institutes of technology in the U.S. receive the second, third, and fourth largest amounts of funds for military research. The total amount awarded to the first four recipients represents over 80 percent of the total allocation shown.

The impact of this militarization of industry, government, and university on social policy, goals, and values grossly distorts social allocations and priorities. As bad money drives out good, so does bad policy. The ensemble of military technical means cannot avoid subverting the validity of social and humanly desirable ends if those in power allow it.

The fundamental interests of the corporate group can readily be seen in Table 7. The Pentagon awarded $45 billion in defense contracts to the Big Ten in 1983 alone. That these large military contracts comprise a large percentage of these companies' total sales (General Dynamics at 95 percent!) powerfully indicates the existence of industrial militarization.

TABLE 6

Top Twenty Universities in the U.S.A. in Military Research for Fiscal Years 1979 and 1980

UNIVERSITY OR UNIVERSITY-AFFILIATED INSTITUTION	FISCAL YEAR 1979	FISCAL YEAR 1980	PERCENTAGE CHANGE
1 Johns Hopkins University	$155,801,000	$163,327,000	+4
2 Massachusetts Institute of Technology	123,724,000	154,564,000	+25
3 University of California (system)	24,159,000	29,679,000	+22
4 Illinois Institute of Technology	23,442,000	26,319,000	+12
5 Stanford University	10,694,000	18,068,000	+69
6 University of Texas	15,072,000	15,772,000	+4
7 University of Rochester	12,848,000	15,480,000	+20
8 Georgia Technology Research Institute	8,360,000	14,758,000	+76
9 University of Dayton	13,564,000	13,859,000	+2
10 Pennsylvania State University	14,562,000	12,226,000	-16
11 University of Southern California	11,872,000	10,260,000	-16
12 University of Washington	8,717,000	10,069,000	+16
13 University of Alaska	9,338,000	8,119,000	-13
14 Carnegie Mellon University	4,536,000	7,335,000	+62
15 University of Illinois	3,727,000	6,797,000	+82
16 University of New Mexico	5,428,000	6,472,000	+1
17 California Institute of Technology	3,309,000	5,428,000	+64
18 Harvard University	1,421,000	4,902,000	+245
19 University of Pennsylvania	3,132,000	4,900,000	+56
20 Columbia University	4,052,000	4,848,000	+20

Source: Burkholder, 1981.

WHAT ABOUT THE RUSSIANS?

"We always exaggerate Soviet power" to the point that the Soviet Union has become a collective bogeyman (Steele, *Washington Post,* Sunday, 25 December 1983, p. 82), a congealed image of a Stalinist regime, politically and militarily invalid in the 1980s. With a few exceptions, the Soviet Union has retreated and retrenched all over the world. In terms of world power trends, the Soviets register a dramatic decline: their influence predominates in just 19 of the 164 countries in the world today (*Defense Monitor* 13, no. 6, 1984). The loss of Soviet importance in China, Indonesia, Egypt, India, and Iraq dwarfs any minor successes they may have made in lesser countries. Since 1956, most Western intellectuals have withdrawn their support of the "Soviet experiment." The West and China supersede Soviet influence and action in all areas, even in Central America. In every way, Soviet influence has waned. Still, the pervasive suspicion of Soviet intentions increases.

TABLE 7

TOP TEN DEFENSE CONTRACTORS	FISCAL 1983 DEFENSE CONTRACTS (MILLIONS)	1983 TOTAL SALES (MILLIONS)	FORTUNE 500 RANK
1 General Dynamics	$6,818	$7,146	46
2 McDonnell Douglas	$6,143	$8,111	42
3 Rockwell International	$4,545	$8,098*	43
4 General Electric	$4,518	$26,797	10
5 Boeing	$4,423	$11,129	27
6 Lockheed	$4,006	$6,490	50
7 United Technologies	$3,867	$14,669	18
8 Tenneco	$3,762	$14,353	19
9 Howard Hughes Medical Institute	$3,240	$4,938	—
10 Raytheon	$2,728	$5,937	59

*Fiscal year end September 30.

The Big Guns of Defense Contracting
The military buys the lion's share of its hardware from the aerospace, electronics, and shipbuilding industries. Some of the fiscal 1983 contracts are multiyear programs, but in general the contracts mirror the relationship of military sales to the total sales of the companies listed.

SOURCE: *Fortune,* 30 April 1984.

The Reagan administration has greatly overestimated every aspect of Soviet capability, and has particularly exaggerated Soviet nuclear warfighting capabilities. As we have stated, the U.S. is the actor and the USSR the reactor in the world dynamics of the arms race. The U.S. has forced a costly arms race on the USSR as part of deliberate policy, as revealed in the defense guidance document. The Soviet Union's heavy bureaucracy and inferior technology make it a grossly inefficient society. This inefficiency plagues the Soviet military systems in all its aspects, from its personnel to its military hardware and software (Cockburn, 1983).

In the last decade, Soviet political leaders have consistently stated that a nuclear war is unwinnable and unsurvivable. They have unilaterally announced a "no first-use" doctrine and literally begged for a freeze, particularly in space militarization. An article in the *Christian Science Monitor* quotes the abruptly dismissed Marshal Nicolai Ogarkov, "The time is here when acquiring new nuclear weapons has no purpose. More weapons fail to enhance deterrence" (*Washington Post,* Thursday, 15 November 1984, p. 1). Doubtless, the Soviets would have made serious concessions on Euromissiles if the U.S. had not insisted on "zero-zero" or had delayed cruise and Pershing II deployment. The U.S. subverted "dual-track" to monorail by making intentionally unacceptable offers (Talbott, 1984), as direct and devious statements by various members of the Reagan administration have attested. For example, in speaking of the findings of the General Advisory Committee on Arms Control concerning alleged Soviet violations of past accords, Colin Gray, an influential member of that committee, challenges "the very notion that the superpowers retain enough common interests in arms control to warrant continuing negotiations" (*Arms Control Chronicle,* no. 4, October 1984).

General John Vessey, chairman, Joint Chiefs of Staff; Caspar Weinberger, secretary of defense; Admirals McKee, Wadkins, and Crowe; John Lehman, secretary of the Navy; Richard de Lauer, former undersecretary of defense for research and engineering; and Dr. Robert Cooper, director, Defense Advanced Research Projects Agency (DARPA) have all stated in official hearings that the U.S. is militarily superior to the USSR in every sector of military capability. (General Frederick J. Kroesen, commander, U.S. Army–Europe, has also downgraded the notion of NATO superiority.) The following actual statements of these top officials have been derived from *Defense Monitor* 11, no. 6, 1982, and *Defense Monitor* 13, no. 6, 1984.

Senator Karl Levin: I am wondering whether or not you would swap U.S. military capability overall, with everything that is included in that phrase, for that of the Soviets?

General John Vessey: Not on your life, not to live there or have his job or his responsibilities or to have his forces in comparison to ours.

Senator Levin: I appreciate your answer. Just focusing on the military capability aspect is your answer that you would not trade?

General Vessey: I would not trade.

> Senate Armed Services Committee
> 11 May 1982

Senator Charles Percy: Would you rather have at your disposal the U.S. nuclear arsenal or the Soviet nuclear arsenal?

Defense Secretary Weinberger: I would not for a moment exchange anything, because we have an immense edge in technology.

> Senate Foreign Relations Committee
> 29 April 1982

Just one of our relatively invulnerable Poseidon submarines—less than 2 percent of our total nuclear force of submarines, aircraft, and land-based missiles—carries enough warheads to destroy every large and medium-sized city in the Soviet Union. Our deterrent is overwhelming.

> President Jimmy Carter
> 23 January 1979

It disappoints me to hear people talk about the overwhelming Soviet conventional military strength. We can defend the borders of Western Europe with what we have. I've never asked for a larger force. I do not think that conventional defense is anywhere near hopeless.

> General Frederick J. Kroesen
> Commander, U.S. Army–Europe
> March 1983

U.S. tactical air forces retain a qualitative advantage over those of the Union in aircraft and weapons and, more importantly, in personnel and training.

> Department of Defense
> *Soviet Military Power, 1984*

The U.S. has maintained its lead in most of the basic technologies critical to defense.

> Richard D. DeLauer
> Undersecretary of Defense for Research and Engineering
> February 1984

These factors led the Chief of Naval Operations to comment, "I am confident, as long as our principal maritime allies do not reduce their capability, that we shall secure both flanks and the North Atlantic against the Soviets."

> Admiral James Watkins
> Chief of Naval Operations
> March 1984

We are clearly ahead of the Soviets in overall space technology.

> Dr. Robert Cooper
> Director, Defense Advanced Research Projects Agency
> 1982

On 24 March 1981, John Lehman, Navy secretary, stated the U.S. Navy forces were "far superior in both numbers and quality."

Because of its structure, history, ideology, and experience, Soviet society has a deeper military tradition than the U.S. As a garrison state that survived the extreme ravages of two world wars, the hierarchical political structure gives rise to paranoia about invasion and subversion. Russian society lives half in the nineteenth and half in the twentieth century, drawn together psychologically by the powerful mystique of "Mother Russia." The Russians resisted the armies of Napoleon and the Third Reich despite their enormous social divisions. The Russian people, from tsarists to communists, fear war above all, but they can be collectively militarized in response to a common threat.

"The engines of the Soviet machine are still turning over, but are sputtering" (Kaiser, *Washington Spectator,* 15 November 1984, p. 1). The Soviet economic system falters on recurring crises of grain shortfalls. With the black market and corruption widespread, the safety net for the needy "is badly torn. . . . The old promises of communist ideology are no longer taken seriously" (Kaiser, *Washington Spectator,* 15 November 1984, p. 1). The Afghan war has turned into a Vietnam-style disaster. East European unrest increases as the Warsaw Pact countries show signs of growing independence. The *New Statesman* speaks of "the existing hordes of old tanks and missiles" in the Soviet military machine. The American threat to the sacredness of Mother Russia keeps Soviet society together. Thus, the policies of the Reagan administration, designed to destroy Soviet communism, keep it alive. The Soviets are being driven into a state of high anxiety that George Kennan described as "the dark suspicion of everything and everyone . . . [as] wicked, hostile and menacing" (Kaiser, *Washington Spectator,* 15 November 1984, p. 1).

By consistently exaggerating Soviet military strength, by consistently conjuring up the Soviet threat, by presenting the Soviets as the "focus of evil," the Reagan administration is forcing desperate men into desperate actions. Desperate men in a desperate age genuinely threaten the entire world: even Reagan's jesting remark "We begin bombing in five minutes" initiated a Soviet high alert, according to the Japanese newspaper *Yomiuri Shimbun.*

Even while the East German leader R. Honneker planned a visit to West Germany and the "return of détente," Ronald Reagan declared that he does not accept the "permanent subjugation" of Eastern Europe. In addition, Reagan helped to sabotage the return of détente by feeding on the Soviets' ultimate fear of a reunited Germany. Since FY Defense Guidance 1984–1988 expressly calls for active subversion in communist Eastern Europe, it is hardly surprising that the Soviets clamped down on improving relations between East and West Germany. A reunified Germany may be part of the plan to destroy the Soviets' "evil empire," but the backfire would be nuclear war engendered by catalytic fear, anxiety, and tension.

Because the USSR is a garrison state, the militarization of Soviet culture is far deeper and more overt than in the U.S. Civilian populations participate in such activities as civil defense and relief operations through such organizations as the Voluntary Society for Cooperation with the Army, Air Force, and the Navy (in Russian, DOSAAF). Russian schools include Soviet military and patriotic education in their curricula. While these practices appear offensive and Orwellian, they are defensive in nature. In fact, civil defense is ineffective (Holloway, 1981), and the people treat it with much cynicism, as Moscow's most popular joke indicates:

"Tovarich, what will you do if there is a nuclear war?"

"Well, I will wrap myself in a white sheet and walk very slowly to the graveyard."

"Why slowly, Tovarich?"

"Well, I wouldn't want to cause a panic!"

Despite any criticism that may be made of the militarization of culture in the Soviet Union, we must respect the courage shown by the Russians during World War II. Many of them fought the "Great Patriotic War" as an expression of their love of Mother Russia, not as an extension of their acceptance of Soviet ideology. Because the Russians lost nearly thirty million people as a result of the Reich's invasion of the USSR, their current paranoia about invasion is understandable.

Soviet civilian activities not only aid the military, but also contribute civilian technical skills to the military-industrial complex. Thus they serve the cause of modernization in the Soviet defense industry, which, as in the U.S., is the most technically advanced production endeavor. Unlike the fascist state, Soviet culture is peace loving at its core; its military-industrial complex aims at the psychological capture of traditional sentiment. Finally, the Soviet military has not captured political power. In every major political crisis requiring a change in leadership, from Beria's decline to Khrushchev's fall in 1964, the military acted only as a partner with the Politburo. The removal of Marshal Zhukov proves that the military and politics do not mix well in the Soviet Union because internal dissension is endemic to both sectors.

Roger Garaudy identified the Soviet system as a "bureaucratic-military complex" because he felt it lacked economic driving force. The powerful linkages between a nation's economy and its military must exist to convert it to a "military-industrial complex." In the U.S. such relationshps are obvious and dynamic. The spin-off and spillover of technology, from civil to military industrialization and back, go on all the time. In the supersecretive neo-Orwellian Soviet state, this does not occur. The key dynamic now spurring militarization of the Soviet Union is the external pressure of the arms race and its dedication to parity. United States policy dedicated to economic suffocation of the Soviet Union through the arms race, an overt program described in FY Defense Guidance 1984–1988 and national security directives, holds danger for the world.

All the evidence seems to support Admiral Kennard R. McKee's candid admission of 15 March 1984, "We are the threat, not they" (*Defense Moni-*

tor 13, 1984, p. 5). Then, what is the game? Only one answer makes sense: the total capitulation and/or defeat of the existing Soviet state, by limited or protracted nuclear war if necessary. Parts of the critical document Defense Guidance FY 1984–1988 are explicit in this regard. The mind-set and group-think of the two major philosophical alliances in America—the Moral Major-ity of the fundamentalist right and the strategic scholars of apocalypse, like Richard Pipes, Richard Perle, Fred Iklé, Colin Gray, et al.—uphold this as a firm belief, religious for the "born again" and "rational" for the "intellectual," but no less insidious in spite of its nature. The political power of these two strange alliances is obvious, attested to by the presidential elections of Novem-ber 1984, the Republican platform, and the powerful political positions attained by some of their members. It is not exaggeration to state that they have "captured" foreign and military policy making in the U.S. Moreover, the writings of influential political-strategic intellectuals carry a consistent, implacable theme in their will to achieve escalation dominance, their support of decapitation strikes, or their more subtle opposition to arms control.

Two superpowers, military cultures and military-industrial states over-armed with hair-trigger weapons of the twenty-first century, are confronting each other with policies and tactics of the nineteenth century. Now more than ever, the mobilization of peace movements is critical if we are to avoid the ultimate holocaust.

The alarming, massive intrusion of militarism into the universities, into the factories, and into the government apparatus of both the Soviet Union and the U.S. has significant psychological parameters. Culture itself becomes infected. The U.S. plan for economic suffocation of the USSR seems to be working, aided by the Soviet Union's vast internal problems; but the psycho-logical end-product could be disastrous for the world.

8

The Greening of the World

Peace-making is not an optional commitment. It is a requirement of our faith.
U.S. Catholic Bishops' Letter
"The Challenge of Peace," 1983

Shall there be womanly times, or shall we die?
Ian McEwan

Peace must become a continuation of politics, by peaceful means.
F. H. Knelman

*What kind of peace do we seek? Not a Pax Americana, enforced on the world
by American weapons of war. . . . I speak of peace because of the new face of
war. Total war makes no sense. . . . I speak of peace, therefore, as the necessary
end of rational men.*
John F. Kennedy
American University, Washington
June, 1963

The emergence of an international network of resistance and protest groups
against the nuclear arms race offers the most hope for peace and disarmament. Opposition takes many forms, from Western European formal neutralism to trade détente, but in its most powerful form the people themselves
manifest their opposition to the nuclear cold warriors by demonstrating in
the streets. By the autumn of 1981 the U.K., Italy, Netherlands, Italy, Norway, Denmark, Belgium, France, and West Germany had witnessed the
largest protest marches in their history. Weinberger drew 250,000 protestors
in Bonn in October 1982. Reagan, called the Neutron Cowboy in Amsterdam,
provided one of his best gaffes and fueled the peace movement with his
remark that he could envisage a nuclear war limited to Europe (Sanders,
1983, p. 324). Only Haig's statement that NATO might set off a "nuclear
bomb for demonstration purposes" (Sanders, 1983, p. 326) received more
attention.

In the face of millions of protestors Major General Robert L. Schweitzer
predicted the "Soviets are going to strike" (Sanders, 1983, p. 325). For this he

was transferred from his post as head of NSC's defense group.

Meanwhile, the antinuclear arms race movement spread across the Atlantic. The U.S. developed its own formal opposition with the Nuclear Freeze Initiative (NFI), a sane response to Reagan's policy of peace through strength and right through might. Four former members of the foreign policy establishment, McGeorge Bundy, Robert McNamara, Gerald Smith, and George Kennan, issued a statement in support of NFI (Bundy, 1983). More recently George Kennan has gone further in his denunciation of current nuclear strategies (Kennan, 1983). The mass protests in Europe in the autumn of 1981 led to Reagan's "zero option" proposal for Europe, while criticism at home in 1982 spawned START, both patently designed to disarm the USSR while rearming the U.S. (The latest "initiative," termed "build-down," is yet another version of the same ploy.)

The leak of Weinberger's Fiscal Year 1984–1988 Defense Guidance document coalesced and reinforced the greatest American citizens' movement in history (Halloran, 1982). On 12 June 1982, at the second UN Special Session on Disarmament (UNSSOD II), three-quarters of a million people gathered outside of the United Nations to protest the arms race. The policies of the Reagan administration had finally reversed the views of the American public: once again, the doves outnumbered the hawks in opinion polls. A majority of people in the U.S., Canada, and half a dozen NATO countries are now in opposition to the position of their governments on nuclear arms policy (Lumsden, 1983). Despite the electoral victories of Thatcher and Kohl, the Reagan clones, in the U.K. and West Germany, the public opposition to their hard-line support of a Pax Americana policy is formidable (Simpson, 1983), but their quiet pursuit of East-West trade, namely, the Soviet gas pipeline deal, is never deterred by rhetoric.

THE GREENING OF EUROPE

Citizens' groups—peace groups, environmental groups, human rights groups, alternatives groups, antinuclear energy groups—became wedded to the movement within the churches opposed to nuclear war and evolved into the green/ecology parties of Western Europe. This represents the flowering of the political ecology of grass roots. The ideology of peace has become politicized and peace has become an extension of politics by nonviolent means. In West Germany, the Green Party won 6 percent of the popular vote in the federal elections of 6 March 1983 and now are represented in the Bundestag with twelve members (Trimborn, 1982). Grass roots are greener in West Germany than anywhere. France had earlier successes with its politicization of antinuclear sentiment (Grossman, 1977; Chaudron and Le Pape, 1979; Touraine et al., 1980; Nelkin and Pollack, 1980). The green/ecology parties have strived to incorporate into their platforms and policies a new world view that incorporates peace, justice, social restructuring, and retooling (Mowlam, 1983). The ecological imperative has become the core of the new paradigm (*The Ecologist,* 1979; Devall, 1980; Porritt, 1984).

THE ORIGINS

The roots of the new green/ecology parties are certainly the citizen-scientist environmental groups that first emerged in the late 1960s and early 1970s (Sax, 1971). The ultimate concern of these groups became the social, technical, ethical, and environmental impacts of the civil nuclear-fuel cycle, the issues of reactor safety, nuclear wastes, and proliferation that haunt nuclear power use (Knelman, 1976; Gyorgi, 1978; Jungk, 1979). In rejecting nuclear power, the green parties posited that certain kinds of technology are intrinsically alienating/dehumanizing, environmentally and socially threatening, and unacceptably risky. The global network that converged and coalesced around these issues incorporated other streams of protest, and tended to cut across traditional political ideologies and constituencies. The radicals without a cause, anarchists and libertarians, the conservative but concerned middle, the threatened farmer/rancher, the public interest groups, the old peace movement and the pacifists, the women's liberation movement, and environmentalists in general mustered a focused attack on civil nuclear power. The debate matured first in the U.S., where the issue of nuclear power came to the top of the environmental agenda. In some ways the present movement has gone full circle. In the early 1950s a nuclear disarmament movement emerged in England that later spread across the world. The early death of this movement can be attributed to a combination of circumstances: the vulnerability of single-issue movements, ideological divisiveness, shifts in the global agenda of issues, from Vietnam to the environment to energy, and the emergence of arms negotiations and treaties, from PTBT to ABM to SALT I.

A paper on the Stockholm Conference on the Human Environment (Knelman, 1972, 1973) and a book on social ecology (Knelman, 1979) analyzed the history of contemporary environmental movements. By 1970 most Western governments, largely in response to citizen-scientist public interest/ environmental activities, created environmental cabinet posts, departments, and agencies. Earth Day was first observed in the U.S. on 22 April 1970. The year 1972 witnessed the publication of the Club of Rome's "Limits to Growth" study, the British Blueprint for Survival, the roots of the Conserver Society studies at the Science Council of Canada, and shortly afterwards the National Survival Plan of the National Survival Institute of Canada. (This author was a major participant in the latter two developments.) The first ecology party was founded in New Zealand (The Values Party, May 1972) and the first United Nations Conference on the Human Environment was held in Stockholm, June 1972.

This author's direct involvement with the ecology parties of New Zealand, Australia, the U.K., etc., his attendance at the 1972 Stockholm parallel conference "Dai Dong," and his later activity with the Fellowship of Reconciliation in Holland and other parts of Europe (and being the founder of CND, Canada, and cofounder of CCNR) enabled him to observe these new movements at first hand, to discuss platforms and policies, and to observe political/ecological composition and divisions. Earlier, in 1960, he had directly participated in the Campaign for Nuclear Disarmament (CND) in the U.K. and maintains communication with the British Ecology Party through the journal *The Ecologist*.

In general, these movements have fallen victim to internal tension among those who favor equity over environment, those who favor environment over equity, those who view the movement as apolitical, and those who wish it to adopt a particular political philosophy, specifically, the "left." These divisions have plagued these movements almost everywhere. Only the powerful cohesion of opposition to making Europe a nuclear battleground has enabled these movements to overcome these conflicts until the present.

In Britain a strong revival of the nuclear disarmament movement has now become part of a Western European network, the European Nuclear Disarmament movement (END). This movement supports the idea of making all of Europe a nuclear weapons–free zone (Gompert, 1980; Bahrs et al., 1981).

The advent of the Reagan administration and the initiation of a new cold-war policy and the plans to fight and win a limited or protracted nuclear war have made the dangers of nuclear war the most profound and compelling issue in the world. Reagan could have won the 1983 Nobel Peace Prize—his administration's policies have spurred the growth of the world peace movement.

Abortive attempts to publicize the antinuclear movement in the U.S. and Canada, such as the advent of Barry Commoner's Citizens' Party in the 1976 U.S. presidential election and the candidacy of a few Ecology Party members in Canada's last federal election, have met with little success. (The Citizens Party received 0.3 percent of the popular vote in 1980.) This interesting difference in political evolutionary form between North America and Western Europe requires further analysis. Every Western European country has evolved into a three- and sometimes four-party system. Socialist and social democratic governments have been common in most of West Europe since World War II. The U.S. has rejected socialism and retains its traditional two-party system. Nevertheless, political forces such as the Nuclear Freeze

Initiative in the U.S. have taken up the nuclear arms race issue. In Canada, a social democratic third party, the New Democratic Party (NDP), resists cruise missile testing and military ties with the U.S. In general, where political parties unequivocally embrace an antinuclear posture, there seems to be less need to create a new political party. For example, in both the U.K. and Canada, Social Democrats have opposed nuclear arms. Where no political party, socialist or social democratic included, adopts an antinuclear platform, new political groups based on the principles of peace and ecology emerge. These are not simple one-to-one correlations. The evolution of ecology parties depends on one main issue: the widespread and proliferating use of civil nuclear power. Where socialist or social democratic parties have supported nuclear power, as in West Germany, France, and Sweden, ecology parties have arisen. Where social democratic parties have supported NATO's 12 December 1979 decision to place 572 intermediate-range U.S. missiles in Europe, peace politics has flourished, often being incorporated into the platform of ecology politics.

The opposition to the nuclear arms race has a much larger "natural" constituency than the movements opposed to civil nuclear power. As a matter of fact, many prominent scientists and political figures active in opposing the nuclear arms race still favor civil nuclear power. Two important examples are the Nobel laureate Dr. Hans Bethe and Sweden's Prime Minister Olof Palme. In general, socialist and communist countries, with some exceptions such as Austria, have been among the most enthusiastic in the pursuit of civil nuclear power, critical examples of the greater priority of economics (and equity) over other issues. The French socialist government under Mitterand supports civil nuclear power and its independent nuclear warfighting forces as strongly as previous conservative governments. The recession tended to reduce the priority of environmental issues more in France than other countries. France, at this time, lags behind the U.S., Canada, the U.K., and West Germany in its opposition to nuclear arms.

West Germany has the most successful ecology party and has become the pivotal region of the nuclear arms debate (Frankland, 1981). West Germany has a higher density of nuclear weapons (mainly tactical) than any country in the world. With implementation of the 1970 NATO "dual-track" decision, it will have the most potent long-range theater nuclear weapon in the West, the Pershing II, capable of hitting many Soviet "hard" targets within five to ten minutes. On Sunday, 28 September 1982, the Greens elected nine members in Hesse and became the nation's third political force. The Greens' four principles of social equity, ecology, grassroots democracy, and nonviolence (*oekologisch, sozial, basis demokratisch und gewaltfrei*) are embedded in an amalgam of left-wing/anarchist philosophy. They identify themselves as the antiparty party. The Greens have a total of seventeen members in state parliaments while the alternatives have nine seats. The Greens now also have twelve members in the Bundestag. Despite their political success, the Greens face powerful ideological divisions between "pure" and "left-wing" ecologists. The "left-wing" insists on adopting a clear but nonaligned Marxist/anarchist ideological base. A few have supported Colonel Khadaffi's "green movement." In general, green/ecology parties have been guilty of not developing comprehensive policies; one wonders what a successfully negotiated arms treaty would do for their future. In West Germany the present prime minister Kohl strongly supports the Reagan administration's policies, as does Prime Minister Thatcher in the U.K. In Britain's 9 June 1983 general election, the opposition Labour Party divided over unilateral disarmament for the country. It is quite possible that some European voters support economic and military policies that embody political contradictions: peace *and* economic growth. Ecology parties, on the other hand, set a unique goal consistent with the principles of ecology. Thus, small ecology parties have emerged in the U.K., Canada, New Zealand, and Australia—all of which have social democratic parties that oppose the nuclear arms race, but pursue traditional economic growth without any clearly defined adherence to ecological principles.

The basic strength of the "green" movements derives from the fact that people of all political persuasions, of all class and institutional affiliations, have come together to oppose the madness of the nuclear arms race and the increasing threat of a nuclear war. Their concern is the great hope of the world, and it may portend a clear shift to an integrated ecological-social policy. The years of the energy crunch and crisis brought movement in that direction and this should happen again in this decade. Conservation, like arms control, is a transitional step to sanity.

France was the first country to obtain an important response to its ecology party, Les Verts. In the 1974 presidential election the ecological candidate Louis René Dumont received 1.3 percent of the popular vote (330,000 votes). By 1977 1200 candidates participated as green party candidates in municipal elections in France, and Les Verts received between 8 and 14 percent of the vote or 2.3 million votes (Grossman, 1977). In Alsace greens formed a majority on the councils and became known as the "Green Tide." A French branch of Friends of the Earth of San Francisco (FOE) facilitated the growth of the movement. Friends of the Earth also went to the U.K., Australia, and New Zealand. Between 1972 and 1975 the Values Party of New Zealand increased their popular vote to a 5.2 percent maximum and elected several local councilors on a platform similar to most of the ecology parties — survival, justice, and community. Austria, Switzerland, Holland, Belgium, Spain, Italy, and the Scandinavian countries have all experiernced strong antinuclear opposition, but ecology parties have arisen only in the U.K., New Zealand, Italy, West Germany, and France.

All of these movements had their origins in the environmental groups of the late 1960s that responded to increasingly visible environmental degradation. By 1970 many of these movements became interested in the campaign against nuclear power, despite their principal concern with specific and often local environmental problems such as air and water pollution from toxic substances and environmentally destructive industrial by-products, and projects. By 1973 these movements shifted their emphasis from symptom to disease and began to view the problem as the natural outcome of industrial, growth-oriented societies. To a degree, these new movements rejected traditional ideology and recognized that both capitalist and communist/socialist states shared a commitment to progress that lacked a policy for environmental protection.

These new ecology parties drew their constituency from the farmers, middle-income professionals, workers, intellectuals, antinuclear militants, consumerists, nonviolents, technological neo-Luddites, concerned scientists, and women's associations. They have the same composition as the environmental movements that spawned them. Initially, these ecology parties opposed civil nuclear power; in the last three or four years, they have increased their opposition to the nuclear arms race. At their best, these new parties hold out a hope for reconciliations that the French identify as "*socialisme d'austerite et autogene.*"

WOMEN AND PEACE

The gender gap in the peace movements indicates that women play a dominant role in these groups. A significantly larger percentage of women than men support the nuclear peace movement and the nuclear freeze and oppose Reagan, Thatcher, and Kohl, the nuclear trio. Women are the mainspring of global peace movements. In many cases their support of such organizations registers their protest against the restrictive norms of society, in education, the workplace, in the job market, and in remuneration, that have culturally evolved in a male-dominated workplace. Further, a substantial amount of feminist theory associates the peace movement with feminism in general, while war seems to be linked to expressions of masculinity.

If one hypothesizes that exploitation carries a cost measurable in the exploiters' lack of humanness and incapacity of caring for the exploited, then the exploitation of women by men may result in a difference in caring. However, extreme exploitation can also debilitate the victims' human spirit. Perhaps man-woman relationships avoid this dehumanization by virtue of the sexual connection, a component absent from racism and other forms of human rights violations based on collective stereotypes. In the developing world, of course, women fall victim to the structural violence inherent in the food-gathering and preparing systems, in persistent compulsory high birth rates, and in their subjugation to male authority. The pervasive rape and spousal battering now characteristic in the U.S. indicate the tenacity of the patriarchal system in the First World. Not surprisingly, some feminists have resorted to changing sex roles or becoming aggressive, even militant, in the struggle for women's liberation. The exploited are not often kind to their exploiters, even when their roles are reversed.

Evidence seems to indicate that androgyny leads to harmony between the traits of both sexes. Men and women in the peace movements may well be more androgynous than the average population. Evidence also indicates that androgyny may affect one's attitude, behavior, and concern for the environment. Children embody the future, and to love and nurture children is to cherish the future. Such an attitude toward children is traditionally a feminine trait. Opposition to nuclear war and the prevention of nuclear war ultimately extends that care and nurture to the environment and the global biosphere.

Superficially at least, feminine traits, possibly a suspect concept, apparently engender a more peaceful and caring response to life, to living things, and to Nature. The "power trip" — the urge to win, to dominate, to exploit, and to fight — is associated with masculinity, particularly in its "macho" form. Maleness is toughness, conquest, and aggression. It despises as weakness feminine qualities in men. Rational and objective men dominate and prevail over women and Nature. Thus, the masculine personality tends to be antiecological, and the feminine more intrinsically ecological in perspective. The linking of ecological awareness and peace seeking appears more natural to the androgynous person, man or woman. Therefore a case could be made for the androgynous person's commitment to peace and environmental protection. Peace movements conceive of peace as either the positive goal of justice and the absence of war, or the limited goal of controlled armaments and the management of war. Therefore, peace movements serve as an enrichment or sensitization of consciousness in the face of widespread injustice and militarization.

In September 1981 tens of thousands of Englishwomen began a sit-down protest at Greenham Common Air Force Base, a U.S. air base designated for the siting of cruise missiles. This incredible example of passive civil disobedience, perhaps the most dramatic, long-lasting demonstration of women for peace, epitomizes the feminist revolution and its impact on the peace movement. Blending the issues of peace and women's rights into a unique nonhierarchical organization, a "nonorganized organization," this remarkable, organic peace encampment demonstrates a collective objection to nuclear war and the U.S. nuclear presence in Britain. Despite multiple evictions, incredible harassment, threats, direct and brutal physical assault, legal action, and even imprisonment, this sit-down lasted for over a year. The Greenham women offer the ultimate expression of resistance to nuclear war. Similar women's peace camps are spreading to Euromissile sites in other countries as major women's groups form in every country of Europe and North America. In Canada, a long-existing organization, Voice of Women, has been involved in the peace movement for some thirty years. The Women's Strike for Peace is a very active organization in the U.S. Every poll in the U.S. confirms the view that significantly more women than men support the twin causes of peace and justice. By contributing to peace efforts in every country, women uphold the ancient Lysistrata tradition and represent the major force for global peace.

AMERICAN EXCEPTIONALISM

All of Western Europe has had socialist and/or social democratic governments or opposition parties; the U.S., to this day, has not. In addition, all of Western Europe has militant left-wing trade unions. By the 1950s, the U.S. trade union movement had purged its left-wing affiliates. In addition, the high level of existing political alienation in the U.S., as evidenced by the consistently low voter turn-out and the absence of left-wing labor unions, contributes to the general theory of American exceptionalism from the ecological/peace movements. Barry Commoner's attempt to lead a Citizens' Party, a form of green/socialist politics in the 1980 presidential campaign, failed. American populist tradition, as evidenced by Eugene V. Debs's campaign and the nine hundred thousand votes for president he received in 1920, is not dead, but has not yet evolved into third-party politics, because of the relative economic success of American "capitalism." Still, the size and vitality of the American environmental movement spawned Earth Day and Sun Day and have kept the environment fairly high on the national agenda of issues. The Nuclear Freeze Initiative (NFI) results from possibly the single largest grass-roots movement in history.

The peace movement as represented by NFI has not required a new party because the Democratic party in general, and some individual Republican congresspersons have carried the issue into the House and Senate. All three Democratic presidential candidates in 1984 subscribed to NFI. Nevertheless one senses Mondale and Hart might have persisted in the precursor cold-war politics of American liberals. The nuclear freeze campaign and the other disarmament and peace groups constitute a powerful movement in the U.S.; yet in 1984, the problem of defeating Reagan was greater than the need for influencing the Democratic candidates to align their policies with public sentiment. Both Mondale and Hart called for such small cuts in the defense budget that the "fat" remaining far exceeded these shallow cuts. While the

Western European peace movements and, in the U.K., Norway, and the Netherlands, the chief opposition parties think seriously of an independent, nonaligned "third path," Reagan and even the relatively peace-oriented Carter cling to the stale, unproductive climate of the cold war and the Soviet Threat.

Something unique about America accounts for the sharp contradictions that divide it. In the U.S. a powerful aversion to centralization coexists within the immense centralization of corporate and financial power. The aversion to bureaucracy in the midst of excessive bureaucracy is an obvious, often disregarded contradiction, as is the irony of belief in "free enterprise" in the face of monopoly and oligopoly. In further contradiction to the American polity, the aversion to helping the helpless (largely a Reagan policy) creates a CARE program for the rich and trade union membership becomes increasingly right wing. The most powerful theme of all in American life is perhaps the materialization of culture. The capture of culture by the "cash nexus" distorts most values, so "green" means not an evolution in politics, but rather the color of cash. Despite all of this, the democratic vitality in U.S. life cannot be stilled or stifled; it may yet assert itself.

The "materialization" of formal politics produces extremely costly charades of image making that exchange form for content. In contrast the ecology of grassroots has its own forms that rely more on people than money. The labor-intensive politics that brings "green" candidates to challenge the perpetual two parties begins in communities. The constituency is there to repoliticize America (Alger and Mendlovitz, 1984).

As a hopeful sign of this repoliticization, some key cities of America have elected reform black mayors, for example, Harold Washington of Chicago. Their election involved the activation of grass-roots community forces to defeat the traditional, previously invulnerable incumbent political machine.

Ronald Reagan's decisive victory in the 1984 presidential elections, unlike his victory in 1980, did not shift power in the House or the Senate. Nor did it bring in a new wave of the New Right, as in 1980. This president still bases his mandate on a minority, in fact, an unrepresentative minority, of potential voters. This is the way the political game is played. Mondale's courage notwithstanding, he proved a relatively weak opponent, particularly in the image battle. Reagan, the made-for-TV president, won this media event. But not even the popular Reagan can keep peace and war from the top of the public agenda. What is now required is a remobilzation of the peace movement, somewhat dispirited by the presidential results. The issues of "nuclear winter" and "Star Wars" afford a new basis for reopening the public debate.

THE GLOBAL AGENDA AND THE NEW PEACE MOVEMENTS

At present in four NATO countries — the U.K., Netherlands, West Germany and Norway—one of the major, traditional parties has opposed the installation of the new Euromissiles. The present governments of two other countries, Spain and Greece, also oppose it. In the U.S. nine states held referenda on the Nuclear Freeze Initiative, and it was supported in eight states. Every country polled by the Atlantic Institute, including the U.S., believed arms control to be as significant as the military balance in the search for security (Lumsden, 1983, p. 100). In five countries, France, West Germany, Italy, Netherlands, and Canada, a significant majority preferred arms control to strengthening military forces (Adler and Wertman, 1981.) Public opinion polls in the U.K., West Germany, Belgium, and the Netherlands indicate a majority of respondents oppose locating Euromissiles on their soil (Lumsden, 1983).

A conglomerate of public groups — scientists' and physicians' associations, environmental, women's, and religious groups, and, to a lesser degree, trade unions — have adapted their agenda to the peace movement. From the beginning of the nuclear age, scientists have had a history of involvement in the peace movement (Grodzins and Rabinowich, 1963). The U.K.'s Medical Association for the Prevention of War is the oldest physicians' group active in the peace movement. Physicians for Social Responsibilty (PSR), an earlier U.S. movement, has now been reactivated and is linked with many similar groups throughout the world, including its branches in the USSR. The Pugwash Conferences are among the earliest attempts on the part of scientific organizations to deal with the issues of nuclear war. Like the more recent International Physicians for the Prevention of Nuclear War, the Pugwash group is international and includes Soviet members. Created by the famous tycoon Cyrus Eaton, the Pugwash group has influenced policy in both the U.S. and USSR and was certainly a factor in the Atmospheric Test Ban Treaty.

In the U.S., Canada, the U.K., West Germany, and the Netherlands, the churches and other religious organizations also oppose the nuclear arms race. Canon Collins was one of the founders of the original Campaign for Nuclear Disarmament in the U.K. in the late 1950s. In 1983 alone, actual, paid membership in CND doubled to over 80,000; in addition, separate local memberships bring the total to over 250,000. If one includes CND affiliates such as unions, women's groups, and professional associations, membership swells to millions. The national membership of CND grows at a rate of approximately 1000 members per week.

The 1984 annual CND conference maintained unity, although it revealed many significant divisions among its membership in regard to (1) relations with NATO; (2) confinement to the single issue of disarmament; and (3) the freeze initiative and British unilateralism (Penner, 1984). Most Britons understand the negative aspect of NATO as a military arm of the U.S., and the actual recommendation that the U.K. leave NATO garnered intense debate. Many believe, with some merit, that NATO can be reformed. This author feels that NATO must be resurrected from U.S. dominance, particularly because of the way it is used by the Reagan administration. NATO is in a period of flux that results from the counterproductive "dual-track" decision. In the next few years, should the Thatcher and Kohl regimes be overthrown and Reagan's warfighting policies defused, NATO might be restructured. However, the military-industrial complexes of NATO countries will undoubtedly exert pressure to maintain their war economies from which they derive such huge benefits. Only a global peace economy would permit the abandonment of military alliances and militarism.

Policy issues are fundamental for the peace movement. By nature, it is an umbrella organization held together not by common ideologies or social programs, but by a common enemy, the dangers of nuclear war. The peace movement's ability to extend its role into more comprehensive policies and, hence, into more formal politics is questionable. As a single-issue organization made up of diverse groups and individuals, moving into the area of multiple or integrated issues and policies could be divisive. This is what distinguishes the peace movement from the ecology/green parties: the greens have one role under the umbrella organization, but also a more primary political function of their own.

In the U.K., the opposition Labour Party favors unilateral disarmament, probably as a result of their political affiliation with Britain's powerful peace coalition. Again, the peace movement's affiliation with an active political party precludes the emergence of a strong "green" party.

While unilateral disarmament makes economic and strategic sense for the U.K., political problems still plague the adoption of this policy. For one thing, any country without second-strike capacity would be better off with a no-strike capacity: the U.S. might close its nuclear umbrella. Reagan is the first isolationist/interventionist president.

The peace movement in the U.S. has a role to play in all elections because war or peace are fundamental alternatives for government; thus, the peace movement must rally behind those candidates who support the NFI. In the 1984 presidential elections, any of the Democratic candidates would have been a better choice in this most decisive time in history. The arithmetic of the U.S. presidential elections makes it imperative that a large turnout be assured — a large popular vote could have defeated Reagan. If the women, the poor, the student, the black, and the senior voters could have been brought to the polls, Reagan might have lost.

Nineteen hundred and eighty-four was a prophetic year that witnessed the death of Soviet leader Yuri Andropov, the retirement of Canadian Prime Minister Pierre Trudeau, and the U.S. presidential elections. Former Soviet Premier Konstantin Chernenko, like his predecessors, had specified what might be put in the "window of opportunity": (1) removal of the new Euromissiles as a first gesture; (2) an underground test ban treaty; (3) a mutual nuclear weapons freeze; (4) a pact banning the militarization of space; and (5) a chemical weapons ban. The last four proposals have won widespread support throughout the world. While one might question the motives of the Soviets on these initiatives, they are worthy of active pursuit. Perhaps a majority of citizens may be willing to remove the new Euromissiles in order to obtain the other four objectives. While new arms talks have begun in Geneva as of 12 March 1985, months of negotiations have shown little progress in arms reduction. Both superpowers seem to be frozen in a state of permanent deadlock.

A THEORY OF GROWTH

Membership in the British CND provides a good indicator of this author's analysis of the rise, fall, and later repatriation of antinuclear peace movements. From its beginning in 1957, CND has grown to a membership of over forty thousand (Lumsden, 1983). Membership reached over fifteen thousand in the 1960–62 period, its first peak. By 1970 membership had declined to just over two thousand and remained between two thousand and three thousand until 1978. Much more rapid growth began in 1980, with a steep rise in membership in the following three years. This has not yet peaked.

The fallout issue, the Cuban missile crisis, and Britain's independent nuclear capacity dominated the early growth of the peace movement from 1957 to 1963. The success of the Test Ban Treaty of 1963 dampened the vitality of the movement. In the middle sixties détente and the stabilization of the nuclear arms race through mutual deterrence caused the peace movement to recede. At the same time, attention began to focus on the problem of nuclear proliferation and thus interest in civil nuclear developments grew. In the late 1960s and early 1970s the peace movements concentrated on the single issue of Vietnam. The 1972 UN Conference on the Human Environment expressed a trend already discernible in the late 1960s: the environment had emerged as a dominant global issue. For many, environmental issues were linked to the hazards of the civil nuclear fuel cycle, and so these two issues tended to be twinned in the 1970s. By 1977 the proposed development of the neutron bomb began to shift interest back to the issue of nuclear war. The modernization of NATO's nuclear forces and the "dual-track" decision of 1979 acclelerated the resurgence of the European peace movements. The U.S.'s failure to ratify SALT II in the wake of the Soviet invasion of Afghanistan intensified fears of a new arms race, but nothing has contributed to the worldwide growth of peace movements more than the aggressive policy of the new Reagan administration. Nineteen hundred eighty-two witnessed the largest peace demonstrations in history in Europe, North America, and Japan.

The above analysis does not entirely correspond to every country involved. Britain, like France, is a special case because it has an independent nuclear warfighting capacity. Thus Britain has consistently faced the issue of unilateral disarmament, which has also undergone a resurgence in the 1980s. Canada and the U.S. have similar patterns of growth and issue. In both countries, environmental movements generally played a more dominant role in citizen action than Western Europe. The Vietnam issue dominated citizen action in the late 1960s, and gradually yielded its place to environmental issues. As the consequences of nuclear war became better known, environmental groups refocused their attention from their opposition to civil nuclear power to their concern about the nuclear arms race and nuclear war. The commercial collapse of civil nuclear power reinforced this shift in concern.

A global agenda of issues impacts dynamically on the ecology of grassroots. Movements of citizens and scientists emerge around a focus of concern. As the nature of nuclear weapons and the nuclear arms race rose to the top of the agenda, public movements, which this author has termed informal politics, began to influence policy. The first wave of this development rose in the late 1950s, peaked with the Cuban missile crisis, and fell after the Test Ban Treaty of 1963. The separate movement of concern over the environment contended with Vietnam as a major focus of activity in the late 1960s, but environment rose to the top of the global agenda by 1970. That pivotal year witnessed the almost universal creation of government departments, ministries, and agencies mandated to protect the enviromment, as governments formally acknowledged the political significance of the environment. The issue was globalized in 1972 by the first of the great global issue conferences of the United Nations, held in Stockholm. A new United Nations Environment Program (UNEP) was created.

The great energy crisis period heralded by the OPEC boycott in December 1973 began a process that changed the nature of the environmental issue. The movement exchanged its concerns with symptoms of environmental degradation for an understanding of the disease; it shifted emphasis from environment to ecology. Civil nuclear power became the focus of attention of the new ecology movements. This movement matured into "green" politics in the middle seventies. The resurgence of the peace movements began in 1979 and experienced great growth from 1980 on. Today the American peace movement focuses on the nuclear freeze.

Peace movements have a broader constituency and a narrower focus of concern than "green" politics, but these two movements overlap and have many key constituents in common. Peace movements as such have not evolved into a formal political party because traditional parties, in almost every case, have adopted the same agenda: the leading Democratic presidential candidates in the U.S., the Labour Party in the U.K., and the Social Democrats in Norway, Sweden, West Germany, Belgium, and the Netherlands.

Despite occasional denouncements or the rare gesture of support, most of the key governments in the nuclear debate view peace movements with alarm and fear. The Reagan administration expresses its dismay in outright attacks; the Thatcher and Mulroney governments and other elitists dismiss the peace movements by alleging that the public necessarily oversimplifies all contentious issues because of its ignorance of the facts. Scientists and experts cannot be dismissed as readily (Chapple, 1982; Fitchett, 1982).

The core vision of the green/ecology parties represents a new world view embodying a revolutionary social paradigm. The dominant social paradigm of progress/growth riding on high technology while still representing the entrenched political economies of the developed world is being seriously challenged for the first time since the Industrial Revolution. The issue of civil and military power has added clarity to the polarization of these contending world views. (The Appendix provides interested readers with further material on the intellectual roots of the green/ecology movements.)

THE FREEZE THAT PRECEDES THE THAW

There is a curious coincidence in Reagan's "victories" regarding arms control. Having lost the early Senate and House votes regarding the MX, the KAL-007 incident accommodated MX (with the help of some liberals who also discovered the fiction of silo "vulnerability" as they had helped scuttle SALT II).

Randall Forsberg published the original "freeze" manifesto in April 1980, the same year a nonbinding ballot initiative on a freeze proposal won three state senate districts in western Massachusetts. The freeze proposal won two-to-one support in thirty out of thirty-two towns at the height of the presidential election in November 1980 (Cockburn and Ridgeway, 1983). Of all the arms control initiatives, the nuclear freeze has found the greatest support.

In 1981 and 1982, second-level strategy advisers raised the specter of outside subversion in Central America. Under their sinister influence, Reagan indulged in a series of attacks on Soviet communism. He suggested a "window of vulnerability" that necessitated definitive U.S. superiority in nuclear and conventional arms. His violent attacks on Soviet communism imply implacable motives, and the subversion of arms control reinforced this suspicion. But this, of course, is the major thrust of the "secret agenda."

The record shows the Reagan administration has moved from stalling to sabotaging arms control. It took one-and-a-half years before public opinion and European alarm forced the administration to the bargaining table with the Soviets at the Intermediate Nuclear Forces (INF) negotiations in Geneva. It soon became evident that because the original "zero-zero" option, START, and "build-down" were designed to be unacceptable to the USSR, they were designed to defeat any arms control agreement. Instead, the U.S. proposals helped to accelerate the growth of the peace movement.

The success of the freeze movement was quite astonishing. By June 1982, the National Nuclear Freeze Clearinghouse in St. Louis noted that some 279 congressional districts had active antinuclear organizations with up to 20,000 unpaid volunteers (Cockburn and Ridgeway, 1983, p. 10). Moreover eleven state legislatures in one or both houses by then had endorsed the freeze.

The nuclear freeze movement in California models successful campaigning by a grass-roots movement. Within three months of the December 1981 deadline, the freeze initiative resolution had collected 500,000 signatures, almost 50 percent more than the 346,00 required to place it on the November 1982 ballot. The California freeze movement adopted some techniques of special interest lobbying: the use of political action committees (PACs), direct mail campaigns funded by using seed money, and the publishing of voters' "hit lists." The freeze resolution passed in California, winning 52.5 percent of the vote.

The late spring of 1982 was a high point in the global peace movements, as demonstrations occurred throughout Western Europe. The 1982 success of Jonathan Schell's book *The Fate of the Earth* indicated increasing public interest in the nuclear arms race. Almost three-quarters of a million people assembled in a Central Park rally in New York 12 June 1982 in support of the UN Second Special Session on Disarmament (UNSSOD II) then in progress.

THE POLITICAL "BAN" WAGON

Within three weeks of the 12 June 1982 rally, Senators Ted Kennedy (D-Mass.) and Mark Hatfield (R-Ore.) issued a book on the freeze initiative that some of Kennedy's speechwriters had written. This version of the freeze, like Mondale's in the second presidential debate on Sunday, 21 October 1984, had the usual, and perhaps necessary, political qualifiers of why the U.S. had to remain strong in the face of the Soviet threat; but it remained unpalatable to the hawks.

Democrats and some Republicans jumped on the freeze bandwagon.

Voters in 8 states and 27 counties and cities, including Chicago, Philadelphia, and Denver, supported freeze referenda. In total, 11 state legislatures, 9 state initiatives, 307 cities, 61 city councils, and the District of Columbia plebiscite have endorsed the freeze. About 2 million Americans have signed freeze petitions, and a total of 30 percent of the electorate had voted on freeze initiatives, referenda, and plebiscites without suffering a major loss (Cockburn and Ridgeway, 1983). By May 1983 a *New York Times* poll showed that 87 percent of the population supported a freeze. Despite the polls only one freeze advocate went to Congress in 1982, Democrat Bob Carr of Michigan who had lost his seat in 1980.

In reaction to the groundswell of interest in the nuclear freeze, Reagan dispatched Paul Nitze to the INF talks in Geneva. Nitze, a notorious hardliner, almost reached agreement with the Soviets in his famous "walk-in-the-woods," but Reagan administration members more hawkish than he repudiated his attempts (Talbott, 1984). In the same way, European and NATO pressures drove Reagan to renew SALT negotiations, renamed START by the cynical, superhawk professional advisers, Perle, Marshall, Iklé, and company. The European reaction stemmed, in part, from General Haig's casual statement on "demonstration shots," (Sanders, 1983, p. 326), while Weinberger, the laconic fundamentalist, announced the manufacture of the neutron bomb on Hiroshima Day, 6 August 1981.

Later in 1981 and the spring of 1982, the very significant leak of the notorious "five-year defense plan," a title possibly derived from Perle's deliberate attempt at irony, prompted a flurry of response. Strangely enough, the response and analysis were not sustained. The freeze movement itself and the peace movements of Europe did not use the leaked material; the Congress did not oppose Reagan. This author believes the defense guidance document, together with the other top-secret memoranda and decision and directive documents, remains at the top of the agenda, and provides a basis for the analysis of the military and foreign policies of the Reagan administration.

AN ANALYSIS OF THE FREEZE AS ARMS CONTROL

Both the right and the left have viewed the freeze as superficial because it is neither arms reduction nor control. Reagan aimed the same criticism at SALT, which is a form of freeze at the ceiling; with the clever advice of Perle and company he introduced the START proposal to reduce arms, not limit them. The attack by the left derives, in part, from its intrinsic distrust of liberal initiatives and Democratic cooptation. The left sees former President John F. Kennedy, the romantic Camelot figure of U.S. politics, as the coldest of cold warriors. It normally denies the uniqueness of the Reagan administration's warfighting policies by pointing out its historical evolution from Schlesinger's "counterforce" through Brown's "countervailing" doctrine. In particular, the left views Carter's Presidential Directive #59 and his Secretary of Defense Harold Brown's Nuclear Weapons Employment Policy 2 (NUWEP-2) as essentially the same nuclear warfighting doctrine as Reagan's National Security Decision Documents #13 and #32.

Regardless of its early formulations, a later interpretation of the freeze concept began with a "halt to the testing, production and further deployment of all nuclear weapons, missiles and delivery systems in a way that can be checked and verified by both sides" (California Initiative); it also incorporated a detailed set of steps to implement the arms reductions to follow. The right's rejection of the freeze is of course predictable, given their commitment to effective superiority and their rejection of the notion of parity. The Reagan administration affirms a "peace through strength" or even a "capitulation through strength" policy. This administration differs from all previous ones not only in its robust language of nuclear warfighting and warwinning policy, but also in its far more dangerous assumption: that nuclear war is necessary to defeat an "evil empire" that can never be trusted to abide by any agreement. Its premise is a self-fulfilling prophecy of destruction.

The technical aspect of the freeze proposal is not often noted. Thermonuclear weapons utilize tritium or H_3, an unwanted by-product of heavy water–moderated reactors (i.e., CANDU). Tritium has a half-life of 12.8 years. Following a freeze, thermonuclear weapons would suffer tritium degradation and become useless in time. Without tritium replacement, a freeze would thus incorporate arms reduction. (The interesting questions of where the tritium for thermonuclear weapons is produced, and whether Canada exports this critical material to the U.S. have not been raised.)

Attaching possible verification qualifiers to the freeze robs it of its power as an attractive initiative. Mondale's stance on nuclear arms as a presidential candidate weakened the freeze position (a) by echoing the president's anticommunism and (b) by indicating Mondale's lack of knowledge on the destabilizing effect of cruise missiles armed with stealth principles. Mondale attacked "Star Wars" for moving the arms race into space, but he proposed a number of races of his own. He never used the best-documented material to differentiate his position vis-à-vis the USSR from Reagan's. Reagan, as we have amply documented, has stated that arms control treaties with the USSR are useless because the Soviets will always lie and cheat and so, short of a U.S. occupation of the USSR to assure on-site inspections of Soviet installations, no arms limitation treaty could be acceptable. Mondale allowed Reagan to distort the military balance, including strategic bombers, as though it were in the Soviets' favor. Nor did Mondale affirm the U.S.'s greater number of deliverable warheads, its better balance in the triad, its lead in the arms race, and the U.S.'s general technological superiority in terms of accuracy, speed of response, and flexibility. Mondale had all the documentation from official sources, including documentation on the secret plans of the Reagan administration, available to him: he chose to use "pot shots" instead of these "big guns."

The freeze movement appears to be an alliance totally concerned with a single issue of peace, a mutual, verifiable freeze in the deployment and development of nuclear weapons at their present levels. The halt of an arms race exploding quantitatively, qualitatively, and into space could lead to deeper cuts in the nuclear arsenal. The incremental reductions would necessarily thaw the superpowers' relationship. No matter if one believes that peace is indivisible and extends from the military to one's own internal being, or that peace without justice, Orwell's world, is intolerable, nuclear war leads the agenda of global issues because it presents a complete, ultimate threat to the entire world. A world after nuclear war has no justice.

HALLOWEEN IS A TIME FOR WITCH HUNTS: "CAMPAIGN '84"

The right responded predictably to the freeze initiative with the old, witch-hunt tactic of the red scare. John Barron of the *Reader's Digest* had written that the "KGB helped organize and inaugurate the freeze." *Barrons, Commentary, Conservative Digest,* and *American Spectator* repeated Barron's allegations. According to the *Reader's Digest,* the KGB's "objective is to secure military superiority for the Soviet Union by persuading the United States to abandon new weapon systems."

Georgia Congressman Larry McDonald and former Congressman John Ashbrook had attempted to revive the House Un-American Activities Committee for some time. With the landslide to the right in the 1980 elections, the use of the red scare tactic broadened. Alabama Republican Senator Jeremiah Denton began to hold hearings on "disinformation" and subversion. Denton even led the *Washington Post* to believe that extreme radicals had infiltrated Peace Links, an umbrella organization. The *Washington Post,* stating it had been led astray by faulty State Department records, retracted its allegations about Peace Links and deplored the witch hunt; however, the damage had been done. As James Thurber once explained about McCarthyism, guilt by exoneration could now be added to guilt by association. Reagan persisted in his attacks. On 11 November 1982, the president stated, "There is no question about foreign agents that were sent to help instigate and help create and keep such a movement going." The FBI's assistant Director for Congressional and Public Affairs Roger Young said that the "President's remarks are persistently consistent with what we have learned" (Cockburn and Ridgeway, 1983, p. 16). By December 1982 the House Select Committee on Intelligence exorcised the witch of communist infiltration of the freeze movement, but it had planted the notion that one colludes with the USSR by adopting a position supported by the Soviets. Obvious "red baiting" came to a halt, only to be transformed to "softness" or "weakness" in the face of the Soviet threat. Reagan intimated Mondale's "soft" stance in the presidential campaign, and Mondale played Reagan's tune: he spent more time echoing Reagan's anticommunism than revealing the bankruptcy, viciousness, and ignorance of Reagan policies. Surely Mondale's advisers failed to properly prepare him with direct evidence to challenge Reagan's ignorance of nuclear arms issues. The generally much better informed Mondale should have known that not all exotic weapons systems need be based in space — they may be ground based. Reagan admitted his ignorance of the technology of weapons systems but inferred that the esoteric science behind them extended beyond the layman's grasp. Any person incapable of a threshold of technical knowledge is unfit to be president of the most powerful country in the world. Reagan's gaffes, garbled facts, and sheer ignorance are typified by his confession to visitors that he had never understood what "this throw-weight business is all about" (Ball, 1984, p. 11). Despite his admitted confusion, Reagan based his proposals for START and "double build-down" on throw-weight.

THE FUTURE OF PEACE

Apparently discrete concepts and analyses from fields as diverse as the humanities, the social sciences, and the natural sciences find conceptual convergence in a common territory that grounds an ecological theory of human, social, and even political development. This common area, this arena of interdisciplinary studies, is also the common battleground for those conflicting ideas that have risen to the top of the global agenda. We contend that the civil and military nuclear debate and the polarization of policies and politics embedded in it are central to global debates on growth, development, progress, and survival—the major conceptual, personal, and social issues of our time.

Because this new world view is regarded as the ultimate subversion of the existing capitalist and communist systems, it may now be the most revolutionary global movement in contemporary times. At best, it addresses the inequities intrinsic to "free enterprise" market economies, the disfranchisement of the individual in communist systems, the loss of community and growth of alienation, and the "colonial war on Nature" conducted by both systems. This ecological society has yet to find meaningful solutions to the barriers of power and decay and to find answers to the politics of transition (Goldsmith, 1972, 1979; Henderson, 1976, 1978; Knelman, 1979).

Do the new ecological movements represent a viable and new stage of political development that genuinely incorporates the persistent themes of human rights, democratic process, and search for community and identity that have characterized political evolution? Or are they a party of one season, failing to persist when the exclusive issues of their concern are either resolved or changed? How does their policy and platform relate to the realities of an emerging postindustrial information society? Are they universal movements independent of the stage of economic and industrial development? Will they evolve into mainline parties or even gain power in some countries? Does the issue of the environment have the staying power to become the major platform of a new politics, or can traditional political systems solve such major problems as the environment?

Because the freeze movement is a coalition opposed to nuclear arms only, it contains natural elements of divisiveness and erosion. They derive in large part from ideological polarities within the movement and the lack of a broad, legitimate platform and program. Their intense, highly focused opposition to civil and military nuclear technology cements their members into cohesiveness; but political development requires the enunciation of clear alternatives defined in politically and economically realizable terms. Idealism alone will not provide a basis for growth.

In addition, the antinuclear movement generally has failed to develop a trade union constituency, often because of conflicts over short-term job security. Unions that have a stake in civil nuclear power often oppose the arms race. In Western Europe, however, despite its large civil nuclear industry and the socialist and communist parties' support of the nuclear option, antinuclear movements have often alienated the trade unions. Coalitions of environmentalists and trade unions have been successful; for example, the "green unions" of Australia joined with the miners' union to oppose uranium development. In the U.S., Mondale, a freeze-initiative supporter, received the AFL-CIO's endorsement for president in 1984.

The peace movements of Western Europe and other parts of the world include the "green" parties but in general have a more focused agenda, i.e., the nuclear arms race and and the issue of Euromissiles. In Canada, the issue has been cruise missile testing.

In the past year, the peace movement of Western Europe has broadened its political base. The once-divided Social Democrats of West Germany and Norway now unite in opposition to the placing of cruise missiles and Pershing II's in Europe. In various countries of Western Europe, particularly the Netherlands, the church is an active leader in the peace movement. European peace movements and their formal political allies wield potent force in Europe, but it is difficult to predict the course these movements will take in the political future of their countries.

While the majority of members of the Western peace movements adopt a "plague on both sides" attitude toward the superpowers since the Grenada invasion, they have intensified their conviction that the Reagan administration leads and initiates the arms race and presents *the* obstacle to arms reductions and control. Despite insinuations and outright attacks from the right, the Western peace movements have not been hurt by their "biased" actions.

"Official" peace movements in Eastern Europe, which never criticize the USSR, are supported by the state and controlled by the government. Some independent movements have surfaced, particularly in Romania and East Germany; more often, the independent "peacenik" is treated as a dissident. Despite these differences, Western and Eastern European peace movements largely agree on the causes of new international tensions. The people of Eastern Europe concerned with peace may march to a different drummer, but they are no less fearful of nuclear war. They share with their American counterparts the knowledge that there can be no winners in a nuclear conflict.

In conclusion, what we have termed "the greening of the world" represents the emergence of a new political entity focused on opposition to the nuclear arms race: the simple legitimation of the public as a critical actor in the theater of public policy. Because the public pays for military policy in more ways than one, the public has the right to be consulted and to play a significant role in the making of that policy. The public has now asserted this right, and this assertion is the most meaningful factor in the race between peace and war. The people have awakened; the people have spoken. Even Mr. Reagan has to listen.

9

The "Star Wars" Scenario: More Fiction Than Fact

Missiles will bring anti-missiles and anti-missiles will bring anti-anti-missiles. But inevitably, this whole electronic house of cards will reach a point where it can be constructed no higher. . . . And when that time comes, there will be little we can do, other than to settle down uneasily, smother our fears, and attempt to live in a thickening shadow of death. . . . Have we gone too far in this search for peace through the accumulation of peril?

General Omar Bradley

Once secure in office, he declared himself Emperor, shutting himself away from the populace. Soon, he was controlled by the very assistants and boot-lickers he had appointed to high office, and the cries of the people for justice did not reach his ears.

George Lucas, *Star Wars*

THE "HIGH GROUND"

Seeking the high ground may be an instinctive capacity developed through the long evolution of the human species, but unquestionably, humans have always sought this vantage point. Applying this fundamental strategy, men have scaled trees, cliffs, and mountains; now they look to space. At the same time, tools, the extensions of human muscle power, mobility, and sensory capability, evolved from the spear and shield to nuclear-tipped ballistic missiles and sophisticated electronic audio-visual monitors. Today, an evolving tool—the fifth-generation computer or artificial intelligence—seeks to match the function of the human brain. The rate, scale, and complexity of technology now transcend any human ability to effect change or allay uncertainty once the machine has been set in motion.

The tools of destruction have always evolved more rapidly than "tools of conviviality." The war machine always consumes new technology more voraciously than the civil machine. The war machine's insatiable appetite devoured the extensions of muscle power, as weaponry extended its killing power through chemical and nuclear ammunition. Technological and social

223

evolution proceeded in a dialectic of mutual reinforcement. The social organizational systems of production and consumption reached higher plateaus with the evolution of nation-states and their policies of war and peace. Production, consumption, and waste achieved new levels of accelerated growth. The war machine soared above ground with the airplane. Only structured exploitation and competition within nations and between nations could provide the resources to support such exponential technological development. The nations of the world have evolved historically into a hierarchy of political and economic power: small, developing countries at bottom; larger, developed countries in the middle; the two superpowers perched on top.

After World War II, world power had become bipolar through ideological division and competition. The war machine intensified its demand for more sophisticated arms. The constraints of earth and even the sky had been overcome; the stars awaited. In 1957, the flight of Yuri Gagarin, the first man in space, launched the Soviet Union into apparent technological ascendancy. This traumatized America. President John F. Kennedy took up the challenge and gave the U.S. a new national mission: to land a man on the moon and beat the Soviets in the new space race.

But technology can never be neutral in its sociopolitical context. From the beginning, nations viewed space as the ultimate advantage for peace and war. Space became a new region for exploitation by those who had the tools to conquer it. In the new frontier of space, the astronaut would replace the traditional American hero of folklore, the cowboy. Given the right mission, the U.S. would re-create the world of Buck Rogers. The macho boys in the White House, in the Pentagon, and in NASA had the "right stuff" in a new cosmology and a new set of toys, with scenarios all created in the comic strips and the movies. The president seems receptive to this kind of world. As with nuclear weapons and nuclear warfighting, the availability of dangerous new technology and the will to develop it further are mutually reinforcing.

In any attempts to control and regulate technology, the techniques of control must be at least as efficacious as the technology itself. In addition, techniques of control require a consensual system of mandated (legal) regulations and the will and mechanisms to enforce them. Large, mutual benefits accrue from such a system. As an example, civil aviation has achieved relative success in the area of national and international control and regulation, despite such problems as accidents through failure to obey regulations or precautions and hijacks. In outer space, however, we deal with a new, uncharted, unregulated, and, as of now, unregulatable "commons."

Our vision, once limited by the scope of the eye, now has technological extensions through a variety of external electromagnetic and optic sensors: electro-optical devices that use the entire spectrum of visible light, infrared and radiation/radar, microwave, X rays, and other radiation. Specially pro-grammed, modified, and digitalized computers process the "raw" data of this extended vision to convert it into usable information. In the words of a famous American spiritual, "there is no hiding place down here," not if a one-foot visual resolution that provides synoptic, repetitive, and three-dimen-sional views of large areas of earth can be achieved from several hundred miles in space. This "ultravisibility" involves both threat and promise. Beyond understanding the nature of modern technology, technological assessment, control, and transfer, we must understand the national and international social, political, and military contexts in which the application of this tech-nology is constrained and/or enhanced.

SPACE: VISION AND REALITY

The late 1960s gave rise to the hope that space would become a "zone of peace" for the "benefit of all." By 1976, the U.S.A., the USSR, and seventy-two other countries had signed the Outer Space Treaty, endorsing the prin-ciple of making space the "province of mankind." The U.S. had put forward this principle as early as 1955; both parties legalized it through SALT I in 1972. Despite this principle, it became established practice to verify arms agreements by "national technical means"—reconnaissance satellites. SALT I also established the principle of nonconcealment. Treaties and lack of trust seem to go together. However, the Reagan administration appears to have made policy out of abrogating those treaties that might impede its version of critical developments. In the same way, the administration cites problems in verification—seldom a technical obstacle—as an excuse for rejecting pos-sible arms agreements.

The superpowers' satellites have multiple functions. Systems for recon-naissance, early warning, navigation, detection, eavesdropping, communica-tions, meteorological and geodetic monitoring, and interception/destruction have become an essential element of strategic doctrine. Space technology allows the integration and centralization of command, control, communica-tions, and intelligence (C^3I) essential for the controlled function of a complex nuclear arsenal. Navigation and geodetic satellites enable missile guidance and target and terrain recognition for unprecedented accuracy. Monitoring weapons tests, "surrogate" wars, and postwar damage assessment are other essential functions of military space technology. At present the U.S. utilizes twelve military communications satellites, assisted by "leased capacities aboard commercial communications satellites" (Spectrum, 1982, p. 53). Its World-Wide Military Command and Control System (WWMCC) utilizes thirty-five large computers, twenty-five communications centers, seventeen million lines of programming code, twelve satellites, and one hundred ground terminals. Each leg of the triad has its own satellite within this system, thus linking all nuclear launches—bombers, SLBM's, and ICBM's. War has become electronicized and decisions computerized.

The special function of Command, Control, Communications, and Intelligence (C^3I), combined with technological developments in computers, satellites, space optics, transmission and reception, and the miniaturization of weapons and computers through microprocessors, has transformed warfare. This year the U.S. will have the world's most sophisticated photosatellite in the world, an updated version of the KH-11, in use since 1977, that will be able to overcome atmospheric interference. The U.S. also has momentum in its development of Very High Speed Integrated Circuits (VHSIC). Coupling this to advances in satellite optical sensors and to satellite missile guidance, i.e., the targeting of sophisticated or "smart" weapons such as cruise missiles, moves the U.S. closer to preemptive strike capacity. In time, the entire U.S. arsenal will be guided from space with incredible accuracy, transforming even smaller yield strategic weapons into counterforce capacity.

THE "TRAGEDY OF THE COMMONS"

Outer space has become the object of a contest between national gain and international benefit, and the great superpower struggle has intensified the heat of that contest. Thus, the commercialization and militarization of space become as inevitable as the race to exploit the natural universe. The United Nations has expressed its concern for the space theater through the UN Outer Space Committee and its Legal Subcommittee, the UN Conference on Science and Technology for Development, and the UN Committee on the Peaceful Uses of Outer Space (COPOUS), which has now convened for nearly ten years. Ostensibly, the 1967 UN Outer Space Treaty (OST) provides guidelines for the international development of space with its hopeful injunction that the use of outer space "shall be carried out for the benefit and in the interests of all countries, irrespective of their degree of economic or scientific development, and shall be the *'province of mankind'*[Italics mine]."

Like the other commons of mankind, the land, the oceans, and the air, outer space offers another arena for the tragedy of environmentally degrading pollution. The increasing numbers of outer space satellites and missiles present the potential for unprecedented environmental hazard, just as the automobile created the unanticipated problems of traffic control and regulation, accidental deaths and injuries, and toxic emissions and smog.

Today's outer space "traffic" includes more than 5000 "objects" and 114 geostationary satellites. While communications satellites usually orbit at approximately 22,000 miles (Linowes, 1981), so-called "spy" or surveillance satellites travel in much lower orbits, at approximately 150 miles. Although spy satellites have remote control devices designed to propel them into higher orbit, i.e., 500 miles, at mission's end, gravity can pull a malfunctioning spy satellite back to earth quickly due to its orbit. Should complete re-entry burn-up not occur, the debris can fall to the earth. Such a possibility occurred with Sky-Lab in 1979; fortunately, its debris fell into the Indian Ocean.

In the past, many satellites used nuclear reactors to supply their energy. Cosmos 954, a Soviet "spy" satellite equipped with a nuclear reactor, disintegrated over a nonpopulated area in the Canadian North in January 1978. Despite this serious accident, the Soviet Union irresponsibly launched another nuclear-powered Cosmos satellite into space. Cosmos 1402 also failed. Although, at the time of this writing, the Soviets have successfully disproved the claim that Cosmos 1402 had orbited out of control and suffered reactor separation, the accident points out the potential hazard in nuclear-powered satellites. The Hiroshima bomb contained about twenty-five pounds of uraium-235; the Soviet Cosmos contained almost three times as much radioactive material, in the form of one hundred pounds of highly enriched uranium. Assuming the "burn-up" is equivalent, "hot" radioactive debris from the reactor aboard the USSR Cosmos satellite would be equivalent to three Hiroshima bombs. Direct radiation from fallout caused an estimated 15,000 deaths at Hiroshima. Therefore, nuclear power plants aboard satellites present a formidable threat, should the satellite malfunction and the debris fall on a populated region. At least three serious failures have occurred aboard U.S. satellites equipped with nuclear plants.

Satellite malfunctioning can cause satellite break-up and release the entire system into low, uncontrollable orbit. Should this system hit the earth over a populated area, it could cause a major, unprecedented, and unnecessary disaster, on the scale of the worst natural catastrophe ever experienced. Even burn-up would not eliminate the fallout problem.

A Soviet nuclear reactor suffered re-entry in 1983, and a failed Apollo mission lost a complete plutonium reactor in the ocean. These incidents point at another, more likely scenario. Assuming that a malfunctioning satellite's re-entry burn-up is minimal, a nuclear-powered satellite in low-earth orbit, such as the U.S. SNAPS-10A, could leave debris that included more than twenty-five pounds of weapons-grade, highly enriched uranium. Such material could be extremely dangerous in the hands of terrorists.

Outer space belongs to no nation, yet it remains open to exploitation by any. Without the guidelines of an international agreement such as the UN Outer Space Treaty, outer space presents the opportunity for short-term strategic gains and the risks of unassessed environmental damage.

THE POLITICS OF SPACE

As of now, the oceans beyond territorial waters, and the airspace over them remain sovereignty-free regimes. (Guedhuis, 1978; Hudcovic, 1979). Principles such as those outlined in the UN Outer Space Treaty now tacitly imply rules governing activities within these regimes, but no encompassing laws concerning the usage of outer space have met with international acceptance and approval.

The most obvious and persistent problem in international space regulation is, who defines and delimits outer space. In other words, should space be open to international development, or is space the exclusive domain of those nations capable of using it (Mitrany, 1966)?

The original 1958 Space Act provides an interesting, revealing aspect of U.S. space policy. The act specified that "international cooperation was second in priority to nationalistic objectives and was to be pursued in the context of broader U.S. domestic and foreign policy goals" (Logsdon, 1981). This basic principle governs the U.S. approach to the emerging "arms race" in space.

The advent of the Reagan administration has introduced radical, new (old) domestic and international policies. Reaganomics embraces supply-side assumptions: the "trickle-down" theory, general deregulation and self-regulation, and private-sector responsibility in diverse areas, from humanitarian activities to the commercialization of new technologies. Reaganomics has its contradictions, of course. "Free-market" principles do not apply to the military, military-related technology, or the crippled civil nuclear industry. All of these have received substantially increased Reagan handouts. In the development of communication satellites, large corporations such as Hughes and AT&T, for example, gained private competence at zero risk through the use of public funds.

Reagan's foreign policy, based on a simplistic ideology, ties aid, trade, and technology transfer to anticommunism. Reagan's supply-side, free-enterprise domestic principles also apply to developmental assistance for Third-World countries. The U.S. offers development assistance only to anticommunist nations or factions. The administration believes that the private sector, mainly multinational corporations, can provide more effective and efficient aid to less-developed countries. Of course, private-sector developmental investments in Third-World countries often result in increased corporate profits for business and "spin-off" benefits for the government, research and development, product testing, quality control, and price reductions.

Not surprisingly, Reagan's policy on outer space follows these operating rules, and has its analog in the administration's policy on the oceans (*The Chronicle Herald,* Monday, 16 August 1982, Halifax). On 30 April 1982,

117 countries at the UN adopted the Law of the Sea Treaty, establishing an international regime for seabed mining. Despite the fact that the treaty had been proposed as a model for such international regimes as Antarctica, the U.S. refused to sign it. Elliot Richardson, a Republican and former negotiator on the Law of the Sea Treaty, accused the Reagan administration of rejecting the treaty because of ideological differences with noncapitalist Third-World governments. The U.S. strongly opposed the disarming of the private sector through the international mining regime. It urged the highly industrialized nations to agree on a set of rules governing national development of the seabed. The gifts of the sea are available to any nation with the technological ability to retrieve them; when less-developed countries achieve that ability, they are welcome to enter the competition. This dominant policy, intensified by the demands of the emerging space race, will govern the U.S. approach to outer space.

Narrow issues of political and military power also motivate the Soviet policy on space; however, the USSR's position equally reflects its relative inferiority in space technology. The USSR has almost consistently advocated a nonsovereign space regime that included the right of transit passage. However, because of its inferior technology, the USSR has sought to limit remote-sensing activities.

Defining the limits of outer space becomes especially problematic, given the technological sophistication of the monitoring devices aboard satellites. The data collected by these satellites accumulate into a massive data-base of information about the world in general, and about each individual nation in it. The "fair use" versus "exploitation" of outer space then translates into further delicate issues: Who owns or controls this information base? Who has access to the information? Is national sovereignty violated if one nation monitors another without permission (Bordouvov, 1977; Kamenetskya, 1977; Brown et al., 1981)?

Given the enhanced risk of unintentional nuclear war, satellites for arms control, monitoring of tests, verification, and validation perform vital functions for peace. However, because of the sensitive issues involved in the "sovereignty of information," a nonpartisan, nonideological agency may have to operate such information-gathering satellites. At the tenth United Nations Special Session on Disarmament, 25 May 1978, the French proposed the creation of a new agency for monitoring arms agreements. Eventually this agency would operate satellites and receiving stations of its own, and thus would be relatively independent of the superpowers. By implication, the agency could have further global functions, such as monitoring global pollution and, possibly, assisting in overcoming the terrible social disparities between the Northern and Southern Hemispheres.

Thirty-eight nations commented on the International Satellite Monitoring Agency (ISMA) proposal in response to a request by the secretary general (Jakhu et al., 1980). Twelve nations, the majority from the Southern Hemisphere, gave unconditional support to the proposal. Only two of the twelve—India *(Wall Street Journal,* Wednesday, 14 May 1980) and Italy— have some national satellite capabilities, but the unconditional supporters also included Sweden, a leader in "peace initiatives." Another twelve nations supported the proposal "in principle." Among them were Japan and West Germany, two leaders in the relevant technology. However, Japan and West Germany, bordering on two potential arenas of global conflict, made their "support in principle" contingent on a successful, international disarmament agreement. Since the probability of achieving a "successful" disarmament agreement is low (UNGA, 1976), one may well question the sincerity of Japan and West Germany's support. Did they endorse the idea of an international monitoring agency, or did they merely attempt to reaffirm their nonmilitary, nonnuclear "images"?

Eleven states refused to make any decision without further clarification. Canada posed sensitive questions about the nature and powers of ISMA: the prior rights of monitored states; the legal status of the collected data, whether raw or processed; its distribution; and economic considerations. It took a leadership position by confronting the conflict between national interests (sovereignty) and international interests. Canada followed a pattern long-observed in UN debates and ran a blocking pattern for the U.S. position. The U.S. and, ironically, Cuba rejected the proposal outright. The U.S. argued that it was impossible for such an international agency to function properly, and that the U.S. would fund the highest proportion of ISMA's immense budget, just as it currently finances the majority of UN activities. In fact, the U.S. viewed ISMA much like it did the seabed treaty, the Comprehensive Test Ban, or, for that matter, its own internal regulatory system: ISMA was not in the best interests of the U.S. The U.S. military satellite surveillance system supersedes any other in the world; not even NASA has such a powerful and extensive ability to collect information.

Ths USSR did not respond, largely because of its ambivalence on arms control verification. The USSR normally aligns itself with the South on most political and international issues. In fact, it had consistently supported the inalienable right of each state to dispose of its natural resources and information relating to them. But like the U.S., the USSR can only maintain its superpower status by retaining its secret, exclusive information base. Thus, it is willing to disseminate low-resolution global sensing data, but not high-resolution local data. As an open society with technological supremacy in these areas, the U.S. asserts that sensing activity should be nonsovereign, and that information about natural resources anywhere should be freely acquired and easily accessible to any interested parties.

Despite the fact that a special, technical group of experts pronounced ISMA technically, legally, and economically feasible, with per-year costs "well under 1 percent of the total annual expenditure on armaments" (UN Document AC/AC.206/14, Annex, p. 14), sufficient resistance to implementation has blocked real progress on the agency. Various disarmament conferences, particularly the second United Nations disarmament conference held in New York on 24 February 1982, offered the opportunity to implement this proposal. Unfortunately, now its time has passed.

THE MILITARY IMPLICATIONS OF SPACE

All technology has the potential for exploitive as well as nonexploitive uses, for military as well as civil applications. In a broad sense, all space-derived information such as data on weather, environment, agriculture, and social and military activities has a direct military function. In space technology, civil and military functions reach a high level of integration, as they have in the shuttle. One-third of the shuttle's applications has been purchased by the Pentagon.

The multiple tradeoffs in a mixed public-private enterprise include those exchanges between the advantages of exclusive exploitation and the benefits of joint-venture sharing. Nevertheless, current pressures lead the "space powers" to attempt to monopolize the commercial and military applications of such enterprises at the ultimate expense of their international benefits. Further, the space powers view international control/regulation attempts as potential impediments to their own commercial, political, and military exploitation.

The impossibility of distinguishing between civil and military uses, and between public and private costs blurs the economics of space activities. The huge cost overruns endemic in public and military technological development, such as Lockheed's development of the space shuttle, do not appear in the development of commercial space applications. Since all space activities including the space shuttle program have intrinsic dual purposes, i.e., civil and military, they lack the cost constraints of pure commercial developments. Often, political and/or military end-purposes, not the purely social or economic costs, determine the cost effectiveness of certain technological developments.

In general, from the very beginning of the space age, the distinctions between civil and military applications have been unclear. Attempting to separate the civil and military uses of outer space is hardly more effective than earlier attempts to separate church and state. Both share the same hardware and techniques. The techniques used for arms verification from space are the same as remote sensing of the earth's resources and environment.

According to an early guiding principle of U.S. space policy, civilian and military space activities were to be carried out in "separate institutional structures" (Logsdon, 1981).

The military, the private sector, and the intelligence agency (CIA) have tended to prefer separate space capacities, but economics often tends to produce cooperative ventures, at least between NASA and the Pentagon. The NASA administration knows the benefits of such cooperation and actively solicits it.

The CIA monitors compliance with strategic arms limitation treaties (SALT, 1971), as well as the earlier Outer Space Treaty (1967), the Atmospheric Test Ban Treaty (1963), and the Non-Proliferation Treaty (1970). Civil-military space technology has both functional and political links. The shuttle development revitalized a moribund NASA, which could not provide its economic support without Pentagon services. The 1985 U.S. defense budget proposes building a permanent, manned space station to become operational by the early 1990s. The transformation of space into a battleground seems assured. While a space shuttle has many commercial functions, it would also correspond to Reagan's "Star Wars" vision of orbital battle stations, armed with exotic weapons such as lasers and particle beams.

The Soviet Union already has primitive space stations. Seven Salyut stations linked to Soyuz and Cosmos vehicles form structures that weigh over fifty tons and can be inhabited for up to six-month periods. Recent reports indicate that the most powerful rocket in the world waits at its launching pad at Gyurtam, USSR, possibly ready to launch a twelve-man space station.

Soviet and American space technologists share a common technological romanticism about space: "To go boldly where no man has gone before" (Captain Kirk, "Star Trek"). NASA scientists have talked about orbiting a "Noah's Ark" containing a store of the earth's genetic material, to prepare the way for future habitation of the moon and other planets. Solar-power satellites (SPS) and "Project Spacewatch," an asteroid detection and destruction system, will assist in the colonizing and exploiting of space. Both superpowers share these technocratic "dreams" while they commonly neglect our planet. By focusing on space, the superpowers gain some respite from critics of their earthly regimes. The superpowers' technological dreams have a most sinister aspect: the law of technological autonomy or "What is not specifically forbidden becomes compulsory." Because of the policy conflicts involved in the nuclear arms race, the militarization of space must be forbidden. The militarization of space tragically involves yet another arms race and contravenes the basic principle of maintaining space as the "province of mankind."

THE RACE TO THE HIGH GROUND

The race to the high ground began at the very outset of the space age. In 1958, only one year after Sputnik, the U.S. established the Advanced Research Projects Agency (DARPA). President Kennedy's injunction to win the space race sparked interest in outer-space technology in both the civil and military sectors. From the beginning the military contemplated and developed two general space systems: first, antisatellite weapons or ASAT's—weapons to destroy satellites in space; second, antiballistic missiles or ABM's—exotic futurist weapons designed to destroy enemy missiles in flight. Conventional and nuclear-tipped missiles were also developed to serve both functions. Two general types of exotic weapons are being refined: lasers of various types and particle beams. These programs are not totally separate. Certain types of ABM's could also be adapted for ASAT application and vice versa. Similarly, exotic space-based ABM's could be used against ground installations or space stations. The Soviets have comparable programs but, in general, they lag behind the U.S. in the entire range of developments.

Antiballistic missiles have a critical need for a variety of sensors that detect and track missile targets in flight. These sensors basically use radar installations of different kinds, functions, and locations and sensitive, infrared sensors that detect heat emissions from rocket firings and missile exhaust plumes. Mosaic infrared sensors are among the most sophisticated of the infrared variety. Code-named "Teal Ruby" by the U.S., these sensors have 100,000 extremely small, infrared sensing cells per square inch of sensor, and may be carried on satellites or deployed from space stations. In addition, they will be provided with data-processing capacity, currently being tested in project "High Resolution Calibrated Airborne Measurements Program" or "HI-CAMP."

DARPA, together with certain key military research institutes such as the Lawrence Livermore Laboratory, provide the vehicles for the militarization of space. Enmeshed in this technological wing of "Star Wars" is a political wing, a combination of militarists and industrialists, many of whom played a leading role in bringing Reagan to power. Of course, the Committee on the Present Danger (CPD) is among the variety of organizations that offers support.

Several other organizations, somewhat less "respectable" than CPD, played an important role in seeking Reagan's election. The membership of the "Coalition of Peace Through Strength" and the American Security Council represented an extreme conservative wing of the "military-industrial complex."

Retired Army Lieutenant Army General Daniel Graham, a key member of CPD and the Coalition of Peace Through Strength and former head of the Defense Intelligence Agency (DIA), plays a dual role. He is the leading military advocate of "superiority." Graham and retired Major General George Keegan, USAF, were key members of "Team B" that set out to sabotage the CIA estimates of the U.S.-USSR military balance. Graham also served as a key supporter of Reagan's advisory task force during the campaign and transition period.

General Graham's second role has been preaching the "Star Wars" posture through High Frontier Inc. In particular, he advocates "directed-energy" weapons, lasers, and particle beams. Together with Edward Teller, Graham has been a major influence on Ronald Reagan; yet even Edward Teller, a prime supporter of "Star Wars," disagrees with Graham's unrelenting optimism. The scientific community has attacked Graham's views for maintaining the fiction of huge Soviet advances in this field.

In the more formal arena, Colonel Charles Heimach, USAF, and key member of DARPA, is the leading proponent of nuclear war survival through outer space. His book *Space Survivability—A Philosophy/Policy Argument,* the bible of the "high-ground" advocates (Karas, 1984, p. 44), reworks the argument of winnability/survivability in a protracted nuclear war by taking the higher ground. Thus, there is "science-fiction" support for Reagan's new cosmology.

ANTISATELLITE WEAPONS: ASAT'S

Space weapons had their place in the long history of fictitious military gaps elaborated earlier. Following Sputnik, the U.S. used fears of a false ASAT gap to commence its own ASAT program in the early 1960s, at least five years prior to the USSR program that began in 1968. To this day, Soviet ASAT's provide few real threats to the U.S. They fire conventional explosives and must co-orbit with their target, a very difficult maneuver. The majority of a total of twenty Soviet tests of their so-called "killer satellite" failed (Aldridge, 1983, p. 222). Their maximum altitude of intercept, 600 miles, renders most U.S. satellites immune, with the exception of "spy" satellites. Considerable evidence indicates the Soviets designed ASAT's for use against the Chinese and for protection of their own satellites (Aldridge, 1983, p. 224). The U.S., on the other hand, concentrates on conquering deep space. Communications satellites for C^3I functions have planned orbits of 70,000 miles, and Vela and Solrad satellites have already reached this altitude. Typically, the U.S. ASAT program was named SAINT, an acronym for Satellite Interceptor, while the Soviet ASAT's, through the uninformed co-operation of the media, are termed "killer satellites." The U.S. had assigned antisatellite strategies to their Nike-Zeus ABM and to their nuclear-tipped Thor missiles in the 1960s (Aldridge, 1983, p. 220), and had successfully tested an ASAT as early as 1959 (*Aviation Work and Space Technology*, 19 October 1959).

Generally speaking, with the exception of payload, U.S. technology has several generations of superiority over the Soviets'. This can be ascertained indirectly by the fact that the Soviets show more interest in a space weapon treaty than the U.S.

The early Soviet launch of Sputnik proved counterproductive to the USSR. The U.S. responded by outpacing the Russians in space technology—microminiaturization, satellite sophistication, microprocessing, and computers—the linkage of computers, photography, satellites, and antisatellite weapons (ASAT's). Despite considerable propaganda about Soviet developments in "Star Wars" weaponry such as lasers and particle beams, the momentum, even in these developments, remains with the U.S.

The unreliable and ponderous three-ton Soviet ASAT interceptor is limited to low orbits and has a poor readiness factor. Launched by a ground-based SS-9 booster, the ASAT has to wait twenty-four hours until the earth brings the target into orbit in position above the launch site. The U.S. ASAT, launched from an F-15 aircraft, presents a rapid threat to the great majority of Soviet satellites. The U.S. ASAT can operate from any air base with maximum readiness. It can also be adapted to a three-stage booster on an F-15 that enables it to reach high orbit. About 67 percent of U.S. military satellites are in geosynchrous (GEO, 22,000 miles above the earth's equator) or higher orbits; the reverse is true of Soviet satellites, which travel in low-earth orbits (LEO, or less than 1000 miles). The U.S. ASAT could even threaten Soviet early-warning and communications satellites. The Soviet ASAT poses no threats to GEO satellites. In general, U.S. satellites are superior to the Soviet, even in payload, if the shuttle is included. Of the 101 Soviet satellites launched in 1982, over 50 percent were out of operation at the end of the year (Johnson, 1983). Soviet photo satellites usually remain in orbit for two weeks, compared to the two years in orbit of the U.S. KH-11 (Jasoni, 1982).

Because of the overlap in the ASAT and ABM development programs, an ABM weapon known as the Exatmospheric or Endatmospheric Re-entry Vehicle Interceptor System (ERIS) has been flight-tested in the Homing Overlap Experiment (HOE). ERIS had knocked out a missile, launched from Vandenberg Air Force Base, near Kwajalein Atoll as early as 7 February 1983 (Aldridge, 1985a). Thus, the U.S. is developing a series of new weapons with multiple functions against objects in space.

The U.S. Senate and House of Representatives have received resolutions that prohibit the deployment of weapons that can damage or destroy objects in space, and that declare a moratorium on the further testing of such weapons (U.S. Congress, Senate, and House, 1983). The Union of Concerned

Scientists convened a special committee of experts that proposed a similar draft treaty on ASAT's (UCS, 1983). This group that includes Carl Sagan, Hans Bethe, John Steinbrunner, Kurt Gottfried, and Herbert Scoville, Jr., argues forcefully that the advantages of such a treaty would outweigh any of its disadvantages.

Existing treaties such as the Test Ban Treaty of 1963 already restrict the use of nuclear-based weapons in space. The ABM Treaty bans antiballistic missile defenses and also protects "national means of verification." This protection could be extended to ban antisatellite weapons (ASAT's).

In August 1981, the USSR submitted a draft treaty proposing a "prohibition on the stationing of weapons of any kind in outer space." This suggested treaty contained ambiguities, and the U.S. has failed to respond to it. The mutual acceptance of any treaty seems based on a response to a collective threat or the existence of parity in arms. It seems obvious that U.S. policy, particularly under Reagan's direction, takes advantage of the significant superiority of American space technology. The current Soviet ASAT cannot be further refined for high-orbit attack; Soviet tests with a "pop-up" ASAT equipped with a homing device have failed (Johnson, 1983). Conceivably, the U.S. ASAT launched from an F-15 aircraft could be modified to have a high-orbit kill capacity (Jasoni, 1982).

DIRECTED ENERGY WEAPONS

The exotic futuristic weapons sought by the second part of the "Star Wars" program incorporate the principles of "directed energy" through the use of high-energy chemical, X-ray, and electrical discharge lasers, and subatomic (neutron or electron) particle beams. These weapons require enormous power sources to overcome a variety of environmental interferences and travel in coherent form across hundreds of miles of space. Lasers and particle beams hit and destroy rapidly moving targets by transmitting energy on impact. No available laser or experimental-beam weapon can travel through space at the enormous speeds (sometimes approaching the speed of light) and with sufficient energy required for use. The "state of the art" of these directed-energy weapons lags far behind its goal. In addition, the significant gaps in knowledge about directed energy and the unpredictable "learning curve," or rate of projected development, make their future deployment and effectiveness uncertain.

An ICBM launched from a silo has five distinct flight phases: (1) boost; (2) post-boost; (3) midcourse above the atmosphere; (4) midcourse after reentering the atmosphere; and (5) terminal phase. An exotic or directed-energy weapon has to destroy the ICBM during one of these phases. A strike during the last phase would be too late: Soviet warheads have a special fuse that causes them to fire if struck. The resulting damage would be enormous. The preferred strategy would use infrared sensors to detect the hot rocket-fuel exhaust and hit the Soviet ICBM's in boost phase, a two-to-three–minute period for current Soviet liquid-fueled rockets. However, as the Soviets convert their rockets to solid-fuel propellants, they can significantly reduce the time of this phase. This greatly complicates the attack problem. The entire process of sighting, aiming, firing, verifying, etc., would need to be accomplished within ninety seconds.

Waiting to strike an ICBM during its midcourse phase presents its own set of problems. Each Soviet ICBM with an average of ten independently targeted warheads could also have about ten penetrating aids, decoys, and radar or infrared opacity. Instead of 1398 targets, directed-energy weapons would have to deal with a "threat swarm" of some 130,000 targets within ninety seconds or less, according to load increase. In addition, because sighting satellites are not stationary in their orbits, only a large number of them, equipped with an equally large number of directed-energy weapons, could "see" all 1398 targets.

The U.S. Defense Advanced Research Project Agency (DARPA) has a so-called TRIAD project, a composite research and development program for three separate projects. The chemical laser project is ALPHA. The means for identifying and tracking fast-moving targets was TALON GOLD, now abandoned and replaced. The third project of the TRIAD program, LODE, or Large Optics Demonstration Experiment, seeks to complete the durable, lightweight mirror necessary to focus and aim a laser weapon. The problem of constructing numerous space-based laser battle stations that orbit in a manner enabling them to detect all Soviet ICBM launches and destroy them in space lies beyond TRIAD's scope.

The Lawrence Livermore Laboratory is conducting an X-ray laser project named "Excalibur," the supposed "brainchild" of Edward Teller. In "Excalibur," a "small" nuclear explosion that produces clouds of X rays must harness and focus these X rays into a concentrated energy beam, a process termed "lasing." As with TRIAD, hundreds of space-based laser stations would be equipped with X-ray laser rod weapons. "Excalibur" deployment would occur prior to an "imminent" missile attack by launching these X-ray laser weapons into space aboard missile boosters. This is called a "pop-up" deployment.

The High Ground proposal, another scenario developed by the Heritage Foundation in 1982, involves two layers of space-based and one layer of ground-based antimissile defenses. The first space-based layer would consist of 432 orbiting battle stations, each armed with forty to fifty nonnuclear homing devices that have infrared sensors that allow them to home in on Soviet missiles and destroy them on direct contact. These are not unlike the current U.S. ASAT weapons. The second space-based layer would be either TRIAD or Excalibur. The third layer would surround each U.S. silo with scores of ground-based antiballistic missiles of a variety of projectiles and rocket-powered interceptors, not unlike the Nike-Zeus and Thor ABM systems. This back-up stage would destroy any Soviet missiles that might penetrate the two space-based ABM systems (UCS, 1983).

The other group of "Star Wars" energy-directed weapons, particle beams, focus concentrated beams of subatomic particles, rather than the light beams of lasers. To create a particle energy beam, a large particle accelerator accelerates the particles to speeds close to the speed of light. Like laser weapons, particle-beam weapons would be installed on satellites in space. Some U.S. scientists and former generals believe the USSR has already developed and demonstrated this type of weapon, but corroborating evidence remains elusive (Stone, 1981; Bova, 1981).

A further variation on "Star Wars" weapons would orbit a huge and absolutely flawless mirror that would target and focus ground-based laser stations' laser beams. Space weapons systems would also have antisatellite capacity and could also be used as ASAT weapons. By destroying satellites that coordinate the "star weapons" functions of targeting selection, aiming, location, etc., the entire C^3I system could be threatened. The very launching of an elaborate ABM system could initiate a preemptive strike by the other side, fearful that its own offensive capacity could be nullified. Finally, the development of space-based antiballistic missile defense (SBABMD) constitutes a direct violation of the 1972 ABM Treaty. All the arguments that led the superpowers to agree not to develop ABM's would now be abandoned, despite their continued validity. Since the arms race has an offensive-defensive dynamic, any development in one aspect inspires a co-development on one side and a counterdevelopment on the other.

The history of MIRV technology is instructive in this issue. The USSR did not imagine that its development of a primitive ballistic missile defense of Moscow would lead to the U.S. development of MIRVed missiles. Nor did MIRV technology remain the exclusive property of the U.S. Eventually, both superpowers furthered the arms race as a consequence of a defense-initiated development by both. The 1972 ABM Treaty recognized this, but the Reagan administration has not learned this lesson.

All of these proposed weapons are extremely tentative. They provide technological obstacles that must be overcome and involve an enormous cost of approximately $500 billion. The current state of the art in exotic weapon technology and power generation lags far behind what is necessary. The launching and construction problems yet to be solved, and the complexity of the system that would have to achieve a very high degree (nearly 100 percent) of kill may never be practicable. No computer, for example, exists that could compute the data necessary to achieve a high proportion kill of missiles in the few minutes available (UCS, 1983, p. 2). But the ultimate limiting factor of "Star Wars" weapons systems may be their vulnerability to attack.

Defenses against exotic "Star Wars" weapons are relatively primitive, cheap, and effective. They range from saturated attacks by drones—particularly effective against Excalibur, because of its self-destruct characteristic—to the use of a variety of penetrating aids, disguising techniques, laser interference or opacity methods. An even more effective countermeasure would launch a massive attack by advanced cruise missiles equipped with radar and laser "stealth" techniques. The proponents of "Star Wars," the president and his ill-advisers included, do not understand the dynamics of the arms race. ABM's will generate anti-ABM's (AABM's) as well as penetrating offenses. The superpowers signed the 1972 ABM Treaty because they then understood that both defensive and offensive weapons development fuel an arms race. All that Reagan's "Star Wars" decision has done is to move the arms race into outer space, thus removing perhaps the last place to hide and committing yet another tragic violation of the global commons.

REAGAN IN THE ROLE OF BUCK ROGERS

In August 1981 the USSR proposed to the United Nations a new treaty banning the placement of any kind of weapon into orbit around the earth (SIPRI, 1981). In contrast, Reagan, in his speech of 23 March 1983, proposed an initiative without proper consultation, seemingly guided by bad advice from unofficial advisers.

President Reagan, in typically misunderstanding the ethos of science and history, sociology, and political science, called upon the scientific community to turn their great talents to "the cause of mankind and world peace" and give us the means of rendering these nuclear weapons "impotent and obsolete." Ralph Nader once said that Reagan was the first president to own more horses than books, but Reagan must have read a lot of Buck Rogers comic books.

Reagan's speech received a dampening response from the independent scientific community. As reported in *U.S. News and World Report* of 5 April 1983, when asked whether the scientific community opposed "Star Wars" for political rather than technical reasons, George Keyworth responded, "That is precisely what I am saying." He went on to note that scientists respond with creativity to such formidable works as planetary transport or controlled fusion, but not to the defense field. The president's new arms race in space would continue regardless of criticism.

On "Meet the Press," 27 March 1983, journalists asked Defense Secretary Weinberger if the "Star Wars" missile defense system was to be total, i.e., *against all incoming missiles of any kind* (italics mine). Compounding the president's technical ignorance, Weinberger responded, "Yes, and I don't see any reason why that can't be done." This level of technological faith is frightening: the principle of technological infallability is hardly a good guide for policy.

On the same day that the president spoke, Major General Donald L. Lamberson, chief of the "directed weapons" program in DOD, appeared before the Senate Armed Services Committee. Lamberson testified that "a constellation of space laser platforms . . . might possess the capacity to negate, say 50 percent of a large-scale ICBM attack on the U.S. strategic forces." Thus, only a mere 2500 megatons would get through the "Star Wars" defenses. So much for Caspar Weinberger's credibility.

On 24 March 1983, President Reagan invited a group of key scientists to the White House to discuss his proposal. As reported in the *New York Times,* Friday, 25 March 1983, the scientists' response was hardly favorable, if not clearly opposed. For example, Dr. Victor Weisskopf of MIT said it "would be extremely dangerous and destabilizing." Richard Garwin simply stated that it wouldn't work. Hans Bethe said, "What is worse, it will produce a star wars if successful," while Simon Remo, one of the developers of ballistic missiles, said, "Who says that this technique will be used only to knock missiles out of the sky?" (Isaacson, 1983).

As reported in the *Washington Post* of Sunday, 27 March 1983, William J. Perry, undersecretary of defense in the Carter administration, described the staggering requirements of a "Star Wars" system. The system would need hundreds of laser-equipped satellites, each having an accuracy of greater than one part per million, to deal with a mass attack. Each laser weapon would have to be ten times as powerful as existing lasers. An operational test of a current generation laser weapon has failed (Coates, 1983). A laser system that large would have to be launched from low-earth orbit (LEO) and brought to high orbit by space shuttles with payloads ten times as great as those of the Columbia generation (Knelman, 1983). According to Perry, the system would have an estimated cost in excess of $100 billion and would require a lead time of at least twenty years. Moreover, even beginning the construction of such a system would lead to a new arms race in space. Obviously, during the launch and assembly stage vulnerability to attack or disruption would be very great. An entire new arsenal would be required to defend the system, while a new generation of offensive weapons would be developed to destroy it. Large numbers of cruise missiles flying at complex, low-altitude formations could elude the system, particularly if it were cloudy, since lasers cannot "see" through cloud or fog. The Reagan administration is interested in arms superiority, not reduction. "That is why the Administration has ignored the promising Soviet draft treaty for controlling weapons in space" (Gottfried, 1983).

Other scientists pointed out that "It is cruel and misleading to hold out such a false hope" (Rathjens and Ruina, 1983). Offense has consistently overcome defense in the arms race and often costs less. "Is it cost-effective to put up a $1 billion 'zap-sat' when an enemy can knock it down with a $100 million homing missile?" (Bell, 1981). A much lower cost "space mine," deployed in orbits adjoining the laser satellites, could neutralize the entire system. Nothing would prevent either side from launching either system if no act of war were declared: all the satellites of both sides would be destroyed with no advantage to either. Again, the static view of the arms race and the notion of attaining significant superiority prompts Reagan policy. Other laser weapon defenses, based on "stealth" principles or "penetrating aids," are possible (Garwin, 1981).

Clearly, a "Star Wars" missile system would violate the ABM Treaty of 1972, a milestone in the movement towards arms control and reduction. Many "off-the-cuff" statements by members of the Reagan administration have intimated that the ABM Treaty might have to be modified or scrapped. This would be a tragedy. The ABM development led to MIRVing, now regretted by many arms analysts, such as the Scowcroft Committee, who now urge de-MIRVing and a return to small, mobile, single-warhead missiles like Midgetman.

The Soviet response to Reagan's "Star Wars" speech was clear. Former Soviet leader Yuri Andropov said, "Should this conception be converted into reality this would actually open the flood gates to a runaway race of all types of strategic arms, both offensive and defensive" (*New York Times,* Friday, 25 March 1983). Many U.S. scientists agreed. Jeremy Stone, executive director of the Federation of American Scientists, said, "The ABM Treaty is not only the most important treaty we have, but it is the foundation for future treaties on offensive weapons . . . . if either side thought the other was going to withdraw . . . each side would have to reserve the right to build whatever weapons it needed to penetrate the defense" (Mohr, 1983).

A more fundamental problem flaws the concept of laser or particle beam weapons in space. This is the hazard of unleashing an electromagnetic pulse or EMP in space. A large megatonnage thermonuclear explosion in space sends out a huge amount of immediate radiation, mainly gamma and X rays, that moves through space in all directions. When this radiation hits the metallic surfaces of satellites in space, it induces very large voltage currents in the electronic equipment that cause disruption and burn-out. An explosion of sufficient megatonnage taking place as far away as geosynchrous orbit (36,000 kilometers) would blanket a huge volume of space with disrupting EMP. Hardening can resist these impacts but not if the blast is very large, i.e., five to ten megatons. Enhanced radiation weapons or neutron bombs would be most effective in generating EMP's. Only very distant orbits might be safe. Neutrons and gamma rays can also penetrate satellites, causing transient radiation effects on electrons (TREE). Following the orgy of atmospheric tests in 1961–62, TREE caused the malfunction of many satellites, probably because of a band of trapped electrons drifting around the earth. Such a band could be deliberately induced by extremely large explosions of enhanced radiation devices.

The Defense Advanced Research Projects Agency (DARPA) has tended to ignore these flaws and concentrate on laser weapons technology. Laser-equipped satellites would probably rely on relay satellites for earth communications and these could be rendered helpless by EMP (Broad, 1982). Hardening against EMP is definitely possible, but only up to a certain point. The cost advantage of exploding a sizable megaton weapon in space is also huge.

It is interesting that neither Dr. Robert Cooper, director of DARPA, nor John Gardner, director of defensive systems at the Pentagon, was consulted on Reagan's speech of 23 March 1983. Reagan was surprised by the scientific community's negative response. Wolfgang Panofsky, head of the Stanford Linear Accelerator, found "Star Wars" "spiritually troubling" (Smith, 1983b), while others said it either would not work, or would lead to a new arms race.

Laser weapons are weather dependent. An attack at the most inopportune time, during heavy fog or clouds, would render the system less than perfect, particularly since the missile would be targeted in the boost phase, its first 250 seconds under rocket power. The laser could follow the rocket's flame and, at that stage, all MIRVed warheads would be destroyed.

Construction of such a complex and massive system would probably take place in low-earth orbit (LEO), or LEO could be a basing station for system construction in geosynchrous earth orbit (GEO) (36,000 kilometers). The space shuttle could bring materials to LEO, but an entirely new generation of space shuttles, with payloads of as much as one order of magnitude greater than the present group (65,000 pounds), would be required. The ABM satellite system would probably be placed in very high orbit, over 200,000 kilometers, making it subject to radiation and micrometeoroid damage (Knelman, 1981). But the real trade-off involved is the inverse square law, true for any light source including laser. The intensity of the beam would be reduced as the square of the distance from the target. On the other hand, LEO laser stations would have a very limited view of the earth's surface. Great numbers of stations would be needed to cover the entire earth's surface. They cannot hover over the USSR, but must pass over in orbit.

No current laser approaches the power that would have to be generated, estimated as much as five to ten megawatts (Kaplan, 1983). This reference has estimated the mass and minimum number of lasers required to defend against a concerted launching of 2000 Soviet missiles. One would have to assume a multiple of this power to assure complete destruction, all other factors being optimal. For a large ten-megawatt laser system designed for "hardened" targets, about 4000 lasers would be required (Kaplan, 1983). Each of these laser weapons would weigh about 100 tons. Total payload would be 400,000 tons. Assuming that there is a reliability problem, to assure high effectiveness, double this amount would be required, i.e., 800,000 tons. Only 4 percent of the laser satellites would be over the USSR at any one time.

Present shuttle capacity, as we have stated, is about 32.5 tons, so this generation of shuttle would require about 25,000 launches. Not only would this be economically prohibitive, but there would be a very real hazard to the ozone layer (Knelman, 1981). Even assuming a new generation of shuttles having payload capacity of 325 tons, we would still require 2500 launches—a prohibitive number. In addition, the satellite laser ABM system could not "see" low-flying bombers, cruise missiles, fractional orbital bombardment systems (FOBS), etc.

As we have also suggested, a large laser system would require command, communications, and relay satellites for coordination and operation or they would require a direct link to earth for C^3I functions. This could be disrupted by a large EMP.

There are other penetrating aids such as decoys, the firing of ground-based lasers, or the development of "stealth" missiles. Finally, missile-hardening technologies could render the missile impervious to even large-power lasers. All of these anti-anti devices are less costly and more easily developed than "Star Wars" and would force a counterdevelopment in the laser ABM system. Thus we would have a new phase of an arms race. True, a relatively few lasers could be employed if coordinated to defend against a counterforce attack in a "launch-on-warning" posture, within a thirty-minute period. Placing a few laser stations in space would then signal that a counterforce first-strike was being planned. Even initiating such a laser ABM project will undoubtedly lead the USSR to develop the broad range of countermeasures discussed: more missiles, hardened missiles, penetration aids, and low-altitude attack weapons. As we have stated repeatedly, the arms race has a double dynamic: it is an offensive-defensive race. Reagan policy takes a static view and aims for superiority, a fiction in a dynamic race. In any case, this debate occurred in a period of the late sixties and early seventies, when ABM systems were being contemplated by the superpowers. The debate ended with both sides foregoing ABM systems as unworkable and destabilizing. In fact, the U.S. has mothballed its only ABM system, Safeguard, that had protected the ICBM field at Grand Forks, North Dakota.

The debate is also reminiscent of the civil nuclear power controversy.

The proponents share a technological theology of perfectibility, a general myopia concerning multiple-order consequences, and a broad ignorance of biological impacts. If technology could produce space-age "zap" weapons sufficiently powerful to destroy missiles in flight, then why not place installations on the ground?

Even *Time*, not known for championing liberal views and generally conservative on most issues, has castigated Reagan's arms policy. "His record is an almost unbroken pattern of self-contradiction, unfair charges against his predecessors and unfulfilled promises . . . . the U.S. position is utterly non-negotiable. It asks everything of the other side, gives practically nothing, and shows practically no flexibility" (Talbot, 1983).

The Soviet Union will probably choose a technologically simpler path, building bigger and more missiles. Thus, an SDI system presently designed to shoot down 80 percent of present missiles will be capable of shooting down only 40 percent in the 1990's (if feasible at all, which is doubtful). We would have another stand-off at far greater levels of offense and defense and far more complex systems vulnerable to error.

The cost to both superpowers of building or matching two "Star Wars" systems designed to stop 80 percent of incoming missiles is obscenely excessive, compared to the cost of reducing their nuclear weapons by 80 percent. But Reagan and company maintain their dedication to superiority.

The "weaker" side might employ still another tactic, particularly against laser defenses: a proliferation of cruise missiles launched under closed cover. Particularly devastating would be an attack on all the major nuclear power reactors in the U.S. Targeting those, together with weapons storage depots and weapons-grade material storage facilities, would introduce a tremendous multiplier effect into an attack.

Striking fifty commercial reactors would release the radioactive debris equivalent to 50,000 Hiroshima bombs. The release of vaporized plutonium-239 alone constitutes an extreme environmental and health hazard. Exposing 200 million U.S. citizens to fallout from 200 kilograms of plutonium would constitute biological warfare of an unprecedented toxicity. Conservatively, inhaling one-millionth of a gram of plutonium could induce lung cancer within thirty to forty years. The above release would create exposures 1000 times as great.

At the same time, cruise missiles could be launched in a "decapitation" attack on the U.S., disrupting C^3I. The Soviets could also explode a super H-bomb in the upper atmosphere, creating a massive electromagnetic pulse (EMP), that would destroy communications.

All of these speculations refute the idea of technological infallibility embodied in the "Star Wars" defense proposal. The only consequence of SDI will be to exacerbate the arms race, increase tension, and make arms control much more difficult.

The usual excuse for U.S. military development, i.e., that the Soviets have it or are ahead, applies to military space technology and, as usual, is untrue. As long ago as 1979, Air Force Chief of Staff Lew Allen referred to the much-touted Soviet "killer satellite" as "having a very questionable operational capability" (Garwin and Pike, 1984, p. 35). The present threatened group of low-orbit photographic reconnaissance and navigation satellites will be transferred to Navstar satellites that orbit at about 20,000 kilometers, out of range for the Soviet ASAT. On the other hand, the F-15–launched U.S. ASAT, launching a miniature homing vehicle (MHV), can attack a much wider range of Soviet military satellites, including all their photographic and electronic-intelligence satellites and even the Salyut space station. The U.S. ASAT could attack eighty of the ninety Soviet military satellites in orbit in 1983; the Soviets threaten only twenty-four of the U.S.'s ninety-four satellites (Pike, 1983, p. 3). Even Soviet communication and early-warning satellites with highly elliptical orbits are vulnerable at the low point of orbit. F-15's can be forward-based and air-refueled; thus, they have global capacity.

Both the U.S. and the USSR are working on more advanced ASAT's, a second generation of these being on the drawing board. Such ASAT's tend towards antiballistic missile capability and even more advanced technology. At a very advanced level ASAT's and ABM's merge, utilizing exotic destructive mechanisms such as lasers and particle beams, which theoretically are perfectibly accurate and instantly destructive. Satellite evasion would be overcome. The ultimate victim of this will be the 1972 ABM Treaty, one of the most important of all arms control treaties. On the "ABC News with David Brinkley," 8 April 1984, Caspar Weinberger stated with candor that he was not a proponent of ABM, an early warning of things to come. This would constitute a dangerous blow to arms stability just as multiple warheads (MIRVing) had done. This ridiculous situation has the U.S. now pressing for deMIRVing and a return to small, single-warhead ICBM's. MIRVing was the response to ABM; now ABM is the response to MIRVing, and so on, and so on, to include anti–space-based antimissile systems (ASBAM).

The moment either side has space-based laser and/or particle beam weapons, the weapons become dual purpose, antisatellite and anti-earth targets. Caspar Weinberger and Ronald Reagan, having rejected the "mutually assured destruction" (MAD) deterrence doctrine, now seek "assured survival," among the most dangerous myths in their nuclear mythology. But anti-ASAT's and anti-SBAM's are the logical consequence of the dynamics of an offensive-defensive race. Reagan and Weinberger appear mad, since AASAT's and ASBAM's are more economical than ASAT's and SBAM's.

Virtually no difference in assessment of the "star wars" policy exists between independent American scientists and Soviet scientists (Pike, 1982;

Sagdeev and Kakoshin [Committee of Soviet Scientist' Working Group on space weapons, defensive and offensive], 1983; Garwin and Pike, 1984; Federation of American Scientists, 1984; Velikhov, 1984). Even the scientists captive inside the Reagan administration do not totally agree. Only a small group of scientists whose credibility is minimal and whose faith is a corruption of the ethos of science advocates SDI.

In a huge bunker beneath the California desert, sixty-five miles south of San Francisco, experiments on exotic weapons have attracted a new breed of "star warriors." Here at Lawrence Livermore, and also in New Mexico's Los Alamos and Sandia laboratories, a group of bright new "boys" enamored of their technolgoical toys conduct the major research development of "Star Wars." The head of the Strategic Defense Initiative (SDI) is Air Force Lt. General James Abrahamson. The chief scientist is Dr. Gerald Yonas while Dr. Robert Cooper is the director of DARPA. They, together with Edward Teller, are true believers in the infallible and omnipotent power of science and technology.

Edward Teller is the only well-known scientist to cast doubt on the nuclear winter studies. This is a predictable position for a man who places inordinate trust in science and technology's ability to accomplish any task. Teller believes we can invent anything we dream. His almost theological support of nuclear power allows him to deny many of the hazards present in the use of nuclear weapons. Teller wrote in his book *The Legacy of Hiroshima* that radiation from weapons fallout was so very small it might even be beneficial to humans. Thus Teller's work at Lawrence Livermore on X-ray lasers, which require large nuclear explosions in space, combines his belief in nuclear warfighting with a notorious disregard for environmental consequences and treaty stipulations. In other comments from *The Legacy of Hiroshima,* Teller notes, "Rational behavior consists of the courage to use nuclear weapons where tactically 'indicated'" and "being prepared to survive an all-out nuclear attack is what we should strive for." This is the most naked assertion of the doctrine of the secret agenda. To use the word rational in this case is to define the irrational; Robert Jay Lifton calls it the "logic of madness." Edward Teller is a key adviser to Ronald Reagan on "Star Wars." Teller's myths are Ronald Reagan's policies. Teller, Reagan, and *Reader's Digest* are the new trinity of the New Right.

C. P. Snow's perceptive essay "The Two Cultures," which described the problem of noncommunication between scientists and humanists, is once more illustrated in the technological optimism of the new cowboys of the cosmos, the architects of "Star Wars." The young physicists who comprise the "O Group" at the Lawrence Livermore Laboratory are the front line to the high ground. They are consumed by an intractable technicism, convinced that anything they dream can be and should be invented. Educated in the space age and trained to great depth with great narrowness, they suffer a societal myopia that confines their operations to a sociopolitical and, even worse, a humanistic vacuum. Technique has become not merely a means, but an end in itself. As Amory Lovins has observed, "What is not specifically forbidden becomes compulsory." The mind-set of the scientists and engineers who have become totally attached to a particular technology is not unlike religion. It is, in fact, technological theology; therefore, it becomes the opposite of the ideal norms of science, doubt and skepticism. The proponents of space defense, like their counterparts who advocate nuclear power, fission, and fusion, are capable of tortuous rationalization in their blind support of their chosen technology, whose "sweetness" is irresistible.

LAUNCHING THE FIRST STAGE

Behind the scenes a twenty-year program to develop a very sophisticated ASAT weapon is coming to a climax. By the end of 1985, USAF will test a compact two-stage rocket, capped by this supersecret weapon, that can be placed in orbits up to 2000 kilometers above the earth. By 1987 they plan to deploy twenty-eight such weapons on the F-15 jet fighters that will launch them into space. This is yet another weapon "that has never been a 'bargaining chip' for arms control" (Smith, 1983b).

The goal of the multibillion-dollar ASAT program is to knock out all USSR ocean reconnaissance satellites in event of a nuclear war, despite Soviet reconnaissance inefficiency and the easy countermeasures that can be taken against ASAT's. Soviet ASAT's have been characterized as largely ineffective (Smith, 1983b, p. 141).

The real targets of the U.S.'s ASAT weapons are the bulk of Soviet early-warning and military communication satellites in relatively low orbit (Molniya orbits). These are highly vulnerable to the U.S.'s limited-range ASAT. A first-strike on these satellites would pose enormous difficulties for the USSR's capacity to transmit orders to its global forces.

Recalling the rhetoric of Reagan's now celebrated (or infamous) "Star Wars" speech of Wednesday, 23 March 1983, one is again tempted to suspect deliberate obfuscation. This must be tempered by our knowledge of honest ignorance. The "focus of evil" perspective and the need to destroy the "evil empire" do not jibe with "Would it not be better to save lives than to avenge them?" and "Is it not worth every investment necessary to free the world from the threat of nuclear war?" At the same time, this same Reagan proposes the largest budget in history to build weapons of global destruction. Even the U.S. may not be able to afford both, because the space-based antimissile defenses (SBAMD) cost as much as $500 billion and have dubious feasibility. Even the term SBAMD is misleading: should extremely powerful laser or particle beam weapons be developed, there is every reason to believe that they would not be confined to space.

In general, the military indulges in the use of seductive language in describing space weapons: Alpha (a chemical laser); Sipapu or White Horse (a neutral particle beam weapon); Talon Gold (an arming and targeting satellite for laser weapons); Antigone, a laser-guided electron particle beam; Teal Ruby (a mosaic infrared sensor satellite orbited by Columbia); LODE (the mirror to focus laser weapons); and Ladar (the combined use of laser and radar) (SIPRI, 1978; Aldridge, 1983, 1985a; Dyer, 1985). According to one analyst, an article that appeared in late 1982 in *Reader's Digest,* Reagan's favorite magazine, prompted his "Star Wars" speech of March 1983 (Dyer, 1984). According to Dyer, Reagan said, "I had the idea kicking around in my head for some time here recently," but we know this is not so, since the "secret agenda" introduced the concept of space-based defenses.

In October 1983 an "expert" advisory committee reported that "with vigorous technology development programs, the potential for ballistic missile defense can be demonstrated by the early 1990's." The committee estimated the cost of such a demonstration at between $18 and $27 billion. Their faith in technology, lead times, and "learning curves" would appear as faulty as their economics. The committee specifically recommended spending $7.7 billion on the Talon Gold, LODE, and Alpha laser weapons in the next five years. The defense against lasers would appear to be much cheaper. "Stealth" principles or laser countermeasures (LCM) could make missiles invulnerable to lasers. In fact, cruise missiles flying under clouds could not be "seen" by lasers. There are, of course, counter-countermeasures such as Project "R"— an X-ray laser, proposed by none other than Edward Teller at the Lawrence Livermore Laboratory (Dyer, 1984), that would involve putting a nuclear device in space, in violation of the spirit of the Outer Space Treaty.

Besides laser weapons, particle-beam, ground-based, and other energy-directed weapons are also to be developed over the next five years at an estimated cost of $6.2 billion. A long-term goal is to develop Air-Launched Sortie Vehicles (ALSV) that would be a form of "space fighter," a space vehicle launched from a Boeing-747 and equipped with exotic weapons (Dyer, 1984).

The "best" estimate of time and money to create these systems is twenty years and $500 billion. This is not necessarily the most reliable estimate; the weapons systems may never be developed. Assuming the impossibility of perfectibility, even if in 2004 the U.S. has a system that can destroy 90 percent of incoming Soviet missiles (excluding cruises), then the U.S. could be struck by an estimated 1500 strategic missiles. Assuming each of these averages ten times the Hiroshima bomb, this represents a mere 15,000 Hiroshimas, or an overkill capacity to destroy the entire population of North America.

Two of the U.S.'s most eminent scientists have initiated a petition to ban all weapons in space (Garwin and Sagan, 1983). Among those who have signed the petition are prominent scientists and Nobel laureates in the relevant areas of expertise: Hans A. Bethe, I. I. Rabi, Edward M. Purcell, and Glenn T. Seaborg; former presidential science advisers Lee A. DuBridge and Jerome B. Wiesner; space scientists E. Margaret Bunbridge, Clark R. Chapman, Thomas M. Donohue, Herbert Freedman, Donald M. Hunter, Christopher C. Kraft, James S. Martin, Jr., Gerry Neugebauer, Bruce C. Murray, Tobias Owen, Gordon H. Pettengill, William Pershing, John A. Simpson, Edward C. Stone, and James Van Allen; arms experts Sydney D. Drell, retired Admiral Noel Gaylor, and retired Vice-Admiral John Marshall Lee, Franklin A. Long, Carson Mark, Phillip Morrison, Wolfgang K. H. Panofsky, George W. Rathjens, Robert R. Wilson, and Herbert York. The petition states in conclusion, "If space weapons are ever to be banned, this may be close to the last moment in which it can be done." Late in May an even more impressive group of U.S. scientists signed a statement opposing "Star Wars." The signatories included over 50 percent of the National Academy of Sciences (NAS) and fifty-four Nobel laureates.

An influential group of computer scientists have joined the large majority of independent U.S. scientists opposing "Star Wars." They argue, quite properly, that a system designed to destroy a high percentage of Soviet missiles would require a huge, complex computer system requiring a program well beyond the capacity of current computer technology. To test and "debug" such a program is realistically impossible. Inevitable residual errors could actually lead to an unintentional nuclear war. A group of computer scientists at the University of Illinois have appealed to their colleagues throughout the U.S. to refuse to work on "Star Wars" (*The Gazette*, Saturday, 13 July 1985, p. B-7, Montreal). But "Star Wars" is the perfect fodder for defense contracts. It will proceed much as an internal memo of High Frontier reveals, i.e., "Star Wars" should "seek to recapture the term arms control and all the idealistic images and language attached to this term" and then wrap it up "with appropriate political and emotional packaging" (*Washington Spectator* 2, no. 13, 1 July 1985, p. 3).

Despite the expert disapproval ranging from pure skepticism to opposition to moving the arms race into space, Reagan's "Star Wars" plans are to proceed (Smith, 1983c). The first step approved some $25 billion for a tracking and targeting system that would simultaneously "pinpoint" thousands of missiles with tens of thousands of warheads. Additional funds will go to multiple weapons—lasers, particle beams, and space-based antiballistic missiles (SBABM). A self-fulfilling prophecy prompted these decisions: most of the consulted scientists who concluded that there were no "invincible" technical obstacles to SDI came from the Pentagon or its principal contractors. The academic community was not invited to participate and the National Academy of Sciences declined to participate; yet these groups represent the most objectively informed sector in the country. "Star Wars" development is deliberately linked to forcing the Soviets into arms negotiations. Moreover, any cooperative development with the USSR, as originally suggested by Weinberger, has been rejected. The powerful lobby behind "Star Wars" includes retired Army Lieutenant General Daniel O. Graham (former director of the Pentagon's Defense Intelligence Agency) and present director of the Heritage Foundation's High Frontier Inc. Like Teller, they are long-time "superiority" crusaders (Scheer, 1983b).

Reagan operates through "kitchen cabinets," and this unjustified informality extends to military policy. Discounting the president's formal science adviser George A. Keyworth II, who in November 1983 stated categorically that the president's "Star Wars" scenario "was feasible" (Smith, 1984c, p. 32), considerable skepticism about SDI appears within the defense bureaucracy. There even appears to be a difference of opinion between the White House and the Pentagon. Caspar Weinberger's untenable and ignorant statement claiming the 100 percent effectiveness of a "Star Wars" missile defense has its own logic. Reagan and Keyworth have made explicit that the new "Star Wars" ballistic missile defenses (BMD) are an *alternative* to offensive systems or, as Keyworth sees it, "a new stability based on, as he [Reagan] called it, rendering nuclear weapons obsolete" (Smith, 1984c, p. 32).

The broad majority of the technical community of experts inside and outside the military dismiss the infallibility notion (Carter and Schwartz, 1984). Moreover, the two secret commission reports, which the public has been assured supported Reagan and Weinberger's proposition, did not agree that there was a foolproof defense against all incoming missiles. One panel of experts, the Hoffman Commission, questions whether a slightly imperfect defense system is attainable (Smith, 1984c, p. 32). It recommends a combination of systems that mixes offensive and defensive systems, with defensive systems that concentrate on the protection of offensive weapons, rather than people. The other group, the Fletcher Commission, merely talks about research, development, and demonstration of BMD systems "effective in the twenty-first century." It acknowledged that a fully perfectible system was impractical, if not impossible.

Amazingly, Caspar Weinberger, the highest official in the defense establishment, and the president himself persist in a delusion, and continue to transmit that delusion to the public as though it were real. On 8 March 1984 Richard De Lauer, formerly the Pentagon's top scientist, told an Armed Services Committee that he could not envisage a BMD system that would eliminate the need for offensive weapons; yet the president and his science adviser persist in their public obfuscation. Thus, the Reagan administration, despite what they say, will certainly put their money (actually, the people's money) into both offensive and defensive systems, attempting to maximize both. The real issue is what SDI development will do to an already heavily deficited budget; it is questionable if Congress will go along with the program. Economic suffocation would be suicidal. The ultimate hypocrisy is the assertion by Reagan and Weinberger that they would freely give such a "perfect" BMD system to the Soviet Union.

THE PRESIDENT WITH STARS IN HIS EYES

To fully understand the "Star Wars" issue, we must bring it back into its real political context. Almost on the eve of the U.S. election in November 1984, the U.S. conducted its first flight of an ASAT weapon, a two-stage missile launched from an F-15 fighter jet over Vandenberg Air Force Base, California. The media almost totally ignored this event; yet a few days before the U.S. election, in an exclusive interview with a *Washington Post* reporter in Moscow, Konstantin Chernenko, then Soviet head of state, made it clear once again that the Soviets oppose the militarization of space.

In a totally predictable manner, the Pentagon began its propaganda campaign to obtain support for "Star Wars" technology early after the 1984 presidential election. The military "brass" used a timeworn technique that ascribes to the USSR what the military really wants to do itself—a common form of double-think, often expressed in moralistic terms such as "the enemy is evil and only the true force of goodness can destroy it." Thus, the Pentagon , announced that the Soviet Union's "program matches the United States in most, if not all, military space activities and aims to surpass it." Both "Star Wars" defenses and antisatellite weapons are involved (Defense Intelligence Agency report, *Gazette,* Wednesday, 5 December 1984, p. A-14, Montreal).

In an interview with the *Washington Post* on 7 November 1984, Reagan was "disarmingly" revealing. He repeated his notion of achieving peace through strength, using economic suffocation and technological superiority to force the Soviets to accept an unacceptable arms equation (Rosenfeld, 1983), a plan we will document. He then said that the Russians "will see the common sense value in [both of] us achieving a mutual deterrence at a lower level." The man who has launched the greatest military build-up in history, and extended the arms race into space indulges in a special form of double-think, Reagan-think. Using the "turn-the-tables" principle of establishing truth, he depicts the other side in terms of "facts"—actions or intentions that reveal what he himself thinks and intends. This gives him the freedom to claim whatever he wishes to be "facts" about the other side, about Nature, about politics and history. This license is the basis of Reagan's "reign of error" (Green and MacColl, 1983). Pollution comes from trees; acid rain is "natural." The New Deal was based on fascism, and John Kennedy's platform, on Marxism. The Soviet Union has a "1300-0 lead" in nuclear arms. Economic growth will eliminate deficits. Peace will be won through strength or, if necessary, war. Governments that rule through terror are friendly if they are anticommunist. United States' military intervention is aid and the USSR's aid is military intervention; U.S. military are "advisers," while the Soviets' are field commanders.

Further statements in his *Washington Post* interview reinforce our knowledge of Reagan's ignorance of nuclear weapon systems and the arms race. He again defended the "Star Wars" initiative and stated, "It's the only system for which a defense has never been created" (Rosenfeld, 1984); and "Since we've proven that it's possible to be *invulnerable* [Italics mine]" to Soviet attack, "they will have an incentive to reduce or eliminate their missiles." No credible expert believes in infallible systems; yet with the size of the nuclear arsenal, anything less would still be devastating. In this case Reagan shows profound ignorance. The Soviets will not defend against defense, but rather evade and/or overcome it. Nor will the Soviets wait until the system is "perfected" before they respond, both offensively against it and to match it. Even Shultz seems to disagree with the president's assessment, but Kenneth Adelman, head of the Arms Control and Disarmament Agency, agrees with Reagan—naturally, since he directs an agency whose mandate is the opposite of its name. It is proper to quote George Shultz, "We reject the view that we should become strong so that we need not negotiate. Our premise is that we should become strong so that we are able to negotiate. Nor do we agree with the view that negotiated outcomes can only sap our strength or lead to an outcome in which we will be the loser" (Rosenfeld, 1984). Please stand up, Richard Perle, Fred Iklé, Edward Rowny, and Kenneth Adelman!

An even earlier White House statement, released about one month before the new U.S.-USSR talks were to open, revealed the unrelenting "hidden agenda" behind U.S. nuclear arms policies. The statement linked the development of the "strategic defense initiative" ("Star Wars") with the possibility that the superpowers might "agree to very deep reductions, and perhaps someday even the elimination of offensive nuclear arms" (Wicker, 1984). Even if one were to ignore the huge weight of independent (and even some Pentagon scientists') expertise indicating that the goals of the program are undesirable, destabilizing, technically and strategically questionable, and excessively costly, one would be left to wonder why such an expensive ($26 billion in the next five years) method for arms control would be so zealously pursued.

In *Foreign Affairs,* November 1984, Robert McNamara, Gerald Smith, McGeorge Bundy, and George Kennan, four of America's elder statesmen, make the same point: "It is possible to reach a good [arms control] agreement or possible to insist on the Star Wars program but wholly impossible to do both . . . . there is literally no hope that Star Wars can make nuclear weapons obsolete" (Wicker, 1984). Simple arithmetic will confirm this, even if one ignores the inescapable fact that the USSR will pursue technologically simpler and far less costly offensive means to overcome space-based defense systems. Let us assume that a technically and operationally feasible version of "Star Wars" is available in 1995. We can also assume that by that time the USSR will have developed 20,000 strategic warheads, including large numbers of advanced cruise missiles, in response to SDI. Finally, assuming against the best independent judgment that 95 percent of all Soviet missiles can be destroyed, we are still left with 1000 warheads that reach targets. Since 100 megatons can trigger a "nuclear winter" and a 1000-warhead targeted attack would be incredibly devastating, we can see the absurdity of the "Star Wars" proposal. Making the absurd assumption that in the above war scenario the U.S. did not launch any of its 20,000 warheads, the destruction of even 10,000 warheads would release an incredible amount of radioactive materials, sufficient to contaminate global ecosystems. The "Star Wars" system could never be tested in its only meaningful scenario, an all-out Soviet attack. "Star Wars" systems would have to work perfectly when used the first time. There would be no point in offering the USSR this technology gratis unless it was a single, technologically perfect system over long time frames. Would a president who believes the Soviets are an "evil empire" that "lie and cheat" give them this sophisticated weaponry in any case? It assumes the perfectibility and stability quite impossible in a dynamic technological milieu. It would make accidental nuclear war almost certain, since boost phase attack might allow less than ninety seconds for detection, decision, aim, fire, and kill. Finally, McNamara, Smith, Bundy, and Kennan quote Richard Nixon, "Such systems would be destabilizing if they provided a shield so that you could use the sword."

The policy of proceeding with such space weapons is spelled out in the "five-year defense plan" and the appropriate National Security Decision Directives. They called for the "prototype development of space-based systems," including antisatellite weapons, and warned that the U.S. might seek a revision of the Anti-Ballistic Missile (ABM) Treaty. These documents also proposed "investment on weapons systems" that "are difficult to counter, impose disproportionate costs, open new areas of major military competition and obsolesce previous Soviet investment" (Halloran, 1982). We have only two conclusions regarding Reagan's "Star Wars" initiative. First, it is a complete and costly hoax, designed to "suffocate" the Soviet economy as the USSR attempts to match or overcome it. Second, it is an expression of technological faith, a belief in technological infallibility—technological theology. To emphasize the seriousness of the decision to militarize space,

Reagan has created a unified U.S. Space Command to control all Pentagon-related activities. While not responsible for research, this agency will operate any future, defensive and offensive space-based military systems. The obvious goal of the U.S. Space Command and the Global Positioning System (GPS), an eighteen-satellite system for targeting every tactical and strategic nuclear weapon in the U.S. system to an accuracy of 10 meters, is U.S. dominance in space. Controlling the high ground is the oldest military strategy, but it again faces the problem of advanced low-flying missiles like cruises probably escaping detection by sophisticated satellites, 22,000 miles in space.

The U.S. may have established a real technological and economic basis for Soviet concern. The Soviets recognize they cannot match the U.S. in either type of endeavor. They are probably aware of the U.S.'s hidden agenda but unsure of whether SDI is a realistic objective or a deliberate dead-end, designed to drain Soviet resources. The U.S. "five-year war plan" spells out both possibilities.

By 15 December 1984, the U.S., feeling more confident than ever, announced it was prepared to discuss "Star Wars" defenses. The U.S. secretary of state George Shultz said he was willing to do so in his upcoming discussions with former Soviet Foreign Minister Andrei Gromyko, beginning 7 January 1985 (*Arizona Republic*, Saturday, 15 December 1984, p. A-7). Shultz also slipped in a meaningful remark, "I don't quite know how you bargain about a research program, but you can talk about it." That the ABM Treaty prohibits the development, as well as the deployment, of missile defenses has already been lost in the fog of "research." The official Soviet news agency Novosti stated that halting the "Star Wars" program could lead to agreements on strategic arms limitations. Apparently the precondition of halting the deployment of the 572 new NATO Euromissiles (cruises and Pershing II's) is no longer necessary for the Soviets. Shultz, using the Roman method of bargaining from strength, made it clear that Euromissile deployment must proceed on schedule. However, neither Belgium nor the Netherlands agreed to accept their joint allotment of 48 cruise missiles for 1985.

HOW CAN THE PERFECT DEFENSE BE NEGOTIABLE?

As the 7–8 January 1985 round of arms talks between the superpowers drew closer, the plot sickened. In addressing foreign journalists, Caspar W. Weinberger clearly responded to the apparent discomfort of his NATO allies, generated in part by senior Politburo member Mikhail S. Gorbachev's visit to the United States. Instead of Reagan's original concept of rendering nuclear missiles "impotent and obsolete" and freeing "the world of the threat of nuclear war," the "Star Wars" plan was to protect U.S. retaliatory capability. In response to open misgivings by President François Mitterand of France and muted objections by British Prime Minister Margaret Thatcher, Weinberger sought to assure them that the new nuclear defensive umbrella would also cover Europe, not merely the U.S. Weinberger candidly rejected the MAD doctrine, stating that deterrence had been ineffective in slowing down Soviet military build-up. Using the biggest myth of all, the notion of a surprise first-strike by Russia, Weinberger now spoke of SDI (and ASAT's) as a "lever to pressure Moscow" by "defenses that could deny Soviet missiles their military objective . . . or deny Soviets confidence in the achievements of these objectives would discourage them . . . and thus be a highly effective deterrent." In characteristic double-think that matched his double-talk, Weinberger said that the Soviets "are now ready to deploy a defense system with capabilities against both aircraft and many ballistic missiles [probably the medium-range weapons]." Always accuse the other of exactly what you intend to do. Finally, Weinberger stated that the Soviets have spent more on defensive systems than on offensive missiles over the last decade (one wonders why), and should they develop an effective strategic defense system "they will deploy it" and would "break out from the ABM treaty." This is a perfect translation of Weinberger's own intentions.

It bears repeating that there appears to be a simple formula to all of this. Reagan or Weinberger accuse the Soviets of doing what they themselves are planning to do, using the excuse that this is what the Soviets are really doing, even if they are not—and they usually are not. The U.S. is planning sophisticated ASAT's and SDI/Star Wars. Therefore you accuse the Soviets of doing so. The U.S. is planning to dump ABM, so you must accuse the Soviets of doing so. When you want to produce MX missiles, you accuse the Soviets of a major build-up with large expenditures for strategic missiles. Suddenly, when you request huge sums for "Star Wars" and ASAT's, you reveal that strategic defense is the major area of Soviet expenditures and effort. You insert a small half-truth, namely, that the Soviets are developing defenses against some Euromissiles (which can hit Soviet targets and are therefore "strategic"), but you do not mention that you initiated such responses. The Pentagon has already accused the Soviets of a large cruise missile build-up, but you will not tell the public that that is in response to your own prior development. The fictitious "window of vulnerability" was used to obtain the MX. Finally, your objective is to reduce the major part of the Soviet triad, its ICBM's (exactly the same attempt that was made in START and DOUBLE BUILD-DOWN), while leaving the U.S. superior in the other two legs of the triad. You even suggest that you might trade away "Star Wars" if the Soviets reduced their ICBM's, knowing you have nothing to trade yet. You proceed to talks with a threat rather than a promise, a sure way to sabotage them.

This same Weinberger assured us that Reagan's "Star Wars" could be

made effective *"against all incoming missiles of any kind* [Italics mine]" ("Meet
the Press," 27 March 1983). Could it possibly be as effective as the attempts
to protect U.S. embassies against pick-up trucks full of explosives? At a
Washington dinner in November, Weinberger debated with his predecessor at
defense, Harold Brown. Weinberger said, "I do believe the strategic defense
initiative [SDI] is achievable. It is well within our technological, scientific,
productive and inventive genius. The search for it is a vital necessity. I hope
the president will pursue it, and I hope it will be supported" (Nelson 1984).
Brown, the conservative scientist, responded to Weinberger, the lawyer and
born-again conservative: "Technology does not offer even a reasonable
prospect of such a capability . . . of successful population defense against
strategic nuclear weapons—or even a high probability of overall success"; and
"political leaders have also a responsibility not to deceive themselves or to
mislead, however unintentionally, the American people."

Earlier we mentioned the use of alleged "gaps" to justify a particular U.S.
arms development or build-up. We have also noted the incredible consistency
with which the Reagan administration has used accusation to justify its own
intended actions. The latest version of the Pentagon's *Soviet Military Power*
(1985) carries this process to the extreme.

Caspar Weinberger, architect of the notorious defense guidance document, took the occasion to set the stage for the selling of "Star Wars." On a
worldwide television hook-up, Weinberger interpreted the new Pentagon report for all who would listen (*San Francisco Chronicle,* Wednesday, 3 April
1985). Weinberger described Soviet research in laser weapons, claiming that
the USSR had "six major research and development facilities and test ranges
. . . with 10,000 scientists assigned to this program." The Pentagon report
claimed the Soviets would be able to test a ground-based laser missile defense
within a decade, and it could possibly be operational by the mid-1990s, "with
high priority and some significant risk of failure." That is double-talk for it
can't happen there. It is also alleged that the Soviets are developing an
airborne laser that "if successful, could be installed in the early 1990s as a
satellite killer." Weinberger continued that "All of this emphasizes the very
extensive work and resources the Soviets are devoting to the very defensive
systems that they propose and say are so very dangerous if we pursue them
. . . . they are not only doing it themselves, they clearly want a monopoly in
this field." To make even more certain that the talks in Geneva fail,
Weinberger likened the shooting of Army Major Arthur D. Nicholson to an
act of murder by the Soviet system (*San Francisco Chronicle,* Wednesday, 3
April 1983).

All the above tends to confirm our earlier analysis. The Reagan administration accuses the Soviets of doing what it intends to do, and forces
Congress and its allies to support this intention; thereby the administration

helps scuttle any possibility of agreement in Geneva. Weinberger has no respect or regard for the scientific and technological merits of "Star Wars," its cost, or the increased insecurity it would cause. He is programmed by the secret agenda.

ONE GIANT STEP BACKWARD FOR THE WORLD: START, GO, OR STOP

As preparations for the resumption of arms talks between the U.S. and USSR evolved, it became clear that the "Star Wars" proposal was part of the larger plan to deceive the USSR and to strengthen the U.S. bargaining position. To carry out such a plan with real effectiveness, you must have a few technologically gullible scientists who are true believers, and very gullible government leaders who can be made to believe. This was not difficult for the Reagan administration. The president himself, Caspar Weinberger, the secretary of defense, and the president's science adviser Dr. George A. Keyworth II have, on many occasions, proclaimed the viability and desirability of a perfect defense system against incoming missiles. Soviet technocrats in government and science became the necessary gullible enemy. Such developments do not evolve in a social, political, or technological vacuum: their major contexts are both closed and open. The hidden agenda is provided by the arcane defense guidance and national security decision documents of the Reagan administration.

In the sixty days between the 6 November 1984 reelection of Ronald Reagan and the two-day arms talk meeting between George Shultz and Andrei Gromyko scheduled on 6 January 1985, speculation was rife and rampant. The media responded to every signal—weak or strong, genuine or planted, announced or leaked—ravening for news of the arms talks. The "Star Wars" issue, launched by Ronald Reagan in his 23 March 1983 speech, has occupied center stage in the media pursuit of information. In fact, the Soviets themselves probably pushed the issue upward on the preliminary agenda. Soviet leaders, from Chernenko to Gorbachev, gradually moved away from their fundamental demand for the removal of cruise missiles and Pershing II's in Europe, to focus more and more on reaching an agreement to demilitarize space.

On can respond to the Soviets with absolute suspicion, or one can recognize the general validity of their fear. The bulk of evidence would support the latter. In general, the U.S. is a generation ahead of the Soviets in all technological aspects of the nuclear arms race; if anything, the U.S. is further ahead in space technology, including the use of satellites for surveillance, monitoring, warning, command, control, communications, and intelligence (C^3I). The Soviets do not use inferior liquid rocket fuels because they prefer to, but because they have little choice. The bulk of Soviet satellites are in lower orbits and have a shorter life and higher rates of failure.

The U.S. finally seemed to recognize the importance of the "Star Wars" issue to the Soviets. By 21 December 1984, the Reagan administration released information through a senior, unidentified official that the U.S. would consider "measures of restraint" in testing the present generation of ASAT weapons, and was approaching the Geneva talks of 7–8 January 1985 in a "serious, flexible and constructive" manner (Wertzman, 1984). The U.S. also resurrected the inevitable strategy of "linkage": the U.S. would negotiate one issue, if the Soviets would capitulate on another. The 21 December 1984 briefing to reporters made it clear that the U.S. would be discussing the arms race "comprehensively," and not in a piecemeal fashion, i.e., the U.S. would "talk about all offensive and defensive weapons in their entirety and completeness." The new Geneva talks hoped to develop a format to pursue three sets of talks on (1) strategic weapons, (2) intermediate nuclear forces (INF) (broken off by the Soviets), and (3) defensive weapons, including "Star Wars" defensive systems.

The Soviets have already made clear their major concern with antisatellite weapons (ASAT'S) and space-based defensive systems (SBDS) or "Star Wars." Both Caspar Weinberger and Ronald Reagan have reaffirmed their belief and commitment to "Star Wars" defenses and SDI. They have put their money ($26 billion) where their mouths are.

In the above briefing to reporters, the senior official made it abundantly clear that the SDI research program was not negotiable. Since you cannot negotiate or trade-off research, and since there were no such U.S. defensive weapons in existence, "it is intellectually obscure what the trade-offs will be." The official added that the research programs would be put on the table for discussion. He hinted strongly that the "Star Wars" might eventually be used as a trade-off against Soviet ICBM's, a return to the fiction of the "window of vulnerability" and the demand for a "margin of safety," i.e. the legitimation of U.S. superiority by treaty.

The denouement was revealed gradually, first by Weinberger, and then by the scientific community in charge of the Strategic Defense Initiative (SDI) or "Star Wars" program. The absolute, perfect defense system was to be substantially scaled down. Some predictable double-talk accompanied this revelation of a giant step backward for the Reagan administration and a giant step forward for the world. The scientists admitted that the change in goals reflected the practical, commercial, and technological limitations of the original proposal. They managed to speak out of both sides of their mouths at the same time by saying that an "impenetrable defense was impossible but it remains a long-range goal" (Broad, 1984). Dr. Gerold Yonas, the scientist in charge of the $26 billion five-year research program, has been quoted as stating that the scaled-down program could be part of the goal of "total protection": "What was missing when we talked about very advanced technology in the next century was that it ignored all the evolutionary steps . . . . there will be opportunities to apply these more limited technologies if the country so desires." Dr. George Keyworth II, the president's science adviser, said, "Now what we're addressing more and more is what people call the transition, from the first deployment to the second and so on." Keyworth talks as though the U.S. were at the deployment stage when the research is still in its infancy, thus compounding the confusion. If one documents the official goals of SDI as stated by high-ranking officials, one recognizes deliberate obfuscation as well as absolute nonsense.

The so-called "transition" or "evolutionary steps" follow the natural and well-known path of research, development, and demonstration (R, D, & D). Apparently everybody in the field knows this but Drs. Keyworth, Yonas, and, of course, Edward Teller. When interviewed, Dr. Ashton B. Carter, the Harvard physicist who wrote the 98-page critique of SDI for the U.S. Office of Technology Assessment (OTA), said that "without explicitly repudiating the president, people are trying to tone it down and turn it into something more realistic" (Broad, 1984). In his report Carter said that SDI "is so remote that it should not serve as the basis of public expectation or national policy."

This defense system's first application, no less technologically questionable than the full system, attempts to defend ICBM's against a Soviet counterforce first-strike, a myth in itself. What we have here is a mythical defense against a mythical attack, but the "buck" will never stop. The fact that they abrogate the most important arms treaty in existence, the Anti-Ballistic Missile (ABM) Treaty of 1967, is casually ignored or, as we also know, is covertly planned by the cold warriors. The ABM Treaty was designed to support mutual deterrence and hence stability. The SDI program is designed to win a nuclear war and serves to destabilize the arms race.

James R. Schlesinger, former secretary of defense now at the Center for Strategic and International Studies at Georgetown University, stated the case uncharacteristically well: "One might be willing to upset the ABM treaty to provide protection to every man, woman and child in North America . . . but to upset it for possible improvements in deterrence is a much more difficult decision . . . . The heart of Reagan's speech was the promise that some day American cities will indeed be safe from nuclear attack . . . but there is no serious likelihood of removing the nuclear threat from our cities in our lifetime or in the lifetimes of our children" (Broad, 1984, p. A-10). Even the 147-page report of the authoritative Center for International Security and Arms Control at Stanford University concluded that the space-based defense plan was technically unfeasible and strategically unsound.

The concern of NATO allies certainly contributed to the reversal of opinion about SDI. All the allies declared their preference for George P. Shultz's more cautious approach. On her way back from signing for the transfer of Hong Kong to Chinese control in 1997, Margaret Thatcher visited Reagan at Camp David. She managed to secure Reagan's "promise" that the U.S. would begin negotiations with the Soviet Union before putting Buck Rogers weapons into space. Accepting this empty promise puts Maggie Thatcher in the top class of the gullible. Since development of SDI is decades away, if ever, negotiations must precede it by the very nature of time. Mrs. Thatcher unveiled a new strategy confusion, returning to the old view of mutual deterrence as the source of stability, even while Mr. Weinberger had been saying, only two days before and again two days later, that deterrence "condemns us to a future in which our safety is based only on the threat of avenging aggression." Weinberger, possibly unwittingly, was playing out the game of believing in the ultimate "impenetrable defense," a form of prebargaining with the Soviets or a deliberate deception designed to draw them into an arms race that their financial or technological resources cannot match. We adhere to our belief that that is the real purpose of "Star Wars." Senator Robert Lugar insisted that every initiative was part of the "bargaining process."

By 23 December 1984, still another layer of information or misinformation was peeled off. Caspar Weinberger, appearing on the ABC news show "This Week with David Brinkley," referred to SDI as "our only real hope for a future without nuclear weapons." On the CBS show "Face the Nation," Robert McFarlane had implied that they might be negotiating over "Star Wars" and expressed a willingness to negotiate—another essential element of double-think and double-talk. If you have the perfect system to overcome the threat of nuclear war, why would you ever negotiate it away? Weinberger had said "I don't exclude anything" from negotiation; yet Weinberger refused to acknowledge that the first stage of SDI would be for ICBM defense. On the evening news of 23 December 1983 Reagan was quoted as saying SDI was to protect people, not missiles. The American people are not that naive. The Russians will be more than skeptical. Perhaps Caspar Weinberger's greatest disservice is continuing the propaganda that the USSR is ahead of the U.S. militarily, including space technology.

Weinberger used the double-talk term "stages" to defend the fact that the first use of SDI would be as an ABM system. He said, "We will not give up SDI. We will discuss it." He also added that there "is no way in the world there can be limits on research" and "deterrence is a flawed strategy." He acknowledged that the Soviets wished to block SDI development. His words revealed that arms control was a one-way street, the road to superiority, and that the U.S. would like to force the USSR to reduce its arms to a state of relative weakness. He said, "We will reduce defensive systems if they reduce offensive." He did not say that the U.S. would give up its offensive system; he said only that if the Soviets reduced their ICBM leg, the U.S. might reduce the scope of its SDI program. Weinberger maintains a position consistent with the broad policy thrust of the Reagan administration. They pursue the goal of "prototype development of space-based systems," while they simultaneously invest "in weapons systems that are difficult to counter, impose disproportionate costs, open new areas of military competition and obsolesce previous Soviet investment" (Defense Guidance Document, FY 1984–1988). The "truth" depends on the observer. We cannot distinguish between true belief and deliberate hoax, except in the broad, general terms we have attempted. But the "disproportionate costs" of the "new areas of military competition" sap the resources of American people who must pay for this insanity and the planet that may have to pay with its life.

On the ABC news shows, Weinberger, ascribing to the Soviets a motive politically valuable to the U.S., said that "Star Wars" "is the one thing the Soviets seem determined to block." At the same time, in characteristic double-talk, Weinberger also said, "We will discuss it in the context of offensive and defensive systems . . . . And the Soviets have a great many defense systems themselves."

In summary, the administration has given contradictory signals about "Star Wars": they would be negotiated against Soviet offensive systems; they would be negotiated against Soviet defensive systems; they would never be negotiated. As a first stage, the U.S. would use "Star Wars" to protect its ICBM's—a scale-back of the original grandiose goal—but it has not scaled back its original intention of developing a completely impenetrable system.

THE WORLD ACCORDING TO GAP

It also became clear that administration policy applied "gap" mythology to space. Robert Cooper, the Pentagon's chief researcher for the Defense Advanced Research Projects Agency (DARPA), had appeared before a closed Armed Services Committee and stated, "I don't think the Soviets are far advanced as to where we stand in many, if not most, of these technologies" (*San Francisco Chronicle*, Monday, 24 December 1984). Many other inside and outside experts agree that the U.S. is ahead in space technology. As Dr. John Kinkaid, the leading U.S. designer of rocket engines for SLBM's, has stated about continued Soviet use of volatile, corrosive, and dangerous liquid fuels, "Whoever thinks the Soviets have stuck with liquids because they choose to do things that way does not know what they are talking about. No one would mess around with liquids if they did not have to" (Lodgaard and Blackaby, 1984, p. 23). Preparing liquid-fueled rockets for launch is time consuming, hazardous, and unreliable. The U.S. developed solid propellants some thirty years ago. The new Soviet solid-fueled test ICBM, SS-X-24, has failed seven times in ten tests. Even Caspar Weinberger, under oath, has attested to U.S. superiority, as have most other high-ranking military and space officials. The same *San Francisco Chronicle* article reported that Richard De Lauer, former undersecretary for defense for research and development, had earlier testified that it would take a decade of accelerated financing to overtake the Soviets. This predictable propaganda supports big defense budgets.

The new arms talks will not be unlike the INF talks or the START talks. The U.S. is negotiating from and for the clear superiority that it calls stability. The USSR is negotiating for parity and a freeze at present levels. Although a majority of the world's people happen to agree with the Soviets in this instance, the Reagan administration's course will not change. Senator John Warner (R-Va.) has stated, "We will have to increase our spending maybe 14 to 25 percent over the next few years to be able to close the gap" (*San Francisco Chronicle,* Monday, 24 December 1984). One can readily see how the defense budget is an extension of the politics of containment, and how conservative Republicans use the "gap" scare to drum up support for an increased defense budget. The only real gap occurs between their words and the truth. How refreshing Barry Goldwater appears, now that he sensibly opposes further MX funding. Even the Committee on the Present Danger (CPD) has been forced back into the battle: a new report issued at the end of 1984 again repeated their false charges of Soviet supremacy. Unfortunately, space has become the new battleground. It will be further militarized unless an agreement emerges to halt it. The U.S. now has the opportunity to end further space militarization, but the wrong U.S. administration is in power.

President Eisenhower's National Aeronautics and Space Act of 29 July 1958 separated civil and military space activities. NASA received operational control over civil programs for space, but the Pentagon wooed NASA into the shuttle program. As the Pentagon gained a decisive stake in the space shuttle, its use shifted from civil to military applications. The Pentagon sought military priority in shuttle use; now, one-third of the shuttle program is directly military in nature. During Reagan's tenure, the Pentagon military space budget has exceeded NASA's by some 30 percent. Reagan's budget and policy for the militarization of space will totally erode NASA's civil application. We will witness secrecy replacing openness. Space science and technology for humanity will be the losers.

The statements made by Fred C. Iklé, undersecretary of defense for policy, at a secret session of the Senate Armed Services Committee held in November 1984, make it clear that the U.S. is resurrecting ABM defenses: "It seems plausible that components of a multi-triad defense could become deployed earlier than a complete system. . . . such intermediate versions of a ballistic missile defense . . . offer useful capabilities" (Biddle, 1984). If we couple this to Weinberger's callous disreard for the ABM Treaty, "I've never been a proponent of the ABM Treaty" (Biddle, 1984), it is also clear that the U.S. is planning a three-tiered ballistic missile defense system. The first layer, capable of deployment in the next five years, would destroy missiles after they reentered the earth's atmosphere, thus creating a large amount of collateral damage from fallout of radioactive debris. The Pentagon has admitted that it seeks point defense, not wide-area population defense, in a booklet, *Near-Term Demonstrations and Deployments* (Biddle, 1984). The destabilization created by the ABM controversy of the 1960s is being reenacted because the Reagan administration is incapable of learning anything from history. If the military deploys an antiballistic missile (ABM) defense system, the Soviets will match it and develop an anti-ABM system to aid missile penetration, an easier task. The U.S. is determined to kill deterrence by seeking superiority in defense and offense. The disturbance of parity will create two new arms races—offensive and defensive—and will leave the U.S. and the world more insecure than ever before. The cost will strain economies but, as we have suggested, that is part of the plan. It is up to Congress and the people to convert this hawk president into a lame duck.

In Geneva on 7–8 January 1985, the two superpowers met to discuss nuclear arms. After fourteen hours of discussion they finally agreed to further negotiations on three separate but linked issues: (1) strategic weapons, under the false acronym START; (2) intermediate-range nuclear forces (INF); and (3) space weaponry. It would appear that the space weaponry issue includes both ASAT's and space-based defensive systems (SBDS) or "Star Wars." The communiqué released by the negotiators said that "the complex of questions on the various types of arms must be considered and resolved in their interrelationship." While media analysts pondered over the meanings and nuances of every formal or informal statement, this author believes that nothing has changed.

The USSR obviously still considers some Euromissiles as strategic or capable of hitting targets on the Soviet mainland. It still believes that parity now exists at present levels of strategic weapons and would like to see a "freeze." The Soviets would certainly view the development of SBDS or SDI with fear and anxiety if it were not completely linked to the removal of all offensive weapons. The U.S. has never stated that it will abandon its offensive arsenal once it has achieved a space-based defensive system against Soviet missiles. The Soviets are very aware of the relative success of a new U.S. infrared–homing system ABM that was successfully tested on 10 June 1984 over Kwajalein Atoll in the Marshall Islands. An unarmed ICBM, launched from Vandenberg, was knocked out by the "Homing Overlay Experiment" (HOE), a first of its kind (Hanley, 1985). In agreeing to discuss linkages, the U.S. has perhaps committed a diplomatic error. Nothing would destabilize the arms balance if the U.S. developed a shield behind which it had a sword against a Soviet sword without a shield. Neither the Soviets nor the U.S. is prepared to negotiate away trump cards. The Soviets' offensive arsenal, particularly its ICBM's, and the Americans' search for a perfect, foolproof defense presumably will not be bargained away, given the depth of mutual distrust. The bargaining chips did not fly during those two days in Geneva.

The U.S. generally argues for "stability" as if it means superiority, due to U.S. "moral superiority." The Russian word *stabilnost* means parity. As ever, the U.S. and the USSR will be talking about different things. The U.S. might bargain away "Star Wars" for clear superiority but, in this author's view, that is unrealistic for both sides. The Soviets will stick to parity—a present freeze minus "Star Wars" and new ASAT's. The U.S. will cling to its secret agenda to defeat the USSR in peace or, if necessary, in war. In all the news stories and public statements emanating from both sides, the deterrent second-strike capacity of SLBM's is never mentioned. The drama goes on; the players read their scripts and act out their roles. No wonder that the public and the media are confused and deceived. Anyone who has read Strobe Talbott's *Deadly Gambits* would instantly recognize that behind the scenes we are now engaged in Deadly Gambits II. The key actors remain the same. The script still contains the supersecret Defense Guidance Plan FY 1984–1988 and SIOP-6, a "maximalist wish list of time-urgent hard targets." As one commander-in-chief put it, "We are being told by our Commander-in-Chief to be ready, at a moment's notice, to destroy all the Soviet Union—everything, everywhere, of any conceivable consequence or time-urgent value. At the same time, we were supposed to climb on board the reductions band-wagon" (Talbott, 1984, p. 256). This is as true today as it was during the planning of the START proposal, a deception then and a deception now. We must face it. The same group, Weinberger, Iklé, Perle, and Nitze, will win the policy struggle again, as they did in the first term. In appearance at least, the Soviets are retreating and even reeling, having been forced back to the bargaining table much as Reagan had predicted. The supersecret plans are still in force. The Reagan administration is not interested in peace per se but in the ultimate defeat of the USSR through any means, including war.

"Star Wars" has become the centerpiece of the new arms talks. This issue has divided the NATO allies, and has been targeted for the largest campaign of opposition in history from America's most eminent scientists. We were therefore fortunate to have discovered Max Kampelman's views on "Star Wars" and arms control. Prior to his appointment as U.S. chief nego-tiator, Kampelman coauthored an article in the *New York Times Magazine* of 27 January 1985. As a founding member of CPD, Kampelman chose to express his views in the company of two other "hard-liners": Zbigniew Brzezinski, former national security adviser to Jimmy Carter, and Robert Jastrow, the high priest of space technology. The article, originally written as individual contributions but jointly edited and rewritten, proves to be extremely revealing. Although Kampelman attempted to have his name removed from the article, the issue had already gone to press.

Kampelman, Brzezinski, and Jastrow once again resurrect the myth of Soviet superiority. Their actual premise is that the Soviets now have a clear first-strike capacity. They compound this misinformation by suggesting that the entire U.S. strategic "triad" would be effectively neutralized in a Soviet attack. They downplay, if not disregard, the enormous U.S. retaliatory force in their invulnerable SLBM leg: some 5000 warheads with a 500-megaton yield, and the first-strike capacity of Trident I and II. They depict the U.S. as having an unshakable "no cities" strategy, while the USSR will most assuredly strike U.S. cities. The former is untrue; the latter, unknown.

The authors propose a two-layer defense. The first layer, a boost-phase attack on Soviet ICBM's, will use "smart" nonnuclear supersonic projectiles, possibly similar to the present generation of ASAT's: launched in pads from some 100 "hardened" satellites, each holding 150 interceptors, four geosynchrous satellites, and ten low-altitude surveillance and tracking satellites. The cost of the first layer is estimated at $45 billion. The second layer, terminal defense, would consist of some 5000 interceptor heat-seeking homing devices and is estimated to cost $15 billion. The double-layer defense system could be operational by the 1990s. Although various means to overcome such defenses are available, the authors commit the unpardonable sin of assuming a static Soviet response. They claim 90 percent effectiveness for their two-layer proposal. Assuming the Soviets merely double their number of missiles by the 1990s, the combined effectiveness would be only 45 percent. Even at the fantasy level of 90 percent effectiveness, we have already pointed out that 10 percent of the Soviet strategic arsenal could release as much as 500 megatons of explosives on the U.S. If the terminal layer is designed to wait for re-entry, then "salvage fuses" could explode Soviet missiles. If the attack took place above the atmosphere, the 30 percent of Soviet missiles estimated to escape the first layer would contain some 45,000 objects, or 100 decoys for every rocket, and many of these decoys could be made to emit infrared radiation. To believe that a heat-seeking interceptor, such as the one tested by the U.S. in June 1984, could handle a "threat swarm" of such proportions is again ridiculous.

Most significantly, the article denies the feasibility of arms control and openly supports the deployment of space-based defenses. Both positions contradict the established bases of the March 1985 talks. The U.S. publicly committed itself to arms control, but "Star Wars" was not to be a bargaining chip; instead, deployment was negotiable. Therefore, the chief negotiator for arms control has publicly subscribed to "skepticism" regarding arms control and to the abrogation of the 1972 ABM Treaty. He proposes ballistic missile, not population, defenses, in contradiction to the president himself.

Kampelman, Brzezinski, and Jastrow's cost accounting is at the same level as their strategic analysis, which, in turn, is as low as the technical basis for such a space-based system. For first-phase attack, they plan to use 15,000 interceptors deployed on 100 satellites, giving the Soviets 100 targets for simple ASAT devices. Only midcourse attack could be feasible with fifteen minutes to strike. Even at supersonic speeds the interceptors might have to travel considerable distances, depending on ICBM orbits. This system has a low technical feasibility. The authors speak of a 5000-interceptor second-layer defense that would have to be effective against some 45,000 objects (430 rockets with ten warheads and ten decoys per warhead) above the atmosphere. The authors say nothing about a combined cruise missile and depressed-trajectory attack because there is no defense against such an attack. They do not mention the U.S. plan to build a total of 8000 cruise missiles. They ascribe reloadable silos to the 1400 Soviet ICBM's. If this is true, the Soviets could fire three full salvos, each launching 1400 missiles, or the Soviets could develop maneuverable ICBM's and false silos by the 1990s. Any midcourse strike would cause a serious radiation hazard.

The article illustrates a problem that goes beyond false accounting and bad technology. Max Kampelman has faith in nuclear superiority; Zbigniew Brzezinski has said, "I don't consider nuclear superiority to be politically meaningless" (Interview, *Washington Post,* Tuesday, 9 October 1979); and Robert Jastrow stands on record as asserting his belief in "strategic superiority matters" (Jastrow, 1983). The combination of Kampelman, a staunch, founding member of the CPD, Brzezinski, a viscerally anti-Soviet, technocratic political scientist, and Jastrow, the worst of the space-science euphorics, represents the true policy basis of the Reagan administration. The millions of people who still have hope for arms control and disarmament will never see it occur under this administration. Reagan's government bases its operations on the secret agenda of superiority and the political and/or economic assassination of the present Soviet system. Everything the U.S. has done prior to the new March 12 talks, from exhortations in favor of MX, to the active selling of "Star Wars," to the published report on alleged Soviet treaty violations, seems deliberately designed to subvert arms control and assert superiority. The destruction of trust prior to discussions in which trust is a necessary component is no accident. The "Star Wars" shield is being proposed at the same time as the procurement of between thirty-one and thirty-nine Tridents I and II, ninety B-1B bombers, forty-five stealth bombers, 2600 advanced, 4068 sea-launched, and 1739 air-launched cruise missiles, 380 Pershing II's, at least ninety MX's, and 1000 Midgetman—a nuclear sword of almost 10,000 new strategic warheads. In their brutal assault on the truth, Kampelman, Brzezinski, and Jastrow say nothing about all of this. Nor do they mention that the U.S. will soon deploy the most accurate first-strike weapon in the world: Trident II. Thus, by deploying SLBM's much closer to Soviet strategic targets, the U.S. will have the capacity for a devastating first-strike against the USSR.

Because of the accuracy and yield of their missiles, just fifteen Trident II–equipped submarines would threaten all 1398 Soviet ICBM's. Thus, the truth of the situation opposes the major premise of this article. "Star Wars" plus first-strike is excessively destabilizing.

THE MAGINOT LINE IN THE SKY

On 2 January 1985, six outstanding experts wrote a letter to the *Wall Street Journal* explaining "Why 'Star Wars' is dangerous and won't work" (Bethe et al., 1985). They cite six solid reasons:

1. Underflying—"Star Wars" cannot address low-flying delivery systems such as cruise missiles, bombers, and "suitcase" nuclear weapons.
2. Overwhelming—It is cheaper and more feasible to increase your attacking missiles than to defend against them, and it is easier and more technologically feasible to shoot down orbiting defense systems than incoming missiles.
3. Outfoxing—It is cheaper to build countermeasures that would overwhelm, elude, or deceive defensive systems.
4. Cost—The $1 trillion cost of "Star Wars" is so prohibitive that it endangers U.S. economic security and cuts into other military systems.
5. Destabilizing—A "Star Wars" shield that the USSR perceives as a U.S. first-strike strategy tactic might tempt them to a preemptive attack. "Star Wars" will also induce a new arms race whose momentum will be more difficult to control. After deployment institutional momentum will take control, producing the juggernaut effect.
6. Imperfectibility—Anything short of a perfectible system will tend to undermine U.S. security, since only a small percentage of penetrating Soviet missiles would be unacceptably destructive. The Soviets will simply build more strategic missiles to increase this percentage for any particular defensive system.

More and more scientists, many of them experts in the field, are rejecting "Star Wars." Richard N. Lebow of Cornell, who taught at the Naval War College and was a scholar in residence for the CIA, said in a speech at the University of California, Santa Barbara, that "it makes no sense" and would lead to a war of greater damage, because cities would become preferred targets (*Santa Barbara News-Press,* Friday, 15 March 1985, p. C-1). Lebow also noted that after a briefing on the devastating consequences of a nuclear war, Reagan appeared "absolutely ashen-faced." Lebow commented, "I suspect 'Star Wars' represents for him [Reagan] a psychological escape from the dilemma. It's an existential means for him to cope with his psychological burden. The problem is that it's an illusory escape."

A politically influential, twenty-member group at Stanford's Center for International Security delivered another blow to "Star Wars" development. After some five months of discussion, the group reached consensus on a 75 percent cutback on the proposed $26 billion to be spent on "Star Wars" in the next five years (*San Francisco Chronicle,* Friday, 15 March 1985). This decision reaffirms that offensive-weapons development will dominate budget spending for the next five to ten years. The Stanford group reiterated their support for the 1972 Anti-Ballistic (ABM) Treaty. They endorsed the idea of selective, but modest research to parallel Soviet endeavors and establish feasibility of aspects of the "Star Wars" program. They supported the development of "space mines" and "mid-course discrimination" techniques to distinguish actual targets from decoys. In effect, the Stanford group called for research that abides by the ABM Treaty and does not threaten the USSR. Although some of the experts are in favor of the Strategic Defense Initiative, their joint suggestions indicate that Ronald Reagan may have to abandon his plans to escape from "his psychological burden."

All of this criticism must be having an effect on Air Force Lieutenant General James A. Abrahamson, the director of the SDI project and, by necessity, a true believer. However, Abrahamson still manages to misinterpret the strategic significance of ballistic missile defenses on grounds that are difficult to believe: "that [SDI], in turn, might increase incentives for both sides to reduce the numbers of ballistic missiles" (Benedict, 1985). If "Star Wars" had an absolutely perfect tie to the space race and each side was convinced of its own invulnerability—both impossible—then Abrahamson's perspective would be correct. Since he must know better, a real danger exists that the arms race in space will spur the arms race on land, sea, and air; it is already happening. Abrahamson boasts about the June 1984 kinetic-energy Homing Overlay Experiment in which a missile equipped with an infrared sensor and fired from Vandenberg over the Pacific destroyed an unarmed Minuteman: "That's about ten times as complicated as hitting a bullet with a bullet."

The Associated Press journalist who reported Abrahamson's assessments has some knowledge of aerospace technology but remains overawed by the "Star Wars" program. Although homing devices may be self-propelled or fired by electromagnetic rail guns, and deployed in space or "pop-up," the

Homing Overlay Experiment is more a delusion than a demonstration. There is a profound difference between the ability to hit one missile, and the capacity to defend against a swarm of thousands of targets in midcourse. Having a weapon is entirely different from having a defensive system.

Vandenberg Air Force Base will become the center of SDI development, and eventually the military will build its own space shuttle there. Placing astronauts in permanent stations in space is the necessary prelude to constructing space-based battle stations. Developing lasers that can see through clouds and focus through huge, optically perfect, space-based mirrors is another project, fraught with technological uncertainty. The mirrors provide simple targets for "space mines." The video-game syndrome is not only trivializing culture, but also encouraging the older "boys" to play with their more deadly technological toys. They are trying to create reality with mirrors, using the excuse that the Soviets also are experimenting with laser technology. However, the same arguments that render U.S. space-based or ground-based laser weapons impractical also apply to the Soviets.

Both sides are also moving towards mobile, more accurate, single-warhead missiles. This would render "Star Wars" even more ineffective since its targets would be mobile. The USSR already seems to be deploying a single-missile ICBM, the SS-25, at two missile fields, and the U.S. is planning the Midgetman. In addition, the U.S. has strategic Pershing II's that are similar in operation. Some existing evidence indicates that the Soviets already are eliminating some of their missiles to remain within the 1400-missile limits of SALT II. The Soviet ten-warhead SS-24's are rail mobile, a basing mode discarded by the U.S. The accuracy of SS-25's is also disputed. The more credible evidence indicates that they are considerably less accurate than the somewhat older SS-24's. In any case, the maneuverable single-warhead ICBM's that can be hidden will present another great obstacle to a "Star Wars" system based on hits in the "boost phase," which can be shortened to less than two minutes. With such short "boost-phase" times and unexpected launchings, lasers will be rendered ineffective. The U.S. will have to go to "mid-course" or "terminal" defenses, each more difficult to defend. The Soviets have now officially agreed to abide by SALT II and have satisfied the joint U.S.-USSR Standing Consultative Committee (SCC). The U.S. also made this decision, attaching the rider that they would respond with "proportionate measures" to alleged Soviet violations.

"Star Wars" received a further rebuke in March 1985 from an unexpected quarter. Sir Geoffrey Howe, foreign secretary of Great Britain, delivered a 27-page speech that expressed strong doubts on the feasibility and desirability of SDI. Howe also showed concern at the abandonment of the 1972 ABM Treaty, which he called "a keystone in the still shaky arch of security we have with the East." While Howe said that the Soviet build-up has "exceeded the reasonable requirements necessary for the defense of the Soviet Union," he continued, "Historical experience has inclined them toward over-insurance" (Will, *Santa Barbara News Press,* Sunday, 24 March 1985).

Sir Geoffrey Howe concluded that "there would be no advantage in creating a new Maginot Line of the Twenty-first Century, liable to be out-flawed by relatively simple and demonstratively cheaper counter measures." In the same week that Howe spoke, West German Foreign Minister Hans-Dietrick Genscher expressed his reservations about "Star Wars." The French have officially voiced similar concerns. In fact, no NATO ally actually supports the SDI proposal.

Reagan exerted every pressure he could to obtain support of his program from NATO and at the Bonn, West Germany, economic summit in May 1985. NATO defense ministers including Howe, who met in Luxembourg on Wednesday, 27 March 1985, heard so many entreaties from Reagan and Weinberger that the NATO representatives unanimously urged "continuing research" on SDI. Caspar Weinberger, the nuclear hatchetman, brushed off Britain, France, and Germany's strong reservations on actual development and deployment. In his usual double-talk, Weinberger called the reservations that Howe had clearly stated "misunderstandings which seemed able to clear up" (*Washington Post,* Thursday, 28 March 1985). Reagan used the same pressure tactics on NATO that he had used on Congress, but again failed to gain NATO's clear support. NATO has now officially rejected endorsement of "Star Wars." At the NATO foreign ministers' conference in Portugal in June 1985, NATO failed to mention "Star Wars" in their final communiqué (*Santa Cruz Sentinel,* Friday, 7 June 1985, p. A-1). Their "misunderstandings" will never be resolved.

THE TWO FACES OF SPACE

The space age has presented the world with two opposing visions (Knelman, 1981). The first view, the ecological perspective, sees our planet as "spaceship earth," a unified planet, with no boundaries or divisions, that shares the common oceans and receives nurture from the sun. The other perspective views the world with with the pirate's eye, gleaming with the greed of an-ticipated plunder; the military eye, seeking out new means and new arenas of destruction; the sovereign eye, seeking only national gain and aggrandize-ment at the expense of all countries and, if necessary, of the entire planet. The technological development of space has two faces, salvation and ca-tastrophe. Attaining legitimate knowledge about the earth, its environment, and resources is an essential part of survival and fulfillment, but the rockets that launch peaceful satellites can be minor modifications of the delivery system of a nuclear holocaust. The satellites in space can allow us to communicate peacefully, to manage resources wisely, to assess and minimize environmental damage, but they too can be armed with new weapons or spy on "enemies." We already invade the privacy of sovereign states, making them less sovereign and less able to resist. The exploitive process of the cold war, previously confined to earth, has moved into space (Garwin, 1981). Technology embodies the principle that information is power.

We are continually torn between narrow, short-term exploitation and long-term sustainability, between exclusivity and sharing, between jealously guarded sovereignty and international cooperation. Thus, one vision perceives the earth as the habitat for a unitary species; the other sees the earth as a complex of conflicting nation-states, all squabbling over territory and each jealously guarding its position in the hierarchy that splits North and South by wealth and power and East and West by ideology. The small force of the many voices of reason and peace grows more rapidly than the speed of global conflict (Moore, 1975; Kopal, 1977; Ferrer, 1977; Ploman, 1978).

The future will decide which face of space the world will encounter. Having militarized the earth, the seas, and the atmosphere, space now seems likely to become a new frontier for waging war from the ultimate high ground. Only the power of the forces of peace can reverse this tendency. The situation is by no means hopeless. The Reagan administration and its captive technocrats stand alone in their defense of "Star Wars."

10

Canadian Complicity in U.S. Nuclear Strategy

It's as if we're long-lost fraternity brothers, trying to catch up on what's been going on for the last 20 years.
                                                    Paul Robinson, U.S. Ambassador to Canada

I confess I like Brian Mulroney. . . . He's a true Canadian patriot . . . [and] a strong friend of the United States.
                                                    Ronald Reagan

The contradiction comes from the fact that these democratic countries (who belong to NATO) don't have the right to raise questions without immediately being seen as disloyal.
                                                    Pierre Elliott Trudeau

The cruise missile testing issue, one of the more dramatic events in the long history of U.S.-Canada relations, can only be understood, or at least analyzed with some credibility, within its broader historical, political, and geopolitical context.* The most constant and persistent theme in U.S.-Canada relations is the struggle between the political forces of nationalism versus continentalism, or national independence from the U.S. versus regional integration with the U.S. This polarization manifests itself in all policy debates, including those concerning the military, trade, foreign interests, energy pipelines, and communications. Literally and figuratively, the tension is between the vertical North-South pull and the horizontal East-West pull, with the Rocky Mountains and the Great Lakes favoring the former. Thus, nationalism often conflicts with regional economics, just as the politics of independence conflicts with the economics of trade. Geography and geopolitics tend to deter-

---

*Among the excellent source books deserving mention, John W. Warnock's *Partner to Behemoth: The Military Policy of a Satellite Canada* (Toronto: New Press, 1970) deals with Canada's military connections with the U.S. through the 1960s. Stephen Clarkson's *Canada and the Reagan Challenge* (Toronto: James Lorimer, 1982) covers the complex range of relations between Canada and the U.S., with emphasis on American policies toward Canada during the first two years of the Reagan administration and the Canadian response to them.

mine Canadian military policies. Canada naturally becomes the nuclear buffer zone for the U.S. and an often unwilling accomplice to U.S. military strategies (Lumsden, 1970).

The nuclear arms race and the emergence of NATO and NORAD have played an increasingly dominant role in U.S.-Canada military relations since Canada participated in the Manhattan Project during the Roosevelt and Truman administrations. The cruise missile issue has a fascinating historical precedent, a nuclear debate in which this author was deeply involved, as were certain other, currently more visible actors. The years 1959–1963, the period of the mythical "bomber gap" discussed earlier, witnessed the debate over siting a U.S. antibomber nuclear missile, Bomarc B, at two sites in Canada— Lac Macaza, Quebec, and North Bay, Ontario—and the Cuban missile crisis of October 1962. In 1959 and 1960, this author chaired what was possibly the first Canadian nuclear disarmament group. The innocuously named Montreal Committee for the Control of Radiation Hazards (MCCRH) had Pierre Elliott Trudeau as a member of its illustrious board of directors.

During 1959–1962, MCCRH focused its concern on two major issues: fallout from atmospheric testing and the Bomarc missile debate. The Bomarc B had failed most of its tests and was an unproven weapon designed for a nonexistent target. Moreover, the siting of U.S. nuclear weapons such as Bomarc B on Canadian territory contributed to the arms race and would have made Canada a primary victim of targeted Soviet weapons, as well as the victim of fallout from exploding U.S. nuclear weapons. The "continentalist" Lester Pearson defeated the "conservative" John Diefenbaker, often the "nationalist" in Canadian politics, on the very issue of Canadian response to the siting of U.S. nuclear weapons in Canada and Canada's support of the U.S. in the Cuban missile crisis of 19 October 1962 (Warnock, 1970, pp. 121–129; 156–195). Bomarc B missiles were finally installed at Lac Macaza on 31 December 1963 (Warnock, 1970, p. 196).

Canada became an accomplice to U.S. nuclear strategy not because of its commitment to NATO—an entirely false proposition—but because of its bilateral arrangements with the U.S. The cruise missile testing issue again raises the question of Canada's position on nuclear weapons, but at a far more serious level. Pierre Elliott Trudeau, then editor of *Cité Libre,* and Gerard Pelletier, then editor of *La Presse,* were among the few editorial voices in Canada to denounce Lester Pearson's stance on nuclear weapons. The famous April 1963 issue of *Cité Libre* not only accused Lester Pearson and the Liberal Party of selling Canada out for campaign support, but also brought these words from Trudeau's immortal editorial: "Since I have observed politics, I do not remember ever having seen a more degrading spectacle than all those Liberals who became 'turncoats' with their Chief, when they saw a chance of regaining power" (Warnock, 1970, p. 195). It is impossible not to note the irony of these words in the light of the cruise missile "testing agreement." We contend that the Canadian alliance with John Kennedy and Robert McNamara was benign compared to Canada's strategic integration with Reagan and Weinberger, CPD, Team B, the "Moral Majority," the New Right, and a holy nuclear crusade (the five-year plan) against the USSR.

The diaries of Charles Ritchie, Canada's ambassador to Washington in 1962, yield a more intimate insight to U.S.-Canada nuclear diplomacy (Ritchie, 1983). According to Ritchie, the government of John Diefenbaker, particularly his minister of external affairs Howard Green,

> has certainly made it abundantly clear that we are against nuclear arms as one is against sin, and this moral attitude is shared by the most sophisticated [Norman Robertson] and the least so among Canadians . . . . It is not only a moral attitude but also hygienic, the two often go together in Canada. Fall-out is filthy in every sense of the word. This reaction, strong in many parts of the world, is particularly strong at home. It is from this soil that our disarmament policy grows . . . but no political leader of any stamp is prepared to go to the Canadian people and tell them they must have nuclear arms or store nuclear arms. This may change with a change of government; if so, gradually. This is a deep difference between us and the United States.

Mr. Ritchie must have been shocked at how quickly Canadian policy changed with Diefenbaker's defeat by the "peacemaker"-turned-powdermaker Lester Pearson; he would have been more shocked at Pierre Elliott Trudeau's alliance with nuclear arms proponents in the U.S.

The "logical" allies for Canada are the majority of the U.S. Congress who support the Nuclear Freeze Initiative and the majority of Canadians who oppose cruise missile testing. The consummate irony is that in allowing cruise missile testing or the siting of U.S. nuclear weapons on Canadian soil, Canada supports the strategic nuclear warfighting forces of Reagan, not its NATO commitment.

Canada's long history of accommodation to U.S. policies, including its nuclear weapons policies, occurs in a larger economic context. The long, undefended border between the countries has encourages tourism and trade. The U.S. is Canada's predominant trading "partner" in all areas of commerce. Canada's abundant natural resources have spurred interest in "energy continentalism." In addition, Canada has served as a "frontier" for U.S. investment and development; many industries became established as "branch plants" of U.S. corporations. Canada's sixty-four military "notes" concerning bilateral arrangements with the U.S. stem directly from the Defense Production Sharing Agreements (DPSA) of 1959. The U.S. agreed to provide Canada with access to the U.S. defense market if Canada would agree to share continental defense, strategic "continentalism," and weapons testing (Warnock, 1970; Clarkson, 1982). These agreements made it inevitable that Canada would approach its own security, and global security, from the perspective of U.S. nuclear strategy and technology. U.S. congressional sources have linked cruise missile testing in Canada with cancellation of a $70 million Canadian payment for F-18A fighter plane research and design, while Canada is purchasing 138 F-18A's from McDonnell Douglas. Litton Systems in Toronto, Ontario, has a $1.2 billion contract for the cruise's guidance system. Thus, Canada's military accommodation to and compliance with U.S. objectives may have various components: pragmatism, deception, ignorance, or belief and rationalization.

THE CRUISE MISSILE: SOME TECHNICAL AND STRATEGIC ASPECTS

Three versions of the cruise missile (CM) are currently under development: the air-launched cruise missile (ACLM's), the sea-launched cruise missile (SLCM's), and the ground-based cruise missile (GLCM's). The so-called "dual-track" NATO decision of 12 December 1979 permitted the U.S. to site operational GLCM's in Europe by the end of 1983. All cruise missiles other than the antiship cruise use an automatic inertial guidance system (made by Litton Systems of Toronto) with a built-in sensor system, TERCOM or "terrain contour matching device," and the same fanjet, air-breathing subsonic engine. The air-launched cruise missile and the nuclear land-attack ship-launched cruise missiles (TLAM/N) have a 200-kiloton warhead. Ground-launched cruise missiles have selectable 10- to 50-kiloton yield warheads. There are also conventional land-attack and ship-attack missiles (Aldridge, 1985b).

Cruise missiles range from fifteen to twenty-one feet in length. Their guidance system, radar-eluding capacity, low-flight capability, and great accuracy make cruise missiles unique. According to a senior weapons specialist, "They have a 100 percent 'kill capacity' against some hardened emplacements" and "are virtually impossible to detect" (Aldridge, 1981, p. 39). The U.S. Air Force and Navy both have the Tomahawk GLCM. Ground-launched cruise missiles can be mounted and fired from mobile, covert launchers. The U.S. originally ordered 3780 ALCM's and 3994 SLCM's (75 percent of the latter are nuclear), providing a total megatonnage of about 1500, more than enough to destroy all urban and industrial targets in the USSR. Updated versions will have ranges up to 2500 miles. The U.S. Air Force ALCM has a range of over 1300 nautical miles, and the Air Force is planning an advanced strategic ALCM (or ASALM), a cruise missile with supersonic capability. These have been kept relatively secret because of their incredible lethality (Aldridge, 1981, p. 42; 1985b). B-52G's and B-52H's can carry twelve externally mounted cruise missiles.

The ALCM's, particularly the faster, longer-range updated version, equipped with Electronic Counter-Measure (ECM) devices (Aspin, 1980), can be considered "first-strike" weapons using the criteria of lethality and probability of kill. Their low radar cross-section of 0.05 square meters and terrain contour matching flight path of less than 100 feet make them almost impossible to shoot down. It is unlikely that silo kills are their intention; their real strategic significance lies in their penetrating capacity against hard C^3I targets. This ability, in effect, nullifies the USSR's excellent bomber defense system and forces the Soviets to develop other, expensive defenses against ALCM's. Even the 464 GLCM's and 108 Pershing II's designated for NATO have critical response- and delivery-time advantages over the cumbersome Soviet SS-20's. The SS-20's reaction time is slow, about one hour, while Pershing II's in West Germany can be launched and hit targets in minutes (Paine, 1981). Although air-breathing GLCM's are subsonic and slow, their accuracy and penetrating capacity make them excellent weapons against C^3I targets. The definition of "strategic" has always been applied to weapons that can hit the national territory of either of the two superpowers; therefore, regardless of semantics such as the LRTNF's designation, Euro-missiles like GLCM's and Pershing II's can hit Soviet territory. Although the USSR tested ALCM's as early as 1979, existing SS-20's cannot hit the U.S. from their current bases in Europe or Asia.

The production of U.S. ALCM's will be reduced from the 4348 planned for 1990, to 1739, augmented by 1500 ACM's (*Defense Monitor* 12, no. 4, 1983, p. 3). The ACM's will also have on-board threat detection equipment and will be capable of evasive action. They will travel at much higher, possibly supersonic, speeds and maneuver through the guidance of terminal homing systems like the Pershing II's, and/or links to the NAVSTAR global positioning system like Trident II. These technological refinements could lead to a counterforce intercontinental strategic weapon with devastating first-strike accuracy and the ability to destroy "hard" targets. One must remember that, in part because SALT II included a protocol to ban deployment of cruise missiles, the CPD sought to defeat its ratification.

The cruise missile was originally one of those perennial "bargaining chips" used by both sides in strategic arms limitation talks. The USSR's "chip" was the Backfire bomber. By 1972, at the time of SALT I, the Pentagon firmly declared the cruise missile off the list of "bargaining chips." Henry Kissinger stated, "I didn't realize the Pentagon would fall in love with cruise missiles" (Ford et al., 1982, p. 30). Nobel laureate Hans Bethe has stated, "Cruise missiles are probably the most accurate weapon that has been invented . . . the most important progress in weapons in the last decade" (Scheer, 1982, p. 273). An independent Canadian expert says, "The cruise missile represents a major change in weapons technology" (Polanyi, 1983). The cruise missile has the capacity for launch from the ground, air, and sea, so it is really three weapons in one and confuses the lines of demarcation between theater and strategic weapons. Cruise missiles are doubly dangerous because they largely defeat any verification potential. Contrary to current misinformation, these missiles can be fired covertly, from a garage or van. Since these missiles can be armed with H-bombs or conventional weapons, misinterpretation of their payload might cause a fearful response.

The Soviets lag at least a generation behind the U.S. in development of GLCM's. The U.S. also has a two-"generation" lead in ALCM's. The U.S. ALCM program escalated the USSR response, as usual; yet again we see raised the fiction of a "cruise missile gap," when actually a new and dangerous increment of the nuclear arms race is being initiated.

The *Defense Monitor* 12, no. 4, 1983, reveals the strategic significance of the cruise missile and dispels the notion that the USSR has such weapons. It notes that the U.S. is "a quantum jump ahead of the Soviets." Two squadrons of sixteen B-52H aircraft, each armed with twelve ALCM's, are already operational, one at Griffis Air Force Base in New York and the other in Michigan. Although this program has had a number of reported failures (Aldridge, 1985b), in a few years the present generation of ALCM's will likely give way to the "Advanced Cruise Missile" (ACM). This weapon will be augmented by "stealth" techniques as well as ECM to make it nearly invulnerable to detection and defense. The 100 B-1 bombers will each be armed with six ACM's. The Senate and the House have now approved the production of the B-1 and a cruise missile budget of nearly $15 billion. All 172 B-52G's and 96 B-52H's will each be equipped with twelve externally mounted cruise missiles, giving a total of 3816 ALCM's when fully operational (Feld and Tsipis, 1979; *Defense Monitor* 12, no. 4, 1982).

Even as early as February 1983, five B-52 aircraft were equipped with twelve cruise missiles each, given defined targets, and were being deployed on a "twenty-four–hour war alert" (*Observer,* Sunday, 6 March 1983, London). The number of ALCM's plus SLCM's roughly coincides with the total (about 3000) C^3I targets in the USSR (Barnaby, 1982). The number of strategic targets estimated by the Pentagon always increases to a number greater than the procurement policy allows. Myth again tends to become policy. The assumption of a limited and/or protracted, winnable nuclear war necessarily means a strategic weapon for every conceivable target, even if it is not strategic or would be destroyed as "collateral damage." One would think that as targets become more precise, the emphasis would shift to conventional weapons, but the U.S. intends to have it all ways. The use of enhanced radiation weapons is prominent in the new warfighting plans. While the Reagan administration argues that accurate weapons designed for "counterforce" targets are more "humane," they plan a huge expenditure on "neutron" bombs, which are the Wall Street weapons, designed to protect property and kill people.

At the level of current orders, cruise missiles would comprise about 25 percent of the total U.S. strategic weapons. This additional threat will undoubtedly accelerate the arms race. Moreover, cruise missiles are difficult to verify in construction, in deployment, and in attack. They may carry nuclear or conventional warheads. They can be loaded onto civil aircraft. These unknowns increase the danger that any cruise missile strike, intended to be "local" or "limited" according to current U.S. doctrine, could be interpreted as a major nuclear attack. Since the cruise can be both a conventional and a nuclear weapon, stockpiling would be misinterpreted. Cruise missiles now armed with conventional warheads can be converted to nuclear warheads (Betts, 1981). The cornerstone of arms control and reduction is thus effectively negated by the inability to verify (*Defense Monitor* 12, no. 4, 1983).

The Soviets are now actively engaged in developing their own ALCM's. A U.S. spy satellite first photographed a new intercontinental jet bomber, the Blackjack, on 25 November 1981 (Aldridge, 1983, p. 58). The Blackjack photograph appeared one month after the Reagan administration's announcement of a B-1 bomber program. The Soviets obviously intended that their new bomber be "seen" by the U.S., just as they now want their A-101 to be "seen" and reported in Jane's *All the World's Aircraft*. The Soviets have consistently bluffed on aircraft since the 1950s, and they do not seem to have learned the hard lesson that an implied threat can cause a real response. While the Soviets have begun testing the cruise missile, they remain perhaps a generation behind U.S. military technology initiatives.

DUAL-TRACK OR MONORAIL

The cruise missile debate arose from a NATO policy decision made during the Carter administration. The argument that the NATO "dual-track" decision of 1979 was a response to the "new" threat of Soviet SS-20's appears spurious. The deployment of the first 108 Pershing II's and 464 GLCM's in Germany and Britain has left Europe more vulnerable and more anxious about security than before. The majority of West Europeans now view the graver threat as deriving not from Moscow, but from Washington. In general, the 1979 decision divided the alliance and led to serious political realignments. The Social Democrats of Norway and West Germany now oppose deployment. Ironically, Helmut Schmidt, as leader of the West German Social Democrats, actively supported deployment.

The deployment of Pershing II's has not only increased the danger of "launch-on-warning" postures and accidental nuclear war, but the deployment of these strategic Euromissiles has also initiated a new arms race. In response, the Soviet Union has moved its SS-20 missiles closer to NATO targets and threatened to deploy SLBM's closer to the U.S. The USSR will continue to develop cruise missiles, and their verification problems will make arms control more difficult. The Reagan administration has integrated Pershing II's and cruise missiles into specific warfighting plans that have nothing to do with the defense of Europe. Both the U.S. and the USSR have incentives to launch first-strikes, the former out of conviction and the latter out of fear. In either case, Europe would become a nuclear graveyard.

An excellent analysis of the deployment decision has been made by one of the best of the nuclear weapons investigative reporters (Smith, 1984b). While that reporter does not entirely agree with this author, considerable evidence indicates that the deployment of operational Euromissiles, called for by the "dual-track" decision, is part of the Reagan plan for the decapitation and economic suffocation of the Soviet Union. It follows the general pattern of the original attempt to achieve significant superiority through the huge defense budgets of FY 1984–1988 that maximized every new weapons development, including space weapons.

The development and deployment of cruise missiles serves commercial and political purposes. Key defense contractors—Boeing, McDonnell Douglas, General Dynamics, and Lockheed—all powerful actors in the military-industrial complex, have the clout to push the cruise. Initially, all three branches of the U.S. military had opposed the missile, but certain other defense intellectuals of the right such as Richard Burt, then with the International Institute for Strategic Studies and now Reagan's assistant secretary of state, helped in selling it (Smith, 1984b, p. 374).

The USSR deployed SS-20's primarily for "routine nuclear modernization," as Paul Nitze and other experts have stated (Smith, 1984b, p. 373). In fact, the modernization flowed from failure. The USSR made futile attempts to develop an advanced, mobile intercontinental missile, the SS-16. The SS-20's were the successful first and second stages of a three-stage rocket. The SS-4's and SS-5's, first deployed in the 1950s, were inappropriate, clumsy, and destined for replacement by more modern weapons. The SS-20's also have a strategic function and are targeted against the strategic forward-based NATO and U.S. forces, as well as strategic targets in Asia and possibly Africa. Like the Backfire bomber, the SS-20 has a range shorter than that required by the traditional intercontinental definition of "strategic," but it can perform strategic functions.

Independent experts believe that SS-20's represented little more than modernization: they neither altered the strategic balance nor constituted a new threat to Europe. They were part of an old Soviet threat. Cruise missiles, on the other hand, particularly Pershing II's, represent a technological and strategic leap of great significance, and many of these same experts anticipated the results of proceeding with deployment. Pershing II's can hit some Soviet targets in a few minutes, leaving no time for validation.

During the years of Soviet LRTNF Euromissile supremacy, the USSR tried to hold Europe hostage in response to overall U.S. missile supremacy. In 1965, the USSR had 733 missiles targeted on Europe (SIPRI, 1982); by 1973, the Soviets had reduced this maximum number to 720 SS-4's, SS-5's, and SS-11's, with over 1000 megatons of nuclear warheads. When the Soviets replaced these obsolete models with new SS-20s, each having three warheads of 150 kiloton yield, the U.S. and NATO discovered the Soviet missile threat. Despite this "threat," and over the objections of the U.S., the USSR and several NATO members reached agreement on a gas pipeline. Former Soviet premier Andropov attempted to forestall deployment of the new U.S. Euro-missiles. He offered to cut back the SS-20's to 162—a number equal to the forward-based missiles deployed by the French and British (Lewis, 1982)—with 73 megatons of total yield. This seemed a fair proposal or at least a serious negotiating step. Between one-third and one-quarter of Soviet LRTNF's have China as their target, and must be based in Soviet Asia. The 162 missiles remaining after Andropov's proposed cutback would include all SS-20's in Europe and in "swing-positions" in the Urals. In contrast, President Reagan proposed nondeployment of the new missiles only if the Soviet Union removed all of its European-targeted SS-20's, completely ignoring the question of French and British missile strength. Clearly the U.S., not NATO as such, negotiates Euromissiles with the USSR.

Cruise missiles were a major issue in every arms negotiations since Vladivostok and SALT I in 1974. Reagan's hypocritical START proposal excluded cruise missiles and bombers and gave the U.S. an enormous advantage. In a personal letter to President Reagan, Rear Admiral G. La Rocque (ret.), director of the Center for Defense Information (CDI), had requested a one-year delay in NATO's "dual-track" decision regarding GLCM's and Pershing II's.

On 3 August 1983, in an address to a Montreal meeting of the United Food and Commercial Workers Union, La Rocque pointed out that the ALCM is not a deterrent, but a counterforce first-strike weapon. He commented, "If they have guts enough in Canada, they ought once in a while to stand up and decide what is right for themselves and not always do what the U.S. wants." The rear admiral also predicted a cruise missile race: "When the Soviets get them—and they will, three to five years down the road—then we too are going to be threatened" (*Gazette,* Thursday, 4 August 1983, p. 1, Montreal).

THE ISSUE OF CRUISE MISSILE TESTING IN CANADA

The cruise missile testing drama played on the wide range of Canadian national and international relations. The main characters juggled their props before a global audience. The Reagan administration misdirected with reference to a NATO decision, which Canada followed. But the "secret agenda," defined by NSDD-32 and SIOP-6, and U.S. economic interests in Canada provided the real script. Trudeau and the Canadian government manipulated long-term Canada-U.S. relations, internal Canadian politics, and the former prime minister's peace initiative. Before analyzing cruise missile testing in Canada, we must dispel the "fictions" and replace them with facts.

1. Contrary to Canadian government assertions, no NATO commitment requires cruise testing, nor has Canada been formally requested to do so. Norway, a staunch NATO member, has refused such testing.
2. The weapon to be tested is not the "theater" GLCM designated for deployment in Europe by the December 1979 "dual-track" NATO decision; instead, it is a strategic weapon, the ALCM, critical to the Reagan administration's plans to fight and win a limited or protracted nuclear war.
3. The testing of an ALCM in Canada can only be viewed within the specific context of the Reagan administration's NSDD-32 and SIOP-6, both nuclear warfighting documents. The latter specifically assigns strategic roles for so-called theater weapons.
4. The actual testing of ALCM's at the Primrose Lake Air Weapons Range on the northern border of Saskatchewan and Alberta provides a unique facility in terms of the flight corridor and the terrain.
5. Official government statements on cruise missile testing have been both contradictory and deceptive. Despite former Prime Minister Trudeau's and former External Minister MacEachen's repeated policy statements that tied cruise missile testing to progress at the Geneva negotiations, a special cabinet meeting in Ottawa on 15 July 1983 disclosed Canada's agreement to test U.S. missiles without reference to NATO. A meaningful settlement on IRTNF's in Europe could have been reached during the remaining five months of the Geneva talks.
6. The relevant document giving the terms of the U.S.-Canada agreement, Note #64, is not a NATO document nor is NATO a party to it. It is a bilateral arrangement in direct support of a superhawkish administration.
7. The testing of ALCM's in Canada will negate any future Canadian role as mediator or initiator of arms reduction and control, and will directly contribute to heating up the arms race. It violates the principles of Trudeau's suffocation policy and the Nuclear Freeze Initiative. It is clearly perceived by independent assessors as contributing to the arms race.

In the light of the above facts there was a history of obfuscation, deliberate deception, and extreme rationalization in the Canadian response to the U.S. request to test cruise missiles on Canadian soil. As early as March 1981 the minister of external affairs in the Trudeau cabinet, Mark Mac-

Guigan, stated categorically that these "argeements" were officially linked to NATO: "We are not doing this for the United States. We are doing it for the Alliance [NATO] we belong to" (*Gazette,* Thursday, 18 March 1981, Montreal). Yet as late as March 1983, former Minister of External Affairs MacEachan denied the existence of any agreement to test cruise missiles (*Gazette,* Friday, 11 March 1983, Montreal). In clear contradiction, this same MacEachan said that cruise missile testing "is needed as part of NATO. . . . I think we are required to do our share as part of the defense of NATO and the Free World" (*Vancouver Sun,* Friday, 11 February 1983).

Furthermore, throughout 1983, official statements maintained that Canada had not signed an agreement to actually test cruise missiles, only an "umbrella" agreement, general in nature. Yet it seemed quite clear from Vice President Bush's statements in Ottawa that "there is no evidence that they [Canada] want to change this agreement . . . . It is important that when the [NATO] alliance takes decisions, the alliance stays together."

Don Sellar, Washington bureau chief for the Southam News chain, disclosed the cruise missile testing issue on 10 March 1982. Seller stated that Canada and the U.S. had signed a five-year umbrella agreement for the testing of a wide range of weapons, including cruise missiles. In the next months, the Canadian government floundered from admission to denial. Fifteen months later, on 8 June 1983, the FBI began an investigation of Don Sellar. According to a UPI release, the FBI has acknowledged their investigation of Sellar. Their interest is definitely concerned with cruise missile testing (Rusk, 1983; Bauch, 1983).

This rather unusual FBI investigation stemmed from more than "extraordinary" fervor on the part of the FBI. United States Attorney General William French Smith personally ordered the investigation at the request of the Canadian government. According to a Washington informant, "The Canadians told the Americans, 'Unless these leaks are stopped, we may not be able to carry on these negotiations [for a framework agreement on the testing of U.S. weapons, including the nuclear-capable cruise missile in Canada]'" (*Gazette,* Tuesday, 21 June 1983, p. A-7, Montreal). According to this release, the agreement was eventually signed at a secret ceremony in Washington on 10 February 1983, and later made public. On 5 April 1983, this author received a copy of Note #64 from the Canadian Department of National Defence (DND), with an accompanying letter from J. Gilles Lamontagne, then minister, addressed personally to a research assistant. The terms of the agreement relate to the Canada/U.S. Test and Evaluation Project (CANUSTEP). The letter states that this test and evaluation agreement is "governed by the terms of the Agreement between Parties to the North Atlantic Treaty Regarding the Status of Their Forces (NATO SOFA) dated June 19, 1951," and bears the signature of Allan Gottlieb, Canadian ambassador to Washington.

Lamontagne's accompanying letter specifically describes the ALCM. Thus there can be no question that this was the missile to be tested, very likely released from an EC-135 aircraft (the military version of a Boeing 707), since the letter also mentioned this aircraft. The letter states flatly, "It is very important to understand that the cruise is not a first-strike weapon, because it is too slow. It is exclusively *retaliatory* [Lamontagne's underlining]." We can conclude that our own minister of national defense ignored the strategic role of ALCM's and that he had obviously neither seen SIOP-6 nor understood it. Lamontagne also failed to distinguish between GLCM's and ALCM's and their relative functions. Both Lamontagne's letter and Note #64 falsely imply that NATO membership required the testing of U.S. weapons. Finally, Lamontagne's letter suggests that the so-called European weapon imbalance provides the USSR with a margin of superiority, since otherwise there is "rough parity." A very senior Canadian military official exploded this myth.

Admiral Robert Falls, a Canadian and former chairman of NATO's military committee, has made a remarkable suggestion. He has recommended that one way out of the arms negotiation deadlock is a *unilateral* reduction by the West (*Gazette,* Tuesday, 28 June 1983, p. B-2, Montreal). No person in a position to know the precise balance of power would make such a suggestion, if it could be construed as weakening his side. We must conclude that Admiral Falls recognizes that the West can initiate a unilateral reduction without risking its security or, possibly, without reducing its superiority. Such a suggestion implies a present superiority in Western strength.

More of the elusive truth about the issue of cruise missile testing in Canada has now emerged. Utilizing the Access to Information Act, the Montreal *Gazette* was able to secure certain cruise-related documents, some of them stamped "classified," from the Department of National Defence. Not all the documents were released, and there were sections deleted from those obtained. Their Saturday, 18 August 1984, *Gazette* published a selection of the above material that enables us to move from conjecture to evidence, unveiling some of the secrecy behind the cruise missile testing issue.

The actual U.S.-Canada talks on an umbrella testing agreement began in June 1978. By December 1981, after receiving a letter from Reagan, Prime Minister Trudeau agreed with the overall testing proposal, and External Affairs initiated a deliberate campaign to rationalize the agreement. Later, the government issued an order effectively commanding a "consistent response" to the public from all branches of government and armed forces.

The most telling memo, a confession written by Ross Francis of External Affairs defense relations on 2 February 1983, contains deleted sections but is nevertheless revealing. It is obvious from this and earlier memos that External

Affairs had some doubts about the political viability of the umbrella agreement. The Francis memo states in part, "Canadian government actions since
then have ensured that a negative decision now would have much more
serious consequences than it would have fifteen months ago." Then it reveals
the real motive for Canada's acquiescence: "While it is difficult to indicate
with any degree of specificity what the [U.S.] Administration would do, there
is no doubt that its disappointment would colour the relationship [with
Canada] in all its facets, including trade and economic." The agreement was
ratified on 10 February 1983.

It would appear that, after the courting period, Canada both solicited
benefits from the U.S. and responded with cowardice at the fear of reprisals
from the Reagan administration. These depresssing actions confirm one's
worst fears about the Trudeau regime's record on peace initiatives. The
testing request occurred during the Carter administration, in the same period
as Trudeau's famous "suffocation" policy speech proposing a nuclear freeze.
The request and its acceptance had nothing to do with the 1979 NATO
"dual-track" agreement. In 1978–79 the request could have been categorically
refused; then, Trudeau could have supported the nuclear freeze without fear
of punitive measures. The arguments later used to justify the agreement,
namely, the NATO commitment, became entwined in a web of deceit. An
entry in memos from the Pentagon on 22 July 1983 expresses its gratitude to
DND for "sustained support and cooperation in securing your government's
approval of *the ALCM test request* [Italics mine], despite the political sensi-
tivity of the program in Canada." Clearly both the U.S. and Canada have
their share of hawks, and the military of both countries has a common world
view. The only hopeful revelation was the additional information revealed in
the 1984 election campaign that some former members of the Trudeau cabinet, i.e., Lloyd Axworthy, Donald Johnson, and possibly Chretien, may
have been in opposition. Turner and Mulroney used lame arguments in
refusing to underwrite the nuclear freeze: Walter Mondale could have become
president and left them out in the real political cold. Their support of the
Reagan administration makes their seriousness about peace questionable.

On 6 June 1983, the U.S. made the specific, formal request to test an
ALCM in Canada. The prime minister said, "The paramaters are well-
known. It is a request which comes under the two-track decision—*at least it
is a request* [Italics mine] Cabinet is considering as relating to the two-track
decision of NATO in December, 1979. And obviously it will involve testing
over some part of Canada" (Rusk, 1983). Once again we have a slip that
could be interpreted as deception. Either the 1979 "dual-track" decision requires testing or it is a cabinet decision; obviously it is only the latter.
According to the author of this report, "The missiles would be launched
from U.S. B-52 bombers flying high over the Arctic" (Rusk, 1983). This is

precisely the strategic first-strike role of the ALCM: targeted against C^3I and economic-political-industrial targets, released from B-52 bombers beyond Soviet bomber defenses, and following a flight path over terrain similar to the Primrose Lake range.

The rationalizations for Canadian testing of cruise missiles are varied and exhibit remarkable convolutions. "Few if any Canadians will ever see a cruise missile in flight," said Gilles Lamontagne, former minister of defense whose public role in the cruise testing debate has been indefensible (Simpson, 1983b).

Which cruise missile was to be tested in Canada was not long in question. It was, of course, an ALCM, and the Canadian government had known it for some time. In Ottawa 23 March 1983, Trudeau told Vice President Bush, "You may get some benefit of our testing the cruise, if we do," as if the issue of testing were still in question. Then Trudeau added, "But it is not to help you; it is because the Europeans have asked us to do this for them" (Hay, 1983). There is no record of such a European request relating to ALCM's. Trudeau vacillated with unusual consistency. In his questionable open letter to Canadians of 10 May 1983, Prime Minister Trudeau, obviously writing in haste and out of a bad conscience, indulged in some weak "red baiting" in his attack on cruise testing opponents, even those among his own party. At least two of his cabinet ministers were opposed.

SOME IMPLICATIONS OF CRUISE DEPLOYMENT AND TESTING

Other aspects of the cruise missile testing issue are important to note. Sometime in the fall of 1980, President Carter requested Canada to test cruise missiles. Shortly afterwards, Mark MacGuigan, then Canadian minister of external affairs, stated for public record that such an agreement had been promulgated and was, in fact, a necessary consequence of the 1979 NATO "dual-track" agreement. The Reagan administration took a very tough stance toward Canada regarding all bilateral matters. The above arrangement gradually expanded into a five-year umbrella "Canada-U.S. Test and Evaluation Program" (CANUSTEP), tabled in the House of Commons on 10 February 1983. Article 4 of this agreement designates the two Departments of Defense as having the exclusive right to draw up the terms of any test. Apparently parliament and Congress are not a party to these decisions on "project arrangements." Article 17 further buttresses this nonaccountability by shrouding in effective secrecy any information on test projects. No information about the tests can be released without mutual consent of the two DOD's; thus, neither parliament nor the people can make any judgments about the nature or purpose of tests. Future tests might certainly include a variety of ABM regimes that in real battle conditions would extend far into Canadian territory. Canada is thus the logical testing site for ABM's and satellite surveillance systems designated to locate and intercept far-distance, incoming Soviet bombers and missiles. The U.S. may very likely use Canada to test U.S. Air Force low-flying bomber accuracy in their SEEK-SCORE program. All of this tends to convert Canadian territory not only into an extension of U.S. (Reagan) nuclear sovereignty, but also into a future nuclear battlefield, laced with corridors for the battle of cruise missiles and low-flying bombers. Canada has already given the U.S. permission to test their Low Altitude Navigation and Targeting Infrared device (LANTIRN) in New Brunswick.

The cruise missile to be tested in Canada was launched operationally as though it were attacking the USSR from a flight path over the North Pole. Launched from a high-flying B-52G or B-52H offshore in the Beaufort Sea, the missile crossed the Arctic shoreline within a 50-kilometer-wide path and continued its 2500-kilometer flight over Canadian tundra and through the Primrose missile range, where its flight pattern and accuracy were monitored. The target could just as well have been the Kremlin.

Unfortunately for Canada, cruise is a two-way street. Inevitably, the Soviets will develop their own cruise missiles. The history of the arms race shows that both sides match weapon for weapon, system for system—the Blackjack bomber for the B-1, the SS-20 add-on third-stage for MX. The undoubted technical and strategic advantages of the cruise include its ability to be "fired" from bombers, i.e., air-launched cruise missiles (ALCM's). The ALCM would suit the Soviets well. The USSR bomber fleet contains 180 Backfire bombers (Tu-22M) that are not genuinely strategic, because their maximum range is just sufficient for one-way intercontinental missions, leaving no margin for evasion. By equipping the Backfires with cruise missiles, they could be converted into true strategic bombers. The only reports on Soviet cruise development indicate an ALCM code-named BL-10, a 2000-kilometer-range SLCM coded the SSNX-21, and a shorter-range GLCM, the SSC-X-4 (Kipling, 1984). The BL-10 would be used in conjunction with the Soviet long-range turbo-prop bombers, the Bear and the Bison, as well as the new secret Blackjack bomber.

The reasons for testing cruise missiles in Canada are also the reasons for firing the BL-10 on a path toward the North Pole and across Canada's Northwest Territories to targets in the U.S. Ironically, this terrain is similar to the Soviet north, having a similar climate and magnetic fields. The Soviets will use similar test areas in their northern region. In projection, Canada would become a battleground of cruise missiles: defenses would have to attempt to knock out Soviet ALCM's over Canadian territory before the Soviet missiles struck U.S. targets. As a partner in the North American Air Defense command (NORAD), Canada is committed to accepting a cruise defense role. Finding the cruise and destroying it with "shoot-down look-down" aircraft will be a difficult task for forward air defenses. Canada's integration with the Reagan administration's plan to force the Soviets to develop cruise missiles of their own (Lodgaard, 1982), as a form of "economic suffocation," could lead to Canada becoming a nuclear battleground. By testing the cruise, instead of opposing it and seeking an agreement in Europe, Canada became, under Trudeau, the unwilling ally of a regime that distrusts him and that he distrusts.

During much of this debate, unreality permeated all sides, as if each part of the debate stood isolated from the full context of the nuclear weapons system and the arms race. Euromissiles are not required to deter conventional attacks by the USSR in Europe. The U.S., French, and U.K. SLBM's can do this, just as Soviet SLBM's can devastate the U.S. if it uses nuclear forces in response to a conventional attack. The mythology is broader than this. Who is defending Canada against whom? Why does Canada need a U.S. umbrella? Is an invasion of Canada by the USSR a realistic assumption upon which to base military policy? If NATO is stronger than the Warsaw pact, why raise the question of the USSR overrunning Europe? SALT II would have maintained deterrence. The Nuclear Freeze would have maintained deterrence and led to reductions. The Reagan policy is an acceleration of the arms race.

Canada has consistently been in the "top-ten" arms merchants to the Third World, selling $406 million of materiel in 1982 (Naidu, 1983). The DPSA of 1958 stated that "Canadian work in . . . production of defense equipment will have to be closely integrated with the major programs of the U.S.A." (Reford, 1968); yet this integration has not been to Canada's benefit. Between 1959 and 1981, under "defense sharing," the U.S. gained a surplus of $400 million in the two-way military trade. Even worse, the major "Canadian" share actually comes through U.S. and other foreign subsidiaries in Canada. These firms have also received large federal grants of public money. During the modern history of Canadian trading with the U.S., Canada has suffered deficits of as much as $31.6 billion between 1974 and 1981 (Naidu, 1983, p. 14). As one critic sees it, "the force behind cruise missile testing in Canada is the militarization of the Canadian industry and the Americanization of the Canadian economy . . . [as well as] the military integration of Canada and the U.S.A." (Naidu, 1983, p. 17). In the reign of Ronald Reagan, this is not mere folly, but a tragedy for Canada and the world.

On Tuesday, 19 July 1983, Trudeau suggested that only a new election, bringing a new government that withdrew from NATO, could change the decision to test the cruise. This is the constant confusion. There is no NATO commitment to flight-test nuclear-carrying missiles. NATO members did not formally request Canada to test U.S. strategic missiles, the ALCM's. In most polls, more than 50 percent of Canadians seemed consistently opposed to cruise testing; thus the government represented a minority. Moreover, U.S.

and European antinuclear groups indicated their solidarity with Canadians opposed to cruise testing (CP-UPC, *Gazette,* Wednesday, 22 July 1983, Montreal). Pauline Jewett put it simply, "Norway remains part of NATO and has refused such testing. . . . He's saying we'll have to leave NATO if we refuse—and that's an absolute lie" (CP-UPC, *Gazette,* Wednesday, 22 July, 1983). Norway, Greece, the Netherlands, and Denmark have all refused to have U.S. cruise missiles on their territory. Greece requested a delay in their decision to deploy 572 missiles. Norway, a very strong NATO member, just refused to test nuclear missiles. Even though none of these countries share a border with the U.S., Mexico, a neighbor state of the U.S., pursues a far more independent peacemaking foreign policy than Canada.

The cruise missile test issue became a global affair integrated into the policy of the antinuclear network in North America and Europe. The Canadian peacemaker "image," whether deserved or symbolic, has been tarnished. Canada is viewed as the lackey of the U.S., without the minimal courage of independence. This undoubtedly will affect Canada's future ability to revive the mediator's role in international affairs.

THE PEACE INITIATIVES OF PIERRE TRUDEAU

Pierre Elliott Trudeau was a pivotal figure in Canadian and international politics. His support of the North-South dialogue that attempted to redress the inequalities between the rich Northern countries and the poor nations of the South earned him the respect of many Third-World countries. Mr. Trudeau made an impressive contribution to global peace initiatives with his "suffocation" proposal, delivered in a speech to the first United Nations Special Session on Disarmament (UNSSOD I) in 1978. Trudeau proposed a mutual freeze on all nuclear weapons testing, development, and deployment, a theme voted on by the United Nations virtually every year. Subsequent realities of U.S.-Canada relations led Trudeau to reconsider his proposal.

The prime minister modified his "suffocation policy" to such a degree as to render it ineffective and harmless. He added that he never meant it to apply unilaterally (United Nations Special Session on Disarmament II, 18 June 1982). Reversing his 1978 UNSSOD I speech, Trudeau made his proposal far less than suffocating and supported the U.S. in its unilateral test of air-launched cruise missiles. This author has always maintained that Trudeau neatly castrated point #3 of the "suffocation policy" by adding the provision "An agreement to prohibit all production of fissionable material for weapons purposes" that applied to those countries intending to make bombs. Canada can neither control the ultimate uses of its uranium exports, nor safeguard its nuclear reactor (CANDU) exports to a degree necessary to prohibit clandestine production of plutonium.

At times Trudeau has spoken out courageously against the Reagan administration. In an interview with the *Toronto Star,* Saturday, 14 May 1983, Trudeau said, "Basically once again they are demonstrating against what they see as the policy of an American [Reagan], who has rightly or wrongly been perceived as war-like, or so hostile to the Soviet Union that he cannot be trusted to look for peace. . . . Unfortunately, President Reagan and some of the people around him have given some justification for these fears." Trudeau was not alone in this judgment. Ronald Reagan was viewed by millions as "trigger-happy, unreliable, an alarming president to have control over nuclear weapons . . . a jumpy hard-liner" (*Economist,* quoted in the *Washington Spectator,* 15 December 1983). Unfortunately, Trudeau retracted his statement after a telephone call from Reagan (*Gazette,* Friday, 27 May 1983, Montreal).

Trudeau made his second major contribution to peace in a speech delivered at Guelph University on 27 October 1983. In his address Trudeau enumerated ten principles of peace. These principles, much like those covered in the Pastoral Letter of the U.S. Catholic bishops, include several that directly contradict current U.S. policy: that nuclear war cannot be won; that nuclear war must never be fought; that security strategies cannot be based on the assumed political or economic collapse of the other side; and that dangers are inherent in destabilizing weapons. The destabilizing weapons Trudeau mentions can only be "first-strike" weapons such as MX, Pershing II's, and air-launched cruise missiles (ALCM's). Mr. Trudeau somehow managed to both test ALCM's in furtherance of Reagan's military policy and condemn them on "principle."

Toward the end of his term in office, Trudeau launched a peace initiative of his own. Unfortunately, the time was not right for Trudeau's proposal. The Reagan administration treated it with open distrust. As a result Trudeau failed to get support for his peace initiative, an essentially sound idea for achieving a dialogue among all parties concerned with the nuclear arms issue.

THE TRUDEAU PEACE INITIATIVE

In his speech at the University of Guelph, Trudeau pledged to devote the rest of his political career to "reducing the threat of war." He seems to have kept his word. Although one cannot yet see any positive results, we are still prepared to give him the benefit of the doubt.

While Mr. Trudeau has specifically set the banning of weapons in space as one initiative, Canada is part of U.S. antisatellite weapon (ASAT) development. The U.S. Air Force's high-flying F-15 Eagle jets will carry a non-explosive miniature homing vehicle (MHV). The entire projected system of 128 ASAT rockets to be readied by 1989 will be controlled from the Space

Defense Operations Center in the Cheyenne Mountains in Colorado. Since this center is integrated with U.S.-Canada North American Air Space Defense, Canada is party to ASAT development. In April 1983, the USSR called for an international agreement banning *any kind of weapons* from space, and in August 1983, the USSR submitted a draft treaty to halt further ASAT development. To date the U.S. has used its usual smoke screen of verification problems to justify its failure to respond. Mr. Trudeau had an opportunity to prove his initiative integrity by publicly requesting that the U.S. stop its present ASAT developments and negotiate a ban with the USSR. In his Guelph speech, Mr. Trudeau stated, "I have in mind a ban on the testing and deployment of these anti-satellite weapons." The five-year "umbrella" testing agremeent with the U.S. (CANUSTEP) represents a most serious step toward Canada's total integration with Mr. Reagan's military policies. Because we have argued that the Reagan administration represents a sinister historical discontinuity in U.S. military policy, no real peace initiative can avoid resisting it. If Mr. Trudeau had followed the logic of his "ten peace principles," they would have collided with the Reagan policies and plans.

Thus despite Trudeau's good intentions, superpower relations worsened. Mr. Trudeau remained firmly committed to the so-called NATO "dual-track" decision even after the Soviets deployed SS-20's in East Germany and Czechoslovakia. Nevertheless Mr. Trudeau's initiative contains the sound elements of banning defensive and offensive weapons in space, preventing proliferation, and ratifying SALT II.

ONE DAY AT DAVOS

On 29 January 1983, former Prime Minister Trudeau attended an international conference at Davos, Switzerland, and participated in a panel on international security. Kenneth Dam, a fellow panelist and deputy secretary of state, said that it was "a misconception that the United States had been steadily building up the number and megatonnage of its nuclear weapons." Trudeau responded that "reduction in itself . . . does reopen the question of quality versus quantity and, incidentally, draws us into the whole question of whether the NATO overall strategy is still the right one. . . . the question is, have we reduced their deadliness?" Trudeau went one step further and said, "Ah yes, but will the U.S. president really order the use of an atomic weapon, even in Europe, if it is going to result in World War Three. . . . I don't know the answer of the president, but one can speculate whether he would want to start World War Three through INFS [Intermediate Range Nuclear Forces] any more than he would through START [Strategic Arms Reductions Talks] weapons" (*Gazette,* Monday, 13 January 1984, p. B-3, Montreal). Former French Prime Minister Raymond Barre, another panelist, broke into Trudeau's conjectures on "flexible response," i.e., "first use," by warning that to merely ask such a question injects doubt about Washington's nuclear umbrella and breeds "neutralism and pacifism." Trudeau then questioned Barre's credibility by again asking whether a U.S. president would respond to Soviet overrunning of Europe with conventional forces by starting "World War Three—an atomic war" (*Gazette,* Monday, 13 January 1983, p. B-3, Montreal). In effect, Trudeau questioned NATO's "dual-track" decision that he willingly supported and that resulted in his decision to allow cruise missile testing in Canada. His contradictions remain profound. As late as 12 January 1984, former Canadian Defence Minister Jean-Jacques Blais, a Northern hawk, spouted the doctrine of accommodation, of being a nuclear protectorate of the U.S., calling it a far less costly policy than bearing "the large financial and political burdens associated with the possession of nuclear weapons systems" (*Gazette,* Friday, 13 May 1984, Montreal). At the same conference, the Canadian chief of defense staff, General C. C. E. Theriault, went even further by speaking of the "disinformation [that] has . . . crept into the debate" over cruise missile testing, and regarding such "massive disinformation" as a Soviet Union plot to conceal the truth about the military balance and the "mounting military threat to the Western world from the Warsaw pact nations led by the Soviet Union." The military chief of Canadian defense was even contradicted by President Reagan, who claimed U.S. superiority in his 1984 "State of the Union" speech. Since it is now well known that the cruise missile to be tested was not the one designated for Europe, but a weapon with genuine strategic significance, one wonders at Defence Minister Blais's "disinformation" when he once again refers to the NATO connection. One expert who should know the truth, Rear Admiral Robert Falls, retired chairman of NATO's military committee, publicly agreed with Trudeau (*Gazette,* Tuesday, 28 June 1983, p. B-2, Montreal). Thus, while Trudeau questioned the doctrines of "flexible response," "escalation dominance," "first use," and "peace through strength," the cornerstones of U.S. policy, his own military and political chiefs of defense talked from the other side of their collective mouths.

It would seem that the Pierre Trudeau of Davos does not seem to be the Pierre Trudeau of the cruise debate, or even the Pierre Trudeau of the Guelph speech, who still clung to traditional NATO policy. Pierre Trudeau felt the winds of change. He seems to have attempted to build a peace movement among nations that would isolate the suicidal policy of both superpowers. In the end, he seemed to have remembered a dream he appeared to have lost.

Despite his own peace initiative, Mr. Trudeau failed to support the "five continent" appeal from the leaders of six nations—India, Mexico, Sweden, Greece, Tanzania, and Argentina—for a comprehensive nuclear freezed that would halt the testing, production, and deployment of nuclear weapons and their delivery systems, a proposal identical to the major thrust of the Nuclear Freeze Initiative. The U.S. rejected the five-continent proposal out of hand (*Gazette,* Wednesday, 23 May 1984, Montreal), while the USSR voiced unconditional support for it (*Gazette,* Tuesday, 29 May 1984, Montreal).

POSTSCRIPT TO THE CRUISE TEST

As this author had predicted as early as the spring of 1983, the air-launched missile designed as a strategic missile to be carried on strategic B-52 bombers was tested over the Cold Lake, Alberta, test site on Tuesday, 6 March 1984. Three more tests took place on 15 January, 19 February, and 25 February 1983. The 2400-kilometer flight lasted four-and-one-half hours. The ALCM traveled down the Mackenzie River Valley, across northeastern British Columbia and, hence, southeast over northern Alberta, and ended its flight near Cold Lake, 290 kilometers northeast of Alberta. This was not the NATO-designated missile; nor was the test requested or required by NATO. This weapon was designated for nuclear warfighting programs, as described in the supersecret U.S. documents SIOP-6 and NSDD-13. In his annual report to Congress, U.S. Defense Secretary Caspar Weinberger mentioned an agreement with Canada that would allow this missile to be tested "in climate and terrain that closely represent the areas of the world where we face the greatest threat" (Sellars, 1984).

This cruise missile testing must be put into the account columns when judging Mr. Trudeau's peace initiative. One day at Davos may not be sufficient to balance the books. Mr. Trudeau has since defended the cruise test, saying that the purpose of the test was to ensure Canada's position as a member of NATO. The leaders of Czechoslovakia, East Germany, and Romania would have been "less inclined to listen to me seriously" if Canada wasn't seen as a member in good standing of NATO (*Gazette,* Wednesday, 7 March 1984, p. 1, Montreal). This compounds the misrepresentation. Trudeau's arguments concerning NATO obligations and/or standing are patently false. His arguments about credibility in Eastern Europe are highly dubious. Mr. Trudeau would have appeared much more credible as a peacemaker if he had rejected the testing of all destabilizing warfighting weapons. Lest there be any doubt concerning these points regarding NATO, this author has been categorically informed by a high-ranking official in the peace initiative campaign that there is no NATO connection to the cruise test conducted on 6 March 1984. Reagan's mythic "window of vulnerability" has not been transformed into Trudeau's "window of opportunity," not because Mr. Trudeau did not try for success, but because Mr. Reagan made certain there could be no success.

While Canada's long-standing role as arms merchant is not publicly known, it is minor compared to the current Canadian pursuit of military/ commercial industrialization. At the very same time that Mr. Trudeau pursued his "peace initiative," the Department of National Defense (DND) received over 50 percent of all federal contracts in the last four years (Beer, 1984). In the fiscal year 1982-83 alone, seventeen of the twenty companies with the highest volume of sales to the federal government sold to DND. Total defense contracting comprised 68.7 percent of all federal government purchases in 1980-81. Even External Affairs, with their paltry funding of "peace" activities, can take credit for $1.5 billion in Canadian military exports per year.

A current movement within the Canadian government and the military seeks to adopt a so-called "wartime mobilization plan" that would make Canada a junior military-industrial state. In six years DND's capital budget has quadrupled. The Conference of Defense Associations (CDA), an active "defense" lobby inside and outside of government, operates in the Ottawa forum. Although CDA is a nongovernment organization, DND, the agency it has set out to influence, gave the lobby $155,560 in operating funds, plus staffing, space, and services, in 1984. Among CDA's allies are Canadian public and private hawks, including our last two ministers of defense, Blais and Lamontagne. The CDA's major political support comes from the ranks of the Tories. The duality of Canadian policy and image—as peacekeeper and powdermaker—renders its peacekeeping attempts futile and its powdermaking capacity counterproductive in terms of economic benefit and industrial strategy.

In its operations and purchases, Canada is a nuclear and chemical weapons state. Since 1976 DND has purchased almost half a million dollars worth of nuclear ordnance of all kinds, and $4.3 million of "military chemical agents." This policy has continued long after the official Canadian promise that all nuclear weapons would be removed from Canadian Forces property (Beer, 1984). This promise does not extend to U.S. nuclear forces using Canadian bases.

Canada's pursuit of high technology includes a high emphasis on military development. A plan for a four-year wartime mobilization program awaits cabinet approval. External Affairs does a major selling and promotional job for military technology. The program director, T. M. Chell, says publicly that Canada only makes "sub-systems," as though these can be separated from the missiles and delivery systems for which they are essential. Regrettably, the mass and mess of misinformation presented through some government ministries and many senior officers in our armed forces reinforces their close collaboration with their counterparts in the Reagan administration.

A PREDICTION—CANADA-U.S. RELATIONS, 1984-1988

Nineteen eighty-four was a prophetic year. Ronald Reagan was reelected president of the United States, Indira Ghandi was assassinated, and Pierre Elliott Trudeau retired. Trudeau and Ghandi had the great intellect and great gifts of leadership rare among world leaders. In Canada, the new prime minister, Progressive Conservative Brian Mulroney, won his election by an overwhelming margin. Superficially, at least, Mulroney and Reagan would seem to be in much closer accord than previous U.S.-Canadian leaders. As U.S. Ambassador Paul Robinson noted at a dinner commemorating the twenty-eighth anniversary of the 1956 Hungarian uprising, "It's as if we're all long-lost fraternity brothers trying to catch up on what's been going on for the last twenty years." Mr. Robert Coates, former defense minister in the new Progressive Conservative government, said that he and U.S. Defense Secretary Caspar Weinberger have "been seeing a lot of each other lately and I love it. Not only do I love it, my Prime Minister loves it" (Gooderham, 1984). Paul Robinson is a Helms Helper. Although Mulroney rushed to assure Reagan of his loyalty shortly after the Canadian election, he also has made some unusual appointments.

Prime Minister Brian Mulroney appears to have pulled off a political coup in appointing Douglas Roche as ambassador for disarmament and Stephen Lewis as UN ambassador. He may have satisfied the peace movement while disarming some of its most eloquent supporters, but the contradiction inherent in these appointments cannot be concealed for very long. On 20 November 1984, Stephen Lewis, voting as Canada's UN ambassador, joined the U.S. and ten other countries in rejecting a UN General Assembly resolution that called for a mutual and verifiable freeze on the production and deployment of nuclear weapons. The vote was 111 to 12. In each of the last three years, Canada, under the Trudeau regime, opposed the same resolution. One wonders how Ambassador Lewis will rationalize his acquiescence to U.S. power. The NDP has consistently supported the freeze initiative, and on his appointment, Lewis said, "I don't imagine you appoint someone who has been a critic or an adversary or at least a partisan of another party and expect the appointment will be applauded if his convictions and personality are simply subsumed in government policy" and "I can't pretend that having accepted this job I've suddenly changed my views over the years" (Cahill, 1984). Sixteen days later, Stephen Lewis voted against the UN freeze proposal that won the support of a vast majority of UN members.

In the article cited above, Jack Cahill quotes Lewis at length on the value of peace initiatives, including Trudeau's suffocation proposal. He quotes Lewis's disapproval of NATO as a military alliance and his antipathy to the policies of Reagan and former U.S. UN Ambassador Jeane Kirkpatrick.

Lewis comments, "Some diplomats do exactly as they are told by their governments and they do it superbly. But I don't think I will be able to do that. . . . I know there will be awkward moments . . . but I also know it's possible to make small compromises." Obviously Stephen Lewis believes in the "small compromises" of voting against the freeze initiative and supporting Canada's generally accommodating role in the military plans of the Reagan administration, including missile testing. In another interview, Lewis says, "When you live life as a socialist in Canada you learn patience. . . . you learn about doing things incrementally" (Delean, 1984). Incrementalism involving backward steps is a rare trick.

Pierre Elliott Trudeau seems always to have understood the issue but was caught in the trap of his own position. In the *Gazette,* Monday, 19 November 1984, Montreal, Trudeau said, "At the beginning, Mr. Mulroney seemed to be buddy-buddy with President Reagan, and that is not a bad policy, for the short-term. . . . But the thing is to know, when it comes to the crunch, when there are fundamental questions, if we can stay buddies and still say the truth. . . . It's not yet proven if Mr. Mulroney can tell the truth, but if he doesn't I predict that Canadians will soon turn against him." Trudeau went on to say that Reagan "gets advice from counsellors who don't want their president to make big efforts for peace because it's not their point of view." He then repeated his accusations that NATO did not really attend to the most important issues, those of peace and war, a charge he had made during the presentation of the Einstein Peace Prize on Tuesday, 13 November 1984, in Washington. He added, "The contradiction comes from the fact that these democratic countries [who belong to NATO] don't have the right to raise questions without being immediately seen as disloyal," a reference to his painful encounter at Davos on 29 January 1983.

Aside from the implicit accusation that NATO is controlled by the U.S., one wonders what the "truth" Mr. Trudeau refers to really is. Is it merely the bad counseling that he mentions? How does his own agreement to test U.S. cruise missiles and other weapons systems in Canada relate to this unspoken "truth"? How does Canada's refusal to vote for the UN nuclear freeze in 1982 and 1983 relate to this unspoken "truth?" How does Mr. Trudeau's refusal to join the "five continent" statement by nonaligned leaders in favor of a freeze relate to this unspoken "truth"? How does Mr. Trudeau's own support of the freeze, as given in his UNSSOD I speech in 1978, relate to this unspoken "truth"? Who speaks the truth when they are in political power in Canada? The U.S. influence over official Canada, including its right to speak the truth, seemed irresistible to even Mr. Trudeau when he was prime minister. Although Trudeau made repeated allegations of U.S. "pressure to conform," Larry Speakes, deputy U.S. press secretary, said, "Our appreciation of international political consultations differs from Mr. Trudeau's."

Mr. Trudeau's Einstein Prize–acceptance speech called for an initiative by NATO that would halt deployment of U.S. nuclear missiles in Europe to prompt a Soviet cutback, but Mr. Trudeau supported "dual-track" even after negative Soviet responses. However, in his acceptance speech, Mr. Trudeau still talked "tough," "O.K., now you see we're not backing down, and when we say we're going to do something we do it. Now let's talk peace." (*Gazette*, Thursday, 15 November 1984, Montreal). In an interview on NBC's "Today " 14 August 1984, Trudeau also said, "If the Pentagon keeps telling him [they will] be able to put engines into space that will destroy the communication center of the enemy, then he won't go to peace. He'll bring us nearer to war." Mr. Trudeau may retire with the satisfaction that Lawrence Eagleburger, who once characterized Trudeau's peace efforts as "akin to the pot-induced behavior of an erratic leftist," has been "retired" as undersecretary of state for political affairs. Eagleburger, like former adviser Richard Pipes, lacked the diplomacy to control the true feelings of the Reagan administration.

Seen in perspective, Mr. Trudeau's policies on arms control and disarmament seem to fall short of their potential to influence mediation. In large part, Mr. Trudeau was constrained by the enormous pressures the Reagan administration and NATO commitments exerted on Canadian policy. These constraints led to a series of ambiguous decisions. Trudeau's original contribution to UNSSOD I seemed to be contradicted by the cruise missile testing agreement. We now know the cabinet was split on this issue. Trudeau's later peace initiatives were contradicted by his refusal to sign the five-continent appeal. In general, his refusal to support a comprehensive freeze seemed out of joint with Trudeau's knowledge and values. The risks of taking a position independent of the Reagan administration are difficult to assess from outside the seats of power. Now that Mr. Trudeau is out of power and it has been made clear that he was neither liked nor appreciated by the U.S. defense establishment, the risk may have been worth taking. Apparently NATO solidarity was also at stake, but Mr. Trudeau had already breached that with his contribution at Davos. He could have gone further and led the fight for Canadian independence within NATO. Pierre Elliott Trudeau was among the most gifted political figures of our time; whether he fulfilled the promise of those gifts must be left to history. One can appreciate Trudeau's talents and still disagree with his policies. One point is valid. The failure to freeze has led to a cruise missile race, a space militarization race, a space-based defenses race, and, in general, a more destabilized universe of weapons, strategies, and conflicts. The failure to recognize the destabilizing effect of the forward-based INF system of Euromissiles robbed the world of new agreements on arms limitations. While the USSR has returned to the bargaining table, it has also deployed air-launched and sea-launched cruise missiles. Forward-based Soviet delivery systems now can launch their own "decapitation" strikes against the U.S. One wonders what Mr. Trudeau really meant when, at a 25 October 1984 dinner in his honor, he warned his successor Brian Mulroney, "to stop kowtowing to Ronald Reagan." Mr. Trudeau's decision to sign the testing agreement is now history. Neither the good will of Joe Clark nor the good sense of Douglas Roche and Stephen Lewis can reverse the military tide.

"Peace initiatives" have not merely been relegated to the back burner—they are not even on the stove. No one seems capable of expending the resources and efforts necessary to make any significant impact on arms control. Lawrence Hegan, research director of the Ottawa-based Canadian Centre for Arms Control and Disarmament (CCAD), has supported Mr. Trudeau's plea for a ban on high-altitude antisatellite weapons (Knox, 1985), calling it "a good Canadian idea which has not been as fully developed or explored as it could be." Robert O'Neill, director of the influential International Institute of Strategic Studies (IISS) in London, sees SDI as a perfect issue for Canadian intervention to curb the U.S. move to militarize space (Knox, 1985). Nor has Canada undertaken an even more natural initiative, to strengthen the nuclear nonproliferation treaty and join the countries who criticize the superpowers for their "vertical proliferation." Atomic Energy of Canada has yet to admit there is a proliferation problem.

The Montreal *Gazette,* Saturday, 1 December 1984, headlined a news story that Canada might ask the superpowers to agree on a ban on cruise missiles, a somewhat unlikely prospect. This would be a somewhat astonishing step, and completely ludicrous, in view of the entire debate on cruise missile testing and CANUSTEP. Canada directly assisted the U.S. in provoking a cruise missile race; in response, the Soviet Union will deploy strategic air-launched and sea-launched cruise missiles throughout 1985–1986 and support deployment in Europe. It is too late. Northern Canada could become a cruise battlefield, as this author originally implied in a paper delivered in May 1983. Since cruise flight paths are a two-way street, national defense and the testing and operating of vastly expanded North American air-defense systems and the North Warning Line are also involved. Canada's External Affairs minister, Joe Clark, admitted that no such initiative is being contemplated and "that a unilateral action by Canada would have no effect." The superpowers' commitment to cruise development and deployment is now irreversible. Clark used a few brave but empty words in saying Canada wants assurance that "any defense that might be mounted to a cruise threat from the Soviet Union would not involve Canada in other aspects that we might not approve." Canadians need not hold their breath waiting to hear a single, public disapproval of any such existing or proposed aspects by the U.S.

Lloyd Axworthy, former Liberal cabinet minister who apparently opposed cruise testing in the first place, said in a Commons debate that he is convinced "the cruise should be put on the agenda [of the U.S.-Soviet arms talks of January 1985], and we should now say 'Look, the best answer is not to have them or to certainly freeze them at their present state.'" In contradiction to Axworthy's implied Canadian resistance to U.S. policy, John Turner, Liberal opposition leader, said in Ottawa that in regards to cruise testing, "The policy of the party remains the same as it was when we were in government" (*Gazette*, Monday, 3 December 1984, Montreal).

The inevitable and increasing Canadian involvement in the Reagan administration's policies will be accelerated. What Mr. Trudeau might have done to criticize these policies privately and publicly, Mr. Mulroney is unlikely to do, despite Stephen Lewis and Douglas Roche (or because of them).

THE WEARING OF THE GREEN OR LET ME SEE THE COLOR

At the 17 March 1985 "Shamrock Summit," two undistinguished leaders of Irish heritage, President Ronald Reagan and Prime Minister Brian Mulroney, met in Quebec City to discuss U.S.-Canadian relations. Three items dominated the agenda—acid rain, trade, and mutual air defenses—but the meeting seemed more typical of a mutual admiration society. Reagan said, "I confess, I like Brian Mulroney . . . he's a true Canadian patriot." Mulroney was "a strong friend of the United States," unlike Trudeau, according to Reagan (Schafer, 1985). Reagan defines a Canadian patriot as one who supports Reagan without reservation, particularly in his defense policy. Canada and the U.S. share a mutual world view. They are two equals, but one is more equal than the other. Mulroney has called the United States (**Reagan**), "our greatest friend, neighbor and ally, period" (Schafer, 1985). Predictably, Mulroney prefers to have Canada bombarded with the cruise and other missiles of a nuclear war, rather than tolerate acid rain, although Mulroney's commitment to the acid rain issue does not coincide with his record on environmental questions. The real issues of concern are economic: trade, balance of payments, and the relative weaknesses and strengths of Canadian-American currency. Since both leaders are supply-siders, their negotiations are made more difficult. Canadian public opinion has forced Mulroney to take a strong public position on acid rain, but one suspects that cosmetics rather than conviction are involved in Mulroney's stance. The integration of Canadian defense with U.S. defense is a necessary consequence of economic subservience and the "benefits" of defense contracts. The "Shamrock Summit" effected an agreement on salmon fishing that benefited the U.S., an agreement on modernizing the North American Air Defense system (NORAD), also beneficial to the U.S., an agreement to make Canada a nuclear battlefield, and predictably a new tactic of delay on acid rain curbs. Settlement of the acid rain issue has been delayed by scientific uncertainty that required "more research"; by governmental reluctance to regulate or to enforce rules against noxious emissions; and now, by the appointment of special acid rain envoys. Similar stalling ploys could lead to an environmental charade of continental proportions: why not appoint envoys to deal with oil and gas spillage, toxic waste, and nuclear winter? Envoys could be dispatched to study every outstanding issue that one side or the other wishes delay. Expressing his approval of such "progress," Reagan said, "I couldn't be more pleased to see us get things under way and off dead center."

Dead center means an exact 50 percent split between the two positions; in Reagan's terms moving "off dead center" means moving 90 percent away from Mulroney's position. This is the general formula for dividing U.S.-Canadian spoils, nine for the first and one for the second. The green, as far as Reagan and Mulroney are concerned, is the color of money, not of the environment. More than $110 billion dollars of bilateral trade is a lot of green.

The "Shamrock Summit" made a clear break from the customary division of costs and benefits. Canada agreed to pay 40 percent of the cost of building a new multibillion-dollar network of fifty-two new advanced radar stations, now called the North Warning System (NWS), to replace the old, obsolete Distant Early Warning System (DEWS). The new North Warning System officially recognized the nuclear battleground status of Canada in a cruise missile war. Reagan also used the occasion to demonstrate his well-known carrot-and-stick approach to the Soviet Union. After yet another short tirade against the USSR that accused the Soviets of violating treaties and human rights and suppressing religion, Reagan added that he was ready to work with the new Soviet leadership for "more constructive relations."

At the same meeting, Defense Secretary Caspar Weinberger stated that defensive missile launches might be placed in Canada: "They would be first placed in the most effective way . . . some might be here, some might be in the U.S. . . . . It just depends on where the most effective technical place is for them to be put" (Belcher and Morrison, 1985). We all know that the most effective technical place would be in the Canadian North, and probably integrated with the North Warning System. There is every reason to suspect this is the case, since in typical fashion this is what the U.S. is accusing the Soviets of doing at Kiasnoyarsk, and the connection between NWS and "Star Wars" is in the books. But Weinberger responded to a question about the placement of nuclear weapons on Canadian soil by saying, "We don't have any way of knowing the details of that . . . . It would depend on the location, size and nature of any potential attack" (Belcher and Morrison, 1985). This is a patent falsehood: it has already been divulged that U.S. contingency plans call for the placing of nuclear weapons in Canada. Moreover, it is a compounded falsehood: SIOP-6 has precise scenarios for every type of nuclear attack.

Since "Star Wars" defenses cannot intercept ground-hugging cruise missiles whose preferred route both ways is via Canada's northland, there is little question that the new North Warning System will be integrated with U.S. defenses against cruise missiles. Moreover, "Star Wars" is designed to take out ICBM's but not bomber attacks, and these will also be "defended" over Canada, a return to the days of the Bomarc. Mid-course interception in the "Star Wars" plan would make Canada the preferred area for sensors, readout stations, and launchers. In 1981, when the NORAD agreement was renewed, an important clause was *removed* without the knowledge of the public or parliament, i.e., "This agreement will not involve, in any way, a Canadian commitment to participate in an active missile defense." The new secret clause, of course, is that Canada will participate, willy-nilly, in "Star Wars" and other defenses, including nuclear-tipped interceptors. The difference between the Liberals and the Progressive Conservatives on this issue is that the Liberals, out of power, oppose participation in "Star Wars."

It is naive to believe that Canada has not already been involved in "Star Wars" research since the field is broad enough to cover much research already under way in Canadian corporations and universities. The only hope, and again it is likely to be vain, is that Canada will adopt a policy of not contracting for "Star Wars" research funds from the official U.S. Strategic Defense Initiative Organization (SDIO), will not allow testing on or over Canadian territory, and will not allow linkages with the North Warning System.

Canada's Foreign Minister Joe Clark was probably being more naive or ignorant than deceitful when he said that "Canada retains the sovereign right to decide whether Canada will allow nuclear weapons here" (Sallot, 1985), and that he has "no reason to believe it might be necessary." The two qualifiers are mutually contradictory, and Mr. Clark must know that in conditions defined as necessary by the U.S., Canada would "decide" to accommodate them.

In a U.S. television broadcast on 15 March 1985, Prime Minister Brian Mulroney stated, "Canada does not have nuclear weapons on its territories nor shall it during the life of this government," but he hedged by adding that any such decision would be a matter of a Canadian sovereign decision (Sallot, 1985). We all know what Mr. Mulroney's sovereign decision will be. Mulroney will agree to have U.S. offensive and defensive nuclear systems on Canadian territories if and when this is requested by the U.S. Acquiescence and accommodation have defined Canadian sovereignty and will continue to do so while Brian Mulroney is prime minister. Mulroney has expressed his admiration for Ronald Reagan; Pierre Trudeau did not.

On Wednesday, 6 March 1985, Paul Nitze, chief adviser to the U.S. on arms control, said that it "remains to be seen" whether "Star Wars" can be tied to the new radar system in Canada (*Toronto Globe and Mail,* Saturday, 9 March 1985, p. 5). But the issue goes deeper than Canadian integration. It now appears clear that SDI and offensive warfighting plans are also to be integrated (Molotsky, 1985). In fact, as we could glean from the "secret agenda," the nuclear "shield" is to have a nuclear sword poised behind it. New Canadian Defence Minister Eric Nielson seems to be following in the footsteps of Robert Coates and his predecessors, becoming a de facto member of the U.S. Department of Defense.

As the high point of the "Shamrock Summit," Reagan and Mulroney, two conservative clones, lead a chorus in singing "When Irish Eyes Are Smiling" on the stage of a great theater in Quebec City. We can conclude that Reagan came, saw, and conquered.

11

Beyond 1984: The Prospects for Peace

Doublethink means the power of holding two contradictory beliefs in one's mind simultaneously, and accepting both of them . . . . it also has to be unconscious, or it would bring a feeling of falsity and hence of guilt. War is Peace.
Ministry of Truth, in George Orwell's *1984*

Political language is designed to make lies sound truthful and murder respectable.
George Orwell, "Politics and the English Language," (1946)

All the existing patterns of human life will have to be improvised to conform with the non-human fact of nuclear power.
Aldous Huxley, *Brave New World*
(Foreword to revised edition, 1946)

The accidental and incidental convergence of technological, political, and social events and developments in the early 1980s brought reminders of the world depicted in George Orwell's novel *1984*. Orwell's novels deal with politics and language, with personal freedom and political authority. Politically, Orwell "was a maverick of the left—all of Orwell can be distilled from a witches' brew of romanticism and pessimism that was his hang-up" (Mullally, 1984). His Etonian, puritanical British middle-class upbringing, his experiences with the Stalinists in the Spanish Civil War, and his rejection by the leftist *New Statesman* led Orwell to become a declassé recluse who vainly attempted to live like the proletarian he could never be. Isolated, bitter, and terminally ill with tuberculosis, Orwell became obsessed with the Soviet threat, a posture common to members of the disenchanted left. In his writing, by "an uncanny coup—he [Orwell] put his signature and claim on a piece of our time" (Steiner, 1983). Now that 1984 has passed, we still seek some guideposts to the future.

Our present-day futurists look to the year 2000 and beyond, hoping that their current, fateful dreams will prepare us in some measure for the unpredictable challenges that await us. Orwell and his contemporaries—futurists like H. G. Wells and Aldous Huxley—left their legacy in informed, often prescient, writings that continue to be relevant today.

All three of these major twentieth-century futurists predicted the three great technological innovations of our time: (1) nuclear technology; (2) information-communications-cybernetic technology; and (3) biogenetic technology. This "triple revolution," as this author has called it, influences the social dynamics of our present and future world and affects and shapes our politics, economics, and culture.

Orwell, Huxley, and Wells foresaw the inherent dangers of this "triple revolution" when it came into conflict with the emergent "fourth revolution," the demands for human rights, distributive justice, and the right to human development and psychosocial evolution. In *1984,* Orwell provides us with a chilling picture of a communication technology powerful enough to determine profound social change. Today, all around us, we can see technology that offers the potential for a Big-Brother society. Huxley's *Brave New World* deals with biogenetics. Its message echoes as we read of recombinant gene research and the production of chemical/biological weapons. H. G. Wells based *The World Set Free* on information from Frederick Soddy's *The Interpretation of Radium and the Structure of the Atom.* Wells's book fired the imagination of Leo Szilard, who eventually patented the schematics for an explosive device similar to the atom bomb. After Hahn and Strassman's 1938 fission experiment in Berlin, Szilard said, "All the things that H. G. Wells predicted appeared suddenly real to me" (Hilgartner et al., 1982, p. 16). The "things" Wells's predicted were "atomic bombs," the "last war" that "would leave hundreds of the world's cities in ruins," fallout and firestorms, the exponential growth in destructive technology, and the inability to mediate conflict—all facts of life to today's informed citizens.

In this chapter, we intend to deal with aspects of the "triple revolution" that offer the world the contradictory fates of salvation and destruction. Following the lead of Orwell, Huxley, and Wells, we will focus on the politics of language and nuclear war.

NUCLEAR POWER AND "BIG BROTHER"

The advent of nuclear power has led to the evolution of a "technological priesthood" (Weinberg, 1972), whose members, often revealed to be petty power brokers, make "Faustian bargains" in a much bigger game (Weinberg, 1972). The widespread accommodation by elite experts acting directly or indirectly for government and industry has been heavily documented (Knelman, 1980b). Because the military use of nuclear power leaves little margin for error and presents a great chance of potential hazard, it reinforces the tendency to exert higher and more pervasive levels of control. The centralization and vulnerability of nuclear power lead to its technocratic management. Like military nuclear power, civil nuclear power also might require a new technological priesthood to manage its safe use in the future. "A permanent cadre of experts that will retain its continuity over immensely long times . . . the Catholic Church is the best example of what I have in mind, a central authority that proclaims and, to a degree *enforces doctrine . . . and has connections to every country's own Catholic Church* [Italics mine]" (Weinberg, 1973). Weinberg's choice of the Catholic Church as a model overseer does not hold up well, now that Catholic bishops are in the forefront of resistance to social terror and the nuclear arms race; however, his point is well taken.

The nuclear establishment represents the most fulfilled Orwellian model of society. "As long as the commercial and military use of nuclear power is internationally sanctioned, governments cannot be denied broad powers to protect their citizens from annihilation by nuclear war or devastation by nuclear accident" (Tribe and Remes, 1980). Safeguards cannot sufficiently prevent clandestine proliferation of nuclear technology and supplies. In an article on the making of the H-bomb in the May 1979 *Progressive,* Howard Moreland said that the classification priesthood of the U.S. Department of Energy, the keepers of the secrets, "do not simply withold the answers, they can also confiscate the questions" (Hilgartner et al., 1982, p. 63). One must not think or speak classified thoughts, even if their sources are all unclassified, according to the euphemism of "information management." These threats to freedom of movement, privacy, speech, and even thoughts have already occurred and are documented (Jungk, 1979; Hilgartner et al., 1982). The intrinsic links between civil and military nuclear power are made functional and organizational. In the U.S. one government department bears responsibility for both civil atomic energy and the production of nuclear weapons; thus, the conflict of interest between the public and the state is institutionalized. The "new tyranny" results from an "unforgiving technology." Such politics in action, accompanied by a necessarily restrictive process and a specialized political language, carries the possibility of a garrison state and a misinformation society.

TECHNOSPEAK AND "NUKESPEAK"

In general, obscurantist and elitist languages tend to evolve from new, specialized technologies such as computer science and cybernetics. This form of language, commonly known as "technospeak," results in part from the explosion and fission of knowledge. It occurs as part of the baggage of the new technocratic management class or technological priesthood. The nuclear age has its own, special form of evolved language that almost perfectly embodies Orwell's double-think, "nukespeak" (Hilgartner et al., 1982), an apt derivation of the Orwellian term "newspeak."

In his 1946 essay "Politics and the English Language," Orwell charged that political language consists mainly of "euphemism, question-begging and sheer cloudy vagueness," while "politics is a mass of lies, evasions, folly, hatred, and schizophrenia." This author analyzed the Orwellian double-think nature of "nukespeak" in dealing with civil nuclear power. "Nukespeak incorporates errors in logic, elements of deliberate deception—apologetics and cosmetics—and the semantics of illusion." It is a "nuclear jargon created to provide an illusion of safety, security and serenity" (Knelman, 1976, p. 85). "Nukespeak" complies with Orwell's definition of political language as "designed to make lies sound truthful and murder respectable." As a language deliberately evolved by the "cult of the atom," "nukespeak" covers up real social and environmental violence to sanitize the brutality and hazards of civil and military nuclear power. It is at once conscious corporate image-building, extreme rationalization, and a vocabulary of deliberate deception (Hilgartner et al., 1982).

The Orwellian rule for political language is sanitize by euphemism, and euphemism prevails in the language of nuclear power. Forbidden words such as "accident," "waste," "pollution," or "disease" are never used in "nukespeak." Accidents are "transients," "events," "significant events," "anomalies," "occurrences," "abnormal occurrences," or, in the extreme, "normal abnormalities." Truth becomes lies. Explosions are "events of rapid disengagement" or "prompt criticality." Toxic waste dumps are "residue areas." Thermal pollution translates into "thermal effects," while pollution itself becomes "environmental impacts." Disease means "health effects"—the euphemism for cancer and genetic malformations. Missing plutonium, the link to clandestine acquisition of nuclear explosives, is "material unaccounted for" or simply "MUF"!

In Orwell's *1984*, the state of Oceania has three powerful ministries, the Ministry of Peace, the Ministry of Love, and the Ministry of Truth. Using the synthetic, simple language "newspeak" and a process of "double-think," the three ministries propagate their corresponding slogans for Oceania: (1) War is Peace; (2) Hate is Love; and (3) Ignorance is Strength. These slogans form the basis for the real catchphrase of the Big-Brother system of government—Freedom is Slavery. This author may be accused of exaggeration, but it seems that the Reagan administration's rhetoric and policy approach these forms of double-think and double-speak.

THE MILITARY MANIFESTATION OF "NUKESPEAK"

The language of the nuclear military establishment increasingly has become a blend of double-speak and jargon. Acronyms abound. Weapons systems receive "natural" names such as "Frogs," "Aphids," "Kangaroos," "Sparrows," "Walleyes," and "Aardvarks." United States' weapons such as "Hound-Dog," "Bambi," and "Fat Albert" sound as innocent as characters from children's cartoons; yet they are used in the war-gaming scenarios the generals play.

The proliferating nuclear arsenal has spawned a new terminology designed to generally obscure the real horror behind each side's intended use of nuclear weapons, or to deliberately create an image of moral superiority from each side's identification with "good." Euphemism is invaluable in attributing "evil" to the other side. For example, the Soviet "Scud" has its counterpart in the U.S. "Honest John," yet both are capable of incredible destruction. Soviet ICBM's are "silo-killers," while U.S. ICBM's have "alleged counter-silo capability" or are merely "paper missiles" (MX). A Pentagon official, commenting on the naming of weapons, said that it is important "to pick a name that nobody will laugh at" (*Los Angeles Times,* Monday, 28 December 1981, p. 7); yet Reagan, disregarding the irony, refers to the MX as the "Peacemaker."

Cold warriors on both sides spew rhetoric in the mirror-image process of piously self-identifying with the "good" and self-righteously attributing "evil" intent to the other. Their words are more than rhetoric: there is a politics to language. Language can obscure an undesirable reality, make the unthinkable thinkable, and ultimately sell a policy that would be unacceptable if understood.

The old policy of nuclear stand-off, "deterrence," has given way to policies of "first use," "first-strike," "demonstration," all designed to lead us to accept the possibility of a "limited nuclear war." Made secure by the "crisis relocation" programs that have replaced civil defense, and emboldened by the "escalation dominance" that has disguised intended nuclear use, finding the will to "move up the ladder of escalation" is easy. A nuclear war can be won and survived.

The military uses Strangelovian terms in its pursuit of victory. The innocuous prefix "mega," as a substitute for "one million," minimizes enormity: in a strike by a ten-megaton weapon, New York would suffer only ten megadeaths. Single missiles designed to carry independently targetable warheads are said to be MIRVed or MARVed. A "theater war" refers to a localized or regionalized nuclear war, not the battle of Broadway. Only "tactical" nuclear weapons would be used in such a "limited" nuclear "theater production." But some "tactical" weapons, excluded from SALT because they were not "strategic," can travel as far as 3000 miles, carrying warheads thirty times as powerful as the bomb that destroyed Hiroshima.

Like the difference between tactical and strategic weapons, the distinction between nuclear and conventional war has disappeared from the minds of the military. Targets are "strategic hamlets" to be destroyed in "surgically clean strikes" under the name of "pacification." Strategies of "preemptive deterrence" or "aggressive defense" echo the philosophy behind much of the Vietnam War, "We had to destroy the village in order to liberate it."

We have reached the ultimate expression of "double-speak" in the twinning of contradictory concepts such as "peaceful aggression," "offensive defense," and "conventional nuclear warfighting." Double-speak reflects double-think, the process of combining rationalization, moral superiority, and deceit. Yet language is more than a deliberate form of deception: it provides direct insights into the rationale and mind-set of the nuclear military establishment.

"Body counts" hold the key to victory and survival. The dead may have been "wasted" through direct hits, "bonus kills" through radiation effects and damages, or victims of "collateral damage"—the corpses left in buildings or factories struck by the neutron bomb. The games generals play with their technological toys of mass destruction incorporate an actuarial attitude toward suffering and a denial of actual devastation. The language used to describe the effects and aftereffects of a nuclear war reflects some fundamental human lack, the absence of concern for the value of life. In the casual calculus of acceptable casualities—"Some estimates predict 10 million [dead] on one side and 100 million on the other. But that is not the whole population" (Rostow, 1981)—ten million deaths can appear benign by fearsome comparison. It is not merely that the numbers are wrong that is disturbing. The entire process of abstraction is inhuman. Paolo Soleri wrote, "Scientific abstraction is a two-edged sword. With one edge we sweep away the mysteries of the universe. With the other we shed the blood of our kin." Perhaps that is the horror. The military planners of the superpowers have forgotten the lessons of Hiroshima and Nagasaki.

There is no sense of kinship among members of a unitary species occupying a small planet. Nuclear war cannot be reduced to physics, flawless rationality, infallible technology, or moral superiority. The abstraction is not only bloodthirsty, but inherently antiecological and antibiological. Reductionistic terms only express the tragedy of quantification that excludes the qualitative aspects of life. There is no concern about the rape of Nature, no caring for the destruction of the innocent, no compassion for the incredible suffering inflicted by a nuclear holocaust. The same callous arithmetic calculations that enabled the Nazi's "final solution" could lead the planet to global holocaust. We will all be victims unless we rise up and speak out. We must all make the avoidance of nuclear war our problem.

THE SPECTER OF NUCLEAR WAR

Ten weeks after the U.S. dropped the first bomb on Japan on 6 August 1945,

Orwell wrote "You and the Atom Bomb," published by the London *Tribune* on Friday, 19 October 1945. In this article, Orwell noted that "We have before us the prospect of two or three monstrous super-states, each possessed of a weapon by which millions of people can be wiped out in a few seconds, dividing the world between them." To counter the threat, Orwell suggested a theory of deterrence or "no first use," "that the surviving great nations make a tacit agreement never to use the atomic bomb" against each other. Orwell never imagined that competition among the superpowers would lead to surrogate wars; nor did he think that the superpowers' nuclear arsenal could be rendered ineffectual in wars fought against countries not equipped with nuclear weapons, such as Vietnam or Afghanistan. Orwell did not begin to comprehend the extensive proliferation of nuclear weapons, which haunts us more than ever, or the catastrophic consequences of using nuclear weapons.

In 1946 Aldous Huxley wrote his foreword to a revised edition of *Brave New World*, some twenty years after its original publication. With incredible prescience, Huxley said, "One vast and obvious failure of foresight is immediately apparent. *Brave New World* contains no reference to nuclear fission . . . . The release of atomic energy marks a great revolution in human history, but not [unless we blow ourselves into extinction and end history] the final and most searching revolution . . . . All the existing patterns of human life will be disrupted and new patterns will have to be improvised to conform with the non-human fact of nuclear power" (Knelman, 1971, pp. 267–68).

The truly frightening aspect of the world situation in 1985 is that we have two superpowers that are both capable of committing mutual suicide through their mutually assured delusions and mutually assured paranoia. One side's identification of the other as the "source of all evil" or as an "evil empire" is not mere rhetoric, but a powerful amalgam of religious belief, ideology, and, in the case of U.S. leaders, a fundamentalist, apocalyptic vision. In his *The Judgement of Nations* Christopher Dawson wrote, "As soon as men decide that all means are permitted to fight an evil, then their good becomes indistinguishable from the evil they set out to destroy." Such a mirror-image judgment by each side transforms war into peace, truth into lies, and love into hate.

Nuclear war has rendered obsolete Clausewitz's famous strategic doctrine, "War is a continuation of politics by other means." Prenuclear wars left winners and losers. A nuclear war has no winners: all sides lose. Even worse, as the ultimate expression of technological colonialism against Nature, nuclear war takes aim at the heart of planet Earth. Inhumanity is given its final expression in the idea that we "must possess the ability to wage nuclear war rationally" (Gray and Payne, 1980). People must possess the passionate and loving ability to make peace an extension of politics. We see a most significant development as people all over the world enter into the theater of peace and become legitimate participants in its drama. The great antinuclear Easter parades of Western Europe and the global activities of October Disarmament Day present real hope.

Some leading U.S. figures have expressed the notion "better dead than Red." Nuclear war serves no national interest. As J. Robert Oppenheimer noted when he witnessed the first atomic test, we have "become Death, the destroyer of worlds." Peace nurtures life; therefore, peace is in everyone's best interests. In the nuclear age, the cause of war serves nothing—even justice is only attainable if survival is assured.

The twentieth century has two dominant images horrifically stamped on its history through newsreel description and documented testimony. Auschwitz and Horoshima combine in the nightmare of our days in the composite picture of genocidal and ecocidal holocaust, the organized murder of an entire planet. Total extinction has become possible through technological means, and technological means become compulsory unless expressly forbidden. Two "civilized" nations committed the twin atrocities of Auschwitz and Hiroshima. These countries, and other industrial civilizations, have waged a long colonial war against Nature. Not surprisingly, they now prepare for the ultimate solution. The world anticipates the final days, not of judgment, but of cupidity and stupidity. The doomsday tinderbox stands ready for the first match that will light the way to destruction. To be or not to be has truly become a soliloquy for civilization.

Our concluding thoughts dwell on the notion that the very existence of large numbers of nuclear weapons in a world divided by mistrust is the problem. Even the "balance of terror" is a "terror of balance" for we cannot live in security under the threatening mushroom cloud of oblivion. We who travel on this nuclear Titanic must mutiny against the captains of the world and steer a new course toward peace, not war. This world can have no future unless the nuclear threat is radically reduced, if not eliminated. This world can have no future as long as there is gross injustice among and between nations. This world can have no future as long as we threaten the environment that supports life on this planet. The problems of war, injustice, and ecodeath are inextricably linked. If we value the future, we must find permanent solutions to all three. To deter or not to deter is not the question; to be or not to be is.

We cannot overemphasize the danger of the Reagan administration's nuclear military policies, the "extreme wrong on the extreme right" (Tsipis, 1982). Their inflammatory holocaust language—from the late Senator Richard Russell's statement, "If we have to start all over again with Adam and Eve, then I want them to be Americans and not Russians, and I want them on this continent and not in Europe," to Energy Secretary James B. Edwards's, "I hope we never get into another war. . . . if we do, I want . . . to come out Number One, not Number Two" (Paine, 1982c)—reflects the most sinister threat to the world. Continued Soviet aggression, whether intentional, paranoid, or both, is an undoubted source of global conflict. But we insist that the Reagan administration is the most serious new factor in the possible precipitation of a nuclear confrontation. Fortunately, the relative openness of U.S. society offers hope that Reagan's warfighting plans can be defeated, and a more meaningful détente policy, resurrected. It is most heartening that Canadians, like Americans and Western Europeans, will continue to apply mounting but peaceful pressure against the arms race and for disarmament.

Much of this book has been directed toward an analysis of the policies and programs of the Reagan administration. Now we must face the significance of four more years of the Reagan regime. The Reagan victory could deal a serious, if not fatal, blow to peace. Unless the U.S. House and Senate firmly oppose the president, the danger of nuclear war could approach 100 percent probability. Even some of the most conservative economists predict terrible consequences from Reagan's huge, dedicated deficits. With interest, the U.S. accumulated deficit could reach a total of $2 trillion by 1988. At the same time, the U.S. balance of payments has become increasingly negative. The major corporations, particularly those in the energy field, are indulging in a $150 billion orgy of acquisition and conglomeration, at the expense of more internal exploration activities—a shortsighted view that disregards the actuality of a continuing energy crisis. The Third-World debt, estimated by some experts to be as high as $400 billion, may never be paid back. In the world as a whole, the sum of these financial disasters is high interest rates and high inflation. Many think that the high level of unemployment is systemic, structural, and permanent. The U.S. economic recovery could collapse by the end of 1985, and Reagan's fiscal policies will probably be seen as the cause of this calamity. These large economic problems are a major source of U.S. insecurity, and military overkill and overskill contributes to it. But we must not despair. Franz Werfel said, "Man's heart is a little mill which grinds and grinds, but can never grind out the last grain of hope." We have reason to hope. In 1985, Reagan's "secret agenda" suffered critical defeats in the MX issue, in the defense budget vote, and, as perhaps a more important indication of the strength of the opposition, in the congressional response to Reagan's position on SALT II.

The media has described Ronald Reagan's decision to comply with the terms of SALT II as a victory of State over Defense, i.e., Shultz over Weinberger, or as an act of Reagan's responsive, if not responsible, statesmanship. Both of these judgments are highly questionable. The great majority of the Reagan cabinet seems dedicated to the policies of the "secret agenda." While Caspar Weinberger is a pure, ultraright ideologue, Shultz and McFarlane are pragmatists as well as conservatives. Fortunately, their practicality sometimes impedes the exercise of their right-wing political philosophy. The victory in saving SALT II belongs to the majority of sane Americans and their representatives, and to the pressure exerted by world opinion and most Western governments. To them also belongs the victory of defeating Reagan's mammoth defense budget.

Throughout this book, we have advised our readers that the "secret agenda" is not untouchable. It has to operate within the reality of political constraints, obstacles, and opportunities. The victories we have cited are defeats for the Reagan administration because they presented constraints and obstacles to the implementation of the "secret agenda." Ronald Reagan is the consummate politician. To believe that he has abandoned the major thrust of the "secret agenda" and its ideological components is naive. Reagan's negative response to SALT II or arms control has not changed; that the political climate has changed is the real basis for hope.

After all we have written about the "holocaust lobby" that has come to power in Washington, America still remains the hope of the world. Despite the current insanity of a holy nuclear crusade dedicated to the destruction and/or capitulation of the Soviet Union, America has the democratic traditions and the necessary freedom to lead the world on the path to peace. Of the two superpowers, the U.S. can more likely reverse the policies of its cold warriors with their deadly plans for nuclear war. The American political system still permits dissent and encourages the participation of those whose powerful voices of sanity raise the alarm. America is the stronger of the superpowers, but with America's strength comes responsiblity. America must take the initiative to end the arms race and to search for the only security, the security of peace. The task is formidable, and the odds are poor, but 1986 can make the difference. If reasonable and caring Republicans and Democrats can achieve majorities in Congress, then we can allow Reagan to wait for the judgment of time. There will be no monuments. The Reagan phenomenon will be viewed as a temporary aberration, the coincidence of accidental circumstances—an eminently forgettable footnote to the history of the world.

References

Abbott, M., and J. Gallagher, eds. 1966. *The Documents of Vatican II*. New York: America Press.

Abrams, N. E., and J. R. Primack. 1980. "The Public and Technological Decisions." *Bulletin of the Atomic Scientists* (June): 44–48.

Adams, G. 1981. *The Iron Triangle: The Politics of Defense Contracting*. New York: The Council on Economic Priorities.

———. 1985. "The Budget: Now or Never." *Nuclear Times* (March): 16–17.

Adams, R., and S. Cullen, eds. 1981. *The Final Epidemic: Physicians and Scientists on Nuclear War*. Chicago: Foundation for Nuclear Science Inc.

Adelman, K. L. 1985. "Arms Control With and Without Agreement." *Foreign Affairs* (Winter).

Adler, K., and D. Wertman. 1981. "Is NATO in Trouble? A Survey of European Attitudes." *Public Opinion* (Aug./Sept.): 126–34.

Aldridge, R. C. 1981. *The Counterforce Syndrome: A Guide to U.S. Nuclear Weapons and Strategic Doctrine*. Washington: Institute for Policy Studies.

———. 1983. *First Strike: The Pentagon's Strategy for Nuclear War*. Boston: South End Press.

———. 1983. Chap. 5 in "Accidental War: The Growing Peril," compiled, edited by A. Newcombe. Peace Research Institute-Dundas, Ontario, draft.

———. 1985a. "Star Wars and First Strike." (March 7) Santa Clara, Calif.: Pacific Life Research Center.

———. 1985b. "Cruise Missile Background Paper" (February 18) Santa Clara, Calif.: Pacific Life Research Center.

Alger, C. F., and S. Mendlowitz. 1984. "Grass-Roots Activism in the United States: Global Implications." *Alternatives* 9, no. 4 (Spring): 447–74.

Alvarez, L. W., et al. 1980. *Science* 208: 1095–1108.

Ambio Advisory Group (Swedish Academy of Sciences). 1982. "The Aftermath: The Human and Ecological Consequences of Nuclear War." *Ambio* 11: 76–176.

Amnesty International. 1979. *Annual Reports*.

———. 1980. *Annual Reports*.

———. 1981. *Annual Reports*.

Arkin, W. M. 1983a."Why SIOP-6?" *Bulletin of the Atomic Scientists* 39 (April): 9–10.

———. 1983b. "Pershing II and U.S. Nuclear Strategy." *Bulletin of the Atomic Scientists* 39, no. 6 (June–July): 12–13.

313

Arkin, W. M. 1983c. "Nuclear Weapons at Sea." *Bulletin of the Atomic Scientists* 39, no. 8:5–7.

———. 1983d. "Nuclear Security: The Enemy May Be Us." *Bulletin of the Atomic Scientists* 39, no. 10 (December): 4–5.

Arms Control and Disarmament Agency. 1978. *An Analysis of Civil Defense in War.* Washington, D.C.: U.S. Arms Control and Disarmament Agency.

———. 1979. *Effects of Nuclear War.* Washington, D.C.: U.S. Arms Control and Disarmament Agency.

Aspin, L. 1980. "Judge Not By Numbers Alone." *Bulletin of the Atomic Scientists* 36, no. 6: 28–33.

Bahrs, R., et al. 1981. *The Dynamics of END.* Nottingham, U.K.: University Paperbacks.

Baldwin, H. 1959. "Washington Finds No Proof Moscow Had Capability to Launch ICBM's." *New York Times,* 25 March.

Ball, G. 1983. "Star Wars." *New York Review,* 14 April.

———. 1984. "Deadly Gambits." *New York Review of Books,* 8 November, 5–11.

———. 1985. "Star Wars." *New York Review,* 14 April.

Barnaby, F. 1982. "Bombed Out of Their Brains." *The Guardian,* 26 December, 6.

———. 1982. "Strategic Nuclear Weapons." Chap. 4 in *The Arms Race and Arms Control,* compiled by Stockholm International Peace Research Institute (SIPRI). New York: Taylor and Francis.

Bauch, H. 1983. "Cabinet Approves Plan to Test Cruise Missiles." *The Gazette,* 16 July, 1, Montreal.

Beer, M. 1984. "Canada's Cold Warriors." *Goodwins* (Spring): 16–121.

Belcher, M., and J. Morrison. 1985. *Washington Times,* 10 March, 1A, 10A.

Bell, T. E. 1981. "Weapons in Space: The Prospect Sets Off Heated Controversy." *Los Angeles Times,* 30 December, 5.

Benedict, H. 1985. *Santa Barbara News Press,* 17 March, B-2.

Bereanu, B. 1983. "Self-Activation of the World Nuclear Weapons Systems." *Journal of Peace Research* 1 (January).

Berger, J. J. 1972. *Nuclear Power.* New York: Dell.

Bergstrom, S., et al. 1983. "Effects of Nuclear War on Health and Health Services." *WHO Publications,* A 36.12.

Bethe, H., and K. Gottfried. 1982. "The Five Year War Plan." *New York Times,* 10 June.

Bethe, H., et al. 1983. "Why Star Wars is Dangerous and Won't Work." *Wall Street Journal,* 2 January.

Betts, R. K., ed. 1981. *Cruise Missiles, Technology, Strategy, Politics.* Washington, D.C.: The Brookings Institution.

Bezold, C., ed. 1978. *Anticipatory Democracy: People and Politics in the Future.* New York: Vintage Books.

Biddle, W. 1984. *Santa Barbara News Press,* 29 December.

Blair, S. 1977. "Handicapping the Arms Race." *New York Times,* 19 January.

———. 1981. "New CIA Estimate Finds Soviet Seeks Superiority in Arms." *New York Times,* December 26.

Boeker, E. 1977. "Public Information on Science and Technology: The Dutch Case." *Science and Public Policy* (December): 558–62.

Boffey, P. M. 1974. *The Brain Bank of America.* New York: McGraw-Hill.

Bonello, C., and G. Roussopoulos, eds. 1971. *The Case for Participatory Democracy.* New York: Viking Press.

Bordouvov, V. D. 1977. "Remote Sensing Satellites: Some Legal Problems of Remote Sensing of Earth from Outer Space." *Colloquium* 20: 496.

Borning, A. 1984. "Computer System Reliability and Nuclear War." In *International Physicians for the Prevention of Nuclear War Report* (October).

Bottome, E. M. 1971. *The Balance of Terror: A Guide to the Arms Race.* Boston: Beacon Press.

Bova, B. 1981. *High Road.* Boston: Houghton-Mifflin.

Bracken, P. 1983. *The Command and Control of Nuclear Weapons.* New Haven, Conn.: Yale University Press.

———. 1984. *The Command and Control of Nuclear Forces* New Haven, Conn.: Yale University Press.

Broad, W. J. 1982. "A Fatal Flaw in the Concept of Space War." *Science,* 12 March, 1372–74.

———. 1984. *Santa Barbara News Press,* 23 December, A-1.

Brodie, B. 1946. "Implication for Military Policy." In *The Absolute Weapon,* edited by B. Brodie. New York: Harcourt Brace.

Brown, S., et al. 1985. *Regimes for the Ocean, Outer Space and the Weather: Towards International Accountability in the Nonterrestrial Realms (NTR's).* Washington, D.C.: The Brookings Institution.

Bryson, R. A. 1984. *Climates of Hunger.* Madison, Wis.: University of Wisconsin Press.

Bundy, M., et al. 1982. "Nuclear Weapons and the Atlantic Alliance." *Foreign Affairs* (Spring).

Bunn, M., and K. Tsipis. 1983. "The Uncertainties of a Preemptive Nuclear Attack." *Scientific American* 249, no. 5 (September): 38–47.

Burkholder, S. 1981. "The Pentagon in the Ivory Tower." *The Progressive* (June): 25–31.

Burt, R. 1981. "The Relevance of Arms Control in the 1980's." *Daedalus* (Winter): 159–77.

Cahill, J. 1984. *Toronto Star,* 4 November, F-1.

Calder, N. 1979. *Nuclear Nightmares.* Harmondsworth, U.K.: Penguin.

Canadian Centre of Arms Control and Disarmament. 1984. *Arms Control Chronicle,* no. 4:14.

Carnesale, A., et al. 1983. *Living With Nuclear Weapons.* New York: Bantam Books.

Carrol, J. D. 1971. "Participatory Technology." *Science,* 19 February, 647–53.

Carter, A. B., and D. N. Schwartz, eds. 1984. *Ballistic Missile Defenses.* Washington, D.C.: The Brookings Institution.

Casper, B. M. 1976. "Technology and Democracy." *Science,* 1 October, 29–35.

Castelli, J. 1983. *The Bishops and the Bomb: Waging Peace In A Nuclear Age.* Garden City, N.Y.: Doubleday Image Books.

Chapple, B. M. 1982. "Perspective on the Peace Movement." *Reader's Digest,* November, 49-54.

Chaszer, E. 1969. *Science and Technology in Social and Political Alienation.* St. Louis, Mo.: George Washington University.

Chaudron, M., and Y. LePape. 1979. "Le Mouvement Ecologique dans La Lutte Anti-nucléaire." In *Nucléopolis,* edited by F. Fagnani and A. Nicolson. Grenoble, France: University of Grenoble.

Clarke, D. L. 1981. "Arms Control and Foreign Policy Under Reagan." *Bulletin of the Atomic Scientists* 37, no. 9: 12-19.

Clarkson, S. 1982. *Canada and the Reagan Challenge."* Toronto: James Lorimer.

Cleroux, R. 1982. "Trudeau Wants to Show USSR West Can Meet a Gun for a Gun." *The Globe and Mail,* 20 March, Toronto.

Coates, J. 1983. "Star Wars Plan Called Into Doubt by Laser Failure." *The Gazette,* 27 April, D-4, Montreal.

Cockburn, A. 1982. "Sure, But What About the Russkies?" Special Disarmament Issue, *Mother Jones,* September/October.

———. 1983. *Inside the Soviet Military Machine.* New York: Random House.

Cockburn, A., and J. Ridgeway. 1983. "The Freeze Vs. Reagan." *New Left Review* 137: 1-14.

Commoner, B. 1974. *The Closing Circle.* New York: Bantam.

———. 1979. *The Politics of Energy.* New York: Knopf.

Crissey, B. L. 1984. "Simulating Accidental Nuclear War." *Applied Computer Science,* January.

Crutzen, P. J., and J. W. Birks. 1982. *Ambio* 11: 114.

Daly, H. 1973. "The Steady-State Economy." In *Economics, Ecology and Ethics,* edited by H. Daly. San Francisco: W. H. Freeman.

Dasmann, R. F., et al. 1973. *Ecological Principles for Economic Development.* London, U. K.: Wiley.

Delean, P. 1984. *The Gazette,* 10 November, B-1, Montreal.

Dentzer, S., et al. 1983. "The Lawyers Hop on Flight 007." *Newsweek,* 19 September, 64.

Devall, W. 1980. "The Deep Ecology Movement." *National Resources Journal* 20: 299-338.

Deudney, D. 1984. "What Goes Up Must Come Down." *Bulletin of the Atomic Scientists* 40, no. 3: 10-11.

Dickson, D. 1974. *Alternative Technology and the Politics of Technological Change.* Glasgow, Scotland: Fontana/Collins.

Dodd, C. H. 1972. *Political Development.* London, U.K.: MacMillan.

Dorf, R. D., and Y. Hunter, eds. 1978. *Appropriate Vision: Technology, Environment and the Individual.* San Francisco: Boyd and Fraser.

Doub, W. D. 1974. "Meeting the Challenge of Nuclear Energy Head-On." *Atomic Energy Law Journal* 15, no. 4 (Winter): 260-64.

Draper, T. 1982. "Dear Mr. Weinberger." *New York Review of Books,* 4 November, 1982.

———. 1983. *New York Review of Books,* 18 August.

Draper, T. 1984. *Present History: On Nuclear War, Détente and Other Contro-versies.* New York: Vintage Books.

———. 1985. "Pie in the Sky." *New York Review,* 14 February.

Dumas, L. J. 1980. "Human Fallibility and Weapons." *Bulletin of the Atomic Scientists* 36 (November): 15–20.

Dyer, G. 1984. "Star Wars 'Toys' Set to Misfire." *The Gazette,* 13 October, B-3, Montreal.

Ebben, S., and R. Kasper. 1974. *Citizens Groups and the Nuclear Power Contro-versy.* Cambridge, Mass.: MIT Press.

Edwards, G. 1982. "Cost Disadvantage of Expanding the Nuclear Power Industry." *The Canadian Business Review* 9, no. 1: 19–30.

Ehrlich, P., et al. 1983. "Long-Term Biological Consequences of Nuclear War." *Science* 222, no. 4630: 1293–1300.

Ellul, J. 1965. *The Technological Society.* London, U.K.: Jonathan Cape.

Energy, Mines and Resources Canada. 1981. *Policy Review of the Nuclear Power Industry in Canada.* Ottawa, Canada.

Enloe, C. 1975. *The Politics of Pollution in Comparative Perspective: Ecology and Power in Four Nations.* New York: McKay.

Esposito, M. P., et al. 1980. U.S. EPA Report, EPA-600/280-197.

Estes, C. F. 1981. Testimony before Senate Committee on Armed Services. 97th Cong., 1st sess. 30 March, 4380–81.

Fedchenko, V., ed. 1977. *Things to Come.* Moscow, USSR: Mir Publishers.

Feld, B., and K. Tsipis. 1979. "Air-Launched Cruise Missiles." *Scientific American,* November.

Fisher, J. M. 1985. *Washington Times,* 19 March, B-1.

Fitchett, J. 1982. "U.S. Arms Buildup Worries Europeans." *International Herald Tribune,* 25 October.

Fitzgerald, F. 1981. "The Reverend Jerry Falwell." *New Yorker,* 18 May, 132.

Ford, D., et al. 1982. *Beyond the Freeze: The Road to Nuclear Sanity.* Boston, Mass.: Beacon Press.

———. 1985. *The Button.* New York: Simon and Schuster.

Frankena, W. K. 1939. "The Naturalistic Fallacy." *Mind* 48, no. 192: 467.

Frankland, E. G. 1981. "Will Germany Go Green?" *Environmental Actions* 12, no. 8: 19–22.

Frei, D. 1983. *Risks of Unintentional Nuclear War.* London, U.K.: Allenheld Osun.

Fried, C. 1970. *An Anatomy of Values.* Cambridge, Mass.: Harvard University Press.

Fritz, S. 1985. *Los Angeles Times,* 20 March, A-1, A-14.

Gardiner, R. W. 1974. *The Cool Arm of Destruction.* London, U.K.: Westminster Press.

Garthoff, R. L. 1984. "The Spending Gap." *Bulletin of the Atomic Scientists* (May): 5–6.

Garwin, R. L. 1981. "Are We on the Verge of a New Arms Race in Space?" *Bulletin of the Atomic Scientists* 37, no. 5 (May): 48–55.

Garwin, R. L., and C. Sagan. 1983. "Ban Space Weapons." *Bulletin of the Atomic Scientists* 39, no. 9 (November): 2–4.

Garwin, R. L., and J. Pike. 1984. "Space Weapons: History and Current Debate." *Bulletin of the Atomic Scientists* (May): 25–115.

Gelb, L. H. 1984. "Is the Nuclear Threat Manageable?" *New York Times Magazine*, 4 March.

Gertenzang, J. 1985. *Los Angeles Times*, 26 March.

Gertler, M. 1982. *Washington Post*, 4 June.

Glasstone, S., and P. J. Dolan, 1977. *The Effects of Nuclear Weapons.* 3rd ed. Washington, D.C.: US DOD and ERDA.

Goldsmith, E., et al. 1972. "A Blueprint for Survival." *The Ecologist* 2: 1–43.

Goldsmith, E. 1977. "The Future of An Affluent Society: The Case of Canada." *The Ecologist* 7: 161–94.

Gompert, D. C., et al. 1980. *Nuclear Weapons and World Politics.* New York: McGraw-Hill.

Gooderham, M. 1984. *The Globe and Mail,* 3 November, Toronto.

Goodman, E. 1983. "National Nuclear Follies Act II." *Miami Herald,* 10 December, 31A.

Gorz, A. 1980. *Adieux Au Prolétariat.* Paris, France: Gallilée.

Gottfried, K. 1983. *Los Angeles Times,* 13 April.

Gray, C. 1979. "Nuclear Strategies: The Case for a Theory of Victory." *International Strategy* (Summer).

Gray, C., and C. Payne. 1980. "Victory Is Possible." *Foreign Policy* 39 (Summer).

Green, M., and G. MacColl. 1983. *Ronald Reagan's Reign of Error.* New York: Pantheon Books.

Greve, F. 1983. "Soviet Pilots Were Clumsy." *The Gazette,* 15 September, A-10, Montreal.

Grodzins, M., and E. Rabinovitch. 1963. *The Atomic Age: Scientists in National and World Affairs.* New York: Basic Books.

Grossman, S. 1978. "The Greens (Les Vertes): The New Dialectic in French Politics." *The Co-Evolution Quarterly* (Winter): 94–98.

Ground-Zero. 1982. *Nuclear War: What's In It For You.* New York: Pocket Books.

Gyorgi, A., et al. 1979. *No Nukes: Everyone's Guide to Nuclear Power,* Boston, Mass.: South End Press.

Haefele, W. 1974. "Hypotheticality and the New Challenge: The Path-Finder Role of Nuclear Energy." *Minerva* 13, no. 3 (July).

Hall, B. W. 1984. "The Anti-Nuclear Peace Movement." *Alternatives* 9, no. 4 (Spring): 475–518.

Halloran, R., et al. 1981. "Weinberger Said to Offer Reagan Plan to Regain Atomic Superiority." *New York Times,* 4 August.

Halloran, R. 1982. "Pentagon Draws up First Strategy for Fighting a Long Nuclear War." *New York Times,* 30 May.

———. 1982. "Interview with Caspar Weinberger." *New York Times,* 9 August.

———. 1984. "Reagan at War." *The Gazette,* 21 January, Montreal.

Halperin, M. H. 1983. "The Freeze Is Arms Control." *Bulletin of the Atomic Scientists* 39: 2–3.

Hancock, T. 1979. "Tomorrow's Political Party." *Conserver Society Notes* 1, no. 4 (Winter).

Hanley, C. J. 1985. *Santa Barbara News Press,* 11 January.

Hardin, G. 1968. "The Tragedy of the Commons." *Science* 162: 1243–48.

Harper, P., and G. Boyle, eds. 1976. *Radical Technology.* London, U.K.: Wildwood House.

Harwell, M. 1984. *Nuclear Winter.* New York: Springer Verlag.

Hay, J. 1983. "Testing the Cruise: To Defend or Disarm." *MacLeans,* 30 May, 22–26.

Henderson, H. 1970. "Politics by Other Means." *The Nation,* December.

———. 1974. "Information and the New Movement for Citizen Participation." *Annals of the American Academy of Political and Social Science,* March.

———. 1976. "Citizen Movements for Greater Global Equity." *International Society of Science* 28, no. 4: 773–88.

———. 1978. *Creating Alternative Futures.* New York: Berkley Wyndhover.

Heritage Foundation. 1984. *A World Without the U.N.: What Would Happen if the U.N. Shut Down.* Edited by Buston Yale Pines. Washington, D.C.: Heritage Foundation.

Hilgartner, S., et al. 1982. *Nukespeak: The Selling of Nuclear Technology in America.* Harmondsworth, U.K.: Penguin Books.

Hohensmeser, C., et al. 1977. "The Distrust of Nuclear Power." *Science,* April, 25–34.

Holloway, D. 1981. "War, Militarism and the Soviet State." Working Paper No. 17. New York: Institute for World Order.

———. 1983. *The Soviet Union and the Arms Race.* New Haven, Conn.: Yale University Press.

Holzman, F. C. 1978. Testimony before U.S. Congress, Joint Economic Committee Hearings, Washington, D.C.

———. 1980. "Dollars or Rubles: The CIA's Military Estimates." *Bulletin of the Atomic Scientists* 36, no. 6: 23–27.

———. 1980. Testimony before U.S. Congress, Select Committee on Intelligence, Washington, D.C.

———. 1982. Testimony before U.S. Congress, House Armed Services Committee, Washington, D.C.

Hooker, C. A., et al. 1981. *Energy and the Quality of Life: Understanding Energy Policy.* Toronto: University of Toronto Press.

Hoyt, R. G. "The Bishops and the Bomb." *Christianity and Crisis,* 9 August.

Iklé, F. C. 1973. "Can Nuclear Deterrence Last Out the Century." *Foreign Affairs* (January): 267–85.

Illych, I. 1973. *Tools for Conviviality.* New York: Harper and Row.

Inglis, D. R. 1984. "Freeze the Cruise." *Bulletin of the Atomic Scientists* 40, no. 1: 48–49.

Isaacson, W. 1983. "Reagan for the Defense." *Time,* 4 April.

Jackson, W. E., Jr. 1982. "Reagan's Unsavoury SALT." *Bulletin of the Atomic Scientists* 38, no. 7: 15–16.

Jacquier, H., ed. 1976. *Appropriate Technology: Problems and Promises.* Paris, France: OECD.

Jagnarke, H. 1973. *Political Development.* New York: Harper and Row.

Jakhu, R., et al. 1980. "International Satellite for Disarmament and Development." In *Annals of Air and Space Law*, edited by N. M. Matte. Montreal: McGill Institute of Air and Space Law.

Jasani, B., ed. 1982. *A New Dimension of the Arms Race*. Stockholm International Peace Research Institute. London: Taylor and Francis.

Jastrow, R. 1983. "Why Strategic Superiority Matters." *Commentary*, March, 27–32.

Johnson, M. 1982. "Debunking the 'Window of Vulnerability.'" *Technology Review*, January.

Johnson, N. L. 1983. "Estimated Operational Lifetimes of Several Soviet Satellite Classes." *Journal of British Interplanetary Society* 34: 280–83.

———. 1983. "The Soviet Year in Space: 1982." Colorado Springs: Teledyne Brown Engineering.

Johnson, R. W. 1984. "KAL-007: Unanswered Questions." *World Press Review*, March, 23–26.

Jopling, D., and S. Gagel. 1971. "The Pattern of Public Political Resistance." *Nuclear News*, March, 32–35.

Juenger, F. G. 1956. *The Failure of Technology*. Chicago: Henry Regnery.

Jungk, R. 1958. *Brighter Than A Thousand Suns*. New York: Harcourt and Brace.

———. 1979. *The New Tyranny*. New York: Warner Books.

Kahler, E. 1957. *The Power and the Abyss*. Paris, France: George Brajeller.

Kahn, D. 1983. "Spy Planes Play Deadly Game With Soviet Defenses." *The Gazette*, 9 September, Montreal.

Kahn, H. 1965. *On Escalation: Metaphors and Scenarios*. New York: Praeger.

———. 1969. *On Thermonuclear War*. New York: Free Press.

Kaldor, M. 1982. *The Baroque Arsenal*. London, U.K.: Sphere Books.

Kalven, J. 1982. "A Talk With Lou Harris." *Bulletin of the Atomic Scientists* 38, no. 7: 3–5.

Kamenetskya, E. 1977. "Cooperation Among States in the Exploration and Use of Outer Space." *Colloquim* 24.

Kampelman, M., et al. 1985. *New York Times Magazine*, 27 January.

Kaplan, D. 1983. "Lasers for Missile Defense." *Bulletin of the Atomic Scientists* (May): 5–8.

Kaplan, F. 1983. *Mutual Delusions*. Boston, Mass.: Council for a Liveable World.

———. 1983. *The Wizards of Armageddon*. New York: Simon and Schuster.

Karas, T. 1983. *The New High Ground*. New York: Simon and Schuster.

Kasper, R. 1976. "Citizens Groups and Nuclear Controversy." *Technology and Culture* 17: 401–4.

Keeny, S. M., and W. Panofsky. 1982. "MAD Versus NUTS." *Foreign Affairs* (Winter).

Kennan, G. 1983. "Zero Options." *New York Review of Books*, 12 May.

———. 1983. "Breaking the Spell." *The New Yorker*, 3 October.

Kennedy, J. F. 1974. *Public Papers of the President of the United States*. J. F. Kennedy, 1963. Washington, D.C.: GPO.

Kipling, B. 1984. "Canada to Be Battleground for U.S.-Soviet Cruise." *The Gazette*, 6 February, B-3, Montreal.

Kneese, A. V. 1973. "The Faustian Bargain: Cost-Benefit Analysis in the Nuclear Fuel Cycle." *Resources* 44: 1–5.

Knelman, F. H. 1971. *1984 And All That.* Belmont, Calif.: Wadsworth.

———. 1972. "Relevant Science." *Science Forum,* June.

———. 1973. "What Happened in Stockholm." *International Journal* 28, no. 1 (Winter): 50–68.

———. 1976. *Nuclear Energy: The Unforgiving Technology.* Edmonton, Alta.: Hurtig Publishers.

———. 1978. "Review Essay on Anti-Science." *Futures Canada* 4, no. 3.

———. 1979. "Canadian Nuclear Energy: Who Needs It?" *Our Generation* 13, no. 1: 23–34.

———. 1980a. "The Science-Technology-Society Complex." In *Human Context of Science and Technology.* Social Sciences and Humanities Research Council, Canada.

———. 1980b. "Adversarial Processes in Scientific Controversy." Background Paper for Report No. 35, *Regulating the Regulators.* Canada: Science Council of Canada, 1983.

———. 1981. "The Myopia of Social Systems: Applied Systems and Cybernetics." In *The Quality of Life: Systems Approaches,* edited by G. E. Lasker, vol. 1. Toronto: Pergamon Press.

———. 1982a. "To Develop or Not Develop Is Never the Question." Keynote Address at 2nd International Conference on Petroleum and the Environment, Halifax, Canada, August 16–19.

———. 1982b. *Energy, Information and the Conserver Society: The Fundamental Questions.* Paper No. 1-13. Montreal: GAMMA.

———. 1983a. "The Mythology of the Nuclear Arms Race: Reagan Policy and Canadian Complicity." Paper delivered to Learned Societies, CPREA, UBC, 30 May.

———. 1983b. "Solar Power Satellites: Social and Political Implications." In *Earth-Oriented Space Activities and Their Legal Implications.* Montreal: McGill Institute of Air and Space Law.

———. 1983c. *Remote Sensing Satellites.* Study commissioned by McGill Institute for Air and Space Law, Montreal.

Knox, P. 1985. *The Globe and Mail,* 5 January, Toronto.

Kohlberg, L. 1971. "From Is to Ought: How to Commit the Naturalistic Fallacy and Get Away With It." In *Cognitive Development and Epistemology,* edited by T. Michel. New York: Academic.

Komanoff, C., and E. E. van Loon. 1982. "Too Cheap to Meter and Too Costly to Build." *Nucleus* 4, no. 1: 3–7.

Komer, R. 1984. *Maritime Strategy or Coalition Defense.* Cambridge, Mass.: Abt Books.

Kowolowski, L. 1984. "Rapture." *Sanity,* July, 29–34.

Kristol, I. 1984. *Wall Street Journal,* 15 December.

Kuhn, T. 1962. *The Structure of Scientific Revolutions.* Chicago: University Press.

Kuznetsov, B. G. 1977. *Philosophy of Optimism.* Translated by Y. D. Khakina and V. L. Sulima, Moscow, USSR: Progress Publishers.

Laird, M. 1962. *A House Divided.* Chicago: Regnery.

Lamb, H. H. 1971. *Climate: Present, Past and Future.* London, U.K.: Menthuen.

Lapp, R. E. 1962. *Kill and Overkill.* New York: Basic Books.

Leaning, J. 1983. "An Ill Wind: Radiation Consequences of Nuclear War." Chap. 11 in *The Counterfeit Ark,* edited by J. Leaning and L. Keyes. Cambridge, Mass.: Ballinger.

Leaning, J., and L. Keyes, eds. 1983. *The Counterfeit Ark.* Cambridge, Mass.: Ballinger.

Leitenberg, M. 1982. "The Numbers Games or Who's on First." *Bulletin of the Atomic Scientists* 38, no. 6: 27–32.

Lens, S. 1977. *The Day Before Doomsday: An Anatomy of the Nuclear Arms Race.* Boston: Beacon Press.

Lewis, A. 1982. "Europe Missile Issue is Political. *The Post,* 31 December, West Palm Beach.

———. 1983. "Reagan Calls on God to Support Missile Stand." *The Gazette,* 13 March, B-3, Montreal.

———. 1984. *The Gazette,* 11 February, B-3, Montreal.

———. 1984. *New York Times,* 12 April.

———. 1984. *The Gazette,* 30 October, Montreal.

———. 1984. *New York Times,* 30 October.

Lewis, K. N. 1979. "The Prompt and Delayed Effects of Nuclear War." *Scientific American* 241 (July): 35.

Lewis, R. S. 1972. *The Nuclear Power Rebellion: Citizens vs. The Atomic Establishment.* New York: Viking.

Lifton, R. J., et al. 1974. *Living and Dying.* New York: Praeger.

Lifton, R. J. 1976. *The Life of Self: Towards a New Psychology.* New York: Simon and Schuster.

———. 1982. "The Psychic Toll of the Nuclear Age." *New York Times Magazine,* 6 September, 52–66.

———. 1982. "Beyond Nuclear Numbing: A Call to Teach and Learn." In *Proceedings of Symposium on The Role of the Academy in Addressing the Issues of Nuclear War.* Washington, D.C.: Hobart and William Smith Colleges et al.

Lifton, R. J., and R. Falk. 1982. *Indefensible Weapons.* New York: Basic Books.

Linowes, D. F. 1981. "Is There a Spy in the Sky: Innovations and Values of Freedom." *Vital Speeches* 47, no. 21 (August 15): 665–68.

Lodgaard, S. 1982. "Long-Range Theatre Nuclear Forces in Europe." Chap. 8 in *The Arms Race and Arms Control,* compiled by SIPRI. New York: Taylor and Francis.

Lodgaard, S., and F. Blackaby. 1984. "Nuclear Weapons." Chap. 1 in *The Arms Race and Arms Control,* compiled by SIPRI. New York: Taylor and Francis.

Logsdon, J. 1981. "The Evolution of the U.S. Space Program: An Inventory of Policy Issues." *Proceedings* of Symposium, McGill Institute of Air and Space Law, Montreal, October 16 and 17.

Longsreth, T. K. 1985. "Report Aims to Sabotage Arms Control." *Bulletin of the Atomic Scientists* 41, no. 1 (January): 29–31.

Lovins, A. B. 1977. *Soft Energy Paths: Towards a Durable Peace.* Cambridge, Mass.: Ballinger.

Lowi, T. 1967. "Making Democracy Safe for the World." In *Domestic Sources of Foreign Policy*, edited by James Resenau. New York: The Free Press.

Lowrence, W. W. 1976. *Acceptable Risk: Science and the Determination of Safety*. Los Altos, Calif.: William Kaufmann.

Luckham, R. 1984. "The Militarization of Culture." *Alternatives* (Winter).

Lumsden, J. 1970. *The Americanization of Canada*. Toronto: University of Toronto Press.

Lumsden, M. 1983. "Nuclear Weapons and the New Peace Movements." In *The Arms Race and Arms Control*, compiled by Stockholm International Peace Research Institute. New York: Taylor and Francis.

Lushbaugh, C. C. 1974. "Human Radiation Tolerance." In *Space Radiation Ecology and Related Topics*, edited by C. A. Tobias and P. Todd. New York: Academic Press.

Manfred, S. 1969. "Technology and Its Critics." Summarized in 5th annual report of Harvard Program on Science and Technology.

Mann, C. 1982. "The Holocaust Lobby." Special Disarmament Issue, *Mother Jones*, September/October.

Marcuse, H. 1964. *One-Dimensional Man*. Boston, Mass.: Beacon Press.

———. 1969. *An Essay on Liberation*. Boston, Mass.: Beacon Press.

McConnell, J. 1981. Testimony before Senate Committee on Armed Services, 97th Cong., 1st sess., 30 March, 4382.

McNamara, R. 1967. "Testimony on ABM Defenses." In *The Antiballistic Missile*, edited by E. Robinowitch and R. Adams. Chicago: Science and Public Affairs, pp. 144–54.

———. 1983. "What the U.S. Can Do." *Newsweek*, 5 December, 48–55.

McNamara, R., et al. 1984. "Star Wars." *Foreign Affairs*, November.

Meadows, D. H., et al. 1972. *The Limits to Growth*. New York: New American Library.

Mearsheimer, J. 1982. "Why the Soviets Can't Win Quickly in Central Europe." *International Security* 7, no. 1 (Summer).

Mishan, E. 1967. *The Costs of Economic Growth*. London, U.K.: Staples Press.

Mitrany, D. 1966. *A Working Peace System*. Chicago: Quadrangle Press.

Mohr, C. 1983. "Scientists Dubious Over Missile Plans." *New York Times*, 25 March, A-8.

Molotsky, I. 1985. "Official Disputes: An Article on Offensive Atom Weapons." *New York Times*, 1 June, 7.

Morrison, D. C. 1984. "Air-Breathing Nuclear Delivery Systems." *Bulletin of the Atomic Scientists* 40, no. 2 (February): 32–39.

Mowlam, M. 1983. "Peace Groups and Politics." *Bulletin of the Atomic Scientists* (November): 28–31.

Mullally, F. 1984. "A Failed Prophecy." *Los Angeles Times*, 1 January.

Naidu, M. V. 1983. "Economics behind the Cruise Missile Testing in Canada." *Peace Research* 15, no. 3: 1–17.

National Academy of Sciences (U.S.). 1975. *Long-Term Worldwide Effects of Multiple Nuclear Weapons Detonations*. Washington, D.C.

Nelkin, D. 1976. *The Politics of Technical Decisions*. London, U. K.: Sage.

Nelkin, D., and S. Fallows. 1978. "The Evolution of the Nuclear Debate: The Role of Public Participation." *Annual Reviews of Energy* 3: 275–312.

Nelkin, D., and M. Pollack. 1979. "Public Participation in Technological Decisions: Reality or Grand Illusions." *Technology Review,* August/September, 55–64.

———. 1982. *The Atom Besieged: The Anti-Nuclear Movement in France and West Germany.* Cambridge, Mass.: MIT Press.

Nelson, L.-E. 1984. *New York Times,* 19 June.

———. 1984. *The Gazette,* 21 November, Montreal.

Newcombe, A., ed. 1983. "Accidental War: The Growing Peril." Draft. Dundas, Ont.: Peace Research Institute.

New Democratic Party. 1982. *Ottawa Report,* 12 March.

Nitze, P. 1976. "Assuring Strategic Stability in an Era of Detente." *Foreign Affairs,* January, 223–26.

Nucleus. 1983. "New Reactor Safety Study. Winter.

Office of Technology Assessment (U.S.). 1979. *The Effects of Nuclear War.* Washington, D.C.: GPO, OTA-NS-89.

Olthuis, J. H. 1969. *Facts, Values and Ethics.* Assen, Netherlands: Van Gorcum.

Origins. 1982. "The Challenge of Peace: God's Promise and Our Response." 28 October: 313, 317.

Paine, C. 1980. "Pershing II: The Army's Strategic Weapon." *Bulletin of the Atomic Scientists* 36, 8 October, 24–26.

———. 1981. "Running in Circles with the MX." *Bulletin of the Atomic Scientists* 37, no. 10: 5–10.

———. 1982a. "The Elusive Margin of Safety." *Bulletin of the Atomic Scientists* 38, no. 5: 11–14.

———. 1982b. "A False START." *Bulletin of the Atomic Scientists* 38, no. 7: 11–14.

———. 1982c. "Nuclear Combat: The Five-Year Defense Plan." *Bulletin of the Atomic Scientists* 38, no. 9: 5–12.

———. 1983a. "MX: Too Dense for Congress." *Bulletin of the Atomic Scientists* 39, no. 2: 4–6.

———. 1983b. "The Freeze and Its Critics." *Bulletin of the Atomic Scientists* 39, no. 4: 5–9.

Paradise, S. I. 1983. "Catholic Doctrine and Nuclear Dogmatics." *Science, Technology and Human Values* 8, no. 3 (Summer): 30–40.

Parsons, T. 1951. *The Social System.* New York: The Free Press.

———. 1977. *The Evaluation of Societies.* New York: Prentice-Hall.

Pearson, D. 1984. "KAL-007: What the U.S. Knew and When We Knew It." *The Nation,* August 18 and 23, 105–9.

Penner, R. 1984. "Cruise, Freeze, NATO Highlights Debate." *The Peace Calendar* 11, no. 1 (February): 1.

Perry, W. 1978. Senate Arms Services Committee, Authorization Hearing, FY 1979.

Peterson, J., ed. 1983. *The Aftermath: The Human and Ecological Consequences of Nuclear War.* New York: Pantheon.

Physicians for Social Responsibility (U.S.). 1981. In *The Final Epidemic: Physicians and Scientists on Nuclear War,* edited by R. Adams and S. Cullen. Chicago: Foundation for Nuclear Science, Inc.

Piel, G. 1963. *The Illusion of Self-Defense in the Fallen Sky: Consequences of Nuclear War.* New York: Wang and Hill.

Pike, J. 1983. *Anti-Satellite Weapons.* Federation of American Scientists, Public Interest Report, November.

———. 1984. *An Assessment of "Star Wars."* Washington, D.C.: Federation of American Scientists.

Pipes, Richard. 1977. "Why the Soviet Union Thinks It Can Fight and Win a Nuclear War." *Commentary,* July.

———. 1980. "Soviet Global Strategy." *Commentary,* April.

Pirages, D., ed. 1977. *The Sustainable Society.* New York: Praeger.

Polanyi, J. C. 1983. "History Will Judge the Cruise Decision." *The Globe and Mail,* 11 February, 7, Toronto.

Pontifical Academy of Science. 1982. *Statement on the Consequences of the Use of Nuclear Weapons.* Geneva, Switzerland, and Rome, Italy: World Council of Churches.

Porat, M. U. 1977. *The Information Society.* Washington, D.C.: U.S. Department of Commerce.

Porritt, J. 1984. *Seeing Green: The Politics of Ecology Explained.* Oxford, U.K.: Basil Blackwell.

Powers, T. 1985. "On Nuclear Winter." *The Atlantic Monthly,* November.

Price, J. L. 1968. *Organizational Effectiveness.* London, U.K.: Irwin.

Primack, O., and F. von Hippel. 1976. *Advice and Dissent.* Scarborough, Ont.: New American Library.

Primack, J., and F. von Hippel. 1979. *Advice and Dissent.* New York: New American Library.

Pringle, P., and W. Arkin. 1983. *S.I.O.P.: The Secret U.S. Plan for Nuclear War.* New York: Norton.

Prins, G., ed. 1983. *Defended to Death.* Harmondsworth, U.K.: Penguin Books.

Proxmire, W. 1980. *U.S. Congressional Record,* 26 August.

Quinn, H., W. Lowther et al. 1983. "Flight Into Darkness." *MacLeans,* 12 September, 18–22.

Rapoport, A. 1963. "Chicken á la Kahn." *Virginia Quarterly Review* 41, no. 3 (Summer).

Rathjens, G., and J. Ruina. 1983. *New York Times,* 27 March.

Rawls, J. 1971. *A Theory of Justice.* Cambridge, Mass.: Harvard University Press.

Reford, R. 1968. "Merchant of Death?" *Behind the Headlines* 27, no. 4, (October).

Reichley, J. 1982. Cover page, *The Brookings Review.*

Reuters News. 1983. "Soviet Pilots Were Clumsy." *The Gazette,* 15 September, A-10, Montreal.

Ritchie, C. 1983. *Storm Signals: More Diplomatic Diaries, 1962–1971.* Toronto: Macmillan.

Rodberg, L. S. 1982. Letter in response to R. Halloran's revelation of "guidance" document. *New York Times,* 10 June.

Roderick, H., and U. Magnussun, eds. 1983. *Avoiding Inadvertent War: Crisis Management.* Austin, Tex.: University of Texas, Lyndon B. Johnson School of Public Affairs.

Rosenfeld, S. S. 1984. *Washington Post,* 8 November.

Rostow, E. V. 1979. "The Case Against SALT II." *Commentary,* February.

Rostow, E. J. 1981. U.S. Senate Confirmation Hearings Committee on Foreign Relations, June 22, 23.

Roszak, T. 1969. *The Making of a Counter Culture: Reflections on the Technocratic Society and Its Youthful Opposition.* Garden City, N.Y.: Doubleday.

———. 1973. *Where the Wasteland Ends: Politics and Transcendence in Postindustrial Society.* Garden City, N.Y.: Doubleday.

———. 1974. "The Monster and the Titan: Science, Knowledge and Gnosis." *Daedalus* 103 (Summer): 17–32.

Rotblat, J. 1981. *Nuclear Radiation in Warfare.* New York: Taylor and Francis.

Rowen, H. S. 1984. *Wall Street Journal,* 4 December.

Rusk, J. 1983. "U.S. Request to Test Cruise Now Official." *The Gazette,* 14 June, 1, Montreal.

Sagdev, R., and A. Kokoshin. 1983. *Political-Military Implications of Prospective American Space-Based Anti-Missile System.* Moscow, USSR: Committee of Soviet Scientists for Peace against the Nuclear Threat.

Sallot, J. 1985. *The Globe and Mail,* 16 March, 1, Toronto.

Saloma, J. S., III. 1984. *Ominous Politics: The New Conservative Labyrinth.* New York: Hill and Wang.

Sanders, J. 1983. *The Peddlers of Crisis: The Committee on the Present Danger and the Politics of Containment.* Boston, Mass.: South End Press.

Sayre, K. M., ed. 1977. *Values in the Electric Power Industry.* Notre Dame: University Press.

Schafer, S. M. 1985. *Santa Barbara News Press,* 17 March.

Scheer, R. 1981. "Interview with Jerry Falwell." *Los Angeles Times,* 4 March.

———. 1981. *Los Angeles Times,* 4 October, V-3.

———. 1982. *With Enough Shovels: Reagan, Bush and Nuclear War.* New York: Random House.

———. 1982. "Pentagon Plan Aims at Winning Nuclear War." *Los Angeles Times,* 15 August.

———. 1983. *With Enough Shovels: Reagan, Bush and Nuclear War.* New York: Vintage Books.

———. 1983. *Los Angeles Times,* 10 July

Schell, J. 1982. *The Fate of the Earth.* New York: Knopf.

Schlesinger, J. 1974. "Flexible Strategic Options and Deterrence." *Survival,* March/April, 86–90.

Schmidt, F., and D. Bodansky. 1976. *The Energy Controversy: The Fight Over Nuclear Power.* San Francisco: Albion.

Schnee, J. E. 1981. "Inventory of Space Activities (Economic)." *Proceedings,* Symposium, McGill Institute of Air and Space Law, Montreal, October 16 and 17.

Schumacher, E. F. 1975. *Small Is Beautiful.* London, U.K.: Sphere Books.

Science Council of Canada. 1976. *Nuclear Dialogue.* Ottawa, Canada: Science Council of Canada.

———. 1977. *Canada As a Conserver Society.* Report No. 27. Ottawa, Canada: Science Council of Canada.

Science Council of Canada. 1983. *Regulating the Regulators: Science, Values and Decisions.* Report No. 35. Ottawa, Canada: Science Council of Canada.

Scott, R. 1984. "Now A Warhead Gap." *Bulletin of the Atomic Scientists* 40, no. 9: 43–44.

Scowcroft Commission. 1983. *Report of the President's Commission on Strategic Weapons,* DOD, B. Scowcroft, chairman. Washington, D.C.: GPO.

Seaman, M. 1966. "Alienation, Membership and Political Knowledge: A Comparative Study." *Public Opinion Quarterly* 30: 353–67.

———. 1967. "Powerlessness and Knowledge: A Comparative Study of Alienation and Learning." *Sociometry* 30, no. 2 (June): 105–23.

Sector, B., and Z. Nauth. 1985. *Los Angeles Times,* 20 March, A-1, A-14.

Sellars, D. 1984. "U.S. Has New List of Weapons for Testing in Canada." *The Gazette,* 7 March, 1, Montreal.

Shabecoff, P. 1983. "Scientists See No Hope in Atom War." *New York Times,* 9 December, A-13.

Shrader-Frechette, K. 1980. *Nuclear Power and Public Policy: The Social and Ethical Problems of Fission Technology.* Dordrecht, Holland: D. Riedel.

Simon, H. A. 1984. "Mutual Deterrence or Nuclear Suicide." *Science* 223, no. 4638, (29 February): 775.

Simpson, J. 1983. "Why the Greens Hope for the Impossible." *The Globe and Mail,* 5 February, 9, Toronto.

———. 1983. "Station More Troops in Europe, Top NATO Official Tells Canada." *The Globe and Mail,* 15 March, 4, Toronto.

SIPRI. See Stockholm International Peace Research Institute.

Sivard, R. 1980. *World Energy Survey.* Leesburg, Va.: World Priorities.

———. 1982. *World Military and Social Expenditures.* Leesburg, Va.: World Priorities.

Skelton, G. 1983. *Los Angeles Times,* 19 March, 1, 14.

Smith, R. J. 1982. "They Have More EMT Than We." *Science* 216, 2 April, 32.

———. 1983a. "Scientists Fault Charges of Soviet Cheating." *Science* 220, no. 4598 (13 May): 696–97.

———. 1983b. "The Search for a Nuclear Sanctuary." *Science* 221, 1 July, 30.

———. 1983c. "Star Wars Get Green Light." *Science* 222, 25 November, 901–2.

———. 1984a. "The Allure of High-Tech Weapons for Europe." *Science,* 23 March, 1269–72.

———. 1984b. "Missile Developments Roil Europe." *Science* 223, no. 4634: 371–76.

———. 1984c. "Weapons Bureaucracy Spurns 'Star Wars' Goal." *Science* 224, 6 April, 32–35.

———. 1984d. "Microchip Problems Plague DOD." *Science* 224, 5 October, 24–26.

Southam News, 1983. "U.S. Ordered Probe on Missile News Leaks." *The Gazette,* 21 June, A-7, Montreal.

Sprout, H., and M. Sprout. 1971. *Ecology and Politics in America: Issues and Alternatives.* New York: General Learning Press.

Starr, C. 1972. "Social Benefit Versus Technological Risk." In *Technology and Society,* edited by N. de Nevas. London, U. K. : Addison-Wesley.

Starr, C., and R. Rudman. 1973. "Parameters of Technological Growth." *Science* 182, 358–64.

Steele, J. 1983. "We Always Exaggerate Soviet Strength." *Washington Post,* 25 December, B-3.

Steinbrunner, J. D. 1982. *Foreign Policy* 45 (Winter): 16–28.

———. 1984. "Launch Under Attack." *Scientific American* 250, no. 1: 37–47.

Steiner, G. 1983. "Books—Killing Time." *The New Yorker,* 12 December, 168.

Stewart, J. 1983. "Trudeau, Mulroney Win Praise for Korean Jet Stands." *The Gazette,* 5 October, Montreal.

Stivers, R. 1976. *The Sustainable Society: Ethics and Economic Growth.* Philadelphia, Pa.: Westminster Press.

Stockholm International Peace Research Institute (SIPRI). 1978. *Outer Space— Battlefield of the Future.* New York: Taylor and Francis.

———. 1981. *The Arms Race and Arms Control.* New York: Taylor and Francis.

———. 1982. *The Arms Race and Arms Control.* New York: Taylor and Francis.

———. 1983. *The Arms Race and Arms Control.* New York: Taylor and Francis.

———. 1984. *The Arms Race and Arms Control.* New York: Taylor and Francis.

———. 1984. *No First Use.* Edited by F. Blackaby et al. New York: Taylor and Francis.

Stone, H. C. 1981. *Confrontation in Space.* New York: Prentice-Hall.

Talbott, S. 1983. "The Risks of Taking Up Shields." *Time,* 14 April.

———. 1984. *Deadly Gambits.* New York: Knopf.

Taylor, B. 1980. "The International Movement." In *Atom's Eve: Ending the Nuclear Age,* edited by R. Hardest and G. L. Moulton. New York: McGraw-Hill.

Taylor, J. W. 1984. *Janes' Defense Weekly,* 14 February.

Teller, E. 1982. "Dangerous Myths About Nuclear Arms." *Reader's Digest,* November, 139–41.

Thompson, E. P., and D. Smith. 1981. *Protest and Survive.* New York: Monthly Review Press.

Thompson, E. P. 1982. "A Letter to America." *The Nation* 234, 10–17 July.

Thompson, S. L., et al. 1984. "Global Climatic Consequences of Nuclear War." *Ambio* 13, no. 4: 236–43.

Toffler, A. 1978. *Anticipatory Democracy.* New York: Random House.

Toth, R. C. 1985. *Los Angeles Times,* 11 March, 1–10.

Touraine, A. 1979. *La Prophète Anti-Nucléarie.* Paris, France: Ed. du Seuil.

———. 1981. *L'Après Socialisme.* Paris, France: Ed. Grasset.

Tribe, L. H., and D. H. Remes. 1980. "Does the Progressive Have a Case?" In Hilgartner et al, *Nukespeak: The Selling of Nuclear Technology in America.* Harmondsworth, U.K.: Penguin Books.

Tribe, L., et al. 1980. "Some Reflections on the Progressive Case: Publish and Perish." *Bulletin of the Atomic Scientists* 36, no. 3 (March): 23.

Trimborn, H. 1982. "Greens Emerge as Potential Political Force in West Germany." *Los Angeles Times,* 21 May, 1-A.

Tsipis, K. 1982. "Extreme Wrong on the Extreme Right." *Bulletin of the Atomic Scientists* 38, no. 4: 3–4.

Tsipis, K., and M. Bunn. 1983. "The Uncertainties of a Preemptive Nuclear Attack." *Scientific American* 249, no. 5 (November): 38–47.

Turco, R., et al. 1983. "Nuclear Winter: Global Consequences of Multiple Nuclear Explosions." *Science* 222, no. 4630 (December 23): 1283–92.

Union of Concerned Scientists. 1983. *Anti-Satellite Weapons: Arms Control or Arms Race?* Cambridge, Mass.: Union of Concerned Scientists.

———. 1984. *The Fallacy of Star Wars.* Edited by J. Tirman. New York: Vintage Books.

United Nations. 1980. Documents A/AC. 105/267, Annex 2, 15 February; A/AC. 105/271, Annex 3, 10 April, Nuclear Power Sources.

United Nations General Assembly. 1976. "Coordination of Outer Space Activities." Report of the General Secretary, Doc. A/AC. 105/166.

United Nations University. 1978. *Goals, Processes and Indicators of Development, A Five-Year Project.* Tokyo, Japan: United Nations University.

United Press International (UPI). 1981. "U.S. Congressional Report on Fake Alarms." 26 May.

United States Air Force. 1982. *Air Force 2000: Air Power Entering the 21st Century.* Washington, D.C.: GPO.

Vaillancourt, J. G. 1982. "The Protest Movement Against Nuclear Energy in Western Europe." *Our Generation* 15, no. 2 (Summer): 14–25.

Valaskakis et al. 1979. *The Conserver Society.* New York: Harper and Row.

Velikov, Y. P. 1984. "Space Weapons: Effect on Strategic Stability." *Bulletin of the Atomic Scientists,* May, 125–55.

Von Hippel, F. 1983. "The Myth of Edward Teller." *Bulletin of the Atomic Scientists* 39, no. 3 (March): 6–12.

Wall Street Journal. 1980. "Satellite Aided U.S. World Crop Production Forecast." 14 May.

Wallace, M. D. 1984. "Accidental Nuclear War: A Risk Assessment." Paper presented to the Second World Congress of Arts and Sciences, Erasmus University, Rotterdam, Netherlands, June.

Warnock, J. 1970. *Partner to Behemoth.* Toronto: New Press.

Weiler, L. S. 1983. "No First Use: A History." *Bulletin of the Atomic Scientists* 39, no. 2: 28–33.

Weinberg, A. 1969. "Social Institutions and Nuclear Energy." *Science* 177, 27–34.

———. 1972. *Science and Trans-Science.* London, U.K.: U.S. International Association for Cultural Freedom.

———. 1972. "Social Institutions and Nuclear Energy." *Science* 177, no. 4043 (July 7): 34.

———. 1973. *Bulletin of the Atomic Scientists* 30, no. 9 (November): 20.

Weinberger, C. 1982. Letter. *New York Times,* 23 August.

Wertzman, B. G. 1984. *New York Times,* 21 December.

Westlake, M. 1983. "On Course For Disaster." *Far Eastern Economic Review,* 13 October, 29–35.

Wicker, T. 1984. "Reagan Has 'Star Wars' in His Eyes." *The Gazette,* 1 December, B-3, Montreal.

Wieseltier, L. 1983. *Nuclear War, Nuclear Peace*. New York: Holt, Reinhart and Winston.

Wiesner, J. 1982. "Is a Moratorium Safe?" *Bulletin of the Atomic Scientists* 38, no. 7: 6–8.

Will, G., 1985. *Santa Barbara News Press*, 24 March.

Willrich, M. 1971. *The Global Politics of Nuclear Power*. New York: Praeger.

Wilson, A. 1983. "SS-20 Off Target." *The Observer*, 3 April.

Wilson, G. C. 1982. "Preparing for Nuclear War Is a Waste of Funds, General Says." *Washington Post*, 19 June.

Winner, L. 1977. *Autonomous Technology*. Cambridge, Mass.: MIT Press.

Winters, F. X. 1983. "The American Bishops on Deterrence." *Science, Technology and Human Values* 8, no. 3 (Summer): 23–29.

Woodwell, G. M. 1982. "The Biotic Effects of Ionizing Radiation." *Ambio* 11, 143–48.

York, H. 1970. *Race to Oblivion: A Participant's View of the Arms Race*. New York: Simon and Schuster.

Zuckerman, S. 1982. *Nuclear Reality and Illusion*. London, U.K.: Collins.

Glossary of Terms and Acronyms

ABM. Anti-Ballistic Missile.

ABMT. Anti-Ballistic Missile Treaty. Part of SALT I, 1972 and 1974, that puts restrictions on ABM interceptors, launchers, and radar.

ABRV. Advanced Ballistic Reentry Vehicle. A new warhead, now called Mark-21 RV, designed for MX and possibly Trident II.

ACDA. Arms Control and Disarmament Agency, U.S.

ALCM. Air-Launched Cruise Missile.

Alpha. A DARPA program to develop a pulsing, chemical high-energy (killer) laser for use in space.

ALSV. Air-Launched Sortie Vehicles that evade or confuse radar.

AMARV. Advanced MAneuvering Reentry Vehicle.

ASALM. Advanced Strategic Air-Launched Missile.

ASAT. Anti-Satellite Weapons.

ASW. Anti-Submarine Warfare.

ATB. Advanced Technology Bomber. The "stealth" bomber.

ATBT. Atmospheric Test Ban Treaty, 1963.

Atosevocom. Automatic Secure Voice Communications.

AWACS. Airborne Warning and Control System. A Boeing 707–type radar aircraft, also called the E-3A.

B-1. A new U.S. supersonic bomber.

B-1B. A version of the B-1 bomber designed as a cruise missile carrier.

B-52. A current U.S. strategic bomber.

Ballistic missile. A rocket-powered missile that coasts through a ballistic arc after being boosted to speed.

Big Bird. A U.S. reconnaissance (spy) satellite.

BMD. Ballistic Missile Defense.

BMEWS. Ballistic Missile Early Warning System.

Build-down. An arms race reduction proposal of the Reagan administration.

C^3I. Command, Control, Communications, and Intelligence.

C^4I. Command, Control, Communications, Countermeasures, and Intelligence.

CBC. Canadian Broadcasting Corporation.

CCNR. Canadian Coalition for Nuclear Responsibility.

CDI. Center for Defense Information, Washington, D.C.

CEP. Circular Error Probability. The radius of a circle that centers on a target and circumscribes the area that has a 50 percent chance of being hit by an incoming warhead.

CIA. Central Intelligence Agency, U.S.

CND. Campaign for Nuclear Disarmament, U.K.

COPOUS. The United Nations Committee on the Peaceful Uses of Outer Space.

Counterforce. A nuclear strategy in which the attack missiles are aimed at the opponent's military forces.

Countervailing. Another name for counterforce, used in Presidential Directive #59 (PD-59) to connote a limited nuclear exchange as opposed to a disarming first-strike.

Countervalue. A nuclear strategy in which the attack missiles are aimed at the opponent's value targets: cities and industrial areas.

CPD. Committee on the Present Danger, U.S.

Cruise missile. A guided missile supported by the atmosphere that uses an "air-breathing" engine and flies like an airplane.

CTBT. Comprehensive Test Ban Treaty.

Damage limitation. A strategic nuclear doctrine intended to limit damage to American cities by destroying Soviet nuclear weapons before they are launched; a euphemism for counterforce.

DARPA. Defense Advanced Research Projects Agency, U.S.

Decapitation. A nuclear attack on the seat of government and the logistics system of a country.

Delta-3. Another version of the Delta class that carries sixteen SS-N-8 missiles.

Deploy. To make a weapons system or component operational.

Depressed trajectory. Short-range launch of SLBM's close to targets.

Deterrence. A nuclear strategy whereby a potential aggressor is "deterred" from attacking because of the massive and unacceptable retaliation that will follow.

DEWLINE. Distant Earling Warning line of radars for bomber and cruise missile warning.

DIA. Defense Intelligence Agency.

Directed energy. A term used to describe high-energy (killer) lasers and sub-atomic particle beams; any other type of energy that is directed to a target to destroy it or render it inoperable.

DOD. Department of Defense, U.S.

DOE. Department of Energy, U.S.

DSCS. Defense Satellite Communications System. A U.S. military communications satellite.

Dual-track. The 1979 NATO decision to place U.S. GLCM's and Pershing II's in Europe while negotiating theater weapons.

EC-135. A special modification of the Boeing-707 airplane that is used for airborne command posts.

ECM. Electronic Countermeasures. Devices for "spooking."

EMP. Electromagnetic Pulse. A high-voltage spike generated by a nuclear explosion that affects the circuitry of missiles and reentry vehicles that travel through the environment of a nuclear blast.

END. European Disarmament Movement.

ERIS. Exatmospheric or Endatmospheric Reentry Vehicle System.

Escalation dominance. The doctrine that the U.S. must dominate every stage of escalation in a confrontation with the USSR, including warfighting.

Evader. A name given to the Mark-500 maneuvering reentry vehicle for Trident I that implies that it evades defensive interceptor missiles.

Excalibur. An X-ray laser weapon.

F-15. A modern U.S. Air Force fighter plane.

FB-111B/C. A proposed stretch version of the FB-111A fighter bombers and the F-111 fighters that carry cruise missiles.

FB-111H. A proposed stretch version of the FB-111A that carries cruise missiles.

False alert. A failure in the Ballistic Missile Warning System.

FEMA. Federal Emergency Management Agency, U.S.

First strike. An unprovoked nuclear attack, usually against missile silos; also called a preemptive strike.

First use. The option of using nuclear weapons first, primarily in response to a conventional threat; also known as flexible response.

Fratricide. The destructive effect of the debris, EMP, etc., from a nuclear explosion that disables subsequent warheads.

FY. Fiscal Year.

GEO. Geosynchrous Earth Orbit, 22,000 miles above the equator; also called earth-synchrous orbit.

GLCM. Ground-Launched Cruise Missile.

GPID. Goals, Processes, and Indicators of Development, a United Nations University research project.

GPS. Global Positioning System (Navstar).

HALO. High Altitude Large Optics. A future satellite-based sensor array for detecting and tracking ballistic missiles, bombers, and satellites.

HI-CAMP. High-Resolution Calibrated Airborne Measurements Program.

HIT. Homing Interceptor Technology. A. U.S. program to develop non-nuclear interceptors that destroy ballistic missiles and satellites.

HOE. Homing Overlay Experiment.

ICBM. Inter-Continental Ballistic Missile.

ISMA. International Satellite Monitoring Agency. A French proposal, UNSSOD I, May 1978, to monitor arms agreements.

ISSS. International Institute of Strategic Studies, London, U.K.

KAL. Korean Air Lines.

KCIA. Korean Central Intelligence Agency.

KH-11. A modern U.S. reconnaissance (spy) satellite.

Kt. A kiloton or 1000 tons of TNT equivalent.

L. Liberal Members of Parliament, Canada.

Ladar. Combined use of Laser and radar.

Landsat. The U.S. earth resources satellite series.

Laser. An acronym for Light Amplification by Stimulated Emission of Radiation, a highly concentrated beam of coherent light.

Launch on attack. A response to a perceived attack.

Launch on warning. A posture whereby missiles are put on automatic (computerized) response.

LEO. Low Earth Orbit, less than 1000 miles.

Lethality. A number expressed as "K" that denotes the ability of a missile or warhead to destroy a hard target: the higher the number, the more lethal the weapon.

LODE. Large Optics Demonstration Experiment. A DARPA program to develop the mirror to steer and control a high-energy (killer) laser.

LRTNF's. Long-Range Theater Nuclear Forces.

MAD. Mutual Assured Destruction. (Originally: Mutual Assured Deterrence.)

Mark-12A reentry vehicle. A new warhead designed for Minuteman III missiles, and possibly for MX and Trident II.

Mark-500 reentry vehicle. A maneuvering reentry vehicle (MARV) being developed for the Trident I missile.

MARV. Maneuvering Reentry Vehicle.

Megaton. The nuclear explosive force equal to one million tons of conventional high explosives.

MHV. Miniature Homing Vehicle. An ASAT weapon based on infrared sensing.

MILSTAR. Military Strategic-Tactical and Relay satellite system. A future replacement for AFSATCOM, SDS, and possibly FLTSATCOM.

MIRV. Multiple Individually-targeted Reentry Vehicle.

Missile-X. A new mobile intercontinental ballistic missile, sometimes referred to as MX, that the Pentagon hopes to put into production.

MRV. Multiple Reentry Vehicle, not independently targeted.

Mt. A megaton or one million tons of TNT that has an explosive force equivalent to seventy Hiroshima bombs.

MX. Missile-X.

NAS. National Academy of Sciences, U.S.

NASA. National Aeronautics and Space Administration, U.S.

NATO. North Atlantic Treaty Organization.

NAVSTAR. The global positioning system of satellites being developed by the U.S.

NDP. New Democratic Party, Canada.

NFI. Nuclear Freeze Initiative.

NORAD. North American Aerospace Defense Command.

NPT. Non-Proliferation Treaty, 1970.

NRC. National Research Council, U.S.

NSC. National Security Council, U.S.

NSDD. National Security Decision Document, a nuclear warfighting plan; also called National Security Decision Directive.

NUTS. Nuclear Utilization: Tactics and Strategy.

OST. Outer Space Treaty, UN.

OTA. Office of Technology Assessment, U.S.

PAL. Permissive Action Link. Inability to detonate a warhead without intervention of head of state.

PAR. Perimeter Acquisition Radar. A phased-array radar formerly part of the North Dakota ABM site; now assigned to NORAD for missile early warning.

PAVE PAWS. An acronym for Precision Acquisition of Vehicle Reentry-Phased Array Warning System. New phased-array radars for detecting submarine-launched ballistic missiles.

Payload. Throw weight.

P.C. Progressive Conservative Member of Parliament, Canada.

PD. Presidential Directives.

Penetrating aids. Devices that overcome ballistic missile defenses.

PINETREE LINE. A line of bomber early warning radars sited in central Canada.

P_k. Probability of Kill.

Polaris. The first U.S. nuclear-powered ballistic missile.

Polar orbit. The orbit of a satellite that passes over the north and south poles of the earth.

Poseidon. A class of U.S. ballistic missile-launching submarines converted from Polaris subs; also, the Poseidon submarine-launched ballistic missile. Successor to Polaris.

P.s.i. Pounds per square inch pressure.

PSR. Physicians for Social Responsibility.

PTBT. Partial Test Ban Treaty, 1963.

Radar. Radio Detection And Ranging.

RV. Reentry Vehicle.

SAC. Strategic Air Command, U.S.

SAINT. Satellite Interceptor. A U.S. antisatellite program of the early 1960s.

SALT. Strategic Arms Limitation Treaty.

SBBMD. Space-Based Ballistic Missile Defenses.

SCRAMJET. Supersonic Combustion RAMJET.

SDI. Strategic Defense Initiative, U.S.

SDS. Satellites Data System. U.S. Air Force communications satelites.

SEATO. Southeast Asia Treaty Organization.

SIOP. Single Integrated Operational Plan. The master targeting plan for nuclear weapons.

Sipapu. An American Indian word meaning "sacred fire." The code name for the Army's neutral particle beam weapon for ballistic missile defense in space; now renamed "White Horse."

SLBM. Submarine-Launched Ballistic Missile.

SLCM. Sea-Launched Cruise Missile.

SOLRAD. A U.S. Navy satellite to measure solar radiation.

Sputnik. The first series of Soviet satellites. Sputnik I was the first artificial satellite in orbit.

SRAM. Short-Range Attack Missile.

SS-7. An early Soviet ICBM no longer in operation.

SS-8. An early Soviet ICBM no longer in operation.

SS-9. An early Soviet large throw-weight ICBM no longer in operation.

SS-11. A Soviet ICBM.

SS-13. A Soviet ICBM using solid fuel.

SS-16. A new never-deployed Soviet solid-fuel ICBM.

SS-17. A new Soviet ICBM.

SS-18. A new Soviet large throw-weight ICBM.

SS-19. A new Soviet medium-weight ICBM.

SS-20. A new Soviet intermediate-range ballistic missile being deployed against Western Europe that uses the first two stages of the SS-16.

SS-24. A new Soviet ICBM or a modernized version of it.

SS-25. A new Soviet single-warhead mobile ICBM.

SSBN. A nuclear-powered ballistic missile submarine.

SSD. United Nations Special Session on Disarmament.

SSGN. A nuclear-powered guided missile (cruise missile) submarine.

SS-N-6. A Soviet SLBM carried on Yankee submarines.

SS-N-8. A Soviet SLBM carried on Delta 1 and Delta 2 submarines.

SS-N-18. A Soviet SLBM carried on Delta 3 submarines.

SS-NX-12. A possible follow-up to the Soviet Shaddock SS-N-3 cruise missile.

SS-NX-17. A Soviet solid-fuel SLBM only deployed on one Yankee submarine.

SS-NX-20. A new Soviet SLBM in development for use on the new Typhoon submarine.

START. STrategic Arms Reduction Talks.

Star Wars. President Reagan's proposal to develop exotic space-based anti-ballistic missiles or Space-Based Ballistic Missile Defenses (SBBMD).

Stealth. An aircraft or cruise missile using new technologies that make it less visible to radar.

Strategic. Having to do with strategy: the planning and directing of large-scale military operations; in the case of nuclear weapons, strategy is global in scope.

Strategic triad. The combination of land-based intercontinental ballistic missiles, air-breathing intercontinental bombers and cruise missiles, and submarine-launched ballistic missiles. Both the U.S. and USSR operate with a strategic triad of land, air, and sea weapons.

Strategic weapons. The long-range weapons in the strategic triad designed for a confrontation between the U.S. and USSR.

Suffocation. A policy to curb the arms race proposed by Prime Minister Trudeau at UNSSOD in New York on 26 March, 1978.

Tactical. Having to do with tactics: arranging and maneuvering military forces in action or before the enemy; usually associated with theater operations in Europe, the Pacific, or the Atlantic.

Tactical nuclear weapons. Short-range nuclear weapons designed to be used in a theater of operations.

TALCM. Tomahawk Air-Launched Cruise Missile. An unsuccessful competitor for the strategic air-launched cruise missile.

Talon Gold. A DARPA program to develop the aiming and tracking system for the high-energy (killer) laser in space.

Teal Amber. A visible wave-length mosaic sensor being developed by the U.S. for use in ground-based satellite tracking.

Teal Ruby. A mosaic infrared sensor being developed by the U.S. to detect and track bombers and cruise missiles from space.

TERCOM. Terrain Contour Matching. Cruise missile sensors that use a digital map stored in their computers' memories to follow the ground terrain and reach their targets.

Throw weight. The weight of a missile after the last booster motor has separated; also called "payload."

Time-urgent targets. ICBM silos that would have to be destroyed before they launch their missiles.

TLAM. Tomahawk Land Attack Missile. A sea-launched cruise missile.

Tomahawk. Name for General Dynamics's cruise missile.

Trident. The new sea leg of the U.S. strategic triad: the new submarine is called Trident; the first and second generation missiles are called Trident I (C-4) and Trident II (D-5), respectively.

TTBT. Threshold Test Ban Treaty.

Tu-95. A Soviet strategic heavy bomber, also known as "Bear."

Typhoon. A new Soviet ballistic missile submarine that will probably carry twenty SS-NX-20 SLBM's.

UCS. Union of Concerned Scientists. A group of scientists concerned with the nuclear arms race.

ULMS. Underwater Long-range Missile System, later renamed Trident.

UNGA. United Nations General Assembly.

UNSSOD. United Nations Special Session on Disarmament.

Vatican II. The Pastoral Constitution of the Church in the Modern World.

Vela. A U.S. satellite in deep space (70,000 miles high) to detect nuclear explosions.

VHF. Very-High Frequency.

VHIC. Very-High-Speed Integrated Circuits.

Warfighting. A term that connotes more aggressive counterforce than "damage limitation."

Warhead. The explosive charge of a weapon. For strategic and tactical nuclear weapons, it is the nuclear bomb; in the case of missiles, the reentry body containing the bomb is often referred to as the warhead.

Warsaw Pact. The Eastern Europe military pact.

White Horse. The U.S. Army's neutral practical beam weapon program for space-based ballistic missile defense; formerly called "Sipapu."

Wimmex. Jargon for the World Wide Military Command and Control System (WWMCCS).

Y. Symbol for the explosive power or "yield" of a nuclear weapon, expressed in kilotons or megatons.

Yankee. A class of Soviet nuclear-powered ballistic missiles submarine that carries sixteen SS-N-6 SLBM's each.

Yield. The explosive force of a nuclear bomb expressed in kilotons or megatons and designated by the letter "Y."

Zero-zero. A proposal to remove the NATO dual-track missiles if the USSR removes all its SS-20's.

Appendix

THE INTELLECTUAL ENVIRONMENT OF PEACE AND GREEN POLITICS

The theoretical framework behind the evolution of green politics relates to the nature and resolution of scientific controversy (Knelman, 1980b). Such controversies do not derive merely from epistemological and ontological issues, but also from paradigmatic influence on policy (Knelman, 1981). They involve logical fallacies such as the "naturalistic fallacy" (Olthuis, 1969), the attempt to reduce ethical questions to those amenable by reference to the natural sciences. The naturalistic fallacy embraces the "fact-value" and "is-ought" dichotomies, although it has larger social implications, such as the rationale for energy policy choices, military strategy, etc. A book on the Canadian nuclear industry attempted to develop a subset of fallacies derived from the naturalistic fallacy applied to civil nuclear power (Knelman, 1976), while a book on the U.S. nuclear power industry dealt directly with the naturalistic fallacy (Schrader-Frechette, 1980). The naturalistic fallacy has many faces, such as the concept of "hypotheticality" (Haefele, 1974), and the use of cost/risk benefit analyses (Sayre, 1977). Both deal with what constitutes acceptable risk in nuclear power development, with the latter concentrating explicitly on the role of values.

In a paper delivered at an international conference on oil and the environment, this author began to develop a process model for the admissibility and recognition of values as a legitimate element in social/environment impact assessment (Knelman, 1982a). The naturalistic fallacy, sometimes described as the "definist fallacy" (Olthuis, 1969), is yet another form of reductionism, if not scientism. The role of the humanities can be particularly effective in social impact assessment when it reveals hidden assumptions, tacit paradigms, intrinsic logical fallacies, methodological flaws, and the attempted separation of "facts" and values. This same approach is equally effective in confronting the mythology of the nuclear arms race (Knelman, 1983a), and the debate over civil nuclear power (Knelman, 1976). There are excellent sources on the naturalistic fallacy (Frankena, 1939; Fried, 1970; Kohlberg, 1971).

341

The conflicting views central to the debate on nuclear power range from those held by the neo-Luddites to the perspectives of the technological pessimists (Kahler, 1957; Dorf, 1978). The spectrum of views includes the perception of technology as intrinsically manipulative and autonomous, subversive of human will (Ellul, 1965; Winner, 1977), or imbued with a fatal reductionist flaw, a spirit of false infallibility and omniscient rationality (Roszak, 1969, 1974; Marcuse, 1964, 1969). The debate expresses the polarization between technological optimists (Weinberg, 1969, 1972; Starr, 1972, 1973; Schmidt et al., 1976; Fedchenko, 1977; Kuznetsov, 1977), and pessimists (Ellul, 1965; Manfred, 1969; Winner, 1977; Knelman, 1978, 1981). The same debate occurs over the issue of nuclear war.

Often, the nuclear debate reduces to two world views. One embraces a faith in technology and the other, a resolute doubt and rejection of technology as its proponents lost credibility (Ford, 1982). The anatomy of the history of the debate are essential elements in the evolution of antinuclear movements (Gofman and Tamplin, 1971; R. S. Lewis, 1972; Ebben and Kaspar, 1974; Patterson, 1976; van Hulst, 1977; Hall, 1984).

Still another current in the debate concerns the nature and control of technology (Knelman, 1980a, 1983a). Concepts of appropriate or alternative technology have been raised (Dickson, 1974; Henderson, 1976, 1978; Jacquier, 1976; Knelman, 1979): "radical technology" (Harper and Boyle, 1978); "relevant science" (Knelman, 1972); "participatory technology" (Carrol, 1971); "anticipatory democracy" (Bezold, 1978); "convivial tools" (Illyich, 1973); "soft-paths" (Lovins, 1977); or "intermediate technology" (Schumacher, 1973). These often embrace a new world view in which social systems and technology match ecosystems and natural processes (Goldsmith, 1971; Goldsmith et al., 1972). These systems have been termed "conserver" or "sustainable" societies (Stivers, 1976; Science Council of Canada, 1977; Goldsmith, 1977; Pirages, 1977; Valaskakis, 1979). This new revolutionary society hopes to overcome the "tragedy of the Commons"—the limits to growth, waste, and complexity and develop a life style of "joyous austerity" in a decentralized, humanly scaled, renewable resources society (Hardin, 1968). Often, environmentalists are insensitive to equity, and equitists (socialists) are insensitive to environment; but sometimes, there is an attempt to fuse the two visions (Bonello and Roussopoulos, 1971; Knelman, 1972, 1973; Commoner, 1974, 1979; Dickson, 1974; Dorf et al., 1978).

Precursor concepts and theories derive from the works of a broad spectrum of scholars who deal with the costs and limits of growth (Mishan, 1969; Meadows et al., 1972) from visions of appropriate development (U.N. University, Tokyo, GPID Project, 1978); from concepts of justice and values (Rawls, 1971; Knelman, 1982a); through democratizing the policy process (Hooker et al., 1981); from ideas of political development (Dodd, 1972); and from the study of social systems (Parsons, 1951) and social paradigms (Kuhn, 1962; Knelman, 1981). This group of sources is by no means exclusive. Alienation theory is very significant (Seaman, 1966, 1967; Knelman, 1982b).

The "naturalistic fallacy" and other issues of ethics and risk have been dealt with in direct relation to the nuclear debate (Haefele, 1974; Knelman, 1976; Sayre, 1977; Schrader-Frechette, 1980; Hooker et al., 1981). In the end, nuclear power became the victim of its bad economics, although the force of the antinuclear movements weakened it greatly (Komanoff, 1982; Edwards, 1982). The issue of credibility was a serious factor (Boffey, 1974; Knelman, 1976). This author has begun to develop a method of credibility analysis as a logical extension of the work on the "naturalistic and definist" fallacies (Knelman, 1981, 1983a).

The major content of the relevant literature on antinuclear movements deals with the nuclear debate in the U.S. (Berger, 1972; Schrader-Frechette, 1980). There are a fair amount of Canadian sources (Knelman, 1976; Ontario Coalition for Nuclear Responsibility—OCNR, 1977). There are some good general books (Willrich, 1971; Enloe, 1975; Gyorgi et al., 1979; Gompert, 1980), and good material on Western Europe (Boeker, 1977; Jungk, 1979; Bahrs et al., 1981; Thompson and Smith, 1981; Nelkin and Pollack, 1982). There are also excellent journals and newsletters in the field, i.e., Canada: Alternatives and Transitions; U.S.: Environmental Action; Citizens Energy Council *Nuclear News, Bulletin of Atomic Scientists;* Sweden: Ambio; U.K.: *The Ecologist;* Netherlands: WISE and disarmament campaigns (world network journal newsletters).

There is very little scholarly material on the green/ecology parties of Western Europe with a few exceptions (Devall, 1980; Taylor, 1980; Nelkin and Pollack, 1982), and some good journal and newspaper articles (Grossman, 1977; Touraine et al., 1980; Taylor, 1980; Gorz, 1980; Trimborn, 1982; Vaillancourt, 1982). Books on the nuclear arms race are proliferating rapidly (Knelman, 1983). There are excellent resource centers such as the U.S. Commission for the Advancement of Public Interest Organizations, 1875 Connecticut Ave. N.W., Suite 1013, Washington, D.C., 20009.

There is a rich literature on the role of the public and public interest scientists in policy and decision making, with respect to technology generally and nuclear power particularly (Primack and von Hippel, 1974; Knelman, 1976; Nelkin, 1976, 1978; Boeker, 1977; Nelkin and Pollack, 1979; Abrams et al., 1980).

The core vision of the green/ecology parties represents a new world view embodying a revolutionary new social paradigm. The dominant social paradigm of progress/growth riding on high technology, while still representing the entrenched political economies of the economically developed world, is being seriously challenged for the first time since the Industrial Revolution (Henderson, 1976, 1978). The issue of civil and military nuclear power has added clarity to the polarization of these contending world views.